Japan's Modern History, 1857–1937

Over the course of the period 1857–1937 in Japan, six distinct stages can be identified as the country moved from Shogun rule and its subsequent overthrow, through industrialisation and investment, to the Meiji Constitution and then from Taishō democracy to Shōwa fascism. In this book, Junji Banno stresses the mutual relationships between each period and, to this end, renames them accordingly: the age of reform; the age of revolution; the age of construction; the age of management; the age of reorganisation; and the age of crisis.

Following this model, the book covers 80 years of history in Japan, focusing on political history and foreign relations, with extensive material on economic development and the foreign influences on political institutions and practices. Based on extensive archival research, *Japan's Modern History* synoptically considers the key trends and their significance over the period 1857–1937. In turn, it presents in detail fascinating information on many of the main leaders and other significant figures, with extensive quotations from their writings, letters and diaries.

This book is a translation into English of a major work of scholarship by a leading historian of modern Japan and it may be considered the apex of Junji Banno's work in the field. As such, it will be of great interest to students and scholars of both Japanese history and history more broadly.

Junji Banno is Professor Emeritus of Tokyo University, Japan.

The Nissan Institute/Routledge Japanese Studies Series

Series Editors:

Roger Goodman, Nissan Professor of Modern Japanese Studies,
University of Oxford, Fellow, St Antony's College

J.A.A. Stockwin, formerly Nissan Professor of Modern Japanese Studies and former Director of the Nissan Institute of Japanese Studies,
University of Oxford, Emeritus Fellow, St Antony's College

Other titles in the series:

The Myth of Japanese Uniqueness
Peter Dale

The Emperor's Adviser
Saionji Kinmochi and pre-war
Japanese politics
Lesley Connors

A History of Japanese Economic Thought
Tessa Morris-Suzuki

The Establishment of the Japanese Constitutional System
Junji Banno
Translated by J.A.A. Stockwin

Industrial Relations in Japan
The peripheral workforce
Norma Chalmers

Banking Policy in Japan
American efforts at reform during the
Occupation
William M. Tsutsui

Educational Reform in Japan
Leonard Schoppa

How the Japanese Learn to Work
Second edition
Ronald P. Dore and Mari Sako

Japanese Economic Development
Theory and practice
Second edition
Penelope Francks

Japan and Protection
The growth of protectionist sentiment
and the Japanese response
Syed Javed Maswood

The Soil, by Nagatsuka Takashi
A portrait of rural life in Meiji Japan
*Translated and with an introduction
by Ann Waswo*

Biotechnology in Japan
Malcolm Brock

Britain's Educational Reform
A comparison with Japan
Michael Howarth

Language and the Modern State
The reform of written Japanese
Nanette Twine

Industrial Harmony in Modern Japan
The intervention of a tradition
W. Dean Kinzley

Japanese Science Fiction
A view of a changing society
Robert Matthew

The Japanese Numbers Game
The use and understanding of numbers
in modern Japan
Thomas Crump

Ideology and Practice in Modern Japan
Edited by Roger Goodman and Kirsten Refsing

Technology and Industrial Development in Pre-War Japan
Mitsubishi Nagasaki Shipyard,
1884–1934
Yukiko Fukasaku

Japan's Early Parliaments, 1890–1905
Structure, issues and trends
Andrew Fraser, R.H.P. Mason and Philip Mitchell

Japan's Foreign Aid Challenge
Policy reform and aid leadership
Alan Rix

Emperor Hirohito and Shôwa Japan
A political biography
Stephen S. Large

Japan: Beyond the End of History
David Williams

Ceremony and Ritual in Japan
Religious practices in an industrialized
society
Edited by Jan van Bremen and D.P. Martinez

The Fantastic in Modern Japanese Literature
The subversion of modernity
Susan J. Napier

Militarization and Demilitarization in Contemporary Japan
Glenn D. Hook

Growing a Japanese Science City
Communication in scientific research
James W. Dearing

Architecture and Authority in Japan
William H. Coaldrake

Women's Gidayû and the Japanese Theatre Tradition
A. Kimi Coaldrake

Democracy in Post-War Japan
Maruyama Masao and the search for
autonomy
Rikki Kersten

Treacherous Women of Imperial Japan
Patriarchal fictions, patricidal fantasies
Hélène Bowen Raddeker

Japanese–German Business Relations
Co-operation and rivalry in the
inter-war period
Akira Kudô

Japan, Race and Equality
The Racial Equality Proposal of 1919
Naoko Shimazu

Japan, Internationalism and the UN
Ronald Dore

Life in a Japanese Women's College
Learning to be ladylike
Brian J. McVeigh

On The Margins of Japanese Society
Volunteers and the welfare of the
urban underclass
Carolyn S. Stevens

The Dynamics of Japan's Relations with Africa
South Africa, Tanzania and Nigeria
Kweku Ampiah

The Right to Life in Japan
Noel Williams

The Nature of the Japanese State
Rationality and rituality
Brian J. McVeigh

Society and the State in Inter-War Japan
Edited by Elise K. Tipton

Japanese–Soviet/Russian Relations since 1945
A difficult peace
Kimie Hara

Interpreting History in Sino–Japanese Relations
A case study in political decision making
Caroline Rose

Endô Shûsaku
A literature of reconciliation
Mark B. Williams

Green Politics in Japan
Lam Peng-Er

The Japanese High School
Silence and resistance
Shoko Yoneyama

Engineers in Japan and Britain
Education, training and employment
Kevin McCormick

The Politics of Agriculture in Japan
Aurelia George Mulgan

Opposition Politics in Japan
Strategies under a one-party dominant regime
Stephen Johnson

The Changing Face of Japanese Retail
Working in a chain store
Louella Matsunaga

Japan and East Asian Regionalism
Edited by S. Javed Maswood

Globalizing Japan
Ethnography of the Japanese presence in America, Asia and Europe
Edited by Harumi Befu and Sylvie Guichard-Anguis

Japan at Play
The ludic and logic of power
Edited by Joy Hendry and Massimo Raveri

The Making of Urban Japan
Cities and planning from Edo to the twenty-first century
André Sorensen

Public Policy and Economic Competition in Japan
Change and continuity in antimonopoly policy, 1973–1995
Michael L. Beeman

Men and Masculinities in Contemporary Japan
Dislocating the Salaryman Doxa
Edited by James E. Roberson and Nobue Suzuki

The Voluntary and Non-Profit Sector in Japan
The challenge of change
Edited by Stephen P. Osborne

Japan's Security Relations with China
From balancing to bandwagoning
Reinhard Drifte

Understanding Japanese Society
Third edition
Joy Hendry

Japanese Electoral Politics
Creating a new party system
Edited by Steven R. Reed

The Japanese–Soviet Neutrality Pact
A diplomatic history, 1941–1945
Boris Slavinsky
Translated by Geoffrey Jukes

Academic Nationalism in China and Japan
Framed by concepts of nature, culture and the universal
Margaret Sleeboom

The Race to Commercialize Biotechnology
Molecules, markets and the state in the United States and Japan
Steve W. Collins

Institutions, Incentives and Electoral Participation in Japan
Cross-level and cross-national perspectives
Yusaku Horiuchi

Japan's Interventionist State
The role of the MAFF
Aurelia George Mulgan

Japan's Sea Lane Security, 1940–2004
'A matter of life and death'?
Euan Graham

The Changing Japanese Political System
The Liberal Democratic Party and the Ministry of Finance
Harumi Hori

Japan's Agricultural Policy Regime
Aurelia George Mulgan

Cold War Frontiers in the Asia-Pacific
Divided territories in the San Francisco System
Kimie Hara

Living Cities in Japan
Citizens' movements, Machizukuri and local environments
Andre Sorensen and Carolin Funck

Resolving the Russo–Japanese Territorial Dispute
Hokkaido–Sakhalin relations
Brad Williams

Modern Japan
A Social and political history
Second edition
Elise K. Tipton

The Transformation of the Japanese Left
From old socialists to new democrats
Sarah Hyde

Social Class in Contemporary Japan
Edited by Hiroshi Ishida and David H. Slater

The US–Japan Alliance
Balancing soft and hard power in East Asia
Edited by David Arase and Tsuneo Akaha

Party Politics and Decentralization in Japan and France
When the Opposition governs
Koichi Nakano

The Buraku Issue and Modern Japan
The career of Matsumoto Jiichiro
Ian Neary

Labor Migration from China to Japan
International students, transnational migrants
Gracia Liu-Farrer

Policy Entrepreneurship and Elections in Japan
A political biography of Ozawa Ichirō
Takashi Oka

Japan's Postwar
Edited by Michael Lucken, Anne Bayard-Sakai and Emmanuel Lozer
Translated by J.A.A. Stockwin

An Emerging Non-Regular Labour Force in Japan
The dignity of dispatched workers
Huiyan Fu

A Sociology of Japanese Youth
From returnees to NEETs
Edited by Roger Goodman, Yuki Imoto and Tuukka Toivonen

Natural Disaster and Nuclear Crisis in Japan
Response and recovery after Japan's 3/11
Edited by Jeff Kingston

Urban Spaces in Japan
Edited by Christoph Brumann and Evelyn Schulz

Understanding Japanese Society
Fourth edition
Joy Hendry

Japan's Emerging Youth Policy
Getting young adults back to work
Tuukka Toivonen

The Organisational Dynamics of University Reform in Japan
International inside out
Jeremy Breaden

Schoolgirls, Money and Rebellion in Japan
Sharon Kinsella

Social Inequality in Japan
Sawako Shirahase

The Great Transformation of Japanese Capitalism
Edited by Sébastien Lechevalier
Translated by J. A. A. Stockwin

Neighborhood Associations and Local Governance in Japan
Robert Pekkanen, Yutaka Tsujinaka and Hidehiro Yamamoto
Translated by Leslie Tkach-Kawasaki

Japan's International Fisheries Policy
Roger Smith

Japan's Modern History
A new political narrative
Junji Banno
Translated by J. A. A. Stockwin

Configurations of Family in Contemporary Japan
Edited by Tomoko Aoyama, Laura Dales and Romit Dasgupta

Japan's Modern History, 1857–1937

A new political narrative

Junji Banno
Translated by J.A.A. Stockwin

LONDON AND NEW YORK

First published in Japanese in 2012 as *Nihon kindai shi*
by Chikuma Shinsho

Published 2014
by Routledge
2 Park Square, Milton Park, Abingdon, Oxon OX14 4RN

and by Routledge
711 Third Avenue, New York, NY 10017

Routledge is an imprint of the Taylor & Francis Group, an informa business

© 2014 Junji Banno

The right of Junji Banno to be identified as author of this work has
been asserted by him/her in accordance with sections 77 and 78 of the
Copyright, Designs and Patents Act 1988.

All rights reserved. No part of this book may be reprinted or reproduced
or utilised in any form or by any electronic, mechanical, or other means,
now known or hereafter invented, including photocopying and recording,
or in any information storage or retrieval system, without permission in
writing from the publishers.

Trademark notice: Product or corporate names may be trademarks or
registered trademarks, and are used only for identification and
explanation without intent to infringe.

British Library Cataloguing in Publication Data
A catalogue record for this book is available from the British Library

Library of Congress Cataloging in Publication Data
[Nihon kindaishi. English]
 Japan's modern history : a new political narrative / Junji Banno; translated by J.A.A. Stockwin.
 pages cm.—(Nissan Institute/Routledge Japanese studies)
 Includes bibliographical references and index.
 1. Japan—History—Restoration, 1853–1870. 2. Japan—History—Meiji period, 1868–1912.
 3. Japan—History—1912–1945. I. Title.
 DS881.3.B349613 2014
 952.05—dc23
 2014006372

ISBN: 978–1–138–77517–6 (hbk)
ISBN: 978–1–315–77395–7 (ebk)

Typeset in Times New Roman
by Swales & Willis Ltd, Exeter, Devon

Contents

Series Editor's preface	xi
Translator's introduction	xiii
Conventions	xv
Map	xvi
Introduction	xvii

1 Reform, 1857–1863   1

'Revere the Emperor, expel the foreigner' (sonnō jōi) *versus
 'support the Shōgun, open the country'* (sabaku kaikoku) *1*
Saigō Takamori and his argument for a 'multi-party alliance' 4
Independent military expedition or multi-party alliance? 10
The rise of sonnō jōi *and confrontation between Satsuma and Chōshū 13*
The confused year, 1862 16

2 Revolution, 1863–1871   21

Rehabilitation of the Saigō Scheme 21
Feudal parliament 24
The Sat–Chō alliance 28
Feudal parliament, or 'overthrow the Bakufu by force'? 34
The end of revolution 39
Dissolution and reconstruction of the 'Imperial Army' 47

3 Construction, 1871–1880   53

*Demanding a blueprint for 'construction': the inspection tour of
 Europe and America by the Iwakura Mission 53*
*'Strong army' and 'public opinion': the split over invading Korea
 and the proposal for a popularly elected assembly 58*
'Prosperous country' and 'fairness and public opinion' 63

x   *Contents*

Split in the Kōgi yoron *faction and the successes of the* fukoku
   Faction 70

4   Management, 1880–1893   83

Political participation by the peasantry 83
Breakdown of the 'prosperous country' line and divisions in the
   constitutional system plan 88
Rehabilitation of the 'powerful military' argument and dispute
   between Japan and China 100
Promulgation of the Constitution and inauguration of the Diet 106

5   Reorganisation, 1894–1924   121

Positive policies and the foundation of the Rikken Seiyūkai *122*
The Russo–Japanese War and expectations of political
   reconstruction 136
The Taishō political change 146
Emergence of Minponshugi *151*
The 'regular procedures of constitutional government' (kensei no jōdō)
   and 'the decade of fidelity in adversity' (kusetsu jūnen) *159*
Confrontation between the Hara Cabinet and Minponshugi *162*

6   Crisis, 1925–1937   174

Bifurcation of domestic politics and foreign policy 174
Clear emergence of crisis and decline of parties: from the Manchurian
   Incident to the May 15th Incident 195
Democracy in a vortex of crisis 204
From 'Crisis' to 'Breakdown' 209

Conclusion   232

Glossary   234
Index   236

Series Editor's preface

As the Nissan Institute/Routledge Japanese Studies Series (the largest current series of books on contemporary Japan) draws towards the end of its third decade, it is highly appropriate that it should be publishing a volume which is a cooperative venture between two of its founding members, Arthur Stockwin (the original series editor and still a series co-editor) and Junji Banno (who served with distinction on the series editorial board for over 25 years). Indeed, this is their second contribution to the series. The first, *The Establishment of the Japanese Constitutional System*, also written by Banno and translated by Stockwin, was published, just over 20 years ago, in 1992. The original, which changed the established view of the emergence of constitutional politics in Meiji Japan, had been published in 1971 as *Meiji Kenpō Taisei no Kakuritsu*. An English translation had been long awaited and was received with great appreciation and excellent reviews.

Japan's Modern History was originally published in Japanese as *Nihon Kindai Shi* in 2012 by Chikuma Shinsho and quickly became one of the most popular surveys of late nineteenth and early twentieth century in Japan. We are collectively once again very grateful to Arthur Stockwin for his translation which reflects his own deep knowledge not only of Japanese history but the appropriate English expressions with which to capture the often subtle nuances of Junji Banno's argument.

Japan's Modern History is an important book for understanding the politics of the period under study. It is also an important interrogation of the whole question of how history is contested and constructed. There are few areas of the world where the objective nature of history is more contested than in East Asia and no countries in that region whose history is more under the microscope than that of Japan. Of course, 1937 was the year when the war in China started and so any history book which addresses the period just before then will be examined more closely than most. But can history ever be objective? Just a simple examination of the arenas of contestation around contemporary histories of Japan throws that question into stark relief. One can imagine many 'intentions' (conscious or unconscious) of historians which every reader should interrogate as they read any history book:

1   History as contested ground, with governments and other bodies seeking to impose particular interpretations ('patriotic or nationalistic history');

xii *General Editor's Preface*

2 History as divisive ground within particular countries (e.g. the divergent messages in Belgian museums in Flanders and Wallonia);
3 History as ground contested between different peoples, nations or governments, thus used as an instrument in international confrontations;
4 History as the national story told through stories of warfare (e.g. alleged over-concentration on World War II in UK school history teaching);
5 History as ideology (e.g. the dialectical processes of historical revolution in Marxism, or neo-liberal interpretations deriving from Adam Smith);
6 History as path dependence: because things have always been done this way, they will inevitably be done like this in the future;
7 History as memorable events or processes (e.g. revolutions), which then serve as rich sources of ideas for the present (or, negatively, blot out other possibilities);
8 History as the heroic stories of great men (and women, but less frequently).

History therefore *is* politics and any attempt to separate the two of them is likely to be artificial. As anthropologists like to point out, it is not the past which determines the present as much as the present which determines the past. History is always being written and rewritten. The Nissan/Routledge series sets out to illuminate issues in contemporary Japan in the light of global, historical and local issues. There are few more important periods for understanding contemporary Japan than the period which is covered in this book. It is invaluable therefore that our guides through it are both experts in the politics of history as well as the history of politics. I have no doubt that it will achieve as many accolades as the first Banno/Stockwin collaboration 20 years ago.

Roger Goodman
Oxford, February 2014

Translator's introduction

Professor Banno is a prolific and widely read writer on the political history of modern Japan, whose many insights into its kaleidoscopic politics from the middle of the nineteenth century until the late 1930s have re-written various aspects of Japanese political history. The current volume, which I have had the honour to translate from the original Japanese, treats 80 crucial years of history with a combination of synoptic overview and fascinating detail. The story being told is one of high drama – the transformation of a self-isolated nation whose political system was based on a balance between the political centre and over 200 semi-autonomous domains into an ambitious modern power with international weight in East Asia and around the world. A regime that had lasted more or less intact for some 250 years from the 1860s was subjected to one of the most spectacular and comprehensive revolutions of modern times anywhere in the world. In Banno's view, this is the only true revolution Japan has ever experienced and, by his cut-off date of 1937, the revolution had degenerated into what he aptly calls the 'politics of small slices' – in other words, extreme political fragmentation that left the road open to reckless military adventure.

The story he tells is one of early attempts at reform, the dynamics of revolution, nation building, consolidation, reconstruction and finally crisis leading to war. Protagonists show enlightenment, bravery, luminous intelligence and far-sighted determination, but also venality, corruption, narrow-minded stupidity and ideological fanaticism. Perhaps this just means that Japan was like any other nation state seeking to make its way in a modernising world, in representing a typical human combination of positive and negative qualities. But in the Japanese case, one detects a difference of scale: the achievements were especially remarkable and the failings surprisingly profound.

One of the most original parts of the book concerns the revolutionary leader Saigō Takamori, tragic hero of many television dramas, who led a revolt against the newly established Meiji regime but was killed in battle in 1877. Banno argues that, in the 1860s, Saigō was a revolutionary leader of unparalleled strategic intelligence, whose contribution to revolution has been underestimated. His great contribution to the cause was to argue persistently and subtly that the Bakufu (military government) would not be overthrown without consolidating an inter-domain alliance, not only at the level of the *daimyō* (domain lords), but also between the samurai (warrior-administrators) of various domains opposed to the Bakufu.

xiv *Translator's introduction*

Even though Saigō was in exile on various offshore islands for several years during the 1860s, his influence on revolutionary strategy after he was released was crucial. On the other hand, once the revolution was accomplished, he was much less at home with the mundane tasks of system building and ended up quixotically attacking the new regime he had helped create.

The Meiji regime was largely pre-democratic and enshrined an elitist patriotic unelected bureaucracy at its core. One such official was Tsuzuki Keiroku, in the storeroom of whose son's house in the 1970s Banno unearthed a challenging defence by Tsuzuki of bureaucratic dictatorship, contrasting rational decision making by educated and dedicated government officials with the unreliability and flakiness of politicians and journalists. Banno is inclined to see parallels in this regard between the 1880s and the early twenty-first century.

Banno punctures the democratic credentials of some politicians and political pundits. These included Hara Kei, Japan's first 'commoner prime minister' (assassinated 1921), and Minobe Tatsukichi, prestigious liberal commentator on the 1889 Constitution of the Empire of Japan. He sees Hara as deeply conservative, opposed to universal suffrage and much less favourable to democratic development than many of his rivals. As for Minobe, he regards him as a poor defender of democratic norms in the febrile political atmosphere of the 1930s.

Although the focus of this book is on political history, it also contains a great deal of analysis of economic policy, most especially policy on taxation, on which Banno has done a great deal of detailed work in earlier monographs. There is a fascinating and well-documented section on the mentality and motivations of younger radical military officers during the 1930s and the book also contains an interesting section on the rise of the political left in the later 1930s (by which time, however, parliament had lost much of its power).

Towards the end of the book's final chapter, Banno introduces the writings in 1937 of a contemporary right-wing (indeed jingoistic) journalist, Mutō Teiichi (a figure largely forgotten today), who predicted with uncanny accuracy the consequences for Japan of attempting to fight a simultaneous war against Russia, Britain and the United States. This, Mutō argued, was "beyond Japan's capacities", and "the National Defence Plan which depends on the Yamato [Japanese] spirit and the divine wind is a load of nonsense". He predicted accurately the appalling destruction that American bombers would unleash on Japanese cities, the terrible burns that would be inflicted by incendiaries, and conditions of near starvation which Banno himself experienced as a child. He does not attempt to cover the period from the beginning of the China war (1937) and the defeat in 1945, but he titles it the 'Age of Breakdown'. He hints at a second 'Age of Breakdown' beginning with the earthquake, tsunami and nuclear meltdown of 11th March 1911.

This book was written in Japanese for a Japanese readership. It is this translator's firm conviction that translating the book should give a subtly different perspective from those written by non-Japanese writers or by Japanese writers specifically for a non-Japanese readership. If the book in its translated form raises questions in the minds of readers that Western-oriented books do not provoke, this project will have been vindicated.

Conventions

Japanese, Chinese and Korean names are given in their original order, with the surname first and the personal name second. In the earlier period covered by this book, however, some better-known individuals are, in places, referred to by their personal names. Again, mainly in the earlier period, some individuals have alternative personal names, which are given in brackets. The revised Hepburn system of romanising Japanese words, including names, is used throughout. To indicate the pronunciation difference between long and short vowels in Japanese, macrons are used over long vowels: principally ō and ū, except in Tokyo and Kyoto.

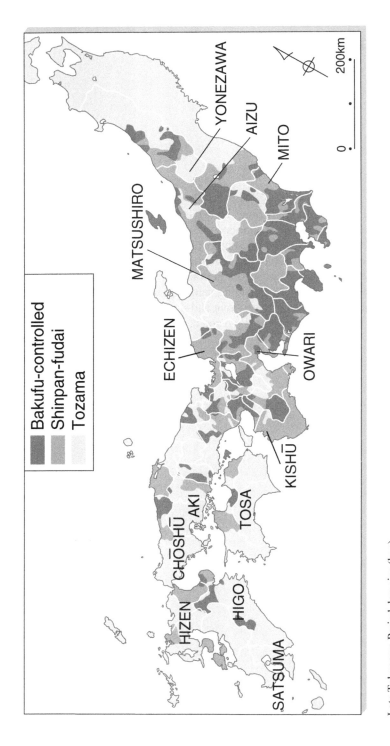

Late Tokugawa Period domains (han)
Important domains named, without boundaries. The three types of domain in the Tokugawa period: Bakufu-controlled, shinpan-fudai (pro-Bakufu domains) and tozama (outer domains, without allegiance to the Bakufu)

Introduction

This book will cover 80 years of Japanese history from 1857 to 1937, dividing it into six stages. Giving individual names to each of these periods in modern Japanese history, we may identify six periods: Union of Court and Shogunate (*Kōbu gattai*) → Revere the Emperor, overthrow the Shogun (*Sonnō tōbaku*) → Invest and industrialise (*shokusan kōgyō*) → Meiji Constitution (*Meiji rikkensei*) → Taishō democracy (*Taishō demokurashii*) → Shōwa fascism (*Shōwa fashuizumu*).

But even if this indicates the characteristics of each period, it fails to show the mutual relations between them. So in this book we shall change their names to the following: Age of Reform (*Kaikaku no jidai*) → Age of Revolution (*kakumei no jidai*) → Age of Construction (*kensetsu no jidai*) → Age of Management (*unyō no jidai*) → Age of Reorganisation (*saihen no jidai*) → Age of Crisis (*kiki no jidai*). 'Union of Court and Shogunate' is equivalent to Age of Reform; 'Revere the Emperor, overthrow the Shogun' to Age of Revolution; 'Invest and Industrialise' to Age of Construction; 'Establish the Meiji Constitution' to Age of Management; 'Taishō Democracy' to Age of Reorganisation; 'Shōwa Fascism' to Age of Crisis.

The course of modern Japanese history

1850	Union of Court and Shogunate	Age of Reform
1860	Revere the Emperor, Overthrow the Shogun	Age of Revolution
1870	Invest and Industrialise	Age of Construction
1890	Establishment of the Meiji Constitution	Age of Management
1900	Taishō Democracy	Age of Reorganisation
1930	Shōwa Fascism	Age of Crisis
1940	Imperial Rule Assistance Association (*Taisei yokusankai*)	Age of Breakdown

Following pre-war history that began with 'Age of Reform' and ended with 'Age of Breakdown, another 'Age of Reform' began with the post-war reforms. Not having engaged in specialist research into the period, I lack the qualifications to speak about the 66-year history since the end of the war. Even so, it seems to me that, although it is difficult to identify an 'Age of Revolution', it is possible to discern over the 66 years of history the following progression: 'Reform' →

xviii *Introduction*

'Construction' → Management → Reorganisation → Crisis, and possibly also Breakdown.

During the six stages of the 66 years since the war, it is my layman's impression that history progressed much like the transitions between the 'Age of Reform' towards a modern Japan, starting in 1857, and going on through six stages in the same order.

Up to 2 December 1872 (Meiji 5), unless otherwise indicated, dates are given according to the lunar calendar. From 1 January 1873 (Meiji 6), they will be given according to the solar calendar.

A further point is that changes in parliamentary seats at elections, frequently discussed from Chapter 4, will be calculated according to the difference in numbers of seats between the time of dissolution and the time of convening. This is because, even in the pre-war period, there were considerable numbers of parliamentarians elected as unaffiliated candidates, who subsequently switched to the party in power.

1 Reform, 1857–1863

'Revere the Emperor, expel the foreigner' (*sonnō jōi*) versus 'support the Shōgun, open the country' (*sabaku kaikoku*)

Uneven course to the Meiji Restoration

When people hear the term 'Meiji Restoration', they generally bring to mind the revival of the monarchy in January 1868 and the Charter Oath in April of the same year. The image of a modern centralised state, absorbing European and American civilisation, having the goal of 'prosperous country, strong military' (*fukoku kyōhei*), as well as 'government in touch with public opinion' (*kōgi yoron*) appeared with great clarity. The latter was also known as a consultative system (*gōgisei*).

Arriving at this, however, required many twists and turns over 20 years or more, while many leaders and thinkers struggled against great odds in this historic cause.

The reason why such a bitter struggle was needed was the appearance of the pro-Emperor, anti-foreign argument stimulated by foreign pressure. Military pressure by the Western powers, symbolised by the arrival of Commodore Perry in 1853, brought together Japanese ancient tradition ('revere the Emperor' – *sonnō*) and a tradition that had lasted 250 years ('expel the barbarian' – *jōi*). When these two 'traditions' were brought together by the Mito school and Yoshida Shōin, as a national policy of 'revere the Emperor, expel the barbarian (i.e. foreigners)' (*sonnō jōi*), a feisty set of national principles was forged.

On the other hand, Japan in the Bakumatsu period, having become accustomed to peace in one country after 250 years of being a closed country, was merely one of a number of small weak countries around the world, and lacked sufficient military and other forces to repel demands from the great powers for the opening of the country. No realistic choice was possible apart from this. For the Bakufu (Shogunate), which controlled Japan, the only thing to do was to open the country. The term used at the time for a combination of support for the Bakufu and acceptance of national opening to the outside world was *sabaku kaikoku* ('support the Bakufu, open Japan').

2 Japan's Modern History

Table 1.1

Date	Event
1842	China loses the Opium War (1840–2).
1851	Shimazu Nariakira becomes Lord of the Satsuma domain (*han*).
1853	Commodore Perry sails into Uraga Bay.
1854	Japan–US Treaty of Harmony and Friendship; similar treaties with Great Britain and Russia; Nariakira goes to Edo in *sankin kōtai*, accompanied by Saigō Takamori.
1856	US Consul-General Townsend Harris resident in Shimoda.
1858	Japan–US Treaty of friendship and Commerce. Ansei purge (~59). Shimazu Nariakira dies.
1859	Saigō Takamori exiled to Amami Ōshima. Hashimoto Sanai executed.
1862	Sakurada Gate Incident. Marriage of a princess to the Shōgun. Shimazu Hisamitsu statement of opinion about reconciliation between the Court and the Bakufu. Teradaya Incident. Saigo returned to Kagoshima and again exiled (Tokunoshima → Okinagarabeshima). Hisamitsu obtains a commission and goes to Kyōto (Hitotsubashi Keiki made regent to the Shogun, and Matsudaira Yoshinaga made political president). The Namamugi Incident (Richardson murder). Samurai from the Chōshū domain set fire to the British consulate.

It was very difficult to overcome the conflict between 'revere the Emperor, expel the foreigner' and 'support the Shogun, open the country'. This was not only a basic conflict in foreign policy; whether to revere the Emperor or support the Shogun also represented a fundamental division within domestic politics. Over the 15 years between Commodore Perry's arrival in 1853 and the Meiji Restoration in 1868, finding how to reconcile these two conflicts was a tremendous struggle.

The four stages of this great struggle

Whether to revere the Emperor or support the Shogun, whether to expel the foreigner or open the country (two rival versions of the national interest) – both these issues developed in stages.

The first stage was the Chinese defeat in the Opium War of 1842. The idea that, emboldened by their victory, the British would in the near future make sure that Japan opened its doors to the outside world appeared crystal clear to a part of the Japanese leadership. From then on some people soon came to propose that Japan should build up a navy, fortresses and a modern army.

The second stage, obviously, was the arrival of the American fleet in 1853 and 1854. Japan could not resist the demand for the country to be opened up, made by Commodore Perry backed by powerful warships. Had Japan refused and gone to war, defeat would have been inevitable. But if the Bakufu, which had always identified national isolation with the national interest, accepted the demand and opened the country, it would lose the legitimacy of its rule.

As for the third stage, at the time of Perry's arrival the American Government merely demanded 'harmony and friendship' without any mention of trade, but from 1857 to 1858, through the first US Consul-General to be posted in Japan, that government pressed hard for the signature of a trade treaty. At this time, in addition to the conflict between expelling the foreigner and opening the country, a conflict was emerging between the Bakufu and powerful domain lords (*daimyō*) over the succession to the Shōgun. This meant that both foreign and domestic policy were simultaneously in a state of confusion. As a result, the Senior Minister (*tairō*), Ii Naosuke, arbitrarily decided to sign a trade treaty between Japan and the US, while the powerful feudal lords and their retainers who were his opponents were subjected to a campaign of wholesale arrests known as the Ansei Purge.

For the time being this ended in a victory for the 'country-opening' policies of the Bakufu. The fact, however, of going ahead without the permission of the Emperor strengthened the links between *sonnō* and *jōi*, while on the other hand, neglect of the opinions of powerful lords led to the emergence of the 'union of Court and Shogunate' argument. Opening the country was seen as desirable, but insisting that to ignore the Emperor and powerful *han* (domain) lords was not to be tolerated became the basis of fierce criticism of the Bakufu, as well as of *sonnō jōi*.

As for the fourth stage, these two different forces criticising the Bakufu – those advocating Union of Court and Shogunate (*kōbu gattai*), and those advocating *sonnō jōi* – clashed head on in the period 1863–4. The Aizu *han*, which supported the Bakufu, and the Satsuma *han*, which supported Union of Court and Shogunate, came together and plotted to isolate the Chōshū *han*, which advocated *sonnō jōi*. These occurrences are known as the 18th August 1863 coup and the Kinmon Incident (1864).

Meanwhile, however, what had been a pro-Bakufu, country-opening argument was replaced by that for unifying Court and Shogunate while also seeking to open the country, whereas the Chōshū domain continued to maintain the national interest argument combining *sonnō* and *jōi*. It was clear that the Chōshū domain on its own was no match, either militarily or economically, for an alliance of the Bakufu with the powerful domains. Even so, for the Chōshū domain, which sought to defend 'national interest', opposing those wishing to open the country as well as opposing the Bakufu was an attractive option. The fact that in the 1864 Kinmon coup the Chōshū domain was given the insulting title of 'Emperor's enemy' was not sufficient to put an end to the *sonnō jōi* problem.

The only way of solving this was to shelve the problem of choosing between the expulsion of foreigners and opening the country, and reduce the choice to one of revering the Emperor as against supporting the Bakufu. If this could be done, then it would make it possible for Satsuma and Chōshū to link hands on the principle of 'revering the Emperor and overthrowing the Bakufu'. If it was possible to wrap up what had been the national interest for about 250 years – namely 'closed country' – in what had been the national interest since antiquity – namely reverence for the Emperor – then the powerful domain lords who emphasised unifying Court and Shogunate were finding that the basis for supporting the Bakufu was becoming less persuasive.

At a time when the conflict between opening the country and expelling the foreigner had been shelved, the demand to respect the views of the powerful domain

4 *Japan's Modern History*

lords in favour of uniting Court and Shogunate mutated into a demand to respect the opinions, not only of domain lords, but also of powerful retainers, to open up political debate. So when 'revere the Emperor and overthrow the Bakufu', and 'open up the debate' became slogans widely used by powerful lords and domain (*han*) samurai, the fourth stage of 'desperate struggle' reached its end, and circumstances moved rapidly on to the Meiji Restoration. My hypothesis is that this happened in 1864, and that its promoter was Saigō Takamori of the Satsuma domain.

Saigō Takamori and his argument for a 'multi-party alliance'

Without a temporary alliance between reformists within the regime and reformists outside the regime, no revolution will succeed. Of course, both before the revolution and after it, these two reformist groups will in many cases struggle with each other. But unless both groups mistakenly think that they both seek the same goals, revolution will not be consummated.

The only revolution that has succeeded in modern Japanese history is the Meiji Restoration. The symbol of 'revolution' is the restoration of the Emperor in January 1868, but its starting point was the 'Ansei Purge' by the Senior Minister, Ii Naosuke, in 1858, and preceding it the 'Ansei Reform'. So through more than ten years of reform from that point until the restoration of the Emperor, reformists inside the regime and reformists outside the regime, clashing fiercely with one another, contested the leadership of reform. In modern Japanese history the former are known as the Unity of Court and Bakufu (*kōbu gattai*) faction, while the latter are called the Revere the Emperor, Expel the Foreigner (*sonnō jōi*) faction.

Change in the reform market place

As we can, however, see if we consider Hashimoto Sanai, samurai from the Echizen domain, who was executed in the Ansei Purge, the reform faction from outside the regime did not have to be an advocate of expelling foreigners. In Japan, before the Ansei Purge, there was nobody more clearly enthusiastic about opening the country than Hashimoto. If we seek to define 'reformers outside the system' including Hashimoto Sanai, then leaving aside the conflict between opening the country and expelling the foreigner, we have to call them pro-Emperor and anti-Bakufu.

Those historians who are familiar with all the details of the decade-long Bakumatsu period may object to regarding Hashimoto Sanai around the time of the Ansei Purge as a member of the anti-Bakufu faction. Not only did he support the Bakufu in its signing of the treaties (thus, opening Japan), but his domestic political reform fitted precisely the *kōbu gattai* model. Moreover, Sanai acted in accordance with the opinions of Matsudaira Yoshinaga, Lord of the Echizen domain, and related to the Bakufu, so that he was not a 'reformer from outside the regime', but a 'reformer from inside the regime'.

On the other hand, in the reform period of more than ten years from 1857 to 1868, something we may call a 'reform market' emerged from time to time. Those calling clearly for restoration of the Emperor and overthrow of the Shōgun just before the Emperor was restored had been no more radical in pursuit of change than Hashimoto Sanai, who in 1857 had been preaching Unity of Court and Bakufu. Unless we take account of this 'reform market' and measure the degree of radicalism of each participant, we may not rate highly the thought of those who were going to die without living to see the Emperor restored. In 1857 and 1858, while the Bakufu was still maintaining its autocratic rule that had lasted for well over 250 years, an ordinary samurai from the Echizen domain (a domain doctor, in his early twenties) urged his domain lord to act and approached the Court. This was an example of 'reform outside the regime', and was a precursor of pro-Emperor activity aimed at overthrowing the Bakufu (*sonnō tōbaku*). In fact, I believe that failure to understand this 'reform marketplace', and taking literally such slogans as *sonnō tōbaku* (Revere the Emperor and Overthrow the Bakufu) and *kōbu gattai* (Unity of Court and Bakufu), constitutes the greatest reason why the history of more than a decade preceding the Meiji Restoration has been distorted.

When we consider how the situation changed in terms of 'reform market' fluctuations, we may discover the seeds of pro-Emperor, anti-Bakufu arguments among the reformers of 1857–8, and discern precursors of 'reformers outside the system'.

What gave me this understanding of the Bakumatsu period was a low-ranking samurai serving a powerful domain lord (the two lowest ranks out of nine), comparable with Hashimoto Sanai, namely Saigō Takamori. The Satsuma domain lord under whom Saigō was working, Shimazu Nariakira, in contrast to Matsudaira Yoshinaga of the Echizen *han*, was an outer lord, but the size of his domain was more than twice that of the Echizen domain (Satsuma 770,000 *koku* of rice produced on its land, Echizen 320,000 *koku*; in population terms, roughly 770,000 as against 320,000). If we offset size against standing, the Satsuma domain had a powerful lord of about the same standing as the Lord of Echizen, while the position of Saigō Takamori, working under his domain lord, was about the same as that of Hashimoto Sanai.

Unlike Hashimoto Sanai, who was arrested during the Ansei Purge of 1858 and executed the next year, Saigō experienced a difficult five years, but in the end fought as a principal leader in the Meiji Restoration. He maintained a consistent position throughout the Bakumatsu period, to the extent that with him there is no need to refer to the previously mentioned 'reform market'.

One of Saigō's key terms throughout the Bakumatsu period was *gasshō renkō* (multi-party alliance). He used this term in two senses.

Shelving the dispute between 'opening the country' and 'expelling the foreigner'

One meaning was of course cooperation between powerful domain lords, centred on the Lord of Satsuma. The structure of friendship between powerful domain

6   *Japan's Modern History*

lords naturally changed with shifting circumstances, but Matsudaira Yoshinaga, Lord of Echizen (later retired), up to the Kogosho Conference at the Palace in Kyoto to restore the Emperor in January 1868, was consistently a target of *gasshō renkō* by the Satsuma domain.

Importantly, however, there was also another kind of *gasshō renkō*. For Saigō, the most important target of this strategy was not the lords of powerful domains, but the 'reform factions' among their retainers. Whether this reform faction among retainers believed in opening the country or expelling foreigners did not matter. Volunteers from any domain who wished to reform the Bakufu were all allies of Saigō. The first real biography of Saigō, *Saigō Takamori den* ('Biography of Saigō Takamori'), published in 1894 by Katsuta Magoyasu, describes as follows the affair of the Shogunate succession in 1856–7:

> Even though there was contestation, over whether to open the country or keep it closed, between Bakufu leaders like Hotta Masayoshi and the Kyoto-based pro-Emperor party, Saigō Takamori did not think this contestation important. What he thought important was the disagreement between the Hitotsubashi Seishi faction, which wished for major reform, and the Kishū faction, which wanted to maintain the ancient laws of the Bakufu. In short, Saigō was not much concerned about whether to open the country or keep it closed.
> (Katsuta Magoyasu, *Saigō Takamori den* ['Biography of Saigō Takamori'], Pelican sha, 1894, 1976, vol. 1, p. 98)

In support of Katsuta's analysis, we may cite the fact that Saigō, who had been exiled to Amami Ōshima at the beginning of 1859 by the Satsuma domain (which feared the difficulties brought about by the Ansei Purge), had sent a list of comrades from other domains to his close friend Ōkubo Toshimichi. In this list the names of eight comrades were given from six domains of Owari, Mito, Echizen, Higo, Chōshū and Tsuchiura (which had close contacts with Mito). These included Hashimoto Sanai from Echizen, who was typical of those wishing to open the country, and Takeda Kōunsai of Mito, who was a hard-line advocate of expelling foreigners. Also, among these eight men, Nagaoka Kenmotsu from Higo, Masuda Danjō from Chōshū (studying under Yoshida Shōin) and Tamiya Jo-un of Owari, Ōkubo Kaname of Tsuchiura were all retainers (*kashin*) and ministers to their lords, so that clearly Saigō's friends were not confined to lower-ranking samurai (letter to Ōkubo Toshimichi dated 2 January 1859 in the old calendar; Rikkyō Daigaku Nihon shi kenkyūkai (ed.), *Ōkubo Toshimichi kankei bunsho*, Yoshikawa Kōbunkan, 1968–71, vol. 3, p. 284.)

This letter was not intended just to send a list of Saigō's friends to Ōkubo. Using the slogan *gasshō renkō* (multi-party alliance), Saigō was trying to persuade Ōkubo Toshimichi of Satsuma, who was stirring up a direct action movement of revenge for the Ansei Purge, that alliances should be struck with lords of other domains, as well as with other close friends. To Ōkubo, who was talking of attacking the Senior Minister, Ii Naosuke, relying only on friends from the Higo and Satsuma domain, Saigō sent the following warning against rash actions:

I hear that you are preparing direct action as soon as you get a report from Hori Chūzaemon about how determined is the Higo domain. But all things considered, I think action should be taken together with the Echizen domain. Not only that, but in my opinion you need to work also with Chikuzen, Inba and Chōshū. Without preparing such alliances, the death of your group will be in vain, and I do not see this death as a matter of loyalty.

(Ibid., p. 283)

In other words, Saigō was trying to persuade Ōkubo that his actions should not just be based on Satsuma and only allying with Higo, but that he should also examine carefully the actions of Chikuzen (today's Fukuoka, 520,000 *koku*), Inba (Tottori, 320,000 *koku*) and Chōshū (370,000 *koku*).

If we put this together with the previously cited list of Saigō's close friends, we see clearly that in writing of the activities of powerful domains he was concerned not only with the actions of the domain lords, but also with the powerful retainers that sustained each of the domains.

Saigō's principal doctrine, while he was seeking to bring several powerful domains together with their powerful retainers in order to press the Bakufu to reform, was 'reverence for the Emperor', which had been the dying wish of Shimazu Nariakira, the former Lord of Satsuma, who had died suddenly the previous year (1858). Saigō made the following explanation to Ōkubo:

On the matter of alliances, I want an alliance of three domains (Mito, Echizen and Higo?), as the late Lord wanted also. He discussed with the three domains, and rendered service to the Court, behaving with resolution. If the three domains are determined to, we should also act strongly together.

Moreover, Saigō thought that, if the Bakufu put pressure on the Court, then pro-Emperor domains would not be limited to Satsuma, Echizen, Mito and Higo. In his words: "If we act together in the way discussed, presumably we should not disregard and abandon the pro-Emperor domains, and I regard it as vital that we should not act in a slovenly way, but rather act together with these domains and thus guard the Emperor" (Katsuta, vol. 2, p. 7).

When we consider the list of Saigō's close friends introduced above, the pro-Emperor domains apart from Satsuma, Echizen, Mito and Higo were Chōshū, Tsuchiura and Owari. Saigō said that if these seven pro-Emperor domains were to enter into an alliance they would be up to fighting the Bakufu led by the Senior Minister Ii Naosuke.

With this in mind, Saigō persuaded Ōkubo that he should exercise caution until it was possible to establish agreement between the pro-Emperor domains. He wrote: "If you become too agitated and act with too much haste, you may create more and more difficulties for yourself, so I urge you to consider the matter very carefully" (ibid.).

8   *Japan's Modern History*

The Saigō letter and the alliance between Satsuma and Tosa

Saigō's thinking in 1859, that if the domain lords and supporters from the pro-Emperor domains made an alliance they would be able to exercise equivalent power and authority to that of the Bakufu, was basically the same as the *taisei hōkan* (the statement by the last Shōgun surrendering power to the Emperor) enunciated eight years later, in 1867. The alliance between Satsuma and Tosa in June of the same year (old calendar) became the basis of the *taisei hōkan*, and in it is written:

> Sovereignty over our whole country rests with the Court. All matters relating to the laws of our Imperial system must stem from the Kyoto Parliament . . . The parliament should be divided into two parts, with members ranging from aristocracy to lower-ranking retainers, honest and pure men should be elected, and besides, the domain lords should also become upper house members in accordance with their functions.
>
> There is no reason why the person occupying the position of Shōgun should perform all the functions of State. Of course he should of his own account resign from his position, join the ranks of the nobility, and restore power to the Court.
>
> (quoted in Banno Junji, *Nihon kensei shi* ['History of Japanese Constitutional Government'], Tokyo Daigaku shuppankai, 2008)

The second article maintained that "The lords should themselves . . . belong to the upper house", and "within an assembly stretching from the higher aristocratic ranks right down to ordinary people", the "higher-ranking aristocrats" must naturally be in the upper house". In other words, lords and marquises should be members of the upper chamber, while: "Sincere and pure men among the retainers" can be members of the lower house. Moreover, Tokugawa Yoshinobu should return to the Court his shogunal powers, and should become a member of the upper house.

If we compare this alliance between Satsuma and Tosa with Saigō's letter to Ōkubo eight years earlier, we see that the two concepts were almost the same. The fact that the lords of Chōshū, Owari and Tsuchiura brought together the lords (and former lords) of Satsuma, Echizen, Mito and Higo under the banner of serving the Emperor, and then that the retainers of the various domains, given the relations of confidence created personally by Saigō, backed up a domain alliance, was a concept linked directly with the Satsuma–Tosa alliance that wished to construct an upper house and a lower house.

Putting this the other way round, to connect the two concepts took eight years.

There are three reasons for these eight blank years. The first is that Saigō, who was constructing a network together with retainers from other domains, was for five years exiled on the islands of Amami Ōshima, Tokunoshima and Okinoerabujima. There were limits, even for Saigō, to operating by remote control while he was confined to these remote islands.

Second, the Satsuma domain retainers under Ōkubo Toshimichi did not sufficiently follow through with his thought and his network. We shall discuss in the next chapter the march to Kyoto, commanded by Shimazu Hisamitsu in 1862, but it is possible to speculate about this from the letter sent by Saigō to Ōkubo, already discussed in this chapter. If there had been common thought patterns and networks between Saigō and Ōkubo, the kind of letter that Saigō wrote would probably not have been necessary.

The third factor was the difference in ability between the former domain lord, Shimazu Nariakira, who died suddenly, and the man who de facto succeeded him, his half-brother Hisamitsu (the domain lord was his eldest son).

The views of Shimazu Nariakira

As is well known, O-yura, the concubine of Nariakira's father, Narioki, worked to annul the claim of Nariakira in order that her own son, Hisamitsu, should become domain lord, and the conservative faction in the domain, including Zusho Hirosato and others, backed her in this. Thus, Nariakira had to put up with an heir presumptive (*seishi*) or successor occupying the position until 1851, when he was 43.

This, however, helped broaden Nariakira's views, as well as his network. Under the Bakufu system of those days, the legitimate wife and heirs presumptive of every domain lord had to live at the domain residence in Edo as virtual hostages.

It was unlikely that the major domain lords coming to Edo, prominent intellectuals and the key Bakufu officials would neglect the descendant of the most powerful domain in the Bakumatsu period. Nariakira received the favours of prestigious domain lords, such as the Lord of Echizen, Matsudaira Yoshinaga (Shungaku), the Lord of Tosa, Yamauchi Toyoshige (Yōdō), the Lord of Uwajima, Date Munenari (Ranzan), the Lord of Hizen, Nabeshima Naomasa (Kansō), and the Lord of Owari, Tokugawa Yoshikatsu (Seisai). He mixed with Iwase Tadanari, a vassal of the Shogun, who was well supplied with information from abroad, as well as with Kawaji Toshiakira, Ōkubo Tadahiro (Ichiō), Egawa Tarōzaemon, Takashima Shirō (Shūhan), Katsu Kaishū and others. He was also in friendly contact with the well-known Mito-*han* Confucianist, Fujita Tōko, and the Matsushiro domain samurai, Sakuma Shōzan, who was a pioneer in Western military studies.

Nariakira, who at last became Lord of Satsuma in 1851, set out for Edo on his first *sankin kōtai* in 1854. On this occasion Saigō Takamori, who was on the lowest of the samurai ranks, was able to accompany him, and as factotum at the domain residence in Edo was delighted to be able to exchange words with Nariakira in the garden. During his three-year stay in Edo he seems to have gained the confidence of Nariakira, and on returning to Satsuma in 1857 Nariakira singled him out and assigned him to negotiations with various reformist domain lords and with reformists in the Bakufu. In the Satsuma residence at that time, the role of discussing with other domains was shouldered by one person, so he was able to talk one on one with those responsible (Katsuta, *Saigō Takamori den*, vol. 1, pp. 62–5).

Saigō, who returned to Kagoshima just after Nariakira, obeyed a new order from him, went to Kyoto and engaged in political activity at the Court. This was the well-known movement in support of Hitotsubashi Yoshinobu. In Kyoto Saigō, on behalf of Nariakira, held a meeting with the Minister of the Left, Konoe Tadahiro, who was the adoptive father of the former Shōgun's wife Tenshōin

10   Japan's Modern History

(known as Atsu-hime), and deepened his friendship with the incumbent priest of the Kiyomizu temple in Kyoto, named Gessho. At the time of the great Ansei Purge in 1858, this was the person who bathed with Saigō in the waters of Kagoshima Gulf.

The views and network of Saigō Takamori in 1857–8 were closely linked with those of the prestigious leader Nariakira. But in July of 1858 (old calendar), Nariakira died of food poisoning, and early in the following year Saigō was banished to Amami Ōshima. Neither with Hisamitsu, Nariakira's deputy who succeeded him, nor with Ōkubo Toshimichi and others, who had remained in Kagoshima, could Saigō's views and network remotely compare with the close links that existed between him and Nariakira. This was an important cause of the political uprising in the Bunkyū era (1861–4), addressed in the next chapter.

Independent military expedition or multi-party alliance?

The domain lords of Mito, Echizen and Owari, who in 1857–8 were supporting Hitotsubashi Yoshinobu alone as successor to the Shōgun from the three houses of Hitotsubashi, Tayasu and Shimizu, regarding their opinions as more important than any blood line, were put under house arrest or forced to retire by the Bakufu, and the Lord of Satsuma, who had avoided such problems, died suddenly. Hashimoto Sanai of Echizen and Yoshida Shōin of Chōshū, as well as a number of other reformist samurai, were thrown into prison and executed. This was the notorious Ansei Purge of 1858–9. Bakufu pressure even extended to the Court, and Konoe Tadahiro as well as other Court nobles (*kuge*) of the faction supporting Yoshinobu were relieved of their posts.

The march to Kyoto commanded by Shimazu Hisamitsu

On the other hand, after the senior Bakufu officials Ii Naosuke and Andō Nobumasa were caught up in attacks by the radical faction, with the incident outside the Sakurada Gate in 1860 and the incident outside the Sakashita Gate in 1862, the various progressive domains began a process of recovery. A famous example of this was the march to Kyoto commanded by the deputy Lord of Satsuma in April 1862 (old calendar). Hisamitsu, borrowing the authority of the Court, went to Edo and persuaded the Bakufu to appoint Hitotsubashi Yoshinobu, who had fought with the 14th Shōgun, Iemochi, to the post of Guardian of the Shogun, and Matsudaira Yoshinaga, the former lord of Echizen, to the post of political president. This was a famous example of a *kōbu gattai* operation taking advantage of the Imperial Messenger Ōhara Shigetomi's journey to Edo.

One factor precipitating Hisamitsu's journey to Kyoto is said to have been the direct action of Ōkubo Toshimichi and others of the Satsuma radical faction. While granting quasi-recognition as 'loyalists' to the Ōkubo group, amounting to some 50 men, Hisamitsu prohibited independent action by volunteers, and in the spirit of 'uniting the Satsuma domain in order to revere the Emperor' led his men to Kyoto.

Reform, 1857–1863   11

The tendency to pressure the Satsuma domain to 'unite the Satsuma domain in reverence for the Emperor' resulted after three years in the release of Saigō from banishment on Ōshima. But Saigō, who returned to Kagoshima in February (old calendar) of 1862, opposed the move led by Satsuma alone to revere the Emperor, and tried to persuade Hisamitsu of the need for a 'multi-party alliance'. In recent research, the fact that Saigō opposed the Satsuma monopoly over the move to revere the Emperor, in favour of a multi-party alliance, has been interpreted as resulting from his three years of exile and his thus being behind the times (for instance, Sasaki Katsu, *Bakumatsu seiji to Satsuma han* ['Bakumatsu Politics and the Satsuma Domain'], Yoshikawa Kōbunkan, 2004, p. 79).

On the other hand, the writer of the first Japanese biography of Saigō, Katsuta Magoyasu, is of the contrary opinion. According to Katsuta, Saigō met Hisamitsu and spoke to him in the following terms:

> Takamori, wishing to report his opinion to Hisamitsu, went to the outer citadel, where he told him that while it was possible that his current plan contradicted the former views of Nariakira, great changes were taking place and the current situation differed greatly from that of earlier times . . . Therefore, altering plans in accordance with the changing times, Hisamitsu should first of all form *a multi-party alliance* with nobles from the great domains, and only after that should he go to Kyoto in order to obtain the imperial command and harmonise Court and Bakufu. Seeking to defend Kyoto through the power of Satsuma alone, and to obtain the imperial command for Satsuma to invite various domains to harmonise Court and Bakufu, has absolutely no chance of success.
>
> (*Saigō Takamori den* ['Biography of Saigō Takamori'], Pelican sha, 1894, 1976, vol. 2, p. 26; present writer's italics)

As background to this interpretation, Katsuta cites a long letter that Saigō sent from his exile on Tokunoshima to Koba Dennai, the Satsuma official resident in Ōsaka (ibid., pp. 44–54). We shall now summarise its main points

Saigō's criticism

The first point is that, in relation to the march to Kyoto by Shimazu Hisamitsu, Ōkubo Toshimichi and others gathered about 50 'loyalists' after Saigō had been moved to Ōshima. In this letter Saigō harshly criticised the understanding of the situation and plan of action of the 'loyalists' as resembling a frog in a well.

> The situation here is completely different from what I expected on the island. . . . Those who call themselves the loyalist faction have been liberated from their subordinate position, they are flushed, and, in a word, are drunk with the world, and seem to be beside themselves. Though they mouth reverence for the Emperor, their loyalty is superficial. They do not understand in what ways their loyalty is going to be expressed, nor can they grasp the situation in which

12 *Japan's Modern History*

Japan is placed. They do not understand how the Bakufu works and they have no comprehension of the state of affairs in other countries, so that their ideas about the world are like those of a frog in a well.

(Ibid., pp. 44–5).

Saigō, three years before, had been freely interacting with progressive officials, lords of major domains and their retainers, and had met powerful Court officials face to face. But over the three years of his confinement the Ansei Purge took place, and there was no opportunity to broaden perceptions and understanding among the loyalist group led by Ōkubo, or to have direct contact with influential people. As a result, Saigō was critical of their thoughtless policy of backing the Emperor from the Satsuma domain alone.

Second, as we have already argued, the basis of Saigō's opposition to the Lord of Satsuma, who sought to back the Emperor alone, was the importance he alone attributed to a 'multi-party alliance', and this position is spelled out by Saigō himself in the same letter. On 15th February 1862, when Saigō met Shimazu Hisamitsu, the domain lord's agent, he argued as follows:

On 15th February, when I was restored to my former duties, I was suddenly called out by the domain lord's agent. What he told me to do was almost impossible to bring about, and greatly differed from my own opinion. What he is planning is just to follow in the steps of the late Lord (Nariakira), *but the present situation is very different from that in the time of the late Lord. . . . Moreover, he does not have friendly relationships with the lords of other large domains.* Without revising the way things were done under the former Lord, there is no prospect for him to achieve his goal. What is needed is to negotiate first with the other lords of large domains, and then enter into a coalition with them to reform the Bakufu. When I advocate alliance with lords from other domains, in other words *a multi-party alliance*, it is difficult to do it with sufficient strength. Without the alliance with nobles of the major domains according to a *multi-party alliance*, this is impossible.

(Ibid., pp. 46–7; present writer's italics)

From this passage it is clear that the idea of being bound by the teachings of Nariakira, without regard for changes in the situation over the three years following Nariakira's death, was accepted by Hisamitsu and the loyalists, but not by Saigō, who was in exile on Ōshima over the same years. Thus Saigō's opposition to Hisamitsu's 'independent march' was part of his 'multi-party alliance' position.

Third, we need to reiterate what we have already shown in section 2, namely that Saigō's idea of 'multi-party alliances' was a double structure. Even while he was held on Ōshima three years earlier, Saigō had sent to Ōkubo the names of 'pro-Emperor samurai', namely eight names from six domains. The common principle of these eight individuals was neither 'opening Japan' nor 'expelling foreigners', but 'revering the Emperor'.

Reform, 1857–1863   13

When Saigō was released and returned to Kagoshima three years later, half of his eight friends had either been executed or had died of illness, but even so, a considerable number of sympathisers had come over to his side. This mantra of Saigō, even after Hisamitsu had retracted his own argument, showed little sign of weakening. Saigō tried to persuade Hisamitsu that, even if he could construct a 'multi-party alliance' consisting only of powerful domain lords (Hisamitsu did not even attempt this), an "unequal national alliance" would not permit either effective administration or structural change. Saigō's mantra was that, unless unity in support of the Emperor were forged, not just among domain lords but also among comrades all over the country, neither revolution nor construction following revolution would be possible (ibid., p. 48).

Seen from this perspective, it is quite clear which approach – that of Shimazu Hisamitsu or that of Saigō Takamori – was spreading. Since Hisamitsu's "independent march" lacked the element of 'multi-party alliance', it could not advance beyond the idea of cooperation between Court and Bakufu – in other words *kōbu gattai*. Moreover, in a paper issued by Hisamitsu himself in March, shortly before the "independent march", interaction by the Satsuma domain with "comrades (*yūshi*) and sympathisers" from various domains was expressly forbidden, and therefore it was not possible to obtain the support of pro-Emperor samurai who wished to establish the superiority of Court over Bakufu in terms of the power relations between them. Hisamitsu's 'march to Kyoto', which entirely lacked the element of 'multi-party alliance' combining both the domain lord level and the level of samurai (*yūshi*), was a very unambitious concept, and its chances of success were extremely low.

By contrast, Saigō's "grand alliance" concept sought to bring about cooperation between powerful domain lords and crossover cooperation between samurai from various domains, whether these samurai wished to 'expel the foreigner' or 'open the country' not being an issue. In a word, the punishment meted out to Saigō by Hisamitsu in 1862 was, for the Satsuma domain, a piece of utter stupidity.

The rise of *sonnō jōi* and confrontation between Satsuma and Chōshū

The rise of the pro-Emperor, anti-foreigner faction in Chōshū and Tosa

Saigō's second exile, which brought together the two key words of 'revering the Emperor' and 'grand alliance' into the slogan 'revere the emperor, expel the foreigner', led to a split between those who wanted to open the country and those who wanted to expel the foreigner. If it had not been for Shimazu Nariakira and Saigō Takamori, it would have been impossible to bring together Takeda Kōunsai of the Mito school and Hashimoto Sanai of the faction that wished to open up Japan.

Hisamitsu went to the Bakufu through the good offices of the Imperial Messenger Ōhara Shigenori, appointed Hitotsubashi Yoshinobu to the Shogunal administration, appointed Matsudaira Yoshinaga as head of administration and in (intercalary) August returned to Kyoto, by which time the situation in Kyoto

14   *Japan's Modern History*

concerning the Court had changed radically. This change in the situation resulted from reasons that Saigō had understood from an early stage.

First of all, powerful *tozama* lords, including those of Chōshū and Tosa, reacted strongly against the independent actions of Satsuma, which refused to participate in a 'grand alliance'. Also, the fact that Hisamitsu's action in punishing Saigō was on account of his interaction with anti-foreigner comrades was much resented not only by domain lords but by progressive samurai from various domains. Here, Satsuma's independent action in sending troops, its attendance on the Imperial Messenger and its reform of the Bakufu created conflict among other domains not only between those who wanted Court and Bakufu to cooperate and those who wished to support the Court and overthrow the Bakufu, but also between those who wished to open the country and those who wished to expel foreigners.

Those who know anything about the Meiji Restoration realise that without belief in revering the Emperor and expelling the foreigner, this great revolution in Japanese modern history would never have occurred. But at the same time, those who have studied the Meiji Restoration in rather more depth probably know that the Chōshū domain, at the centre of the 'revere the Emperor, expel the foreigner' movement, dropped its advocacy of expelling foreigners on the occasion of the attack on Shimonseki in 1864 by the four nation fleet. While showing friendly feeling towards the pro-Emperor, anti-foreign faction, Saigō was right to have a policy of waiting for anti-foreigner sentiment to collapse.

When, however, Saigō was transferred from Tokunoshima to Okinoerabujima, this scenario went haywire.

First, when Shimazu Hisamitsu led his troops to Edo, it was just after Mōri Motonori, who had been staying in the Edo mansion of the Chōshū domain, had set out for Kyoto on the invitation of the domain lord Takachika. The Chōshū domain frankly refused to cooperate with this independent action. Moreover, in the Chōshū domain, Nagai Uta, famous for the 'policy of opening the country and expanding Japanese territory' (1861) had been ordered to do penance. Kido Takayoshi, Takasugi Shinsaku and Kusaka Genzui (pro-Emperor, anti-foreigner) held the reins of power in the domain.

When we look at this with contemporary eyes, Nagai's policy was difficult to fault. The Court should support the signature by the Bakufu of a number of trade treaties, should work towards *fukoku kyōhei*, and while waiting for success, on the other hand, thought Japan should branch out overseas. Moreover, Nagai argued that when the Court (in ancient times a contributor to great achievements in Asia) argued that its own original doctrine was similar to the isolationist policies of the Bakufu (in power for less than 300 years), it was putting the cart before the horse.

In foreign and defence policy, Nagai's argument was close to that of Hashimoto Sanai four years previously, but his approach to domestic politics was conservative, based on the aim of promoting cooperation between Court and Bakufu. The central element in domestic politics was the Bakufu, whereas the Court merely played a supporting role, powerful domain lords were not included in the planning process, and samurai from the domains were out of sight entirely. It was on

Reform, 1857–1863 15

this point that Nagai differed from Saigō's friend of four years before, Hashimoto Sanai. Saigō, whose aim was a horizontal alliance between those wishing to open Japan and those wishing to expel the foreigner, regarded Nagai Uta as a rascal who was attacking those who supported the Emperor and who wished to overthrow the Bakufu (Katsuta, *Saigō Takamori den*, vol. 2, pp. 51–2). In the letter to Koba Dennai that Saigō sent from his exile on Tokunoshima, he evaluated Nagai in the following terms:

> When [Nagai] left for Kyoto, he had backing from the Bakufu. He persuaded the Court to change its previous behaviour with regret, and submitted papers to the Court in which he argued that the Court should approve the trade treaty, and if it did so, the Bakufu would refrain from punishing the nobles. Together with the retainers of our domain, he insisted that the Court should drop those foolish ideas. Even in the Chōshū domain, opposition to Nagai is arising. I have certainly heard this from Shishido Samanosuke, the responsible officer of Chōshū stationed in Ōsaka.

During his only two months of freedom, Saigō learned the outline of the policy of expansionism on the part of Nagai Uta of the Chōshū domain, and came to the support of the pro-Emperor, anti-foreigner tendency opposed to Nagai within the same domain. The Chōshū domain made Nagai change his position and accept the pro-Emperor, anti-foreign position of the domain, as well as putting pressure on the Court. Around this time a similar thing was happening in the Tosa domain. In similar fashion to Nagai in the Chōshū domain, Yoshida Tōyō, an upper-class retainer, had been working for the aims of a prosperous country (i.e. domain) and a strong military, and with this in mind supported the opening of Japan, but he was assassinated by Takechi Hanpeita and others of the Tosa Imperial Party, which revered the Emperor and advocated expelling foreigners (April 1862). The Tosa Imperial Party, backing the domain lord, Yamanouchi Toyonori, in July marched with 2,000 troops and entered Kyoto.

Setback for the pro-Emperor domain alliance

Thus, in Kyoto, a split became increasingly evident between Satsuma, which combined a desire to open the country with a wish to combine Court and Bakufu on the one hand, and the Chōshū and Tosa domains, which combined anti-foreigner with pro-Emperor sentiment, on the other.

It was this situation that was coming to worry Saigō the most, in the period before he was banished to Tokunoshima. Saigō's policy was to forge a multi-party alliance between a grand alliance at the level of domain lords, including the lords of Chōshū and Tosa, and an alliance at retainer level, including Takasugi Shinsaku and Kusaka Genzui of Chōshū and Takeichi Hanpeita of Tosa.

Shimazu Hisamitsu, who rejected both of Saigō's proposals and capriciously condemned him to banishment, was the person most responsible for this confusion. Moreover, while Saigō was banished to Ōshima, the *Seichūgumi*, set up by

16 *Japan's Modern History*

lower-ranking samurai from Satsuma, including Ōkubo Toshimichi and others, gradually came to accept Hisamitsu's "independent action by the domain of reverence for the Emperor", which expressly forbade a horizontal alliance of samurai from various domains. This stimulated further confusion.

In the middle of all this, Arima Shinshichi, an old friend of Saigō who had been in contact with the anti-foreign factions in various domains, was attacked with six other samurai at the Teradaya in Fushimi by Narahara Shigeru and others of the *Seichūgumi*, in what became known as the 'Teradaya Incident'. This contributed to the isolation of the Satsuma domain in the pro-Emperor movement. Shimazu Hisamitsu, who thus lost the support of the Court, Chōshū and Tosa, as well as all the pro-Emperor, anti-foreign samurai, on 23rd (intercalary) August, immediately after reporting to the Court about a degree of reform taking place within the Bakufu at Edo, left Kyoto for Kagoshima. This represented the collapse of Hisamitsu's pro-Emperor position by the Satsuma domain alone.

The confused year, 1862

Katsu Kaishū and Yokoi Shōnan

Even though it is impossible to decide whether the faction wishing to open Japan to the outside world was left wing, or whether the anti-foreign faction was left wing, if we do call the conflict between them a 'left–right struggle' then ever since Saigō's banishment any combination of left and right reformers had disappeared. In Kyoto the anti-foreign faction at Court and pro-Emperor, anti-foreign factions in Chōshū and Tosa, had become influential, while in the Bakufu and in domains that were favourable to it those who wished to open the country were suppressed.

In the Bakufu Ōkubo Ichiō (Tadahiro), one of those who wished to open up Japan, suffered a loss of status. Katsu Kaishū, naval *bugyō* (administrator), noted the following in his diary entry for November 1862:

> Yesterday (5th November) Ōkubo became *bugyō* in charge of military affairs. This man is one of the outstanding Bakufu officials. Happily he was recently given exceptional promotion to the position of secretary to the Shōgun, but today he has been moved to this military position. They say that Ōkubo is a pioneer among those who speak of opening the country, along with Oguri Bungo (Kōzukenosuke) and Okabe Suruga (Nagatsune), and rumour has it that the Court dislikes them. Apparently that is why he has been moved. Ah, in many ways those who focus on the issue of whether to open the country or not do not understand the real situation. Now our nation is facing real peril, and unless the Court appoints able persons to its staff, rather than just following the crowd, and takes the correct path, great reform will never be achieved. The argument over whether or not to open the country, just like the controversy over war or peace at the time of Commodore Perry's visit in 1853, is a useless discussion.
>
> (Katsube Mitake, et al., *Katsu Kaishū zenshū* ['Complete Works of Katsu Kaishū'], Keisō Shobō, vol. 18, pp. 14–15)

Reform, 1857–1863   17

Kaishū's argument – in seeking to shelve disputes about whether to open the country or keep it closed, and in seeking a radical reform of the regime centred on the Court – was close to the arguments of Saigō that we discussed earlier. The difference between them lay in their evaluation of the samurai who wished to revere the Emperor and expel the foreigner. Saigō, by shelving the question of opening the country, aimed to create a national alliance of samurai cutting across domain loyalties. By contrast, Katsu, as naval administrator, rejected pro-Emperor, anti-foreigner arguments as 'populist', advocated appointing those who had exceptional knowledge at the top of the Court government, and aimed at top-down reform. As we shall show in the following chapter, Saigō and Katsu argued the question of taking up this 'populism' only after Saigō was released from his second period of exile.

Whether to open the country or expel the foreigner was the same question as whether to maintain friendly relations with foreign countries or open hostilities with them. If this were so, then no country would find 'war' its 'national interest', and conversely, to continue friendly relations at no time could be in the national interest either. This reasoning on the part of Kaishū was consistent with the arguments of Yokoi Shōnan (Heishirō), who as the brain behind the Lord of Echizen had been appointed to the position of political president in the Bakufu. When Kaishū visited Shōnan in November 1862, the following discussion took place:

> On 19th (November) I went to work. I met Mr Yokoi Shōnan. My question to him: "At present everyone is talking about opening the country or keeping it closed. To talk about opening or closing the country is the same as discussing the question of war or peace. It is only a question of vocabulary. What is the advantage in that?"
>
> Mr Yokoi replied: "Yes, you are right. For some time we should refrain from arguing about this issue. Expelling foreigners addresses the basis of the nationality of our country. But we should certainly not think that we should give priority to national construction and prohibit foreigners from staying in our country (killing foreigners will not help to defend our nationhood). We should not be obsessed by the vocabulary of opening the country. The business of constructing Japan must be conducted through a unified nobility and by preparing our great Navy. At present nobody is giving thought to this, which is regrettable."
>
> (Ibid., p. 17)

Here Yokoi Shōnan expressed the 'shelving' argument more clearly than Katsu Kaishū: "For some time we should refrain from arguing about this." Secondly, the "unified nobility" spoken of by Yokoi was the same as Saigō's "alliance of retainers". Moreover, the "anti-foreigner" expression in Yokoi's "Expelling foreigners addresses the basis of the nationality of our country" suggested that it was necessary to foster support for the nation among the people.

Two years before his discussion with Katsu, Yokoi Shōnan wrote his famous "Three points concerning national interests". In his argument he divided "prosperous country" from "strong military", the first later forming the template

18   *Japan's Modern History*

for the 'investment and promotion of industry' of Ōkubo Toshimichi, while the latter was the precursor of the naval development programme of Katsu Kaishū, the naval administrator. So that now, in this discussion between the two men, Saigō's 'alliance of retainers' was explained by the expression 'unified nobility'.

On the other hand, not only in Katsu but also in Yokoi, the expression of a national horizontal alliance of samurai was lacking. As is clear if we compare it with the previously mentioned proposal for an assembly in the 'Satsuma–Tosa alliance', Yokoi's idea of a unified nobility could lead to an 'upper house', but not a 'lower house'. As we have already pointed out, the importance of a 'lower house', in other words a horizontal alliance of samurai from all over the country, was also lacking in the Satsuma domain *seichūgumi* that emerged while Saigō was in exile. These were proponents of a 'single domain action of reverence for the Emperor' on the part of Shimazu Hisamitsu, who had forbidden Ōkubo Toshimichi to interact with samurai from other domains.

The Seichūgumi *and the* Mitategumi

Nevertheless, the horizontal alliance of samurai across the country premised on shelving differences over "opening or closing the country", which Saigō had proposed to Shimazu Hisamitsu shortly before he was exiled to Tokunoshima, would probably not have been possible if Saigō had not been exiled. I believe that, whatever the extent of Saigō's ability, it would have been extremely difficult to maintain in a horizontal alliance between samurai who supported opening the country and samurai who wanted to expel the foreigner.

One reason for this was that lower-ranking samurai of the Chōshū domain had created an organisation of lower-ranking samurai proclaiming the need to expel foreigners. Much like the *seichūgumi*, formed in 1859 in Satsuma in support of an 'alliance within the domain favouring the Emperor', the *Mitategumi* was formed in the Chōshū domain in 1862, centring on the policy of expelling the foreigner. The *Mitategumi* was founded when Mōri Motonori, the son of the Lord of Chōshū, tried to persuade Takasugi Shinsaku, Kusaka Genzui and Inoue Kaoru to give up plans to kill foreign embassy officials, who at the weekend would stroll around Kanazawa Hakkei – now a part of Kanagawa prefecture.

This resembled the foundation of the *Seichūgumi* in Satsuma, but the *Mitategumi* differed from the *Seichūgumi* in that it did not fall under the control of the domain lord. The blood pledge of the *Mitategumi* was, to put it favourably, an association opposed to foreigners; but speaking unfavourably, it was a terrorist organisation for attacking foreigners. The one thing that the Chōshū domain was united on was the aim of forming an alliance within the domain to expel foreigners, but different methods could be used to carry this out in practice.

A typical example of this was when the British consulate was subjected to arson. The *Mitategumi* carried this out immediately after they had been persuaded to stop attacking foreigners in Kanazawa Hakkei by the successor of their domain lord. The new consulate in Shinagawa Gotenyama had at the time only just been completed, but the consular staff had not yet moved in. Thirteen men of the

Reform, 1857–1863 19

Mitategumi, including this time also Itō Hirobumi, broke into and burned the empty British consulate, which was guarded only by a few Bakufu officials. This took place around midnight on 12th December 1862.

Hisamitsu's written opinion

A person today comparing the Satsuma military force of about a thousand men marching under the banner 'domain alliance in honour of the Emperor' with the torching of the British consulate at Gotenyama by just 13 samurai calling for the expulsion of foreigners, would undoubtedly declare the Satsuma domain the winner. But in (intercalary) August of 1862, Shimazu Hisamitsu, returning to Kyoto in triumph from his great mission, was coldly rebuffed by the Court, by powerful domains and by samurai from various domains.

The reason for this is clear from a reading of Hisamitsu's written opinion sent as a report to the Emperor immediately after returning to Kyoto. In this he accepted reform of the Bakufu in the sense that it had already, following Hitotsubashi Yoshinobu's accession to the position of Shogun, appointed Matsudaira Yoshinaga as political president, and had denied the need for other powerful lords to combine on the initiative of the Court. He also severely criticised the arguments of samurai from various domains, mainly supporting expulsion of foreigners, as "the rantings of yokels", and he urged the Court not to accept any of their suggestions (Katsuta Magohisa, *Ōkubo Toshimichi den* ['Biography of Ōkubo Toshimichi'], Dōbunkan, 1910, vol. 1, p. 335).

I would now like to go back to Saigō's arguments before his second exile, which we have already investigated. He tried to persuade Hisamitsu that a military expedition by Satsuma alone, without an alliance with some other powerful domains, could not succeed, and also that in such an alliance inter-domain cooperation between powerful samurai was essential. For this he was returned to exile.

Lacking these two elements, Hisamitsu's written opinion sought to persuade the Emperor that expelling the foreigner was wrong:

> The question of expelling foreigners is the big issue of our time, and is the origin of the divisions between the Court and the Bakufu. Moreover, in Kantō, since the treaties are already signed, declaring that foreigners are to be expelled will not be accepted. . . . The reason for this is that if, as well as concluding treaties we were to declare war, the foreigners would act in an immoral and tyrannical fashion, the allied nations would immediately get together, send dozens of warships and attack violently not only in the seas off Edo, but also inland ports, and invade indefensible inland areas. . . . We are not well prepared for naval warfare, so the chances of victory are extremely small.
>
> (Ibid., pp. 342–4)

On the face of it this seems a very logical argument. In the Japan of that time, incapable of building a single warship on its own, the idea of declaring war on the Western powers was simply crazy.

20   *Japan's Modern History*

But from the viewpoint of this book, starting with our investigation of why political reform failed in 1857 and 1858, Hisamitsu's written opinion was a tower built on sand. What the 'Ansei reform' aimed at was for powerful domain lords and powerful samurai to cooperate, and while operating within the Bakufu structure, to construct a new political system. But four years later, in 1862, the reform envisaged by the Satsuma domain excluded powerful lords and powerful samurai; the Court also gave up on expelling foreigners and could only think of strengthening relations between Court and Bakufu. In other words, if Hitotsubashi Yoshinobu, who had a brilliant reputation, and Matsudaira Yoshinaga, the former Lord of the Echizen domain, could be appointed respectively as shogunal guard and political president, it was as though reform had come to an end.

2 Revolution, 1863–1871

Rehabilitation of the Saigō Scheme

Councillors' conference

Moving into 1863 the Court activities of the pro-Emperor, anti-foreign faction centred on the Chōshū domain were becoming effective, and in opposition to them the Satsuma domain had shifted from a pan-domain, pro-Emperor approach towards a policy of alliance between various domain lords and their retainers. The way this happened is analysed in detail in chapters 3 and 4 of the previously mentioned work by Sasaki Katsu, *Bakumatsu seiji to Satsuma han* ('Bakumatsu Politics and the Satsuma Domain'), Yoshikawa kōbunkan, 2004, pp. 123–8.

Chapter 3 of this same work, entitled *Bunkyū sannen to Satsuma han* ('1863 and the Satsuma domain') makes clear that the 18th August Court coup d'état occurred not by force of Satsuma arms, but rather by the strength of various domains – Aizu, Tottori, Okayama, Tokushima and Yonezawa – which were unhappy with the control over the Court being exercised by the Chōshū domain. This was the realisation of the alliance urged on Shimazu Hisamitsu by Saigō Takamori a year earlier (pp. 179–84).

Another important point to note is that a horizontal alliance of samurai from various domains, strictly forbidden a year before, proceeded in a positive fashion while preparing for the August political change. This point is brought out in detail in a letter to Ōkubo Toshimichi by the Satsuma domain Court liaison official, Murayama Matsune, cited in the same book. Rather than reproducing it again, I refer the reader to pp. 164–6 of the book, and will summarise it below:

(1) On arriving in Higo (Kumamoto) on 6th April, by chance I ran into the domain samurai Tokutomi Tadasuke (Ikkei, father of Sohō and Roka). This man is a disciple of Yokoi Shōnan, and has been my friend for many years. Together with him I also met Mitsuoka Hachirō (Yuri Kimimasa).

(2) The position of Echizen and Higo is to open up the country, but the rights and wrongs of this are for the future, and at any rate for the time being our domain should revive its alliance with these other two domains.

(3) The reputation in Kyoto of the domain lord of Echizen, Matsudaira Shungaku (Yoshinaga), is bad, and violence by the Chōshū domain is increasing, so that

22 *Japan's Modern History*

if the three domains forge an alliance and go to Kyoto, military conflict and bloodletting will be hard to avoid. The present plan should be finished in three or four days, so it will not be necessary for a large number of people to spend a long time in Kyoto, but in order to help the situation there a certain number of troops will be necessary.

At the political change that took place in Kyoto on 18th August, when pro-Emperor, anti-foreign faction *kuge* and samurai from the Chōshū domain were expelled from Kyoto, the Echizen and Higo domains did not mobilise troops but rather those domain lords who acted as guards or police for Kyoto – namely the domains of Aizu and Yodo, also Tottori, Okayama, Yonezawa, Tokushima and Tosa. The number of Satsuma troops involved was around 150.

Even so, what seems worth noting in the letter from Murayama Matsune to Ōkubo is the point that a multi-party alliance between the class of domain lords and domain samurai, largely absent since Saigō's return from exile, was once again making an appearance. In this it is worth noting that the Satsuma domain samurai Murayama, in talking with Tokutomi Tadasuke of the Higo domain and Yuri Kimimasa of the Echizen domain, was aiming at an alliance of the three domains. As we have repeatedly pointed out, it was a multi-party alliance not only at domain lord level, but also at the level of domain samurai that was the essence of the Saigō plan.

Table 2.1

Year	Era name and year	Events
1863	Bunkyū 3	War between Satsuma and Britain; 18th August political change; councillor system (began 1864).
1864	Genchi 1	Saigō Takamori released, returns to his domain; Ikedaya riot; Kinmon revolt; First punishment of Chōshū; Four nation shelling of Shimonoseki; Saigō discussion with Katsu Kaishū.
1865	Keiō 1	Second punishment of Chōshū announced; Imperial treaty sanction.
1866	Keiō 2	Satsuma-Chōshū Alliance; Punishment of Chōshū lifted.
1867	Keiō 3	Satsuma–Tosa Agreement; Shōgun returned his power to the Court.
1868	Meiji 1	Proclamation of Imperial Restoration; Institution of three ranks (President (*sōsai*), Senior Councillor (gijō), Junior Councillor (*sanyo*) – see above, 1863; Struggle at Toba and Fushimi; Boshin war, to 1869; Bloodless opening of Edo Castle; Charter Oath; Change of era – era to change with each reign.
1869	Meiji 2	Tokyo becomes the capital; Battle of Goryōkaku (Hakodate); Ezochi becomes Hokkaidō.
1870	Meiji 3	Engineering Ministry established.
1871	Meiji 4	Three domains contribute troops (establishment of Imperial Guard); New currency edict; Abolition of domains, introduction of prefectures; Japan-China Friendship Treaty.

Revolution, 1863–1871   23

After the pro-Emperor, anti-foreign faction had been driven out to Chōshū in the August political change, a conference at the domain lord level of the two levels of the multi-party alliance, held at the end of 1863, showed that at this level it had become somewhat institutionalised. A 'conference of councillors' (*sanyo kaigi*) was set up including, apart from Tokugawa Yoshinobu, Matsudaira Katamori of Aizu and the domain lords of Echizen, Tosa, Uwajima and Satsuma.

But this conference of councillors, which was not accompanied by a conference at samurai level supporting domain lords as a whole, was abolished a mere two months later without having made any concrete achievements. Domain lords from Tosa, Echizen, Uwajima, Satsuma and elsewhere resigned from the conference and returned to their respective domains. Even though the Bakufu and powerful domain lords, without their close advisers, had gathered and held meetings at the Imperial Palace in Kyoto and at the Nijō Castle, nothing had come together. As a result, the power of the Bakufu in Kyoto was restored. The powerful Lords of Satsuma, Echizen, Tosa and elsewhere, who had plotted to enter central politics under the banner of 'alliance between Court and Bakufu' (*kōbu gattai*), found themselves consigned to oblivion in the struggle between the Bakufu, which had seized Kyoto, and the pro-Emperor, anti-foreign faction that had coalesced at Chōshū.

Pardon for Saigō Takamori

Saigō's supporters of the Satsuma domain, placed in a tough situation, over two years sought to persuade Shimazu Hisamitsu to grant a pardon for Saigō Takamori, who was in exile on Okinoerabu island in Kagoshima Bay. It was essential that his rights be restored to Saigō, who had come to argue that if they were mired in the disputes between the pro-Emperor, anti-foreigner faction and the faction that was pro-Bakufu and wanted to open the country, then the disputes between these two factions should be shelved, and they should rally round the slogan of overthrowing the Bakufu and restoring the Emperor.

As I have repeatedly stated, Saigō had powerful allies and friends both among the anti-foreign faction and among the country-opening faction. He was a consistent advocate of a 'multi-party alliance', and engaged in practical activities for this aim.

On the other hand, he had twice been frustrated by the arbitrariness of Shimazu Hisaakira, deputy lord of the domain. What Saigō needed when he was released from exile at the end of February 1864 was not only a plan and a network, but also the power to carry out the plan. In this sense the appointment of Saigō, just after his release, to the position of 'military service official' (*gunfuyaku*) is important. Katsuta Magoyasu, in his *Saigō Takamori den* (Biography of Saigō Takamori), wrote as follows about Saigō in the period after his release:

> The first time that Hisamitsu sentenced Takamori to the penalty of exile, he was certainly angry at Takamori's activities . . . but he also perceived that Saigō was an exceptionally knowledgeable and principled man. Therefore, when he was put under pressure by the resented pro-Emperor party, he

24 *Japan's Modern History*

summoned Saigō, and from then on mostly entrusted him with matters of state, including reorganising the bureaucracy.

After Hisamitsu returned home, those who remained in Kyoto were the young nobleman Shimazu Zusho (Hisaharu), the chief retainer Komatsu Tatewaki, the military service official Saigō Takamori, the military affairs *bugyō* Ichiji Masaharu, the chief executive secretary Yoshii Tomozane, and other samurai (*yūshi*) and military officers. They were given the task of guarding the Imperial Palace, and the person effectively in charge of directing this work was Saigō. Ōkubo followed Hisamitsu back to Kagoshima, devoted himself to work within the domain, repelled the conservatives, and managed to bring about cooperation between the domain and those who had stayed in Kyoto. Opinion in Satsuma had greatly changed, and from this the great work of Restoration may be said to have originated.

(Katsuta, vol. 2, pp. 93–4)

The phrase saying that Hisamitsu summoned Saigō overcome by 'the resented pro-Emperor party' is revealing. Two years before, Hisamitsu sent Saigō into exile because he opposed his idea of a multi-level alliance. But neither Hisamitsu's march to Kyoto (1862), nor the consultative association of powerful domain lords (1863–4), achieved any spectacular results. Moreover, during the increasingly bitter conflict between the pro-Emperor, anti-foreign faction and the pro-Bakufu faction, Satsuma's influence was actually declining. In the midst of this, Hisamitsu, pressured by the "exasperation around the pro-Emperor party", summoned Saigō and assigned to him an important role.

Saigō returned to Kagoshima from Okinoerabujima as a kind of 'triumphal Shogun', was assigned to the Satsuma domain residence in Kyoto, and controlled the military forces of the Satsuma domain. Just as Katsuta wrote, "opinion in Satsuma greatly evolved", and "the great work of the Restoration may be said to have originated from this (the restoration of Takamori's rights)". Incidentally, Komatsu Takeaki, Ichiji Masaharu, Yoshii Tomonari, Ōkubo Toshimichi, whose names we have already introduced, and others, taken together, worked as a unified group under Saigō for four years up to the restoration of the monarchy, and never wavered. The Meiji Restoration is often termed a 'revolution by lower-ranking samurai', but the 'revolution by lower-ranking samurai' in Satsuma began with the restoration of the rights of Saigō Takamori at the beginning of 1864.

Feudal parliament

The Kinmon revolt (Kinmon no hen)

Saigō's main idea after accomplishing his aim of fomenting a revolution of lower-ranking samurai was probably to bring about a horizontal alliance with lower-ranking samurai from various domains. But because of the political change of 18th August 1863 while Saigō was in exile, the lower-ranking samurai of the Chōshū domain were hostile to Satsuma. To aim at a horizontal alliance with Takasugi

Revolution, 1863–1871   25

Shinsaku, Kido Kōin, Kusaka Genzui and others was virtually impossible even for Saigō.

On this point, Katsuta's *Saigō Takamori den* introduces the following episode. It was at the time when the Chōshū forces, on their way to the Kinmon revolt (July 1864), were gathering in a Kyoto suburb.

> At that time Kusaka Michitake (Genzui) and Maki Izumi (pro-Emperor, anti-foreign) were at the Tenryū Temple. Matsuda Michiyuki (samurai from the Tottori domain), told them about the fact that Saigō was coming up to Kyoto. Maki said that if Takamori were recalled Satsuma's policies would quickly change. But since he could see that Satsuma's policies had not changed, he found it difficult to believe that Saigō had been recalled. He was very doubtful that Saigō was coming up to Kyoto.
>
> (Katsuta, p. 104)

This is nothing more than a single episode, but it shows that Saigō, who was aiming for a multi-party alliance including samurai who revered the Emperor, was trusted by the pro-Emperor, anti-foreigner faction of the Chōshū domain.

On the other hand, Saigō's 'multi-party alliance' argument had to be fulfilled both at the level of domain lords and at the level of radical samurai. But as shown in the direct action of the Chōshū domain, the first level, namely an alliance of powerful domain lords, was decisively absent. Obtaining Chōshū support for the Satsuma approach just on the basis of expectations by Chōshū samurai was something that even Saigō was unable to deliver. All that Saigō could achieve while conflict was intensifying between the Bakufu and the Chōshū domain was to do nothing until the doctrine of 'revering the Emperor' was clarified.

The immediate reason why some 1,800 soldiers from Chōshū came from Fushimi, Saga and Yamazaki to the Imperial Palace in Kyoto was the Ikedaya riots that occurred the previous month (June). Ever since the failure of attempts between January and March of the same year by powerful domain lords to interfere in the politics of the Court and of the Bakufu, Hitotsubashi Yoshinobu, Guardian of the Shogun, sought to maintain security in Kyoto on the basis of the Bakufu's own power, adding the *Shinsengumi* of Kondō Isamu to the Aizu domain (worth 280,000 *koku* of rice) and the Kuwana domain (110,000 *koku*). The Ikedaya riot occurred when 77 members of the *Shinsengumi* attacked Kido Kōin of Chōshū and about 20 others who were hiding at an inn in the Nijō district of Kyoto and plotting to wrest power back. The march on Kyoto of the Chōshū forces in July was designed as an act of revenge, but for the Satsuma forces led by Saigō neither of these incidents was more than a private struggle, not a public one.

Nevertheless, in a show of strength 1,800 soldiers from Chōshū marched on the Imperial Palace in Kyoto, resulting in the 'Punishment Decree' from the Palace against Chōshū. For the Satsuma domain, while the possibility of restoring relations with the Chōshū pro-Emperor, anti-foreign faction remained for the future, for the time being Chōshū had to be attacked. The Satsuma forces, now increased to some hundreds of soldiers, working together with the forces of the

26 *Japan's Modern History*

Aizu, Kuwana and other domains based in Kyoto, defeated the forces of Chōshū and others that were attacking the Imperial Palace.

If this were all, it would be essentially the same as a year earlier when Saigō was still in exile. If reconciliation with the Chōshū pro-Emperor, anti-foreign faction were not possible in the near future, Saigō's goal of bringing about a multi-party alliance including samurai could not be achieved. After the 1864 Kinmon revolt, Saigō and the Satsuma domain faced deadlock.

The Saigō–Katsu discussion and the assembly argument

A chance to resolve this deadlock emerged with a discussion between Saigō and Katsu in November of the same year.

As we have already noted, between March and July Saigō was in charge of military service at the domain residence in Kyoto, but because of his five years out of circulation he had lost his network of contacts with the 'enlightenment faction' within the Bakufu. For instance, he had never had a meeting with the former naval *bugyō* Katsu Kaishū, and in this he was behind the chief retainer (*karō*) Komatsu Taiteki and Yoshii Tomozane. Director of Konando (supervisors of the private life of the Lord). With an introduction from Yoshii, Saigō visited Katsu in Kyoto on 11th September.

At their first meeting on this day Katsu apparently did not form any particular impression of Saigō (*Katsu Kaishū zenshū*, vol. 18, p. 216). For Saigō, it was different. In a letter to Ōkubo Toshimichi, he wrote as follows about this meeting:

> When I first met Katsu, I found him a really amazing man, I was at first intending to attack him, but I found myself bowing to him. I would say that he has a capacity for ingenuity that I have seldom encountered. He is a man with a brave disposition, and is more able than Sakuma (Shōzan). Even though Sakuma is outstanding in learning and knowledge, in terms of present practice Mr Katsu is a person I really admire.
>
> (Rikkyō Daigaku Nihon shi kenkyūkai (ed.), *Ōkubo Toshimichi tsū kankei bunsho* ['Materials Relating to Ōkubo Toshimichi'], Yoshikawa Kōbunkan, vol. 3, p. 312)

The reason why Saigō admired Katsu to this extent is not sufficiently expressed in this letter to Ōkubo. This is shown by the fact that Saigō's assertion over several years that there should be a multi-party alliance was heard favourably by Katsu, who spoke of a "council of four or five wise domain lords" to establish the 'national interest'. Just one point is worth noting, namely that Saigō understood Katsu's view as advocacy of a permanent regime: "This policy means establishing assembly politics (*kyōwa seiji*) on a permanent basis" (ibid.).

It is clear that he meant systematising 'assembly politics on a permanent basis', but what he meant by 'assembly politics' is not evident. From the perspective of several years of argument up to that point by Saigō, "a council of four or five wise men", and so on, does not easily translate into "assembly politics". Indeed,

Revolution, 1863–1871 27

this probably meant little more than the idea of a multi-party alliance that he had been using for some time.

The meaning of what he called 'assembly politics' is clear from a letter sent to Ōkubo Toshimichi by Yoshii Tomozane, who accompanied Saigō to Kaishū's place. In this letter, Yoshii writes as follows:

> The argument of Ōkubo of Echizen (Ōkubo Ichiō, former Bakufu Army *bugyō*), of Yokoi (Shōnan) and of Katsu (former Navy *bugyō*) is that we should *attack Chōshū and proclaim the crimes of Shogunate officials* simultaneously, bring together national talent and set up a *deliberative assembly*, including *lower-ranking samurai, representing the national voice and establishing the national purpose* right now, as there is no other way to recover the prosperity of our nation . . .
>
> (Ibid., vol. 5, p. 342; present writer's italics)

The initial phrase "We should attack Chōshū and proclaim the crimes of Shogunate officials" implied that the first Chōshū war should be brought to a conclusion in the form of both victory and defeat. Later Takasugi Shinsaku and other Chōshū samurai who trusted Saigō would revive negotiations with Satsuma.

The next point about a "deliberative assembly" and "lower-ranking samurai" coincided with Saigō's consistent argument that there should be a two-level alliance between domain lords and between samurai. In another place attached to this Yoshii writes "Saigō will give you more details".

Incidentally, Ōkubo Ichiō, Katsu Kaishū and Yokoi Shōnan were representative of the Enlightenment faction within the Bakufu. Yokoi was a Kumamoto domain samurai, and was famous as the brains behind Matsudaira Yoshinaga, the former lord of Echizen. Yoshinaga, however, was not just the former lord of Echizen, and we should not forget that he exercised a great deal of influence within the Bakufu as Political President. Reading Katsu Kaishū's diary from 1862 to 1864, it is easy to understand how much Kaishū, the Bakufu minister, admired Yoshinaga. It can also be understood from Katsu Kaishū's diary of the same period that Kaishū expected great things from Komatsu Taiteki, who was *karō* of the Satsuma domain and who had been introduced to him by Yoshinaga.

If we put all these things together, we can see that relations of trust had existed for some time between Yoshinaga, the Bakufu Political President, Tatewaki, Chief Retainer of the Satsuma domain, Yokoi, Katsu and Ōkubo Ichiō – the three men who formed the enlightenment faction within the Bakufu – and although he was different from them, Saigō, who was the great hope of lower-ranking samurai from many different domains, was added to this list in September 1864. As we have already discussed, in the Katsu–Saigō discussions on that day, the two of them agreed that war between the Bakufu and Chōshū should be looked on as a private quarrel, and that two assemblies should be set up, one between domain lords and the other between retainers (upper house and lower house). On the question of seeing the Bakufu–Chōshū struggle as a private quarrel, in their understanding that Chōshū, which was anti-foreigner, should be pressured to change its

28 *Japan's Modern History*

line may be seen the genesis of the Satsuma–Chōshū alliance that came about in January (old calendar) 1866.

Abandonment of the anti-foreigner position of the Chōshū domain

As is well known, the first clash between Chōshū and the Bakufu ended in victory for the latter, but after that the Satsuma domain quickly came together with Chōshū. The beginning of this development was when, through mediation by the Tosa domain *rōshi* (independent samurai) Sakamoto Ryōma, both agreed that the Chōshū domain should purchase rifles from the Englishman Glover under the name of Satsuma. In a letter from Ōkubo Toshimichi to a Satsuma samurai studying in England, dated August 1865, he wrote of the anger of powerful domain lords against the Bakufu, and also about the change of line on the part of Chōshū from anti-foreigner to opening the country:

> Since the (first) Chōshū war, the so-called aggressive extremist party have mostly opened their eyes, and have come to their senses over their insistence that foreigners must be expelled. They have come round to the general view and are generally advocating the opening of the country. I hear that the more discriminating of the domains (Saga, Echizen, Tosa, Uwajima etc.) are looking positively at commercial law (trade).
> (Katsuta Magohisa, *Ōkubo Toshimichi den* ['Biography of Ōkubo Toshimichi'], vol. 1, p. 646)

If the Chōshū domain abandoned its anti-foreigner position, Chōshū and Satsuma could unite to overthrow the Bakufu. If Hizen, Echizen, Tosa, Uwajima and other major domains pursued the aim of opening the country and concentrated on commercial law (trade), then the major domains including Satsuma could unite under the slogan *fukoku kyōhei* (prosperous country, strong army). In these circumstances if the Bakufu were unsuccessful in the second Chōshū revolt, then its authority and power throughout the country would quickly collapse.

These circumstances, for Saigō, who had been consistently advocating a multiparty alliance, were an excellent opportunity to establish a new regime. In addition, Saigō and Yoshii had been learning the idea from the already mentioned Bakufu enlightenment faction – Ōkubo Ichiō, Yokoi Shōnan and Katsu Kaishū – that the 'multi-party alliance' should be upgraded to a 'public assembly'. The Sat-Chō alliance of January 1866, and the June 1867 Satsuma–Tosa alliance, were for Saigō the fulfilment of his 'multi-party alliance'.

The Sat–Chō alliance

Particulars of the alliance

However successful the major domain lords were in forming a 'multi-party' alliance', they could never succeed in overthrowing the Bakufu if they continued

Revolution, 1863–1871   29

to exclude the Chōshū domain (producer of 360,000 *koku* of rice). This domain sounded the slogan 'expel the foreigner, overthrow the Bakufu' and was itself at daggers drawn with the Bakufu. As shown by the term *kōbu gattai* (Alliance of Court and Bakufu) popular in the Bakumatsu period, it was only when the Bakufu and the domains could cooperate in supporting the Court that an end might be put to this division. The Sat-Chō alliance of January 1866 was epoch-making as an 'alliance' in that it broke down the barrier.

On the other hand, the attitude of Satsuma to this important alliance is not well understood. Komatsu Taiteki, Saigō Takamori and Ōkubo Toshimichi, who exchanged many letters while they were living apart in Kagoshima, Kyoto and Edo, gathered at this time in the domain residence in Kyoto to meet Kido Kōin and his party, so no letters between them during this period survive.

If we follow the way the alliance was constructed based principally on documents from the Chōshū side, the outline is as follows.

At the end of 1865 the Satsuma Minister Komatsu Tateaki and the Military Commander Saigō Takamori sent a secret messenger (Kuroda Kiyotaka) to the leader of the Chōshū anti-Bakufu faction, and proposed to improve relations between the two domains through the visit to Kyoto of Kido Kōin. By chance Sakamoto Ryōma, a leaderless samurai who had defected from the Tosa domain but was greatly trusted by the Satsuma domain, was at Shimonoseki in Chōshū, and together with Kuroda did his best to persuade Kido. Kido, however, refused to be persuaded. In Chōshū at that time, in the middle of a civil war with the Bakufu, various armed units including the *kiheitai* of Takasugi Shinsaku (others were the *yūgekitai*, the *shūgitai*, the *giyūtai* and various other irregular units) were exercising power, and among them there was strong feeling not only against Aizu, but also against Satsuma.

Nevertheless, perhaps because among them Saigō's reputation remained exceptionally high, Takasugi's *kiheitai* and the *yūgekitai* reacted positively to Kido's visit to Saigō. As a result, Miyoshi Guntarō and Shinagawa Yajirō of the *kiheitai*, Hayakawa Wataru of the *yūgekitai*, among others, accompanied Kido on his journey to Kyoto.

The Satsuma side worked hard to welcome Kido and his entourage when they arrived at the Satsuma residence (Komatsu house) in Kyoto in January 1866. The senior vassal of the domain Shimazu Hisahiro, the chief minister Katsura Uemon, and below them in rank Komatsu, Saigō, Ōkubo, Yoshii Tomozane and others cared for them diligently and engaged with them in discussions concerning affairs of State.

They did not, however, broach the subject of an alliance between Satsuma and Chōshū. At that time it was Chōshū that was in a difficult situation because of the recent second assault on Chōshū by the Bakufu. Therefore Satsuma had no reason to ask for an alliance with Chōshū. But for the same reason, it would have been humiliating for Kido to plead distress and beg for an alliance.

Kido Kōin's six articles

The man who brought about a resolution of the competing positions held by the two domains seems to have been Sakamoto Ryōma. For it was Ryōma who later,

30 *Japan's Modern History*

at Kido's request, certified as authentic the 'Six Articles of Agreement for Cooperation between Chōshū and Satsuma', the text of which does not remain in the Satsuma archives.

Kido's original draft and Sakamoto's authenticated draft were presented in an NHK 'taiga' drama series in 2010, but there is only one remaining text of the famous Sat-Chō alliance. I think it might perhaps be unnecessary to reproduce here this well-known document, but for this writer who has followed Saigō's long-standing dream of an inter-domain samurai alliance with the aim of 'revering the Emperor and overthrowing the Bakufu' (not 'revering the Emperor and expelling the foreigner') it is something that ought not to be omitted.

The six articles of Kido Kōin's text are as follows:

1   When war [with the Bakufu] breaks out, [Satsuma] shall rapidly mobilise over two thousand troops, which will join troops currently in Kyoto; about one thousand will leave for Naniwa (Ōsaka), and they will take control of both Kyoto and Ōsaka.
2   When we come to the point of victory, at that time the Satsuma domain shall report to the Court, on behalf of the Chōshū domain, that the charges against the Chōshū domain are false.
3   If defeat in the war seems likely, [Chōshū] for a year and a half shall never give up, and in the meantime, Satsuma shall without fail expend its utmost efforts to prove that the charges against Chōshū are false.
4   When the Bakufu forces return to Edo, this shall be reported to the Court, and quickly efforts shall be made for all false charges to be dropped by the Court.
5   When the Satsuma troops have been sent to Kyōto, if Hitotsubashi, Aizu, Kuwana and other domains should needlessly interrupt the work of protecting the Emperor, maintaining morality and making great efforts, then there will be no alternative [for Satsuma against the Bakufu] to engage in a decisive battle.
6   When the false charges are dropped, the two sides shall sincerely come together, and it goes without saying that they shall expend their utmost efforts on behalf of the Emperor, so that by whatever means both sides, having the goal of restoring the Imperial prestige to its full brightness, shall act with sincerity and expend great efforts towards the goal of restoring the Imperial prestige to its full brightness.

> (Kido kōdenki hensanjo (ed.), *Shōgiku Kido kōden*
> ['Official Biography of Kido Kōin'], vol. 1, pp. 598–9)

As is evident from a first reading, it has the hallmarks not so much of a covenant as of a document of affirmation made in Chōshū (Sasaki Katsu, *Bakumatsu seiji to Satsuma han* (Bakumatsu Politics and the Satsuma Domain), pp. 324–5). It was a kind of 'reverse memorandum' from the Kido camp, saying: "Look, Komatsu Taiteki and Saigō Takamori of Satsuma definitely promised these six articles to Kido Kōin."

Revolution, 1863–1871   31

If we take another look at these six articles of the Sat-Chō alliance, famous as the starting point for the restoration of the Emperor in January 1868, we notice that nearly all of them relate to the 'false charges' against Chōshū as disloyal. This is the case with article 2: "at that time the Satsuma domain shall report to the Court that the charges against the Satsuma domain are false"; while in article 3 the phrase: "and in the meantime (Satsuma) shall without fail expend its utmost efforts etc." relates to the same thing. Articles 4 and 6 constitute a condition directly proclaiming the need to wipe out 'false accusations'. When in conjunction with article 4 we consider the meaning of "decisive battle" in article 5, it becomes clear that if the Bakufu, along with the Aizu and Kuwana domains and others, continued to treat Chōshū as disloyal, then Satsuma and Chōshū would use force against them. (Concerning the history of interpretations of the Sat-Chō alliance, see Iechika Yoshiki, *Saigō Takamori to bakumatsu ishin no seikyoku* ['Saigō Takamori and politics in the Bakumatsu and Restoration Periods'], Mineruba Shobō, 2011, pp. 107–9).

This problem may be summarised as a question of whether Chōshū was giving precedence to the Court clearing up the 'false charges' against it, or was putting first the task for Satsuma and Chōshū of overthrowing the Bakufu, along with Aizu and Kuwana. If the return of political rule to the Emperor (*taisei hōkan*) (by the last Shōgun) in October 1867 had included a restoration of the honour of Chōshū, then perhaps the Restoration of Imperial Rule (*ōsei fukko*) coup d'état two months later would not have taken place.

This is not to be found in the archives, but Saigō Takamori was passionate about the six articles and, faithful to his plan for reform, by means of a multi-party alliance involving both major domain lords and their retainers, strove to work out a way of restoring the honour of the Chōshū domain.

Conference of major domain lords

The Sat-Chō alliance worked in favour of Chōshū at the time of the second Chōshū assault in 1866, but this did not succeed in delivering a fatal blow to the Bakufu. Following the death from illness of the Shōgun Iemochi, Hitotsubashi Yoshinobu, who had ended the war with Chōshū, continued to treat Chōshū as disloyal even after the end of hostilities.

Yoshinobu, moreover, once the war had finished, pressed the Court to hold a conference of major domain lords, as had previously been urged by Satsuma, Echizen, Tosa, Uwajima and other domains. He was in fact proposing a structure that was taken as the reverse of Saigō's pet project of a multi-party alliance.

As for those who were designated powerful domain lords not by themselves but by the Bakufu, they did not go to Kyoto if they happened to be ill, but simply sent their deputies. In Satsuma, Hisamitsu did not go to Kyoto himself, but sent Komatsu Tateaki and Saigō Takamori as his deputies (they arrived in Kyoto on 28th October 1866).

But when we come to 1867, Saigō counterattacked. In the middle of February, he went by himself to Tosa and conferred on methods of opposition with the

32 *Japan's Modern History*

previous Tosa domain lord, Yamanouchi Yōdō, as well as the Uwajima Lord Date Munenari. On the occasion of his visit Saigō, following his pet project, emphasised discussion not only with domain lords, but also with important retainers. Indeed, in Tosa he exchanged views over policy with Fukuoka Takachika.

On the basis of these preparations, the Lord of Satsuma, Shimazu Hisamitsu, who in October of the previous year had declined the divine call of the Court and described the Bakufu as 'diseased', went up to Kyoto with Saigō Takamori and over 700 men. On 25th March they left Kagoshima, arrived on 2nd April in Ōsaka, and reached Kyoto on the 12th. Having received prior persuasion from Saigō, the reform domains of Echizen, Tosa and Uwajima agreed this time to leave for Kyoto.

At the conference of powerful domain lords held in May 1867, the points of dispute between the Bakufu side and the four domains, including Satsuma, were extremely clear.

The Bakufu side boiled down the aims of the conference of powerful domain lords to resolving the question of opening a port at Hyōgo (Kōbe), which had been postponed over a long period in opposition to the Western powers, and also to "suppressing as quickly as possible" the Chōshū domain through a regime of national unity. By contrast, the four domains saw as their primary aim, not suppressing Chōshū, but restoring its honour, and they also took the view that the question of opening the Hyōgo port through a regime of national unity was acceptable *provided that Chōshū also participated*. Saigō himself, faithful to the six articles drawn up a year before, continued to assert that the prime aim should be to lift the 'false charges against Chōshū' (Katsuta Magohisa, *Saigō Takamori den*, vol. 3, p. 119).

The fact that for more than a year from February 1866 the central point of dispute had been whether or not to lift the 'false accusations against Chōshū' might seem incredible. But we should note that the phrase used over and over again was 'false charges'. If the Court and powerful domain lords had admitted that Chōshū's offence was a 'false charge', they would have had to bring into question instead the offence of illegal assault by the Bakufu against the Chōshū.

The alliance between Satsuma and Tosa

If we locate the 'Satsuma–Tosa alliance' of 26th June in the above-mentioned arguments at the 'Conference of four domain lords' (Satsuma, Echizen, Tosa, Uwajima) of around May 1867, it becomes evident that power relations between the Bakufu and Chōshū had been moving greatly in favour of Chōshū. Specifically, its fourth article proclaims: "There is no reason why the affairs of state should be in the hands of the Shōgun. From now on he should relinquish his position and renew his allegiance to the domain lords, while political power must naturally revert to the Court" (Sasaki Katsu, *Bakumatsu seiji to Satsuma han*, p. 370).

A further key point in the Satsuma–Tosa alliance agreement is of course the provision for a two-chamber system comprising an upper house and a lower house. Specifically, "The parliament should be divided into upper and lower chambers, and parliamentarians should range from marquises at the top rank to samurai retainers and the common people at the lower ranks. Men of pure morality should

Revolution, 1863–1871   33

be elected, and moreover domain lords should be assigned duties in the upper house according to their work."

While Gotō Shōjirō, a major official (*sansei*) representing Tosa, was writing a draft of the alliance agreement, it is well known that he used as reference the 'eight shipboard policies' compiled by Sakamoto Ryōma, travelling with him in the same ship from Nagasaki to Hyōgo. But the threesome of Komatsu Tateaki, Saigō Takamori and Ōkubo Toshimichi, who participated in the meeting as representatives of Satsuma, had a detailed knowledge of the 'public assembly' concept put forward by the Shōgun's vassal Ōkubo Ichiō (Tadahiro) – I have touched on this in relation to the first meeting between Saigō and Katsu Kaishū in September 1864 – and the principal retainer (*karō*) Komatsu Taiteki in February 1866, at the Satsuma domain residence in Kyoto, listened to an explanation of the 'public assembly' concept from the Elder Statesman of the Echizen domain, Nakane Yukie.

In any case, in June 1867, when the 'public assembly' idea was proposed by Sakamoto Ryōma and Gotō Shōjirō of Tosa, Komatsu, Saigō and Ōkubo from Satsuma had already made substantial preparations for it.

As is well known, the June alliance of Satsuma and Tosa and the 'White Paper for Return of Political Power to the Emperor' (*taisei hōkan ken hakusho*), which the Tosa domain had presented to the Shōgun in October, had almost the same content. Despite this, even though Satsuma, in alliance with Chōshū, had sent troops to Kyoto, it is uncertain that they had decided to launch a coup d'état for Restoration of Imperial Rule (*ōsei fukko*).

Though I am writing 144 years after these events, I am not the only researcher to entertain such a doubt. The Satsuma military commander with the rank of military administrator (*bugyō*), Ijichi Masaharu, a supporter of Saigō Takamori, immediately after the return of political rule to the Emperor in October expressed the same sort of doubt to Ōkubo. This was his statement of opinion in November 1867 (3rd year of Keiō). He argued as follows:

> Understanding the recent trends, the Tokugawa has at last repented its past grave offences, and decided to resign from the position of Shōgun in order to return its power to the Court. If we consider these circumstances, we should not accuse it too harshly, as this seems to me unfair. I think the Court should accept the Shōgun's resignation peacefully, and appoint him to the top position in the assembly of domain lords. It would be against the Imperial Way to doubt its evil intention without evidence. The Court should treat the former Shōgun in a broadminded fashion. I do not think the idea of reducing the stipends from the Tokugawa lands is appropriate. . . . On the question of land and so on, things are as they have been, but expenditures for maintaining peace internally and externally should also be borne by the Tokugawa domain. The basis of restoring the Emperor system requires respect for human feeling, and following the principles of fairness and diligence, there must be strict regulations under the law.
>
> (*Ōkubo Toshimichi kankei bunsho* ['Materials relating to Ōkubo Toshimichi'], vol. 1, pp. 60–1).

34   *Japan's Modern History*

The phrase in this text "the basis of restoring the Emperor system" does not mean that it was a statement of opinion written after the Restoration of Imperial Rule (*ōsei fukko*) on 9th December. As is shown by the annotation at the end, "November Keiō 3", for Ichiji, *taisei hōkan* meant *ōsei fukko*.

If this is so, then argument over the resignation of Tokugawa Yoshinobu's Lord Keeper of the Privy Seal and the return of territory (*jikan nōchi*) did not occur first with the *ōsei fukko* coup d'état. The hard-line faction pursuing *jikan nōchi* in order to attack Yoshinobu, and not being satisfied with the *taisei hōkan* in October, existed within the Satsuma domain. From what we have already established, we may say that the core of this hard-line faction was Saigō Takamori and Ōkubo Toshimichi.

What Ijichi, the right-hand man of Saigō, did not understand (why was Saigō not satisfied with *taisei hōkan*?) is also unknown to me, writing more than 140 years after these events. Even so, we may perhaps speculate that the key issue, already noted, of restoring the honour of Chōshū may have pushed Saigō and Ōkubo into a hard-line position.

Following the submission of the request for *taisei hōkan*, Tokugawa Yoshinobu resigned his position of Shōgun and stepped down to the position of *daimyō* (domain lord), and even though, following the provisions of the alliance between Satsuma and Tosa, the *kuge* (Court nobles), *daimyō* (domain lords), including Yoshinobu, together with their retainers, had set up a two-chamber parliament, the position of Chōshū as 'disloyal' was unchanged. So long as the present regime of a 'Court' that had designated Chōshū as 'disloyal' did not change, the six articles of the Sat-Chō alliance of January 1866 could not be put into practice. Unless Satsuma and Chōshū, together with the forces of the Court that were backing them, effected a coup backed by force, it would be impossible to restore the honour of the Chōshū domain.

'Feudal parliament' or 'overthrow the Bakufu by force'?

Formation of the 'Imperial Army' (kangun)

Between the proclamation of *ōsei* fukko on 9th December of the third year of Keiō (3rd January 1868), and the military struggle at Toba and Fushimi on 3rd January of the first year of Meiji (27th January 1868), there were 24 days. On 27th December (of Keiō 2), a military parade before the Emperor was held in front of the Imperial Palace (*goshō*, in Kyoto), involving the four domains of Satsuma, Chōshū, Tosa and Aki (Hiroshima). The character of this parade helps us understand the tangled political situation between the *taisei hōkan* and the *ōsei fukko* and up to the fighting at Toba-Fushimi, just south of Kyoto. The diary of Tani Tateki, who had participated in the parade as officer in charge of the Tosa forces, includes the following passage:

> On 27th (December) we held a parade of Imperial inspection in front of the Hinogo (Kenshun) gate, involving the forces of Satsuma, Chōshū, Tosa and

Aki. As one would expect, all the Satsuma troops were wearing identical uniform and headgear, and they were preceded by a band consisting of large and small drums, as well as flutes, in the English style. They paraded with dignity before the Emperor, they were brave and lively, and were freezing the gall bladders of the Bakufu supporters. Following Satsuma came the Chōshū troops after which were the forces of Aki. But we only had two small platoons, we had no regular uniform and our troops acted in the old Dutch style. This reflects a most regrettable aspect of our forces. . . . Satsuma's armoured battalion brought up the rear. Such a magnificent military parade I have never seen before. Our (Tosa domain) government is exceedingly indifferent and does not realise that war is approaching before our very eyes.

This account by Tani Tateki, who was leading the Tosa forces, is important in revealing the differences between *taisei hōkan* and *ōsei fukko*.

First of all, this Imperial military parade was a demonstration of the fact that an 'Imperial Army' had been formed, and that it was a challenge to the Bakufu forces at Ōsaka Castle. In Tani's words, it was "freezing the gall bladders of the Bakufu supporters".

Second, it shows that the two-level alliance advocated since 1857 by Saigō Takamori had substantially changed its meaning from the alliance between Satsuma and Tosa of June 1887. The idea of an 'upper house' of powerful domain lords was retained at the Kogosho Conference (9th December), but a horizontal alliance of lower-ranking samurai was now not treated as meaning the establishment of a 'lower house', but as an amalgamation of armed forces from various domains to overthrow the Bakufu. So during the Boshin war, the occasion for which was the fighting at Toba-Fushimi, the armed forces of various domains grew rapidly in relation to that of the domain lords.

From this perspective, the argument concerning whether Tokugawa Yoshinobu should be allowed to participate in the conference, on the night of the Kogosho Conference (which proclaimed *ōsei fukko* – Restoration of the Emperor), between Yamanouchi Yōdō, former Lord of the Tosa domain, and Ōkubo Toshimichi of Satsuma, representing the anti-Bakufu forces, was extremely important.

Peaceful road or military road?

As research by Sasaki Suguru (*Bakumatsu seiji to Satsuma han* ['Bakumatsu Politics and the Satsuma Domain']) has shown, during nearly six months between the Satsuma–Tosa alliance of June 1867, through the *taisei hōkan* of October, up to the *ōsei fukko* of 9th December (3rd January of the third year of Keiō), the course of events was so complex that it cannot be brought together into a single line of narrative. Within the Court, within the Bakufu, within the Satsuma domain, there were divisions between a hard-line faction and a moderate faction, and the only unified force – united in the aim of overthrowing the Bakufu by force – was the Chōshū domain, to which was applied the insulting epithet of 'disloyal'.

36 *Japan's Modern History*

The dispute between a peaceful approach and a military approach was not confined to disputes between high-ranking conservative factions and low-ranking radical factions. The peaceful line of Ijichi Masaharu, discussed earlier in this chapter, given that he was a lower-ranking samurai and a very close adviser to Saigō Takamori, shows in an extreme fashion the complexity of these disputes over which way to proceed. Since this is an important point, we shall try to recapitulate it simply.

The threesome of Komatsu Tateaki, Saigō Takamori and Ōkubo Toshimichi, in order to bring about the fall of the Shogunate, left Kyoto together in October, aiming for Satsuma via Chōshū. Those who replaced them in charge of the Satsuma residence in Kyoto were Yoshii Tomozane and Ijichi Masaharu. In November Ijichi wrote a letter to Ōkubo fully supporting the *taisei hōkan* of Tokugawa Yoshinobu. As we have noted earlier, the content of the agreement was that Tokugawa Yoshinobu should return his administrative powers, but also that he should retain the position of Lord Keeper of the Privy Seal and lands with a total rice production capacity of 8 million *koku*. Moreover, he would be appointed President of the upper house, consisting of Court nobles (*kuge*) and powerful domain lords. For Ijichi, this was what was meant by *ōsei fukko*.

It is hardly likely that the threesome round Saigō, when they returned together to Satsuma, would not have conveyed to Yoshii and Ijichi their aim in mobilising the forces of the three domains plus the Aki domain. In other words, for Ijichi, both *ōsei fukko* and three-domain mobilisation (*sanhan shuppei*) were designed to bring about a new regime consisting of an upper house over which Tokugawa Yoshinobu would preside and a lower house consisting of samurai from powerful domains.

Moreover, the precise nature of the new regime was not known concretely by its creators. The Satsuma–Tosa alliance agreement of June 1867 clearly laid out in theory the aim of creating a two-chamber assembly consisting of upper and lower houses. It did not go so far as to define how many domain lords and their retainers would be selected as members of the two houses. If all the 300 domain lords were to become upper house members and all the domain retainer representatives were to become members of the lower house, that would have almost exactly corresponded to the numbers in the House of Peers and House of Representatives that were set up in 1890. The difference between the two was that in the lower house agricultural village landlords were included, and these also predominated among electors.

Of course the difference between a lower house consisting of retainer representatives throughout the nation, and the House of Representatives including many landlords of agricultural villages, was hardly a minor one. But what I wish to say at this point is that the proponents of the plan do not seem to have really thought in terms of all domain lords becoming members of the upper house and their retainer representatives becoming members of the lower house. Towards the end of November, the three domains of Satsuma, Chōshū and Aki (Hiroshima) gathered in Kyoto and Ōsaka. The Tosa and Echizen domains were principal architects of the *taisei hōkan*. The idea that the lords and their retainers of about 300 domains apart from the five domains mentioned here would become members of the upper and lower houses and thereby each have an influence equal to that of the five major domains was surely unrealistic.

For those who have looked at the course of events after the councillor system was introduced at the end of 1863, it is easy to imagine that the 'upper house' would be limited to powerful Court nobles and powerful domain lords (or their fathers), while the 'lower house' would be confined to retainers of the major domains. After the establishment by the Kogosho Conference of the three officers – President (*sōsai*), Senior Councillor (*gijō*) and Junior Councillor (*sanyo*) – the *gijō* was assigned to the upper house and the *sanyo* to the lower. Among the *gijō*, if we exclude Court nobles, then domain lords, former domain lords and fathers of domain lords of Owari, Echizen, Aki, Tosa and Satsuma amounted to five (later the Lord of Chōshū was added); among *sanyo*, if once again we exclude Court nobles, there were three each from the above five domains, in total 15 (later three samurai from Chōshū were added). Rather than an assembly, this should be called a government, and was the realisation of the 'public assembly' argument of the Bakumatsu period.

The problem is that the *sanyo*, who were the lowest rank of the three, were colleagues of the leaders of the four domain forces that had paraded in front of the Kenshun Gate, as mentioned at the beginning of this chapter. Now samurai of the Satsuma and Chōshū domains and those of the three domains that had seized control of the 'armed forces' had become junior councillors (*sanyo*) in the government. For the *sanyo*, who had seized control of the 'armed forces', grasping the real power in the three-rank system was the natural outcome. At least until the split over the issue of invading Korea in October 1873, the 'Imperial Army' (*kangun*) and the *sanyo*, which later became *sangi* (also translated as 'councillors'), became one and the same thing and were promoting the Restoration reforms.

The military strength of the Bakufu

In military strength, however, the combined forces of Satsuma and Chōshū were no match for the forces of the Tokugawa house, based at Ōsaka Castle. Since the *Bakufu* had sufficient military power, if it had accepted the demands of the Court and avoided a frontal collision with the Court, as well as with Satsuma and Chōshū, it would have been able to defeat them peacefully. In other words, if the Tokugawa house had become the head of a new government in conformity with the Court demands, the forces of Satsuma and Chōshū, which were smaller in number than those of the *Bakufu*, would have suffered from weakened legitimacy. But in the end, the make-up of the new political system could not be resolved without war between the Bakufu and Sat-Chō.

As was clear with the military parade at the Kenshun Gate described at the beginning of this section, the four domains of Satsuma, Chōshū, Tosa and Aki were preparing for a military clash with the Tokugawa side. But in fact, the latter were doing the same.

The Court, wishing to avoid a military confrontation, up to 16th December tried to soften the decision taken at the Kogosho Conference on the 9th. It amended

38 *Japan's Modern History*

the decision to mean that if the position of Lord Keeper were returned to the new government then it would be unnecessary to return that part of the Shōgun's territory. What was necessary for the Tokugawa would be to pay a certain amount of the government expenditures in the same way as other domains would do. If this was brought about, Tokugawa Yoshinobu and the representatives of his retainers should be added to the ranks of the *gijō* and *sanyo*, and in order to make an official decision to this effect an Imperial Order was conveyed to Yoshinobu.

The Tokugawa side, however, rejected this compromise proposal. To Nakane Yukie (*sanyo*), a senior retainer of the former Lord of Echizen, who had been entrusted by the Court as its proxy to proceed to Ōsaka Castle and show this compromise proposal, Nagai Naoyuki, a high-ranking official of the Bakufu, gave a decisive rejection in the following terms. Since this is an important document for understanding the background in which the Bakufu had ventured forth in the fighting at Toba-Fushimi, I want to reproduce it here even though it is a trifle long.

> Basically this letter is unreasonable, since (the post of Lord Keeper) is an independent position unrelated to the Shōgun, therefore your proposal that the Shōgun should relinquish this position is out of the question. Moreover, on the question of Bakufu land, from the time of the *taisei hōkan*, our Lord (Yoshinobu) was already prepared to shoulder the burden of some part of government expenditures, and to support a Court regime with the cooperation of various domains. But your high-handed way of issuing orders is impossible to accept. We cannot escape the conclusion that the question both of resigning his position and of reducing his land holdings is unacceptable. . . . First of all Iga (the Senior retainer Itakura Kazukiyo) and I (Nagai) do not agree with this. If the Imperial Court, regretting the past, were to return to the position it took before 9th (December), there would be room for negotiation, but since responsibility for devising this unacceptable plan stems from the actions of these two traitors, it is our urgent duty to exclude these two traitors, and we have sufficient strength to strike the Satsuma residence, and if there is even a slight provocation, we are bound to make a rapid attack . . .
>
> (Katsuta Magohisa, *Saigō Takamori den*, vol. 4, pp. 14–15).

The document clearly reveals the hostile reaction of the Bakufu leaders against the *ōsei fukko*, but since some parts of the letter are rather hard to understand, I will summarise it in my own fashion.

The first point made by the senior retainer Nagai Naoyuki in his statement was that since there was no connection between the office of Shōgun handed back at the time of the *taisei hōkan* and the official Court position of Lord Keeper, there was absolutely no need for the Lord Keeper to resign (resigning his post – *jikan*). Moreover, appropriately burdening other domains with "things of use to the government" was something that the Bakufu side spoke of at the time of the *taisei hōkan*, and there was no case for this to be ordered once again (rejection of granting land – *nōchi*). The Court was creating the pretence of making concessions to

Revolution, 1863–1871 39

the Bakufu, but all this amounted to was "quitting posts and reducing land (*kōkan sakuchi*)", so that the demands were impossible to accept.

The second point was that the Bakufu was both ready and well enough armed to attack the Sat-Chō 'traitors'. And also, however much Tokugawa Yoshinobu might wish for a moderate line, it is important that the Shōgun's councillor Itakura Katsukiyo, and he himself (the Junior Councillor Nagai Naoyuki), say firmly that they do not accept this. Also the phrase "we have sufficient strength to strike the Satsuma residence" is a remarkably concrete expression.

If we bring together Nagai's hard-line position and the military parade of Satsuma, Chōshū, Tosa and Aki described at the beginning of this section, it becomes clear that the achievement of *ōsei fukko* by peaceful means was little more than an illusion on the part of centrist forces. At the time of *ōsei fukko*, the warship captain Enomoto Takeaki wrote as follows to Katsu Kaishū about the Bakufu side and the Sat-Chō side:

> Our Tokugawa men are likely to be assisted by Aizu and Kuwana without question, while Ii, Kishū, Tōdō, Ōgaki, Kaga and so on all contribute to national strength and will probably assist us. Toshū and Echizen seem to be neutral and uncommitted. I hear that Inaba, Owari and Bizen have of course long been supporters of Chōshū and Satsuma. Happily, so far as our Tokugawa forces are concerned, if we count our forces together with the forces of the former reliable lords, our forces amount to three times those of the forces of Satsuma, Chōshū, Tosa and Aki (the total force strength of the four domains was only 6,000).
>
> (Katsube Shinchō, *Katsu Kaishū zenshū*, vol. 18, p. 446)

The confidence of the junior councillor Nagai Naoyuki is explained by this background.

The end of revolution

Reform faction and conservative faction

Over the six months covering the Satsuma–Tosa alliance of June 1867, the *taisei hōkan* of October and the *ōsei fukko* of December, the reform faction and conservative faction constituted the two extremes of a single movement. The plan for the new power structure broadly emerged with the Emperor at the peak of it, below him the Court nobles (*kuge*), powerful lords including Tokugawa Yoshinobu (and their deputies), who were to populate the upper house, and the reformist sections of their retainers, who were to populate the lower house.

So far as the upper house is concerned, the new system resembled the system of *sanyo* introduced at the end of 1863. Since, during the operation of that system, the Shōgun in his official position listened with respect to the opinions of the most powerful domain lords, it seems to have differed greatly from the position set up at the *taisei hōkan*. But if Tokugawa Yoshinobu assumed the number two position

40   Japan's Modern History

(for instance, deputy president or speaker, in the 'three-rank system' (*san shoku sei*) consisting of president (*sōsai*), senior councillor (*gijō*) and junior councillor (*sanyo*), worked out at the time of the *ōsei fukko*, then this was practically the same as the earlier *sanyo* system. If Yoshinobu, who, as the head of the Tokugawa house, controlled what were officially 8 million *koku* of rice and 8,000 retainers (*hatamoto*) but in fact probably half of that number, occupied the position in the new system of head of the *gijō*, then the lower-ranking samurai of Satsuma and Chōshū, who could only become *sanyo*, had no means of expressing their opposition. This meant putting in place the Alliance of Court and Bakufu (*kōbu gattai*) advocated by the powerful domain lords of the 'reformist faction' throughout the Bakumatsu period.

On the other hand, for the lower-ranking samurai of the three domains of Satsuma, Chōshū and Tosa, who could only attain the lowest rank in the central government (or could only become lower house members at the stage of the Satsuma–Tosa alliance), it was necessary to push forward the key point in the broad framework of the lower house, namely that *sanyo* = lower house, and grasp real power on this basis. Moreover, after Saigō Takamori was able to escape the oppression of Shimazu Hisamitsu and return to his domain, 'lower-ranking samurai' became 'the military' by another name. If we examine the activities of Saigō, who had become the de facto commander of the Satsuma military force in 1864, and of Ijichi, who had become military administrator (*gunyaku bugyō*), this becomes clear in itself.

Something similar may be said about the activities of Shinagawa Yojirō and Ōmura Masujirō, after the Sat-Chō alliance at the beginning of 1866. The 'lower house' became the 'councillors' (*sanyo*), and later the 'military authorities' (*gunbu*). And then, even in the Tosa domain, which had been a central supporter of Yoshinobu's 'Alliance between Court and Bakufu' (*kōbu gattai*), in dispute with the former domain lord Yamanouchi Yōdō and Gotō Shōjirō, who had the assigned rank of councillor, the Tosa domain's 'military authorities' (*gunbu*), namely Itagaki Taisuke and Tani Tateki, and others, began to work towards cooperation with the *gunbu* of both Satsuma and Chōshū.

The lower-ranking samurai of Satsuma and Chōshū, moving in the direction lower house → *sanyo* → *gunbu*, who had paraded before the Emperor on 27th December in the third year of Keiō (1867), changed from being the *gunbu* of the various domains and became the new government's Imperial Army (*kangun*).

The new Meiji Government set up in January of the fourth year of Keiō, which became the first year of Meiji (1868), found itself in a state of confusion over these confrontations between 'right' and 'left'.

There are several ways of referring to Tokugawa after Yoshinobu had returned his powers as Shōgun to the Emperor, but I would like to refer to him as 'the Bakufu leader' up to the ordinance depriving him of his powers on 7th January 1868, and for the later period as 'the former Bakufu leader'. Again, since within the regime set up by the *ōsei fukko* there was much perturbation from the clash of the two extremes, I want to make a distinction between the new government on the one hand and the Satsuma and Chōshū domains on the other.

Revolution, 1863–1871   41

The demands of the Satsuma and Chōshū domains were for Yoshinobu to 'surrender his post and give up his lands' (*jikan nōchi*); in other words, Yoshinobu should give up his post of Lord Keeper and return the so-called '8 million *koku* of rice-producing land' to the Emperor. But the Bakufu's position was that *jikan nōchi* had not been decided with the participation of the Bakufu and the domains that supported it, namely Aizu and Kuwana, and that the decision was made by the government that arose from *ōsei fukko* and, moreover, Satsuma and Chōshū had forced this policy onto the new Emperor, who was only 17; therefore the decision had no legitimacy whatsoever. The two extremes of the new government confronted each other directly over *jikan nōchi* and *Sat-Chō no shii* (independent decision making by Satsuma and Chōshū).

Tactics and strategy of overthrowing the Bakufu

As I have already indicated, since the Bakufu forces that had returned to Ōsaka Castle were about three times the size of the combined forces of Satsuma, Chōshū, Tosa and Aki, there were no reasons for the Bakufu to accept *jikan nōchi* and join the new government. They insisted that the Emperor should hold a national conference of domain lords, including Yoshinobu, to decide there the costs of the new government which should be borne by the domains in proportion to their respective capacity to pay.

If this Bakufu proposal had passed and the conference of domain lords had been assembled under the Emperor, the influence of the Satsuma and Chōshū forces would inevitably have suffered a severe reverse. This was not only because of the participation of Tokugawa, Aizu and Kuwana, in other words, of all the Bakufu forces, but in addition because the influence of the 'moderate faction', namely Echizen, Tosa and others, would have increased. The power within the new government of *gijō* (the upper house) would have overwhelmed that of the *sanyo* (the lower house). In a word, it would have meant the fall from power of the 'Sat-Chō anti-Bakufu faction'.

In a little more than three weeks of the new government between the ōsei fukko of 9th September of the third year of Keiō (3rd January 1868) and the fighting at Toba-Fushimi on 3rd January of the first year of Meiji (27th January 1868), it appeared from an outside perspective to be still pressured by the hard line of the Bakufu side. Against Nakane Yukie, who had been involved in a plan to create a compromise between the Bakufu and the Sat-Chō side, the Bakufu continued to press for a return to the situation before the *ōsei fukko*, and it asserted that even if war should break out and if it became an enemy of the Court (*Chōteki*), there would be no problem because 'the winner becomes the official army' (Nihon shiseki kyōkai [ed.], *Boshin Nikki* ['Diary of the Boshin War'], Tokyo Daigaku Shuppankai, 1973, p. 18).

The forces of Satsuma and Chōshū, which had brought about the restoration of the Imperial regime (*ōsei fukko*) in the coup of 9th December, persevered in defending negotiations between the upbeat Bakufu and the faint-hearted Echizen domain. Even Saigō Takamori, the key advocate of overthrowing the Bakufu by

42 Japan's Modern History

force, conceded that Yoshinobu would be acceptable to him as councillor (*gijō*), taking part in the regime, if he were to agree to resign from his post of Lord Keeper and to hand over land (*jikan nōchi*) (Katsuta Magohisa, *Saigō Takamori den*, vol. 4, p. 9).

The aim, however, of Saigō and others was to make military action a priority against the Bakufu forces, which were pleased with their reaction to the weak-kneed new government. When the Bakufu forces, taking part in a challenge to the Sat-Chō side on 23rd December, set fire to the Satsuma residence in Edo, Saigō wrote to Tani Tateki, leader of the Tosa forces: "It has started. Quickly tell Inui (Itagaki Taisuke) about this" (Shimauchi Toshie [ed.], *Tani Tateki ikō* ['Writings of Tani Tateki'], Seikensha, 1912, vol. 1, p. 58). When the Bakufu forces started their action, it was time for the forces of Satsuma and Chōshū to grasp control of the new government. Falling into the trap set by Saigō Takamori and Ijichi Masaharu (and Ōmura Masujirō was also mentioned), the Bakufu forces at Ōsaka Castle launched an action. For Yoshinobu to report to the Emperor his position on resigning his post and returning his lands, attendant forces of over 15,000 men accompanied him to Kyoto. Since the Sat-Chō forces engaged with the Bakufu at Toba and Fushimi amounted to only 4,000 men, the Bakufu forces were numerically superior by a factor of four to one (Sasaki Katsu, *Boshin sensō* ['The Boshin War'], Chūkō Shinsho, 1977, p. 22). Even so, the fighting at Toba-Fushimi that began three days later resulted in victory for the Sat-Chō forces in a mere two days.

As a number of researches have clearly shown, superiority or inferiority in firearms determines victory or defeat, but there is research showing that the Bakufu forces, which were overwhelmingly superior in number, made a tactical error in not splitting off some of their forces along a different road, but rather concentrating all their troops along the two roads at Toba and Fushimi (ibid., p. 28).

If we examine the whole course of the Boshin war for the nine months that it lasted from its beginning, we have the feeling that the Satsuma forces of Saigō Takamori and Ijichi Masaharu and the Chōshū forces of Ōmura and Shinagawa shaped their strategy so that in several situations they would wait until the time was ripe and then bring all their forces together. It even seems that as a background to this strategy they were consistent in giving absolute priority to striking a devastating blow against the Bakufu forces, while deliberately ignoring minor situations. While the period of just over three weeks between the *ōsei fukko* on 9th December and 3rd January at first sight looks like a time of inaction, the concentration of troops at Toba-Fushimi may well have been the first stage in such a strategy.

Towards a bloodless liberation of Edo Castle

The same kind of story appears in the bloodless liberation of Edo Castle (14th March), resulting from the meeting between Katsu Kaishū and Saigō Takamori. At the same time that this took place, rather than disarming the former Bakufu forces all at once and moving to attack the Aizu domain, the Bakufu forces with their naval vessels, arms and ammunition hastened to flee into Kantō and Tōhoku, and there is evidence that this was deliberately ignored.

Revolution, 1863–1871 43

The Tosa domain forces, which marched along the Nakasendō (central mountain road), broke down the Bakufu forces at Kōfu and made camp at the Owari domain residence at Ichigaya, were becoming increasingly unhappy with the dilatory treatment resulting from the magnanimity of the Tōkaidō expedition High Command led by Saigō Takamori. At that time Tani Tateki, who was assisting Itagaki Taisuke, the staff officer of the Nakasendō High Command, in his capacity as *Ōmetsuke* wrote of this dissatisfaction in the following terms:

> The Tōkaidō vanguard High Command is entering Edo Castle in order to capture it, and forces of various domains are defending its outer gates. . . . Today the High Command entered the Castle with a very small force of guards. Altogether there are senior staff officer Saigō Takamori, and about 30 or 40 others. Among the officials of the former Bakufu, those attending to their duties are Katsu Awa (Kaishū), Ōkubo Ichiō, and Yamaoka Tetsutarō, This gang on the surface is declaring its allegiance, but behind the scenes is stirring up their ruffians in order to escape, so that their forces are scattered to all directions. . . . But the Tōkaidō Expedition High Command is not putting its feelings on this point, believes what Katsu is telling them, and is extremely indecisive in everything. These ruffians are devising schemes, are spiriting the guns, large and small, from inside the Castle, sending them on boats from Fukagawa, and linking up with Aizu, are fleeing to Tōhoku. . . . The High Command (Saigō Takamori) and others are extremely indecisive and therefore no countermeasures are being taken, so that they are allowing these ruffians to scatter in all directions.
>
> (Shimauchi Toshie, *Tani Tateki ikō*, vol. 1, pp. 90–1).

Tani Tateki, of Tosa, who belonged to the Nakasendō Expedition High Command, attributed responsibility for the fact that the former Bakufu forces had carried away weapons and ammunition from Edo Castle and transferred them to Kantō and Tōhoku, to the "indecisiveness" especially of the Tōkaidō High Command, and in particular of Saigō Takamori, its chief of staff. This criticism was directed against the decision of Saigō to halt the all-out attack on Edo Castle on 15th March, and also placed responsibility for the subsequent unnecessary six months' war in Tōhoku onto Saigō and his men. In Tani's words:

> If he had attacked on 15th March, not postponing it, given that the Bakufu's preparations were inadequate and its opinions were divided, it would not have been difficult to take the Castle. Once he had attacked the Castle in strength, malcontents would have been discouraged, and the events in Yashū and Ōshū would not have occurred, nor would the later Ueno war, so that this is most regrettable.
>
> (Ibid., p. 92.)

Tani's criticism at first sight appears to hit the nail on the head. If we assume that the price paid for the bloodless liberation of the Castle was the subsequent

44   *Japan's Modern History*

six months' war in Tōhoku, as well as the Aizu war, then the accounts do not balance.

But if, as Tani argued, an all-out attack on Edo Castle had taken place, and all the Bakufu forces from the *hatamoto* to the Aizu domain had surrendered, then what kind of situation would have been created? The reasons for confiscating the lands of leaders of the pro-Bakufu domains in Kantō and Tōhoku, who had given up resistance by force and had sworn 'allegiance' to the Court, were in Saigō's view difficult to justify. Even if the fall of Edo Castle had resulted in the overwhelming victory of the government forces, control of Kantō and Tōhoku by the new government might well have existed in name only.

Criticism of Saigō's 'lack of action and lack of policy' (*mui musaku*) was also directed at the *Shōgitai* barricaded at Ueno Mountain. Since the Chief of Staff of the High Command entrusted Katsu Kaishū and other former Bakufu leaders with the pacification of the *hatamoto* and other former Bakufu forces, they despised the Imperial Army, and subsequently the 3,000 men of the former Bakufu army gathered at Ueno. It is said that the alleged flexibility and lack of resolution on the part of Saigō was demonstrated also by the fact that at the end of intercalary April the new government in Kyoto sent the Chōshū military strategist, Ōmura Masujirō, as military executive officer, to Edo, and Etō Shinpei of the Hizen domain, who was held in high regard by Sanjō Sanetomi from the time of banishment, also went to Edo as a delegate of Sanjō.

But when, two months after the liberation of Edo Castle, on 15th May, the government forces decided on an all-out attack, the Bakufu forces stationed below Edo Castle, apart from those people aiming at another chance to get at Aizu, gathered at Ueno. A 'do nothing' strategy until the enemy was fully gathered together, and then once the enemy was gathered to strike hard, seems to have been based on the same kind of approach applied at the time of Toba-Fushimi. In fact, the government forces, which included the forces of Satsuma, Chōshū, Kumamoto, Bizen, Kurume and Sadohara, overwhelmed the former Bakufu forces in a single day.

The Tōhoku war

Why the present writer is in sympathy with the strategic concerns of Saigō is because of a feeling that the latter's fundamental aim was to bring those forces that had supported the Bakufu back into the fold. The difference between the *ōsei fukko* aimed at preserving the former Bakufu forces and the *ōsei fukko* aimed at destroying them in a civil war hardly needs explaining.

This policy, which should be called Saigō's strategy, was thoroughly worked out during the Tōhoku war, which was the biggest conflict in the Boshin war. Following Ueno, the former Bakufu forces, which were also defeated at Utsunomiya, regrouped at their greatest stronghold, the Aizu domain.

At the level of 'tactics', Saigō's performance was clumsy. He sent to Tōhoku a small force of the 'Imperial Army' under an Imperial prince attached to the Sat-Chō High Command, and he thought that if he were to order a number of

Revolution, 1863–1871 45

domains in Tōhoku, including Sendai, Yonezawa, Satake (in Akita) and Nanbu (in Morioka) to crush Aizu, the affair would reach a quick conclusion (Katsuta, *Saigō Takamori den*, pp. 142–3).

As Sasaki Suguru, in *Boshin sensō* (The Boshin War), has analysed in detail, circumstances completely betrayed Saigō's optimism. First of all, the Sendai domain, which would be at the centre of an attack on Aizu, was making efforts to mediate between the Court and Aizu.

Second, compared with the forces of the Expedition High Command centred on the three domains of Satsuma, Chōshū and Tosa at the time leading up to an attack on Edo Castle in March, the staff available for an assault force against Aizu was too weak in terms of the quality and size of the Sat-Chō forces upon which it was based. At first, it seemed probable that Kuroda Kiyotaka of Satsuma and Shinagawa Yojirō of Chōshū would take command of the operation. These two men had been the creators of the Sat-Chō alliance in 1866, and were well established in the eyes of the Court. But for reasons that remain unclear, they did not take up their posts, and Ōyama Tsunayoshi of Satsuma and Sera Shūzō of Chōshū – neither of whom were well known in the Bakumatsu situation – took over the responsibility (Sasaki, *Boshin sensō*, pp. 71–2). Moreover, the total strength of the Ōu pacification force, based on Sat-Chō contingents, was scarcely 400 men. This was less than one-tenth the size of the four-thousand-strong government army of Satsuma, Chōshū, Tosa and Aki that had tangled with the Bakufu force of 15,000 at the earlier Toba–Fushimi conflict. As far as later military strength was concerned, a policy emerged of recruiting locally in the Sendai, Yonezawa and other domains.

This meant that the various domains in the Tōhoku region belittled the government army, and gave their backing to Aizu. On 3rd May an alliance was formed of 25 domains, including Sendai, Yonezawa, Morioka, Nihonmatsu (Fukushima) and Akita, which between them accounted for about 430,000 *koku* of rice (ibid., pp. 121–2).

The apparent aim of the alliance was to demand fair sanctions and magnanimity to the Aizu and Kuwana domains against the High Command. But it is clear that its underlying aim, should the High Command reject this demand, was that the 25 domains would unite to defend the Aizu domain. Ōyama Tsunayoshi of Satsuma, who had commanded the Satsuma forces, had battled the Shinjō, Akita and Tsugaru domains. It is said that of his force of a little over 200 officers and men, only just over 50 men remained alive. Even his biographer Katsuta Magohisa, who records in detail the great exploits of Saigō Takamori, has to admit Saigō's tactical failures:

> When the domains of the Ōu region formed an alliance, so that by combining the forces of Aizu, Kuwana and the Bakufu they could take on the government forces, the most urgent thing was to hasten to Hokuetsu and Shirakawaguchi. The arrival of this news in Edo ended the measures against Tokugawa, the Ueno force settled down and the day came when they were able to return to Kantō quite peacefully. At first Takamori wished to subdue

46   *Japan's Modern History*

the forces to be sent to Ōu, but he had specially chosen personnel for his staff, and found himself with only a small force from Satsuma and Chōshū. Thus the main responsibility for the danger in which Ōyama and others were placed lay with Takamori.

(Katsuta, Saigō Takamori den, vol. 4, pp. 146–7)

Nevertheless, what Saigō did in the face of this crisis was not to lead his own Satsuma forces stationed in Kyoto to Shirakawa and Akita, but rather to return by ship to Kagoshima from Ōita with Shimazu Tadayoshi (June).

Government forces or domain troops?

It is difficult to explain this curious behaviour of the Satsuma domain in the terms that I have previously used of allowing time for the enemy to regroup and then mounting an all-out attack at the place where they had assembled. Of course, if we only focus upon the ultimate result, the 'Saigō strategy' argument holds up reasonably well. When the 25 domains of Ōu, brought together to protect Aizu, to which the Hokuetsu domains were now added (thus forming an alliance of the Ōu and Hokuetsu domains), had been attacked and forced to surrender by a newly reinforced three-domain army of Satsuma, Chōshū and Tosa, and when on 22nd September the Aizu domain had been forced to surrender, the *ōsei fukko* government centred on these three domains became a central government both in name and in reality.

On the other hand, if we examine what happened, not from the perspective of the result, but rather of the process, the 'Saigō strategy' argument concerning the Tōhoku war seems unconvincing. And when we focus on process, the reasons for the abolition of the domains and establishment of prefectures (*haihan chiken*), occurring three years later, becomes evident.

I wrote earlier that the 'Imperial Army' was formed at the time of the parade in front of the Kenshun Gate by the four domains of Satsuma, Chōshū, Tosa and Aki. But this referred to what happened formally, and in fact the Court did not bear the cost of these forces. The cost of the four domain forces was borne by the domains themselves.

This situation did not change even after the bloodless liberation of Edo Castle. Even though, with the measures taken against the Tokugawa house, land yielding 6,300,000 *koku* of rice out of 7,000,000 became the property of the new government, it was not sufficient to fund in their entirety the costs of the government army based on the forces of the four domains. The new government merely succeeded to the status hitherto held by the Bakufu, while three-quarters of the whole country continued to be held by fewer than 300 feudal lords (*daimyō*). What each domain continued to hold was land rent and soldiers (samurai). The greater part of military expenditure disbursed between the fighting at Toba-Fushimi in January and the suppression of the Ueno Shōgitai in May was borne by each of the anti-Bakufu domains.

No materials are known that would clearly indicate that the reason Saigō, together with Shimazu Tadayoshi, returned south to Kagoshima rather than pro-

Revolution, 1863–1871   47

ceeding north to Ōu was to recruit domain troops by reconstructing the domain finances. But the diary of Tani Tateki, the military leader of the Tosa domain, whom we shall next discuss, does indirectly indicate the motives of Saigō and the Satsuma domain lord for returning home:

> 13th (June). At this time our troops received the order to leave for the north. But for financial reasons we had to reject this. I very secretly think that the domain lord should have sent troops, certainly to Ōu, and also to the Echigo domain. It is a shame that our domain should only be going to Ōshū. I explain that this is the correct thing to do. Even though everyone is agreed on this, it is just this one factor of military finance that is difficult.
>
> (Shimauchi, *Tani Tateki* ikō, vol. 1, p. 133)

Later, Tani went to Kyoto, received a promise from Iwakura Tomomi to "pay for military expenditure", returned to Tosa, conducted a "reconstruction of the forces proceeding to Hokuetsu", and at the beginning of July set out for Echigo at the head of five platoons from the Tosa domain.

The reconstruction of the Tosa forces mentioned in Tani Tateki's diary, and the previously described return to Kagoshima by Saigō Takamori, occurred at almost the same time. The three domains of Satsuma, Chōshū and Tosa that formed the main strength of the 'Imperial Army' in the four months from the January fighting at Toba-Fushimi to the Ueno Shōgitai attack in May incurred major expenditure of both troops and financial resources, and in order to conduct the Tōhoku war effectively the military leaders of each domain had to return home and contrive to put their domain finances in order, and remobilise the 'Imperial Army' in their respective domains.

The reconstructed Tosa domain forces in the middle of July set out for Edo, and at the end of the month arrived at Shirakawa. On the other hand, Saigō, who had returned to Kagoshima, set out for Akita and Niigata at the beginning of August, leading the reconstructed Satsuma forces, arriving on the 11th. The 'Imperial Army' was now well prepared to attack the Tōhoku-Hokuetsu alliance.

As is clear from the above, the delay on the part of the new government in subduing Tōhoku sprang from the fact that the 'Imperial Army' was, both in its force composition and its finance, mainly supported by the three domains of Satsuma, Chōshū and Tosa. The new government did not yet possess a true 'Imperial Army'.

Dissolution and reconstruction of the 'Imperial Army'

The return home of the 'Imperial Army'

The 'Imperial Army' that began its attack on the Aizu domain on 20th August had been reconstructed by Satsuma and Tosa, and perhaps by Chōshū. In terms of the standing of its High Command, the number of its officers and men, and the fire power at its disposal, it was incomparable with the 'Imperial Army' that had

48 *Japan's Modern History*

existed hitherto. The High Command consisted of Ōmura Masutarō of Chōshū, alongside the much praised Satsuma military strategist Ijichi Masaharu, and Itagaki Taisuke, Supreme Commander of the Tosa forces. We should not neglect to mention that Itagaki, who later was to become famous in the Popular Rights Movement, was at this time a military leader on a par with Saigō Takamori and Ijichi Masaharu.

The numbers of troops in the forces of the six domains including Satsuma, Chōshū and Tosa at the start of the all-out attack was around 2,000, which was no fewer than at the time of the fighting at Toba-Fushimi. Moreover, since the Aizu domain, defeated at the beginning of operations, sought to adopt a siege strategy, it was time for Satsuma to bring into play Armstrong guns and other heavy weaponry.

Subsequently, while Aizu continued its siege strategy, the 'Imperial Army' persuaded the Yonezawa and Sendai domains to surrender, so that the troops of these two domains were added to those of the government, and the total number of government troops rose to 30,000 (Sasaki Suguru, *Boshin sensō*, p. 159). The Aizu domain, isolated, held out in siege conditions for about a month, then formally surrendered. Apart from Hokkaidō, the whole of Japan was now under the control of the new government.

At that very moment, however, the 'Imperial Army' was dissolved and most elements in it returned to their respective domains. Tani Tateki, as the central man in the Tosa domain, who was present at the handing over of Aizu Castle on 23rd September, returned with others to Edo one month later on 24th October. In his diary for the 27th, three days later, he wrote: "The former soldiers all returned home on a borrowed British ship" (Shimauchi, *Tani Tateki ikō*, vol. 1, p. 172). The expression "former soldiers" means the Tosa troops which in March left Tosa for Edo, but the remaining Tosa anti-Bakufu forces that had subdued Aizu also returned to Tosa on 2nd November. The Tani diary for 5th November is important in showing the real situation of the 'Imperial Army':

> On the 2nd (November), the returning soldiers left Edo on the ship *Yūgao* (Moonflower). They reached home on the 5th. The lord came to the Chidōkan and accorded them an audience. He expressed his thanks for our services. The force was then disbanded, some went wild with joy and they all returned to their homes. Today, I met my parents and was so happy that I couldn't utter any words for a while. This evening the taste of *sake* is especially beautiful."
>
> (Ibid., p. 172)

In this way the 'Imperial Army' was easily disbanded, the troops all returned home, and their domain lord and former domain lord continued to control them as before. The situation would be the same with the Satsuma domain forces. In the new Meiji regime which had won victory in the Boshin war, forces capable of mounting a military offensive had disappeared throughout the land, but on the other hand, both military capability and financial resources were almost unchanged from those of the previous Bakufu regime. The Chōshū domain had

Revolution, 1863–1871   49

been suffering from the financial burdens imposed by the 'Imperial Army', just like the others. But in the case of Chōshū, by the strength of a half-private military grouping that brought together lower samurai and the upper ranks of the peasantry, they had on two occasions repulsed attacks by the Bakufu; the Chōshū part of the 'Imperial Army' was much more extensive than that of Satsuma or Tosa. It is true that in the case of Satsuma and Tosa, the burden of the 'Imperial Army' was considerable, but since it was the samurai class that was mobilised, their salaries could be financed from established house records. In Chōshū, by contrast, which had mobilised various half-official, half-private forces (*kiheitai, yūgekitai, seibutai, shinbutai, chinbutai, kenbutai*, etc.) as their 'Imperial Army', the wages of this 'Imperial Army' following victory and their return to the domain became a new financial burden on the domain.

One year after victory in the Boshin war, the Chōshū domain dissolved these miscellaneous forces, reorganised their personnel, absorbed them and united them into domain forces consisting of four battalions (November 1869). The various existing forces fiercely resisted this, and until they were completely suppressed in March 1870 Chōshū was in a state of de facto civil war. Moreover, even when the Chōshū domain had reorganised their officers and men into a proper army, it was still the Chōshū military force, and not the 'Imperial Army' of the Meiji Government. This was exactly the same for Satsuma and Tosa.

Fragility of the centralised government

In order for the new regime to create a centralised government both in name and in reality, each domain needed to give to the centre the land tax that it separately controlled. But since the Bunkyū era (1861–3), it was uncertain whether the domain lords and their retainers, who maintained an affinity with the line of *kōbu gattai* (alliance between Court and Bakufu), would on their own initiative cede their tax-raising powers to the new government. If the 'Imperial Army' that had defeated the Bakufu army in the fighting at Toba-Fushimi, and had forced the surrender of Aizu in the Tōhoku war, had become the property of the new government, then no doubt the backdrop of military strength would have hastened the transfer of tax-raising powers from each domain to the new government. However, the main strength of the 'Imperial Army' reverted to the armies of Satsuma, Chōshū and Tosa, and each of them was under the control of its domain lord.

There was only one thing that the new government could do. It could make the 'Imperial Army' independent of the domains, reorganise it as a proper 'Imperial Army', and on the strength of that hasten to transfer the land of the domains throughout the country to the Court. In February 1871 (old calendar), more than 6,000 troops were contributed by the Satsuma, Chōshū and Tosa domains, so that the first of these aims was accomplished, and in July (old calendar) of the same year, with the abolition of domains and creation of prefectures (*haihan chiken*), the second was brought about as well.

In a situation where the 'Imperial Army' had returned back home, and the power to raise land tax was, as before, in the hands of each domain separately, *ōsei fukko*

50　*Japan's Modern History*

only existed on paper. This also affected the 'eight ministry system' that the new government set up in July 1869.

This 'eight ministry system' consisted of the Minister of the Right (udaijin), four councillors (*sangi*), and ministers for foreign affairs, domestic affairs, finance, the armed forces and justice (*keibu*). Ministers of the five ministries were restricted to princes, Court nobles (*kuge*) and lords of major domains, so that it was not a regime based on the ability of incumbents to carry out their duties. Also, among the councillors, who in 1869 and 1870 amounted to eight, six of them (excluding Ōkubo and Kido) had been little-known personages in the Bakumatsu period.

Iwakura Tomomi, who between the *ōsei fukko* and the Boshin war backed the military actions of the three domains of Satsuma, Chōshū and Tosa from within the Court, was dissatisfied with this regime. In a letter to Ōkubo Toshimichi written in November 1870, he wrote: "Until today we have had to listen patiently to the calls from other domains that an end should be put to the despotic attitudes of Satsuma and Chōshū". Restrained by criticism of Satsuma and Chōshū from other domains that had supported the civil war in the time between the *ōsei fukko* and attack on Aizu, it had become unavoidable that councillors and nobles should be appointed from domains other than Satsuma and Chōshū. The eight ministry system put in place after the Boshin war was a system of government that excluded men of talent, and focused on balancing nobles, powerful domain lords and men of power from outside Satsuma and Chōshū.

Dissatisfaction on the part of the former Imperial Army and supply of troops by the three domains

Dissatisfaction with this kind of regime was expressed by Saigō Takamori, head of the Satsuma military force, who had returned to his own domain. At the end of September 1870, the councillor Saitō Toshiyuki, of Tosa origin, conveyed the news to Sasaki Takayuki, also from Tosa: "Saigō, who is making a lot of noise in Kagoshima and thinks that the present Court administration is irrational, will inevitably lead his troops to Kyōto to cleanse the government, and he is likely to leave for Kyōto in the next few days" (Sasaki Takayuki, *Hogo hirohi – Sasaki Takayuki nikki* ['Dust Hole – Sasaki Takayuki Diary'], Tokyo Daigaku Shuppankai, 1973 vol. 4, p. 434). At the beginning of October this story was transmitted to Kido Kōin, Ōkubo Toshimichi and Iwakura Tomomi.

Iwakura Tomomi, Ōkubo Toshimichi, Kido Kōin and others reacted swiftly to Saigō's activities. While preventing Saigō from marching on Kyoto, which could well have resulted in a 'second Boshin war', they sought to use his activities to reconstitute the 'Imperial Army'. The 'presentation of forces from the three domains' of January 1871 was the result.

In December 1870, the Deputy Head of the Court (*dainōgon*) Iwakura Tomomi, as Imperial Messenger, went to the Satsuma and Chōshū domains and set about persuading them to supply troops to the Court. He was accompanied by Ōkubo Toshimichi and Kawamura Sumiyoshi (Navy Under-Secretary [*shōho*]) of Satsuma and Yamagata Aritomo (Army Under-Secretary) of Chōshū. Shimazu

Revolution, 1863–1871 51

Hisamitsu of Satsuma met the Imperial Messenger but on grounds of illness made Saigō accompany him to Chōshū. Incidentally, while at first he was only asking for troops from Satsuma and Chōshū, it is said to have been Saigō who persuaded him to add troops from Tosa (Katsuta, *Saigo Takamori den*, vol. 5, p. 42). Both at the time of the Boshin war and at the time of the transfer of troops to the Court, Saigō continued to value Itagaki Taisuke of Tosa.

As a result of this, Iwakura ended his mission at Chōshū, and the task of persuading Tosa was left to Saigō, Ōkubo and Kido as his deputies. Thus in January 1871, the transfer of troops from Satsuma, Chōshū and Tosa to the Court (*goshinpei no setchi*) was accomplished.

The transfer of troops was connected with abolition of domains and establishment of prefectures because of financial issues. If the cost of the troops transferred from the three domains had been met by the land rent from the three, there would have been no need to abolish the domains, and thus the troops would not have been under the direct command of the Emperor (Imperial Forces – *goshinpei*). So long as these Imperial Forces were paid for by revenues from the domains, they would not bear fruit merely by assuming an impressive name. In order to establish the Imperial Forces in both name and substance, there had to be a spectacular increase in government revenues.

Executing the plan to abolish domains and establish prefectures

The Ministry of Finance, which basically had to fill the coffers of the central government out of the seven million *koku* of rice from the lands of the former Bakufu, had already been anxious even before the establishment of the Imperial Forces. Ōkuma Shigenobu, the Vice Finance Minister, and Itō Hirobumi, the Deputy Minister, contacted Kido Kōin, the top man in the Chōshū domain, to achieve a reform of the Finance Ministry structure so as to make all expenditure, except for that already decided, subject to the Ministry's agreement. This meant a regime of dictatorship by the Ministry of Finance.

Prefectural governors in charge of lands that had been under direct control of the Bakufu reacted strongly against this dictatorship by the Ministry. But this quarrel between the Ministry of Finance and the prefectural governors was no more than a storm in the seven million *koku* rice bowl of the former Bakufu. So long as the domains retained their revenues from land rent, whether this was a Finance Ministry dictatorship or de facto local control, there would be no fundamental resolution of the problem. With the transfer of forces, the central government had succeeded in attaining sufficient military strength to overpower the domains. It was logically essential to mobilise this strength and concentrate the collection of land rent in the hands of the central government.

Those who felt acutely the need for abolition of the domains and establishment of prefectures in order to bring about central concentration of power were not confined to the Ministry of Finance. Among the samurai from Satsuma and Chōshū who were in charge of military affairs for the new government after the military units had returned home from the Boshin war, Saigō Tsugumichi of

52 *Japan's Modern History*

Satsuma and Yamagata Aritomo of Chōshū, in March 1869, had been ordered to make an inspection tour of military systems in Russia, France and Great Britain, from which they returned in 1870.

In their eyes the 'Imperial Army', amounting to fewer than 7,000 men, was too weak. The 'Imperial Army' might be capable of defending the Court, but in order to defend the security of Japan, it was necessary to place 'army camps' in key locations. Moreover, even if domestic uprisings could be put down by the 'Imperial Army' and by 'army camp troops', they would be no use for security against foreign threats. Although they did not formally advocate introducing conscription until after the replacement of domains by prefectures, the concept was born when these two men returned from the European tour of inspection in September 1870.

Thus, among Finance Ministry officials who were followers of Kido Kōin (including Ōkuma Shigenobu, Inoue Kaoru, Itō Hirobumi), and officials of the Army Ministry who had just returned from Europe, advocacy of moving from transfer of troops from the three domains to abolishing the domains in favour of prefectures grew stronger. The former aimed to concentrate the raising of finance in the centre, while the latter wanted the military power to be grasped by the central government.

Abolition of the domains and establishment of prefectures (*haihan chiken*) marked the ending of the 'Age of Revolution' that had begun around 1864. The influence of the domain lords who within the concept of an assembly would have created an upper house was gradually diminishing, and later the domains themselves were forced to dissolve. When the lower-ranking samurai overthrew the Bakufu and ended the regime of the domains, the Bakumatsu-Ishin (Restoration) revolution that they had led was complete.

Completing the revolution, however, was not the only thing needed to create a new regime. The season changed from 'revolution' to 'construction'. Moreover, the quality of the leaders of the revolutionary period was different from that of the leaders of the construction period. The time of Saigō Takamori would also come to an end.

3 Construction, 1871–1880

Demanding a blueprint for 'Construction': the inspection tour of Europe and America by the Iwakura Mission

Renewed recognition of investment and promotion of industry (shokusan kōgyō)

On 12th November 1871, a large mission consisting of Iwakura Tomomi as Ambassador Plenipotentiary, Ōkubo Toshimichi, Kido Kōin, Itō Hirobumi (leading councillor at the Industry Ministry) and Yamaguchi Naoyoshi (Deputy Councillor at the Foreign Ministry) as Deputy Ambassadors Plenipotentiary, together with 48 delegates of vice-minister or director rank from various ministries, as well as six male and female visiting students, left Yokohama by ship, bound for San Francisco. This was a mere four months after they had put into effect the abolition of the domains and establishment of prefectures – the biggest reform in Japanese modern history. The fact that so soon after 'revolution' about half of the central figures in the new government should have embarked on a mission of inspection to Europe and America to last for over a year may seem not merely bold but positively rash. For what purpose did they undertake this in a fashion that at first sight appears so impetuous? They must have considered the possibility that in the course of events the government might have completely changed and that they would not have been able to return to power.

Ōkubo Toshimichi and Kido Kōin, who over the three years and more between the *ōsei fukko* of January 1868 and the abolition of domains and establishment of prefectures had been pivotal leaders of major reform, nevertheless decided to take more than a year for an inspection tour of Europe and America.

Before investigating the circumstances that led to this plan and the determination to follow it, I want to look at the mission in terms of what its members learned in Europe and America. It was 14th July 1872 when one of the deputy ambassadors, Ōkubo Toshimichi, arrived in Liverpool from Boston. In a letter Ōkubo sent three months later to Saigō Takamori and Yoshii Tomozane in Japan, he made clear that his aim was to inspect the modern factories of Great Britain. In other words, this was an inspection tour to 'promote investment and industry' (*Shokusan kōgyō*).

54 *Japan's Modern History*

Table 3.1

Year	Era name and year	Events
1871	Meiji 4	Abolition of domains, establishment of prefectures.
1872	Meiji 5	Imperial Army reconstructed as Imperial Guards. Lifting of prohibition on long-term trading in fields and rice paddy. School system proclamation. Railway built between Shinbashi and Yokohama. Adoption of solar calendar. National bank law.
1873	Meiji 6	Proclamation of conscription ordinance. Ordinance on land tax. Split over question of invading Korea (five councillors including Saigō Takamori resign). Ministry of the Interior established.
1874	Meiji 7	Petition to establish a popularly elected assembly. Ōkubo Toshimichi decides to send an expedition to Taiwan. Railway built between Ōsaka and Kōbe. Saigō founds a private school in Kagoshima. Compatibility clause between Japan and China.
1875	Meiji 8	Ōsaka Conference (Ōkubo, Itagaki, Kido Kōin). Formation of Patriotic Society (Aikokusha). House of Elders (*genrōin*) established. Imperial Proclamation on gradual establishment of a constitutional system. Treaty exchanging Sakhalin and Chishima. Kanghwado (Kokado) Incident.
1876	Meiji 9	Kanghwado Treaty (treaty of friendship between Japan and Korea). Ordinance banning wearing of swords. Ōkubo makes proposal concerning national foundation culture. Measures to gradually abolish payment of salaries for former samurai *Shinpūren*, *Akizuki* and Hagi uprisings. Uprisings by peasants in Mie prefecture and elsewhere.
1877	Meiji 10	Land tax reduction (to 2.5% of land value). Seinan war (Satsuma rebellion). *Risshisha* petition.
1878	Meiji 11	Ōkubo assassinated. Three new laws for prefectures.
1879	Meiji 12	Abolition of Ryūkyū domain. Okinawa prefecture established. Education ordinance.
1880	Meiji 13	Assembly establishment alliance. Regulations on gatherings. Resolution to freeze land rent for five years.

During my travels here (29th August to 9th October), I have seen amazing and remarkable things. In every city there are great factories, of which the most flourishing are the Liverpool shipyards, the Manchester cotton spinning machine factories, the Glasgow steel works, white sugar machinery at Greenock, paper works in Edinburgh, the Newcastle steel works (this was established by the same Armstrong that invented the Armstrong rifle and cannon; he is still alive and was the man who showed us round this factory), the Bradford silk spinning and woollen weaving machinery works, the Sheffield steel works (which mainly manufacture steam train wheels and all kinds of tools), also a silver factory, a Birmingham beer factory (it is said that the annexe to this factory is 20 leagues [80 km] distant), a glass factory, and an enormous salt mountain in Chester. The complexity of these machines is extraordinary. There is not enough time to list all these factories, large and small, but they are sufficient to show why Great Britain is so prosperous and strong. What has struck me most forcibly is that even in the remotest places roads and bridges have been built, convenient for horse-drawn vehicles obviously, but also there is nowhere that trains cannot go.

(Katsuta Magoya, *Ōkubo Toshimichi den* ['Ōkubo Toshimichi Biography'], Dōbunkan, vol. 3, pp. 48–9)

The greater part of this was directly linked with the public and official works conducted by the Interior Ministry that Ōkubo had himself established on his return, and the last part was a reaffirmation of the public works being carried out by the Engineering Ministry, which had already been fully established in 1870. Production of domestic goods to compete with imports from Europe and America by setting up modern government-run factories (industrialisation for import substitution), as well as improvements to infrastructure, resulted from what Ōkubo had seen and heard in Great Britain.

The importance of mechanised factories, roads and railways had been noted by those who had been on inspection tours of Europe and America before Ōkubo. But in his case, as the most powerful man in the Meiji Government, he was in a position to put the results of what he had seen and heard into practice. But this was not all, since Ōkubo's passion for modern factories was no trivial matter. During his tour of Scotland, which took scarcely 40 days, he actually investigated 13 factories. His passion was of a quite different order from that of Japanese ministers who go on foreign inspection tours in the twenty-first century.

As shown in the book *Meiji ishin* ('The Meiji Restoration') that Ōno Kenichi and I wrote together, after the opening of the ports throughout the Bakumatsu period the most powerful domains worked to foster traditional manufacturing in order to create the financial resources for the import of warships and weapons (in pursuit of a 'strong military' [*kyōhei*]). Ceramics, crude wax and tea in the Hizen domain, silk products and paper in the Echizen domain and camphor, paper and dried bonito in the Tosa domain are representative examples.

Whether it was the development of traditional industries for export or the substitution of domestic manufactures for imported goods (import substitution) that was the principal focus of Ōkubo's Home Ministry is disputed even among Japanese economic historians. But if we distance ourselves from issues concerning the real economy and examine the problem from the perspective of refashioning national goals it is indisputable that Ōkubo returned to Japan attaching great importance to the modern factories and infrastructure that he had seen in Great Britain. 'Promotion of investment and development of industry' (*shokusan kōgyō*) – in other words 'prosperous country' (*fukoku*) – had been introduced as a national goal of equal importance to 'strong military' (*kyōhei*).

Constitution rather than parliament

As for Kido Kōin, of the former Chōshū domain, who stood alongside Ōkubo at the centre of Meiji Government, what did he return with from his overseas tour of inspection? The answer is that he recognised the importance of a 'constitution' as the basic law for national government.

56 *Japan's Modern History*

As we have already seen in Chapters 1 and 2, the proposal to establish an assembly began from an extremely early stage, and from 1863 to 1864 became the common goal of many reformist and revolutionary leaders. So it did not in fact begin with the famous 'white paper for the establishment of a popularly elected assembly' in the name of Itagaki Taisuke in 1874.

However, the argument during the Bakumatsu period for an assembly was premised on the continuation of rule by the Bakufu. The idea was that decisions should be taken, not only by the Bakufu, but also reflecting the opinions of an upper house of domain lords and a lower house of their retainers.

With *ōsei fukko*, however, the Bakufu disappeared, and with the abolition of the domains and establishment of prefectures the domains also ceased to exist. Power in the new government was held by the retainers in the powerful former domains of Satsuma, Chōshū, Tosa and others, so that the grounds for an assembly were much weaker than during the Bakumatsu period, and the new rulers only answered to the Emperor. Even if the Bakumatsu assembly argument had been amended and a new assembly put in place, the very basis for the legitimacy of the central government when the assembly was straining to represent 'public opinion' would have been rendered quite fragile.

Inada Masatsugu, in his classic among classics *Meiji kenpō seiritsu shi*, wrote as follows about Kido Kōin's goals in his inspection tour of Europe and America:

> When Councillor Kido joined the Iwakura Mission as Deputy Ambassador, and toured America and then several European countries, he seems to have been the most passionate of all members of the mission concerning constitutional questions. The day after he arrived in Washington, 22nd January 1872, he wrote in his diary: "I was given the order to investigate military and cultural matters. Ga Noriyuki of the secretariat is assisting me. However, at the time of the Meiji Restoration, I proposed that the Charter Oath of five articles should encompass domain lords, the aristocracy and the bureaucrats. With this Charter Oath, the Japanese people understood the general direction of our nation, but at the present time the Charter Oath of five articles is not enough and a much clearer basic law must be put in place. Thus, at this destination, I want to investigate *what is regarded as the basic law of each country*, and *its structure of government*, and I have informed my secretariat about my decision."
>
> (Inada Masatsugu, *Meiji kenpō seiritsu* shi ['History of the establishment
> of the Meiji Constitution'], Yūhikaku, 1960, vol. 1, p. 195;
> present writer's italics)

It is clear that the italicised phrases mean 'constitution' and 'cabinet system'. Aoki Shūzō, who had been his junior as a Chōshū samurai and was now a member of the Consulate in Germany, had done some work on this, and had served to restrict Kido's constitutional research to a focus on the Prussian Constitution. Professor Inada's previously cited book points to the following noteworthy fact:

Construction, 1871–1880 57

On 9th March, Kido went to Berlin, and was met by Aoki and others. . . . The most significant point in his diary entries was: "From three o'clock I was introduced by Aoki to Professor Rudolf von Gneist. I learned an enormous amount from our conversation." . . . It is interesting that, nine years before 1882, when Itō (Hirobumi) received his teachings, Kido too was impressed when he listened to a lecture from von Gneist, probably about constitutional questions.

(Inada, p. 196).

As Inada says, Japan's Prussian-style Great Japanese Imperial Constitution is thought to have been established on the basis of constitutional research conducted by Itō in Germany and Austria between 1882 and 1883. Of course, this fact itself is not incorrect, but Itō's choice of Germany for his research into constitutions had an earlier history. Also, Inoue Kowashi, Chief Secretary of the *Dajōkan*, had advocated the introduction of a German-style constitution into Meiji Japan, and it is well known that this was in 1881, a year before Itō travelled to Europe. But there was an earlier history to this as well.

After Kido, who became a fan of a German-style constitution during his tour of Europe and America, returned to Japan in 1873, what he emphasised was that the establishment of an assembly should be a matter for the future, but the first thing to do was to enact a constitution. What a constitution should do was to prevent government policy being formulated in an arbitrary fashion, but to guarantee to the people that it should follow fixed rules, and it should also make clear the scope of authority of each government instrumentality. Kido writes about this in his diary in September 1873:

In a constitution where power is shared between the Crown and the people, the fundamental point is that it is to be recognised by the common people. Today, however diligent our Emperor may be, he has only had a few years since the Restoration. It will be necessary to allow a considerable period of time to elapse for the people's knowledge to improve and for a popular assembly to be established. . . . In this way, if we are able, through the wise decisions of the Emperor, through judging public opinion, through regulating national administration, through exercising jurisdiction and controlling the arbitrariness of the authorities in ruling the country, *even though today it may be called an autocratic constitution*, in the future it will become the basis for a joint rule constitution in which the people are consulted, and it should be the foundation for broad happiness of the people.

(Inada, p. 198; present writer's italics)

If we divide up the reformist and revolutionary slogans of the Bakumatsu, namely 'strong military, prosperous country' (*fukoku kyōhei*) and 'governmental fairness and public opinion' (*kōgi yoron*), each into their two constituent parts, then Ōkubo had returned from his year-long travels emphasising 'prosperous country', with his detailed inspection of modern factories, while Kido had returned stressing

58   *Japan's Modern History*

'governmental fairness'. But how did Ōkubo and Kido deal with the two remaining elements, namely 'strong military' and 'public opinion', maintained by the government leaders while they were away?

'Strong military' and 'public opinion': the split over invading Korea and the proposal for a popularly elected assembly

Change in the meaning of 'strong military', and the foreign invasion argument

As we have previously written, if we separate Ōkubo's 'prosperous country' from 'strong military', its meaning changes from what it had meant in the Bakumatsu period.

As I already showed in the last chapter, 'strong military, prosperous country' meant in the Bakumatsu period that large domains should export their local products to Europe and America, and should import warships, cannons and rifles, so that 'prosperous country' was merely a means towards 'strong military'. In the previous section we demonstrated that it was Ōkubo Toshimichi during his inspection tour of Europe and American that had so radically altered this definition.

But during the time when he was occupied with the Iwakura Mission in 1872 and 1873, the meaning in Japan itself of 'strong military' was also undergoing change. The *fukoku kyōhei* of the Bakumatsu period, which meant trying to import warships, cannons and rifles, did little on behalf of *fukoku* (prosperous country), but served the interests of *kyōhei* (strong military). The thinking about 'strong military' on the part of the government that had taken over in the absence of those who were away on the Iwakura Mission was a call to support the 'revolutionary army' that provided the impetus for domestic revolution between the Boshin war and the abolition of the domains and establishment of prefectures.

Among the central personalities of the government at this time was Itagaki Taisuke who, as a product of the Tosa domain, was friendly with Gotō Shōjirō, key proponent of the argument for an assembly in the Bakumatsu period. Moreover, Professor Inada, in his *Meiji kenpō seiritsu shi* (History of the Establishment of the Meiji Constitution), maintains that Saigō himself until around 1872 supported Itagaki's proposal to set up a national assembly (vol. 1, p. 111).

This means that the two key personalities who had taken over the government while the Iwakura Mission was away had on the one hand given substance to what had been the Imperial Guards in the form of the Boshin army corps, and on the other hand had been advocating the establishment of an assembly ever since the Bakumatsu period.

Sudden rise of the 'foreign invasion argument'

Among the members of the Iwakura Mission, Ōkubo returned in May 1873, Kido in July, and the leader of the expedition, Iwakura, returned to Japan on 13th September. This was the turning point after which the caretaker government and the returned members of the Mission began a struggle for power over their differences respecting national goals.

The 'strong military' of the first years of Meiji was not a forward-looking approach towards a steady build-up of military strength but, as we have already written, was a backward-looking way of respecting the views of the distinguished participants in the civil war of 1868 and in the replacement of domains by prefectures in 1871. But what were these views? If the 'revolutionary forces' that had subjugated the whole of the territory of Japan were to be useful to Japan right now, they must send expeditions to Taiwan, Korea and Sakhalin (known in Japan as Karafuto). The Imperial Forces (*goshinpei*), which had backed the abolition of the domains and establishment of prefectures with military force, were reorganised as Imperial Guards in March 1872, but the man who was appointed to be chief of staff of the Imperial Guards, thus Chief of the High Command, was the councillor and Army general Saigō Takamori. At that time Kuroda Kiyotaka, who strove hard under Saigō in the Boshin war and for the replacement of domains by prefectures, confronted the great power Russia as Hokkaidō Development Minister, while Kirino Toshiaki, Chief Commander of the Kumamoto army camp, planned to defend the Ryūkyūs by attacking Taiwan, and was eyeing Qing (Ch'ing) dynasty China – a great power. Also, the Foreign Ministry of the central government was intending to force Korea to enter into diplomatic relations with the new Meiji Government. Territorial issues between Japan and Russia, Japan and China, Japan and Korea – that even now, early in the twenty-first century in which this book is being written, all still remain unresolved – suddenly came to prominence early in 1873 as a result of the military-backed demands of the Restoration government.

As everyone knows, 'revere the Emperor and expel the foreigner' was one of the central slogans, alongside 'prosperous country, strong military' and 'fairness and public opinion', of Bakumatsu politics. 'Expel the foreigner', however, in this instance was entirely directed against the gunboat diplomacy of the great powers, and had nothing to do with territorial issues.

The sudden emergence of territorial issues in 1873 was brought about by the hand of the military leaders of the former Satsuma and Tosa domains, which had supported the Boshin war and the replacement of domains by prefectures with military force. Thus, as we have already seen, Kuroda Kiyotaka of the former Satsuma domain became passionate about the Sakhalin issue; Kirino Toshiaki, also of Satsuma, placed great importance on Taiwan; and Itagaki Taisuke of the former Tosa domain took a forward position in relation to Korea. In 1910, nearly 40 years after that time, in the book *Jiyūtō shi* ('History of the Liberal Party') whose production was supervised by Itagaki himself (the book is a compilation), Itagaki wrote briefly about the circumstances of that time:

> At the time when the 'invade Korea' argument suddenly appeared, Kuroda Kiyotaka, as the principal Hokkaidō development official, was administering the task of unlocking the northern gate, and Kirino Toshiaki, the Kumamoto camp commander, garrisoned the western border. Kuroda, however, knowing that our fishermen on Sakhalin were being shot by Russian soldiers, wished

60 *Japan's Modern History*

to engage with international issues, and Kirino, seeing that inhabitants of the Ryūkyūs, which came under the jurisdiction of the Kumamoto camp, were being massacred by aborigines from Taiwan, using this as a pretext wished to send an army to invade Taiwan. They plotted to go to the capital jointly to engage with the authorities. But when they arrived in Tokyo, they learned that a cabinet decision had been taken to invade Korea, and seeing that their own proposals were not going to be adopted, they were very unhappy.

> (Itagaki Taisuke, compiler, *Jiyūtō shi* ['History of the Liberal Party'], Iwanami Bunkō ban, 1957, vol. 1, p. 62)

As we shall point out later, Kuroda strongly supported not only action on the Sakhalin problem, but also Kirino's desire to invade Taiwan, but it is true that these two men, both followers of Saigō, were not adherents of the 'invade Korea' position.

Saigō's 'invade Korea' argument

Saigō himself, however, advocated sending a plenipotentiary envoy to Korea. Japan's counterpart in the Sakhalin issue was Russia, one of the great powers. Since Taiwan was not a dependency of Qing (Ch'ing) dynasty China but was part of the territory of China proper, even though it was Saigō who was pursuing this he ought not to have wilfully pursued coercive measures before the return home of the Iwakura Mission.

Even so, the option of doing nothing did not exist for Saigō. Not only for Kuroda and Kirino, but also for the Boshin military groups and now the Imperial Guards, there were no longer any enemies to be conquered. Even though the Imperial Army had become the Imperial Guard and was stationed in Tokyo, there was no work worthy of the name left for them to do. Since their Supreme Commander and hero of the Boshin war was Saigō Takamori, both dissatisfaction and expectation was directed at him. In Saigō's own words, this was the situation: "The search for justice was fundamental to overthrowing the Bakufu, and as the basis for the Restoration, but now that we have reached the present situation, some are saying that justice has not yet been achieved. If this situation continues, they say, our actions in overthrowing the *Bakufu* will be pilloried as meaningless. They now attack me for this, and I am embarrassed" (*Itagaki Taisuke ate shokan* ['Letter to Itagaki Taisuke']), 3rd August 1873, in Itagaki Taisuke, compiler, *Jiyūtō shi* ['History of the Liberal Party'], Iwanami Bunkō, 1957, vol. 1, p. 65).

Here Saigō emphasised the Korean issue, which had no direct connection with either Russia or China. Korea at that time was a dependency of China, but this dependency was something of a formality, and Korea was neither an allied country nor a colony. If a struggle broke out between Japan and Korea, the possibility of China intervening was slight.

In Korea at that time, there was a reaction against Japan which was exerting pressure for the Koreans to sign a commercial treaty, and this burst forth in various forms. At the end of May 1873, Hirotsu Hironobu, the seventh-ranked secretary of

Construction, 1871–1880 61

the Japanese Foreign Ministry, stationed in Korea, informed his home government that with Japanese commercial firms conducting secret trading activities, Japan had been officially designated a 'lawless country'. Within Japan, in the middle of June, Ueno Kagenori, who was Deputy Foreign Minister, reported to Sanjō Sanetomi, the Prime Minister, that the Korean public and private sectors were deepening their obstruction of trade with Japan, and demanded that he issue instructions for policies to counter this. Taking hold of this situation, Saigō himself, who was both councillor and Commander of the Imperial Guard, pressed Sanjō to authorise him to go to Korea in the role of plenipotentiary envoy (3rd August). The so-called 'invade Korea' argument had become consolidated along the lines developed by the government during the absence of its key members on the Iwakura Mission.

What Saigō was really thinking is susceptible to two completely contrasting interpretations. The first interpretation identifies him as the pioneer of 'great deeds on the Continent', such as accompanied the Sino-Japanese war of 1894 and the Russo-Japanese war of 1904. In fact the origin of this theory was remarkably early, and had already appeared just before the Sino-Japanese war. In 1893 Sasa Tomofusa, a member of parliament belonging to the *Kokumin kyōkai*, who had inspected Seoul in Korea, had the opportunity to meet with the Chinese consul in Korea, Yuan Shikai. The two of them discussed the great deeds of the two nations on the Continent, and during this exchange Sasa expressed himself as follows:

> Our country's Saigō Takamori is a first class hero in East Asia, and unless he meets an untimely death, our Japan will not only subdue Korea, but will be able to attack the Asian continent.
>
> (Sasa kokudō sensei ikō hankōkai [ed.], *Kokudō Sasa sensei ikō* ['The Writings of Sasa'], Kaizōsha, 1936, pp. 128–9).

In 1877 Sasa, leading volunteers in the Seinan war, joined Saigō's forces, and was put in gaol, so we should not simply reject his portrait of Saigō.

On the other hand, Mōri Toshihiko's controversial 1979 book *Meiji 6 nen seihen* ('The Political Change of 1873'), expressed a view of Saigō totally at odds with that of Sasa. Mōri demonstrated, on the basis of vast quantities of material, that Saigō did not support the 'invade Korea' argument, nor was he an advocate of aggression against Asia.

The fact is that Saigō opposed Itagaki's proposal to send troops to Korea right away, and instead advocated the despatch of an envoy to Korea, unaccompanied by warships, demanding that he himself be given plenipotentiary powers for this purpose. Moreover, as I have already explained, Kuroda and Kirino, both of them followers of Saigō, were much more interested in Sakhalin and Taiwan than in the Korean question. It follows that the Mōri thesis that Saigō's proposal to send an envoy to Korea was designed to prevent the despatch of troops has considerable persuasive power.

The idea that both of these contradictory interpretations of the 'invade Korea' argument are persuasive shows that before the return of the Iwakura Mission Saigō

62   Japan's Modern History

had in a sense gone against his own opinions and had come to show the flag for the Boshin military groups. Saigō in the Bakumatsu period had worked hard to bring about a consensus in favour of overthrowing the Bakufu and establishing a feudal assembly, but he was not an advocate of expelling foreigners. Now, however, not only had the Bakufu and the domains disappeared, but also the former Satsuma forces, which had become the Imperial Guard, were now losing interest in the need for an assembly.

Advocacy of a popularly elected parliament by the former Tosa domain

Itagaki Taisuke and others of the former Tosa domain, who controlled one wing of the Imperial Guard, supported Saigō's plan to send an envoy to Korea (the so-called 'invade Korea' argument), but such support alone would make it impossible for them to reverse their inferiority to the former Satsuma forces under Saigō. Moreover, Ōkubo, who divided the forces of the former Satsuma domain between himself and Saigō, as I have already explained, had learned from Europe and America the importance of economic growth (prosperous country), and returned home in May 1873. Later, Kido Kōin of the former Chōshū domain, who together with Satsuma had backed the Meiji Government ever since the *ōsei fukko*, as we have already seen, was advocating the establishment of an 'autocratic constitution' as the basic law of Japan. Itagaki Taisuke, who was less keen than Saigō in his support for 'strong military', was also behind Satsuma and Chōshū in his support for 'prosperous country' and 'constitution'.

What the less influential Tosa forces put forward was a petition in January 1874 to establish a popularly elected assembly. This was an extension of the 'feudal assembly argument' which had been proposed jointly by Itagaki and Gotō Shōjirō of the former Tosa domain, but its particular characteristic lay in the idea of a 'popularly elected assembly'. On 17th January 1874, at the beginning of the 'Petition to Establish a Popularly Elected Assembly' presented to the Chamber of the Left (the pre-Meiji legislative body), the following sentence made the position clear:

> Those people having the duty to pay tax to the government also have the right to support or reject what the government is doing.
> (Itagaki Taisuke, compiler, *Jiyūtō shi* (History of the *Jiyūtō*), vol. 1, p. 90)

The eight notables who signed the petition, from Tosa (including Itagaki Taisuke), Echizen, Hizen, and elsewhere, were all former samurai, and did not possess "the duty to pay tax to the government".

For this reason, there is room for doubt concerning how far this phrase was really genuine. The fact that post-war historians have seen this as a dubious form of 'samurai popular rights' makes a certain amount of sense.

On the other hand, once this declaration had been made it attained a momentum of its own surpassing the real intentions of its proponents. By 1874, both the Bakufu and the domains had disappeared, and the status system of 'samurai, peasant, artisan and merchant' had been simplified into one of 'samurai descendants' (shizoku) and 'commoners' (*heimin*), so that the effect of the phrase was something absolute. This was because among these two status groups the only 'people having a duty to pay tax' were 'commoners' (mainly agricultural landlords).

The decision of the 'absent government' (the government in Tokyo while the Iwakura Mission was away) to send Saigō as an envoy plenipotentiary to Korea was rescinded after the Iwakura Mission returned, and on 23rd October 1873 Saigō, Itagaki, Soejima Taneomi (a former Hizen domain samurai), Etō Shinpei (the same) and Gotō Shōjirō (a former Tosa samurai) all resigned their positions as councillors. Of these all except Saigō were involved in sending the petition to the Chamber of the Left in favour of a popularly elected assembly on 17th January 1874.

Since the gap between these two dates was less than three months, the fact that Itagaki suddenly changed sides after his defeat on the proposal to invade Korea to the diametrically opposite proposal of establishing a popularly elected assembly has given him a bad reputation among historians of modern Japan. This is seen as an opportunistic shift from 'national rights' to 'popular rights'.

On the other hand, it takes time to compose a formal petition. Moreover, Itagaki was acquainted with Komuro Shinobu and Furuzawa Shigeru, who had just returned from Great Britain, by the introduction of Gotō Shōjirō, who had been a proponent of parliamentary politics since the Bakumatsu period. The 17th January petition had been written in first draft by Komuro and Furuzawa, and then Soejima Taneomi, a specialist in Chinese characters, had revised it. Unless it had been first devised immediately after his resignation as councillor on 23rd October, it could not have been completed by 17th January of the following year.

As we have shown up to the previous chapter, Gotō Shōjirō of Tosa was a consistent advocate of a parliamentary system during the Bakumatsu period, and it has been pointed out that Itagaki Taisuke, who was in charge of the 'absent government', also became a supporter of the assembly idea around 1872 (Inada, vol. 1, p. 111). It may be said that Itagaki, who was the principal councillor, along with Saigō, in the absent government, had an interest both in invading Korea and in establishing a popularly elected assembly.

Thus, between the split over invading Korea in October 1873 and the 'Petition to Establish a Popularly Elected Assembly' in January 1874, Ōkubo and Kido, back from their travels, were proclaiming 'prosperous country' and 'constitution', whereas Saigō and Itagaki, who had been in charge of the 'absent government', advocated 'strong army' and 'assembly', and were at loggerheads with the Iwakura Mission.

'Prosperous country' and 'fairness and public opinion'

Compromise between Ōkubo and Saigō: towards a Taiwan expedition

The dispute, however, between the 'prosperous country' argument of Ōkubo and the 'strong military' position of Saigō did not last long. Yoshii Tomozane,

64 Japan's Modern History

Kuroda Kiyotaka, Saigō Tsugumichi and others supported Ōkubo's opposition to the idea of invading Korea, but since the Bakumatsu period they had worked under Saigō to overthrow the Bakufu. Moreover, although they opposed invading Korea, they took a stronger line than Saigō over the Taiwan and Sakhalin questions. Major Generals Shinohara Kunimoto and Kirino Toshiaki, who acted together with Saigō when, defeated over his proposal to invade Korea, he resigned as councillor and several dozen men under them from the Imperial Guard, were of course strong advocates of overseas conquest. Ōkubo Toshimichi, enthusiast for economic development and founder of the Home Ministry, was surrounded by supporters of overseas conquest from Satsuma, not only outside the government, but also within it. Ōkubo, who promoted 'prosperous country' and halted proposals to 'invade Korea', in other ways was not in a position to resist the 'strong military' argument.

The origins of the proposal to invade Taiwan lay in the murder of 54 Ryūkyū islanders in November 1871, and in the violence against four fishermen from Oda (now Okayama) Prefecture who had drifted to Taiwan. So far as the latter were concerned, the grounds for sending a large military force were too weak, but the real objective lay with the former. The objective of sending troops to Taiwan was to fulfil the duty of government, given that the Ryūkyū islanders were Japanese, and the government was their sovereign.

At that time, however, the Ryūkyūs also had links with China, and China did not regard Ryūkyūans as Japanese. The Chinese government accepted that inhabitants of their dependency of Ryūkyū had been murdered on their territory of Taiwan, but they rejected the idea that it was Japanese that had been murdered.

As is clear from this, the objective of sending troops to Taiwan was to place the Ryūkyū islands under Japanese sovereignty, but this brought with it the danger of confrontation with China, the great power of Asia, which regarded the islands as their dependency. For Japanese supporters of the 'strong military' position, who wanted military struggle in East Asia, it was this that created a positive objective for sending forces to Taiwan.

The Taiwan expedition was carried out in May 1874, at the behest of none other than Ōkubo Toshimichi. It was a large undertaking, with 3,600 men on six warships. An important point is that of the 3,600 men, volunteers recruited in Kagoshima by Saigō after the split among supporters of a Korean invasion were in the majority. According to *Seinan kiden* (first part of volume 1), these Kagoshima volunteers were said to have constituted the main strength of the 'invasion force', alongside the Kumamoto *chindaihei* (an Army division) led by Tani Tateki (Kokuryūkai honbu [ed.], *Seinan kiden* ['Seinan war History and Biography'], vol. 1, part 1, Kokuryūkai honbu, 1908, p. 600). The fact that three years later these two leading comrades had become enemies at the time of the fighting over Kumamoto Castle must have been beyond their imagination.

Three factors are important in relation to this expedition to Taiwan.

First of all, the slogans 'prosperous country' and 'strong military', which in October 1873 had been diametrically opposed to each other, came together again in 1874. As we shall explain later, this was, from the perspective of Ōkubo, whose

Construction, 1871–1880   65

priority was economic development, a compromise forced upon him, but a head-on confrontation between Ōkubo and Saigō was avoided. The powerful regime that emerged as a result of this amalgamation of 'prosperous country' and 'strong military', which many researchers have termed an 'Ōkubo dictatorship', emerged only for a short period.

Confrontation between Ōkubo and Kido

Second, in the debates about invading Korea, Ōkubo and Kido, who had argued for priority to be given to domestic matters, and for a time agreed on this, came to a parting of the ways over the Korean expedition. The first argument of Kido in opposition to the Taiwan expedition was that when the Iwakura Mission returned to Japan and its members opposed the idea of invading Korea, Ōkubo apparently said that he wanted "to stop the Korean expedition and support the Ministry of Home Affairs". He criticised him for changing his view from 'prosperous country' to 'strong military' (*Seinan kiden*, vol. 1, part 1, p. 590).

Another criticism was that a mere seven years after the Meiji Restoration, Japanese national and financial strength was insufficient to withstand a war in East Asia. As he put it, "If we send troops, the resources to send them to the battlefield and their cost on the battlefield means it will be difficult to succeed in our plan" (ibid., p. 587).

Kido was critical of Ōkubo's lack of knowledge of the dependency status of the Ryūkyū islands:

> In my opinion, Ryūkyū feels half Chinese. I have listened to Ryūkyū people who tell me that they think of Japan as their father and China as their mother. I think they will say to the Chinese that they think of China as the father and Japan as the mother. The fact that they resort to both these extremes is permissible, given that their situation is that of a weak country, but we should not look at them as the same as people in Japan. The domestic country (Japan) is the basis, and the power of which they are a dependency (China) is marginal. Putting what is basic as secondary, and what is marginal to the fore, is not the right way of making policy.
>
> (Ibid., p. 588)

From this position, Kido Kōin, representing the forces of the former Chōshū domain within the Meiji Government, resigned his position as councillor in April 1874. This represented a split in the Iwakura Mission, now returned to Japan, a split between the 'prosperous country' and 'constitution' factions, and a split between Satsuma and Chōshū, which between them had engineered the Meiji Restoration.

Advocates of making war on China among Ōkubo's supporters

The third important factor concerning the Taiwan expedition was the support for making war on China among the hard-line faction. In fact the Sino-Japanese war

66 Japan's Modern History

that broke out 20 years later, in 1894, was foreshadowed by the desire to wage such a war in 1874, and this desire was strong in the new government. Moreover, these hard-liners, even after the split over the question of invading Korea, remained within the government, and included Kuroda Kiyotaka (Hokkaidō Development Minister) and the de facto Navy Minister, Vice-Minister Kawamura Sumiyoshi, both of whom supported Ōkubo. In September 1874, when Ōkubo was negotiating in Peking as Ambassador Plenipotentiary towards a settlement of the Taiwan question, Kuroda wrote as follows to the Prime Minister Sanjō Sanetomi concerning the question of going to war with China.

> When we received an urgent message from Ōkubo that war has already been decided, we immediately revealed the unreasonableness of the Chinese government, spoke loud and clear about their crimes, publicised this at home and abroad, and in conformity with the laws of war based on the legal systems of all nations, argued that measures against them must be taken, that right away a ruthless and rapid attack should be launched against the Emperor of China, without giving them time to prepare their defences.
>
> *(Sanjō ke bunsho* ['Materials on the Sanjō House'], held in the National Diet Library, Tokyo, 50/11)

This was a call for hostilities to be launched against China, based on a declaration of war.

Kuroda's view was a clearly thought-out approach to the system of military leadership in preparation for war with China. He argued as follows:

> His Majesty the Emperor should himself take control of the basic elements of military affairs as Generalissimo, and he should quickly issue an edict that this is the sovereign's will, so that all the people are as one. The duty of the Supreme Commander is to accept reverentially the Imperial Will and control military affairs. Prime Minister Sanjō must fulfil this duty.
>
> There needs to be one institution to assist the Supreme Commander, allocate military personnel to their respective posts and plan the method of attack. For this purpose, when the day arrives to begin hostilities, he must rapidly despatch a proclamation, summon Army General Saigō, the sixth-ranking Court official Kido, and seventh-ranking Court official Itagaki, entrust matters also to the councillors Yamagata and Ijichi, to Major General Yamada (Akiyoshi), to fourth-ranking official of the Navy Ministry Ijūin Kanehiro and others. The Bureau (the so-called General Staff Bureau) must be established, mainly to devise strategy"
>
> (Ibid.)

This was an extremely practical proposal to establish a General Staff Bureau bringing together military leaders from Satsuma, Chōshū and Tosa, under the Generalissimo and the Supreme Commander, as a strategic headquarters for the China war.

Construction, 1871–1880 67

What is worth noting here is that with Japan likely to be at war with China (the great power of Asia) the controversy over whether to invade Korea and the question of establishing a popularly elected assembly as well as the dispute over whether to send troops to Taiwan were all forgotten, and the heroes of the Boshin war were all mobilised. Saigō Takamori, Kido Kōin and Itagaki Taisuke, all of whom for various reasons had resigned from the government, were enlisted as key figures.

Among the four men who, apart from the three mentioned above, were listed as members of the General Staff Bureau, I have already referred in the earlier chapters to Yamagata Aritomo and Ijichi Masaharu. As for the two others, Yamada Akiyoshi and Ijūin Kanehiro, they were, respectively, from Chōshū and Satsuma, and had distinguished themselves during the Boshin war. It is worth remembering that, apart from Itagaki, six out of the seven figures renowned in the Boshin war were from Chōshū and Satsuma. The government in 1874 was essentially a Sat-Chō domain government.

When he called for war against China, Kuroda was well aware of Japan's naval weakness. As already explained, 'strong military' in the Bakumatsu period meant increasing military strength by exporting local products and importing warships, cannons and rifles. By contrast, 'strong army' at the beginning of the Meiji period meant relying on existing military strength and going to war with neighbouring countries. But Kuroda had been made aware that if Japan were to wage war against China – a great power – the 'strong army' of early Meiji had serious weaknesses. He argued as follows:

> At the beginning of the war we must attack their navy with our fleet, to destroy their ports, and open up the way for the Army to attack. . . . At present, we have to fulfil our missions with no more than ten battleships, so we must organise a reserve fleet. There are about 100 steamships under the control of various ministries (each ministry and the Development Office) and in private hands. We must choose the most appropriate ones, acquiring one fifth of the total.
>
> (Ibid.)

Perhaps because the Army during the Boshin civil war had acquired practical fighting experience, Kuroda did not express particular anxiety. But whereas in the Bakumatsu period each domain had competed to acquire warships, now in the Navy the situation was deteriorating.

Kawamura Sumiyoshi, who, like Kuroda, was a naval vice-minister, argued for a war against China, but he was more of a Saigō admirer, to the point that while Saigō was back in Kagoshima he proposed to Sanjō, the Prime Minister, that he should call him back and appoint him as 'Supreme Commander' in charge of both the Army and the Navy. Kawamura's reverence for Saigō in the autumn of 1874 was one of the factors that destabilised Saigō's judgement when he raised his private army two and a half years later.

By contrast with military men connected with the former Satsuma domain, Yamagata Aritomo, Army Minister (and Lord) from the former Chōshū domain,

68　*Japan's Modern History*

made clear to the Prime Minister, Sanjō, that he could not bear responsibility for this kind of reckless war (*Ōkuma bunsho* ['Ōkuma's Papers'], vol. 1, p. 75). The confrontation between Ōkubo and Kido concerning whether to send troops to Taiwan reflected rivalry between Satsuma and Chōshū.

Military men from Satsuma, including Saigō, who had secluded himself in Kagoshima, in 1874 genuinely wanted to make war on China, but Kido Kōin's desire to draw up a constitution, and the proposal by Itagaki Taisuke for a popularly elected assembly, led to no action at this period. In a word, the shop selling 'Fairness' and 'Public Opinion' was forced to postpone its opening ceremony.

Rapprochement between Kido and Itagaki

When, however, as the result of Ōkubo's five rounds of negotiations with China in Peking, he concluded compatibility provisions between the two countries, so that war was averted, the situation changed. Cracks appeared in the linkage between 'prosperous country' and 'strong military', whereas 'Fairness' and 'Public Opinion began to converge.

It was Inoue Kaoru, of the Chōshū faction, who worked on those close to Itagaki, advocate of a popularly elected assembly, to comply with the views of Kido, proponent of the need for a constitution. It is uncertain from what date Inoue, known for his torching of the British consulate and his secret voyage to Great Britain in the Bakumatsu period, and in the early Meiji period as an active member of the Ministry of Finance, began to develop an interest in a constitution and a national assembly. But from the autumn of 1874, when he engineered an alliance with the advocates of a popularly elected assembly, until the end of his life, he was an advocate of the gradual development of constitutional government. Inoue held discussions on board a ship bound for Ōsaka with Komuro Shinobu and Furuzawa Shigeru, who had drafted the 'Petition to Establish a Popularly Elected Assembly'. This was the day after Ōkubo's triumphal return to Yokohama, having wrapped up the negotiations in Peking. Hard on the heels of the celebrations of Ōkubo's return – he being a proponent of economic development ('prosperous country') – he met with Komuro and the other advocates of an assembly for a meeting on board ship. The nature of this meeting was described in detail in a letter from Inoue to Kido.

He first of all expressed to Kido his request that he should strive to ensure that the Taiwan expedition was the last such conflict with neighbouring countries. He wrote: "In your letter you expressed your opposition to a war against Korea, and other wars in the future, so please tell Itō, Yamagata and others that the exercise of wealth and power, attempts to spread enlightenment, and unnecessary expenditure should be avoided" (Inoue Kaoru kō denki hensankai [ed.], *Segai Inoue kōden* ['Biography of Inoue'], Naigai shoseki, 1934, vol. 2, pp. 614–15).

Another method of restraining Satsuma was alliance with Tosa to advocate a popularly elected assembly. Since the Bakumatsu period, there had been alliances between Satsuma and Chōshū, and between Satsuma and Tosa (the Sat-Chō Alliance, the Sat-To Alliance), but this was the first time that Chōshū had linked up with

Construction, 1871–1880 69

Tosa. The policy basis for this new alliance was the propinquity between Kido's argument for a constitution and Itagaki's advocacy of an assembly. According to the expression used by Inoue, "Blending Itagaki's argument with that of yours (Kido), if we set up an assembly in accordance with our country's traditions, and have an assembly that gives sufficient power to government, I think that we can have cooperation (with Itagaki and others)" (ibid., pp. 618–19).

The conversations between Inoue, Komuro and Furusawa on board ship between Yokohama and Ōsaka had the following content, according to Inoue:

> I have just arrived at Ōsaka together with Komuro and Furusawa. They agreed to exclude *sweet potatoes* from the government in order to improve the administration. Itagaki is said to have come to Ōsaka. . . . Komuro and Furusawa requested that I invite you (Kido) to Naniwa (Ōsaka), and then they would ask Itagaki to come quickly so that we can discuss the way forward . . ."
>
> (Ibid., p. 614–15; present writer's italics)

The meaning of *sweet potatoes* can easily be guessed.

Two 'Ōsaka conferences'

The shipboard discussions between the three men were continued on 22nd January 1875 between Kido, Itagaki, Inoue, Komuro and Furukawa. Kido wrote about it as follows in his diary:

> At eleven o'clock I went to Inoue and after an hour we visited Itagaki together. Komuro and Furusawa were with Itagaki. We expressed our thoughts concerning their popularly elected assembly argument, and we also listened to their opinions, then around eight o'clock we reached Inoue and held discussions with him, and at eleven we returned.
>
> (Nihon shiseki kyōkai [ed.], *Kido Kōin nikki* ['Kido Kōin Diary'], Tokyo Daigaku shuppankai, vol. 3, p. 144)

In response to the results of the five-man conference held on 22nd January, Kido held a discussion with Ōkubo on 9th February and gained his agreement on "the basic principle of a constitution, involving the creation of a popular assembly and so on, and on gradually forming the basis of a parliament" (ibid., p. 151). In addition, on 11th February Ōkubo held a conference, inviting Kido and Itagaki, and the three men agreed on a plan for the Imperial Proclamation to "establish gradually a form of constitutional government structure" of 14th April.

The 'Ōsaka Conference', famous in Japanese history, pointed to this three-man conference of 22nd February. I cannot disagree with the view that had Ōkubo, the central pivot of the government at the time, not been in agreement, then neither the resumption of their councillor positions by Kido and Itagaki in March, nor the Imperial Proclamation in April, would have been possible, and the 'three-man conference' in February ought to be called 'the Ōsaka Conference'. Even so, it

70   *Japan's Modern History*

would be a mistake to conclude that under the leadership of Ōkubo Toshimichi, advocate of 'prosperous country' (meaning investment and economic development), a step towards constitutional government had been made.

It is true that Ōkubo, who had returned from China having narrowly averted war, had lost the support of the Satsuma faction in the Navy and the Army, which was hoping for war, and that Kido and Itagaki (proponents respectively of a constitution and of an assembly), had brought round the isolated Ōkubo to agreement with a first step towards constitutional government. In this regard, we should not forget the importance of another 'Ōsaka Conference', namely the five-man conference held between Chōshū and Tosa on 22nd January.

Split in the *kōgi yoron* faction and the successes of the *fukoku* faction

In any period it is unlikely that cooperation between radicals and moderates will last long. This was the case in 1875. Itagaki and others of the radical faction in August pressed Kido and Inoue "to fulfil the goal and timetable of establishing a true parliament in order to carry out the February Ōsaka agreement" (Furusawa Shigeru kankei bunsho ['Furusawa Shigeru Papers'], National Diet Library, p. 31). To this Kido countered that in the Imperial Proclamation of 14th April it was clearly written that "a constitutional system should be gradually introduced", and that "progress should be pursued with moderation and there should be no hasty experimentation" (Letter to Inoue on 1st September, in *Segai Inoue kōden*, vol. 2, p. 664).

In this way the alliance between the two men was being decisively ruptured at the end of September. Kido himself argued that "the Ōsaka Conference was a complete failure, and I am ashamed of my hasty decision" (Itō Hirobumi kankei bunsho kenkyū [ed.], *Itō Hirobumi kankei bunsho*, Hanawa Shobō, vol. 4, p. 270).

The Kanghwado (Kokado) Incident

In September 1874, when the alliance between radicals and moderates was breaking down, the Kanghwado Incident took place. Today the truth about this incident has been fully established by historians from documentary materials.

In October 1874, the Meiji Government put an end to the Japan–China confrontation over the Taiwan issue, and in February 1875 sent envoys to Korea in order to attempt a solution to problems in Japan–Korea relations. In contemporary parlance, this was a business meeting. Negotiations, however, went badly, and in May Hirotsu Hironobu (a sixth-ranking officer of the Foreign Ministry) demanded of the Japanese government that it threaten Korea with military action, writing as follows:

> One or two of our warships ought to be sent, making surreptitious voyages between Tsushima and their country (Korea), they should be used to survey a sea route and demonstrate to them our will.
>
> (Gaimushō, *Nihon gaikō bunsho*
> ['Official Documents on Japanese Foreign Policy'], vol. 8, p. 72)

Construction, 1871–1880   71

In July the Japanese–Korean negotiations arrived at an impasse, and when most of the Japanese delegation returned home, the Navy put into practice Hirotsu's proposal. This was the despatch of the survey ship *Unyō* under the command of Inoue Yoshika. On 20th September, when the *Unyō* dropped anchor near Kanghwado island, the captain and others went in boats to Ch'ojijin (Sōshichin), where, coming under fire from a gun battery, they returned to the ship for a while and on 21st they landed on the island and attacked it, then on 22nd they captured the Yŏngjongsŏng (Eishūjō) Castle.

For the people of North and South Korea, this Kanghwado Incident, as the first step in the Japanese assimilation of Korea 35 years later, is still remembered (NHK, *Nihon to Chōsen hantō 2000 nen* ['2000 years of Japan and the Korean peninsula'], NHK, 2010, vol. 2, chapter 10). Even for Japanese who know this history, this continuity is undeniable. Also, it is entirely clear from Japanese materials that the attack from the gun battery on the warship *Unyō* was seen as a blatant challenge by the Japanese side.

As we have already explained, however, Kido Kōin, who returned to the government as a result of the Ōsaka Conference, opposed both the 'invade Korea' argument in 1873, and the Taiwan expedition of 1874. Moreover, one of Inoue Kaoru's motives for engineering Kido's return to government was to make sure that "in future we do not wish to fight other wars with Korea or elsewhere". It is difficult to believe that the Meiji Government was united in perpetrating the Kanghwado Incident.

Despite this, after the Kanghwado Incident took place Kido was converted to a hard-line position against Korea. He explained this conversion in the following way:

> When the debate took place (in 1873) about invading Korea, I deeply regretted that domestic politics was not more advanced, and argued that domestic politics should be given priority and foreign policy relegated to a lesser position. Besides (at that time), there was no clear reason to punish Korea by invading it. Now, however, since it has attacked our warship, Korea has clearly become our enemy. Here perhaps, even though we still have limited capacity in our internal politics, we cannot merely reflect on our internal circumstances and refuse to address foreign issues. We therefore now have to change our fundamental position.
>
> (Gaimushō, *Nihon gaikō bunsho*, Gaimushō, vol. 8, p. 125)

One reason for Kido's change of opinion was the weakening of the base of power with the split in the group that favoured a popularly elected assembly. Moreover, the dissatisfaction of the Saigō faction in Kagoshima and the military element in the central government at having had to swallow that they were being sidestepped was rekindled by the Kanghwado Incident. This was one of the reasons for Kido's change of position.

Moreover, at this stage not only the former Imperial Guard faction led by Saigō, but also the former Minister of the Left, Shimazu Hisamitsu, who may be regarded

72 *Japan's Modern History*

as the former head of the domain, supported an invasion of Korea. Apart from Ōkubo Toshimichi and a handful of ex-Satsuma people who occupied important positions in the central government, a majority of both upper- and lower-ranking former samurai from Satsuma supported the 'invade Korea' argument.

The Kanghwado Treaty

Both Ōkubo, who felt isolated, and Kido, of the former Chōshū domain, who had lost the support of popular assembly advocates, had very little room for manoeuvre. The road chosen by Ōkubo and Kido was to implement a hard-line policy towards Korea, and thus avoid a war with Korea, in order to separate off the legitimate armed forces from the irregular samurai bands of Kagoshima and elsewhere. This time Kido gave his full support to the foreign policy of brinkmanship that Ōkubo had attempted with the Taiwan expedition the previous year.

In concrete terms, in treaty negotiations with the Korean government Kido supported Ōkubo's appointment of the hard-line but highly popular Kuroda Kiyotaka as plenipotentiary, and of Inoue Kaoru, a supporter of Kido representing the moderate Chōshū faction, as Deputy Ambassador Plenipotentiary. The delegation the Japanese government sent thus consisted of both hard and soft elements, and was accompanied by army officers amounting to nearly half the supporting staff positions.

This is not just speculation on the part of the present writer. In reading the following extract, it becomes clear that this was Ōkubo's own scenario. In a letter to Itō Hirobumi of December 1875, Ōkubo wrote as follows:

> I am concerned with the response of Inoue Kaoru. . . . The purpose of now sending the government delegation is without exaggeration to give overall priority to peace. . . . We must definitely assist his strenuous exertions, and I earnestly entreat you to put your best efforts into this cause. . . . I have also talked intensively with Kuroda, so I do not believe that he would appeal to barbarous actions during the negotiations, but we should pay attention to his own personality. We are unable to change our personalities, so to compensate for his weak point is something that the government must concern itself with.
>
> (Itō Hirobumi kankei bunsho kenkyūkai,
> *Itō Hirobumi kankei bunsho*, Hanawa Shobō, vol. 3, p. 233)

In this context, when we read the phrase "we should pay attention to his personality", it is clear that the personality of Kuroda was too audacious, and since there was a risk that commercial treaty negotiations might turn into war, it was Ōkubo's intention to place Inoue Kaoru as his deputy in the same delegation.

Thus the delegation – in which Kuroda had plenipotentiary powers, Inoue had the powers of a deputy plenipotentiary and the full contingent numbered 30 – travelled in six vessels, defended by 260 military personnel, to Kanghwado.

Since this was a negotiation to conclude a commercial treaty, accompanied by a large military force, there is no room for doubt that it was a typical example of

Construction, 1871–1880 73

'gunboat diplomacy'. Moreover, the contents of the Kanghwado Treaty (Japan–Korea friendship pact) included opening the main ports and allowing Japanese to reside freely in Korea, and so on. This was forced on Korea by Japan, which itself had been coerced by the great powers. When the American consul in Japan criticised this 'gunboat diplomacy', the Foreign Minister, Terashima Munenori, replied: "This is like the measures taken when, for instance, your country's Commodore Perry arrived at Shimoda. What we have done is in order to conclude a treaty whose central purpose is peace" (Gaimushō, *Nihon gaikō bunsho*, vol. 8, p. 153).

In the Kanghwado Treaty, however, there was one provision that went beyond 'gunboat diplomacy'. This was article 1, which read: "Korea is an independent country, and has equal rights with Japan". The original Japanese intention was not to write "Korea . . . has equal rights with Japan", but rather to formulate the article as "Korea is an independent country". Stating in a treaty that Korea, which had been dependent on Qing (Ch'ing) China over a long period, was "an independent country" brought out the seeds of conflict between Japan and China over Korea.

The Kanghwado Treaty, concluded in March 1876, in its immediate aftermath fanned new flames in relations between Japan, China and Korea, but within Japan it brought an end to the 'invade Korea' argument that had been promoted by the 'former revolutionary forces' over the two years from 1873. The seeds of conflict with China disappeared temporarily as a result of the mutual provisions between Japan and China in 1874. And now, with the Kanghwado Treaty of 1876, points of dispute between Japan and Korea ceased to exist for the time being.

For the 'former revolutionary forces' led by Saigō Takamori, the 'enemy' to be suppressed, following on from the domestic 'enemy', was now neighbouring countries, but this 'enemy' too had disappeared. At the beginning of 1877 Kirino Toshiaki, who had been Saigō's right-hand man, criticised him in the following terms: "The idea of the Great Master (Saigō) that we should await the opportunity for foreign troubles is an outdated story" (Nihon shiseki kyōkai [ed.], *Ōkubo Toshimichi bunsho* ['Documents relating to Ōkubo Toshimichi'], Tokyo Daigaku shuppankai, vol. 7, pp. 496–7).

Impasse of the 'foreign invasion' faction and the 'constitution faction'

For Kido Kōin and others who allied themselves with Ōkubo Toshimichi after Ōkubo had broken with the popular assembly faction of Itagaki Taisuke, the conclusion of the Kanghwado Treaty removed their raison d'être. As Kido had expected, the Kanghwado Incident did not become the invasion of Korea. For Kido, who in 1873 opposed the plan of Saigō and others to invade Korea, and in 1874 also opposed the Taiwan expedition proposed by Ōkubo and others, this really made sense.

Already, however, apart from breaking ranks with the assembly faction, with the proposal of Kido and others to establish a constitution, the kind of pressure that existed around the time of the Ōsaka Conference of 1875 was dying out. Just as Kirino Toshiaki, Saigō's right-hand man, had begun to harbour criticism of

74   *Japan's Modern History*

'the Great Master', Inoue Kaoru, having backed Kido and brought about the success of the Ōsaka Conference, experienced a deep sense of frustration after the Kanghwado Treaty was signed.

In a letter to Kido on 2nd April after the treaty had been concluded, Inoue showed he was in a complicated state of mind when he wrote: "Because I sincerely place the maintenance of peace as my primary goal, I agreed with reluctance to go to Korea as deputy to Kuroda, and discarding my reputation, all I wanted to do was to keep a balance between the war argument and the peace argument" (*Segai Inoue kōden*, part 2, p. 71). Since joint understanding with the recipient was the premise of this letter, I cannot make a complete analysis as a third party. With this as a premise, I should like to explain that Inoue's phrase as "discarding [his] reputation" and becoming deputy to Kuroda was just to maintain a balance between the argument for war and the argument for peace.

Inoue's appointment as Deputy Ambassador Plenipotentiary occurred after Kido and Itagaki had been the central figures in an alliance, which had broken down with the Kanghwado Incident, between 'constitution' and 'assembly', and for Inoue this may be seen as his ultimate service. Inoue, who returned home in March following the conclusion of the Kanghwado Treaty, was appointed to a three-year-long tour of various European countries to investigate financial and monetary matters. Of course, this was something that Inoue very much wanted.

It is clear that this Western tour was compensation to Inoue for having become Deputy Ambassador to Kuroda "discarding [his] reputation". But the biggest reason why Inoue wished to go on a three-year tour of Western countries was probably his feeling of hopelessness, because the strength of the 'constitution' and 'assembly' arguments were in decline around the time of the 'Ōsaka Conference'. By the conclusion of the Kanghwado Treaty in 1876, while Kirino Toshiaki was acutely conscious of the setback to his own faction, Inoue Kaoru of the 'constitution' faction, despairing of returning to power in the near future, went off on an inspection tour of Western countries.

The age of Ōkubo Toshimichi

Since Itagaki Taisuke and other advocates of a popularly elected assembly had left the government before the Kanghwado Incident occurred, the 'prosperous nation' faction led by Ōkubo Toshimichi was able to take over the centre of government. In April 1876, when Inoue received the order to proceed on a three-year Western tour, Ōkubo, who was both councillor and Home Minister, submitted a proposal to the Prime Minister, which may be regarded as the platform of the 'prosperous country' faction.

In this proposal, Ōkubo emphasised the importance of ability in the contemporary political world: "What is called an empire throughout the world, possessing the right of independence and self-determination, is based on actual power." He asserted that the essence of power was not to be found in "governance, laws, military preparations and education", but in "the statistics of exports and imports". Industrial and economic strength were the basis for 'independence' and for 'empire'.

Construction, 1871–1880 75

For Japan, however, which had only just begun to modernise, it was not possible simply to hand over industrial development to the free enterprise of private companies. While recognising that for government to develop industries was not "the proper way of politics", Ōkubo argued that in Meiji Japan it was necessary to employ "unorthodox methods suitable to the age [in which we are living]". (Satō Seizaburō,

" '*Shi no chōyaku' o koete*" [Going beyond the 'leap of death'], Toshi shuppan, 1992, p. 184). Since this view contrasted with his previously cited opinions in 1872 when he saw over British factories, I will reproduce his words here:

> When we survey the affairs of state and the level of capabilities, we see that after the ups and downs following the Restoration, now that we are at the beginning of reform, people's knowledge has not advanced and private industry has not progressed. This is because the economy is not yet prosperous, trade has lost its equilibrium year on year, sources of profit have not yet been opened up, and the amount of production is declining month by month. . . . In working to stimulate industrial development and to encourage trade, we must nourish in depth the bases of the economy and find the way to promote profits from trade. If this is not done by government efforts, is left to the private sector, and goes through a process of procrastination, it will be extremely difficult to stem decline.
>
> (*Ōkubo Toshimichi bunsho*, vol. 7, pp. 79–90)

This way of thinking was remarkably similar to that of the 'development dictatorships' of many Asian countries after the Second World War.

Even so, during the two and a half years between 1873 and early 1876, Ōkubo was not able to embark on this kind of scheme, which he had brought back with him from Europe and America. In the succession of foreign struggles, from the 'invade Korea' controversy, through the Taiwan expedition to the Kanghwado Incident, the idea of foreign adventures promoted by the 'former revolutionary forces' of Saigō Takamori and others had not been overcome. Even though it is true that Ōkubo and others placed renewed emphasis on 'development', there was now less and less reason for describing the basis of his power as 'dictatorial'.

For Ōkubo at this point, conclusion of the Kanghwado Treaty in March 1876 was a perfect opportunity. While the 'foreign invasion' faction and the 'constitution' faction had lost ground, the 'prosperous country' faction alone was in fine shape.

The Seinan war

Advocates of economic development, however, did not retain the high ground for very long. The 'foreign invasion' faction of Saigō Takamori and others took the initiative, not to engage in foreign invasion, but rather to launch a 'domestic war' against the Japanese government.

76   Japan's Modern History

In this book we have described the group of Saigō and others as 'Boshin military group', 'former Imperial Guards', 'former revolutionary forces', 'strong military faction', 'foreign invasion faction' and so on. Even though I realise that it would be easier for the reader to be presented with a single name, I have been beset by the feeling that I wanted to express their characteristics by reference to the particular circumstances of the time.

The lack of consistency, however, in the present writer's expressions, also becomes an explanation for Saigō's popularity in so many different directions. With the inclusion of those who had experienced the Boshin war and those who had been part of the Court forces – the same thing as the Imperial Guard – as well as discontented samurai who went along with the proposal to invade Korea, participants in the Taiwan expedition, supporters of the Kanghwado Incident, and finally also those who were in tune with the 'Petition to Establish a Popularly Elected Assembly' in 1874, many who were dissatisfied at various times with the Meiji Government placed their expectations on the enterprising spirit of Saigō Takamori. The Hyōron Shinbun, which was at the far left wing of the 'popularly elected assembly' position, published the following assessment in January 1876:

> Today throughout the country, countless millions of people differ from the government's policies, are forming societies and establishing parties, are calling for a return to the feudal system, or are advocating popular rights, and oppose this government covertly. Nevertheless, their power is weak and insubstantial, and they always try to act in conjunction with the Kagoshima party. They are asking themselves what is the situation in Kagoshima, and what Saigō is doing. Given that their arguments are completely different from each other, and since they are not able to combat the government without emotionally relying on Saigō, they can do nothing. This is because those who are dissatisfied with the present government have no possibility of acting unless they work with the Kagoshima party.
>
> (*Hyōron Shinbun*, no. 67)

As we have already argued, uprisings attacking the weak-kneed character of the government in its foreign policy towards Korea and China were impossible in 1874. Despite this, dissatisfied elements scattered around the country continued to rest their expectations on action by Saigō.

Moreover Saigō, ever since he was defeated over the 'invade Korea' argument, was organising a strong private army. The private school that he founded in 1874 was one example. Even though it was called a school, it was both an infantry school and an artillery school, the former being commanded by Shinohara Kunimoto, Commanding Officer of the former Imperial Guard, and the latter by Murata Shinpachi, formerly responsible for artillery in the Satsuma domain. Apart from this, he donated the prize money he had received for his meritorious services during the Boshin war towards the establishment of a school for officers (infant school). If we compare the mobilising power at the time of the Seinan war in

Construction, 1871–1880 77

1877 (government troops 46,000, Saigō's forces 30,000), it is obvious that Saigō's forces were inferior, but even so, given that they were from the single prefecture of Kagoshima, these were quite impressive numbers.

Moreover, Saigō had sympathisers harbouring expectations of him within the government forces. Ichiki Shirō, who on the side of Shimazu Hisamitsu had witnessed in Kagoshima the departure of the Saigō forces for the front, wrote as follows in his *Teichū jōranki* (A Record of the 1877 Riot):

> 11th February, year 10 (four days before the Saigō forces set forth), sunshine followed by rain, cold. . . . Saigō says, Kawamura (Sumiyoshi) is 40 or 50% on our side. In Kumamoto there is Kabayama Sukenori (army camp chief of staff). It is said that if our forces advance in Hikyō (on the border of Kumamoto prefecture), the camps of one or two large battalions may come over to our side.
>
> According to Fuchibe (Gunpei), among Kumamoto samurai, there is a prospect for three or four thousand men. Saga, Fukuoka, Akitsuki, Kurume and others, the four provinces of Tosa, Chōshū, Tottori, Ōmi, or again Shōnai, Wakamatsu and Ishikawa prefectures must rise up one after the other . . .
>
> Ōyama (Tsunayoshi, Kagoshima prefecture Governor) says, in Kumamoto a set of five boxes of food are waiting. In Shimonoseki, Kawamura and others should be waiting. We may arrive in Tokyo while enjoying cherry blossoms.
>
> (Kagoshima ken ishin shiryō hensanjo [ed.], *Kagoshima ken shiryō: Seinan sensō* ['Historical Materials of Kagoshima Prefecture: The Seinan War'], Kagoshima ken, 1978, vol. 1, p. 895)

In this optimistic assessment of the future, some things were well founded and some not. It was ludicrously optimistic to believe that samurai in Shōnai and Wakamatsu were sympathetic. The samurai in both these domains hated as their enemy in the Boshin war, not Ōkubo and Kido in the government, but rather Saigō and his Satsuma military forces.

But as we have already seen in the Taiwan expedition, the Navy Vice-Minister, Kawamura Sumiyoshi, just about two years earlier had been a fanatical admirer of Saigō. At the time of this Taiwan expedition, Kabayama Sukenori, going to Peking as the subordinate of Ōkubo Toshimichi, who had plenipotentiary powers, was expected by Saigō and others to break off the negotiations in order to precipitate a Japan–China war. A scenario in which Kabayama abandoned Commander Tani Tateki and went over to the Saigō forces, those forces having captured Kumamoto Castle and reached the strait between Shimonoseki and Moji, with the Navy Minister Kawamura commanding a warship there, would have been quite possible a mere two years earlier.

Nevertheless, as I have argued repeatedly, with the conclusion of treaties between Japan and China, and between Japan and Korea, there was no longer any pretext for the legitimate forces of the Army and Navy to side with insurrectionary forces. Kabayama and Kawamura were now unable to betray the government forces.

78 *Japan's Modern History*

The outcome of the insurrection

Success or failure of the attack by the Saigō forces against Kumamoto Castle was determined by the time element. On the government side, it took time to send army camp soldiers to Fukuoka. One week after Saigō had raised his army, the government forces reached Hakata (Fukuoka) from Kōbe port, but out of nine expeditionary groups only two, amounting to about 4,000 men, arrived.

On the other hand, at the beginning of April, when the defenders of Kumamoto Castle had endured over 40 days of siege, the government forces had been successively reinforced. The besieged forces were given millet rice twice a day to eat and rice porridge once a day, but civilian officials and others had to put up with millet rice once a day and rice porridge once a day. This siege strategy on the part of the defenders of the castle had paid off. On 15th April, when the rear forces aiming at the Kumamoto Castle succeeded in entering it through the Yashiro Port, the Saigō forces, which for 40 days had succeeded in halting the forward forces, withdrew to Kiyama mountain to the east of Kumamoto Castle.

The insurrection, which might well have succeeded, ended at that point. But it took more than five months for the Saigō forces finally to be subdued. When the Saigō troops committed suicide or surrendered on 4th September, this was more than seven months after they had originally set out from Kagoshima. The main reason why it took over five months after the victory of the government forces to the final suppression of Saigō's troops was their ferocity, since one in five of them were veterans of the Boshin war.

At first the government leaders themselves were completely lacking in confidence in the results of the conscription system launched in January 1873. The plan to recruit and train 30,000 peasant soldiers was gradually fulfilled, but the fact that within less than four years from the inception of the plan they would have to fight against the Satsuma forces which had been involved in a civil war for more than ten months was far beyond what they had anticipated. On 13th March, while the fighting over Kumamoto Castle was continuing, the Minister of the Right, Iwakura Tomomi himself, expressed his disquiet in the following terms:

> The far western traitors are advancing with impetuous ferocity, they only understand death, and we have to deal with them with *bullets and stockades*. As seen in recent battles, their strong points were skirmishing, sniping, swordsmanship and close combat. Even though the strength of our officers is ten times greater than theirs, it is difficult for *our conscripts* to match their particular skills.
>
> (*Ōkubo Toshimichi bunsho*, vol. 8, pp. 16–17; present writer's italics).

The meaning here is that peasant soldiers recruited by conscription were unable to combat the Saigō military force by fighting to expel them from Kumamoto Castle, and thus all they could do was to shoot at them with *bullets* from the *stockade* within the castle.

Because of this capacity difference between the rebels and the government forces, it took five months to conduct a mopping-up operation against the Saigō

Construction, 1871–1880 79

forces, and in the final attack on Shiroyama around 12,000 government troops, in four brigades, surrounded 372 Saigō troops. Thus the government expenses of waging the Seinan war amounted to about 41,000,000 yen, and in order to raise this sum the government issued 42,000,000 yen in inconvertible paper money.

The victory of the 'prosperous country' argument

With victory in the Seinan war, the government, centred on Ōkubo Toshimichi, following the 'assembly faction' and the 'constitution faction', had succeeded in suppressing the 'strong military' faction. The age of 'prosperous country', in its full flowering, had arrived, centred on 'investment and industry'. The issuing of 42,000,000 yen of inconvertible paper money that I have already mentioned brought about a deterioration in government finances. Also, in the Japan of the time, dependent on imports of industrial goods, the creation of inconvertible paper money, equivalent to the issuance of deficit public bonds, badly affected the balance of payments. I shall write later about the mechanism of this, but at this point I want to draw attention to the fact that the high noon of the 'prosperous country' faction was limited in time.

Even so, the defeat of the 'strong army' faction in both domestic and foreign policy brought believers in economic development to their height of influence in the late 1870s. This is demonstrated in an extreme form in the following extract from a statement of budgetary demands by the Army Ministry in 1878:

> First of all, not only do the Home Ministry and the Hokkaidō Development Ministry promote agriculture and industry, while public works to develop communications and railways incur a huge cost for a period at the time of their construction, but they generally earn profits for the public and private sectors. But in the case of expenditure on the army, it is like throwing money into water and fire, since hardly any of this money is repaid even in the long term. Talking just in financial terms, we belong to a useless behemoth, and there are even people who argue that the armed forces ought to be disbanded.
>
> (*Ōkuma bunsho*, vol. 3, pp. 336).

Of course, this extract was an introductory section in tune with contemporary trends, and later on the opinion is presented that "[a]t present things are peaceful in our country, but if we survey the recent situation in the East, we see that the time will come when things will not pass uneventfully and safely". Even so, it is extraordinarily unusual to read a budgetary demand statement from the military that is so humble. At the end of 1877, when the struggles with China and Korea had been settled, at least for the time being, and Saigō's military forces had been suppressed, even the Army must have acknowledged that 'investment and industrial development' was the issue having the utmost priority.

The first step towards industrialisation was when industrial bonds were issued in May 1878 to a value of 10 million yen (face value 12.5 million yen).

The greater part of this 10 million yen was used for railway building under the

80   *Japan's Modern History*

jurisdiction of the Manufacturing Ministry, and for the construction and repair of roads and harbours under the control of the Ministry of Home Affairs. At a time when the Tōkaidō line had been built only between Shinbashi and Yokohama and between Kōbe and Ōsaka, so that travellers between Tokyo and Ōsaka had to go by ship, the completion of a communications network was the major premise of 'investment and industrial development'.

The Home Ministry, using the ordinary budget, imported two modern spinning machines from Great Britain, and also worked to promote traditional industry. The former was aimed to reduce imports of cotton goods, while the latter was to increase exports of products manufactured in Japan.

Twin deficits

Ōkubo's promotion of industry, however, because of falling tax revenue unconnected with its success or failure, fell into terrible difficulties two years after his death. Japanese direct taxation up to 1887 was land tax levied entirely from landowners, being a direct tax payable in cash. By land tax reform that took place between 1873 and 1880, landowners were given land coupons stating clearly the amount of tax they should pay on the land they owned. Because there was no adjustment of prices in this system, the amount of tax collected went down in times of economic prosperity and increased in times of economic downturn. To put the matter in an extreme form, it was a system in which, if you were aiming at healthy tax revenues, there was no other way than to apply deflationary policies.

Nevertheless, the financial policy of the government from the middle of the Seinan war was to issue inconvertible paper money and industrial loans, and this stimulated inflation. Since the majority of land tax payers were rice-growing landlords, the government would suffer a loss and the landlords a gain whenever the price of rice rose. In 1876, the year before the Seinan war, the rice price was 5.13 yen per *koku*, but in 1880 it had risen to 10.57 yen per *koku*. In other words, in the space of four years it had more than doubled. Since the land tax was completely unchanged, landlords had benefitted from a 50 per cent increase in revenue (effective tax reduction), whereas the government had suffered an effective fall in its tax revenues of 50 per cent.

This rapid decrease in government tax revenues brought about a decline of confidence in the yen, and reflecting this, imports became more expensive. In twenty-first-century Japan, which is dependent on exports, a 'cheap yen' signals favourable business conditions, but for Japan in the second decade of Meiji (1877–87), needing to import weapons, textile-making equipment and cotton cloth, a 'cheap yen' led to a deterioration in the balance of payments with an increase in imports. Japan in 1880 was troubled by 'twin deficits' in finance and balance of payments.

After Ōkubo Toshimichi, the central figure in the 'prosperous Japan' faction, was assassinated in May 1878, 'investment and industrial production' policies were directed by the trio of the Finance Minister, Ōkuma Shigenobu, the Hokkaidō Development Director Kuroda Kiyotaka, and the main figure in the Ōsaka financial world (originally from Satsuma), Godai Tomoatsu.

Construction, 1871–1880 81

Problems in revising the land tax

Of these three men, it was Godai Tomoatsu who felt most deeply the weakness of the land tax system for the government. In a statement of opinion drafted by Godai at Kuroda's demand in August 1880, Godai asserted that the most important reason for the crisis in the government's finances lay in the fixed cash payment system established for the land tax by the government in the revised taxation regulations of 1873. He argued as follows:

> When we look today at reform of the revised land tax payment system, we cannot escape the conclusion that the Meiji Government made a great mistake. However it may be, the revised payments system has meant that the peasantry alone has become extremely prosperous, attaining a degree of prosperity that is truly extraordinary. If we research the real conditions . . . and make calculations on the basis of the rice price, the peasantry pay a mere one tenth of the tax they used to pay; this gives them an enormous income, and continues to increase their prosperity to a startling degree.
>
> (*Godai Tomoatsu denki shiryō* ['Biographical Materials on Godai Tomoatsu'], vol. 4, p. 159)

The proposition that compared with the period before the land tax reform, revenues from land tax had fallen to 'one tenth' of what it had been may be somewhat exaggerated.

Nevertheless, the government, fearing both the Seinan war and opposition to land tax revision, in other words simultaneous insurrection movements by former samurai and peasants, lowered the land tax from 3 per cent to 2.5 per cent of land value in 1887 just before Saigō's insurrection. From that time on the land tax became five-sixths of what it had been. If we add the effective fall of 50 per cent (one half) in land tax revenues caused by the doubling in the price of rice already referred to, land tax in 1880 was five-twelfths of what it had been at the time of the revision, in other words it had fallen by 42 per cent. Thus since a reduction in the national land tax created a reduction in the proportion of local taxes accounted for by land tax, although 'one-tenth' is an exaggeration, it is demonstrable that the tax burden falling on the peasantry was around 'three-tenths' of what it had been before the revision.

So since this statement of newly rich people racing to buy foreign imported goods that they had hitherto not been able obtain neglected period and country, Godai specifically asserted that peasants in 1879 and 1880 had begun to purchase high-quality items of clothing manufactured in Europe and America. In his words: "The peasants have attained prosperity and generate luxury in clothing and food, and very evidently they have sufficient wealth to spend competitively on imported goods. . . . But this is quickly reflected in an imbalance between exports and imports" (ibid.).

There was an opposing argument to the argument of Kuroda (Godai) that the main reason for the trade deficit (imbalance between exports and imports) around 1880 lay in the purchase of foreign goods by agricultural landlords who had become rich as a result of a real fall in their rates of taxation. This was the

82 *Japan's Modern History*

assertion that the importation of foreign goods by government, including imports of weapons and ammunition as well as imports of machinery for programmes of industrial development, amounted to a far higher figure. Inoue Kaoru, councillor and Manufacturing Minister, who argued for financial retrenchment, represented this way of thinking.

The rights and wrongs of these positions, however, are not the issue. The question is that land tax reform – the great reform in the taxation system by the Meiji Government – when it was actually put into operation caused a major impasse in government finances. Godai's opinion paper showed that the issue of the age had shifted from 'construction' to 'management'.

Breakdown of the 'prosperous country' faction

The simplest and most effective way of overcoming the financial crisis resulting from the expense of the Seinan war and the halving of revenue from land tax was to increase land tax. But the Meiji Government was not a dictatorship. This was a 'flexible frame' government encompassing those who advocated 'strong military', those who emphasised 'prosperous country', those who thought 'constitution' was imperative, and those who saw the importance of 'assembly', all of them running the government through alliances that changed according to time and circumstances (see Banno Junji and Ōno Kenichi, *Meiji ishin* ['The Meiji Restoration'], Kōdansha, 2010).

However, as a result of an exchange of letters with the comparative economic historian Saitō Osamu, I have begun to believe that even if Japan had been a dictatorship, it would have been difficult to raise the land tax. This is because land tax was a single direct tax, and uniformly affected agricultural landowners from Hokkaidō to Okinawa. Between these taxpayers there was absolutely no conflict of interest. Even in an ordinary 'dictatorial state', it would probably have been impossible to impose an increase in taxation.

The fact of having built a taxation system in which taxation could not be increased was perhaps, from the viewpoint of statesmanship, as Godai wrote, "the greatest mistake in financial policy by the Meiji Government".

Since the government had issued a huge amount of inconvertible paper money, faced a decline in its tax revenues because of inflation, and in addition was unable to increase taxation, the 'prosperous country' faction could hardly continue. Government Decree No. 48 (Reduction of expenditure on ports, roads and water works), and the Factory Sale edict (sale to the private sector of government-operated enterprises in cement, mines, spinning and shipbuilding), both issued in November 1880, symbolised the end of the road for the development ('prosperous country') faction.

The 'Construction period', characterised by policy conflict between devotees of 'prosperous country', 'strong military', 'constitution' and 'assembly' came to an end in 1880.

4 Management, 1880–1893

Political participation by the peasantry

Sluggish progress of 'samurai popular rights'

In the three successive periods of 'reform' → 'revolution' → 'construction' that we have investigated up to the previous chapter, the principal activists were the samurai (*bushi*, *shizoku*), whereas the voices of the peasantry were only heard occasionally in uprisings and similar actions.

From around 1880, however, it had become impossible to provide stable government while ignoring the voice of the peasantry. One of the reasons for this lay in the following unexpected item in the 'Petition to Establish a Popularly Elected Assembly' of 1874: "Those who have the duty to pay tax to the government possess the right to approve or disapprove of government acts." As we have already explained in Chapter 3, direct taxation at that time was confined to the land tax, so that "those who have the duty to pay tax" were mainly independent farmers and village landlords, while samurai were not included. Leaders of the Tosa faction, who since Bakumatsu times had proposed a 'samurai assembly', ended up advocating a 'peasant assembly' against their own interests.

The argument for a 'peasant assembly', which up to 1874 had only been a matter for discussion, in line with the increasing wealth of the landlords (as explained at the very end of the previous chapter), suddenly took on a certain reality. Peasants who had become prosperous not only bought foreign items for their everyday needs, but also wanted to have their voice as taxpayers reflected in politics.

After the 'Petition to Establish a Popularly Elected Assembly' in January 1874, Itagaki Taisuke and others of Tosa samurai background set up in their home territory of Kōchi prefecture a popular rights association, the *Risshisha*. They hoped that similar popular rights associations would be established throughout the country, but those who gathered at the inaugural congress were only a small number of samurai associations. The *Jiyūtō shi* (History of the Liberal Party), supervised by Itagaki, writes as follows of the inaugural congress:

84 *Japan's Modern History*

Table 4.1

Year	Meiji era year	Event
1874	7	Establishment of the Risshisha.
1875	8	Establishment of the Aikokusha, based on the Risshisha.
1877	10	Risshisha petition.
1878	11	Nationwide speech tour to revive the Risshisha and the Aikokusha. First Congress of the Aikokusha.
1879	12	Second Aikokusha Congress. Kōno Hironaka visit to Tosa. Third Aikokusha Congress.
1880	13	Launch ceremony for the Kōjunsha. First Congress of the *Kokkai Kisei Dōmei*. Kataoka Kenkichi and Kōno Hironaka and others issue petition to establish a parliament. Second Congress of the *Kokkai Kisei Dōmei*.
1881	14	Ōkuma Shigenobu petitions for a constitution and parliament. Kōjunsha publishes 'private draft' constitution. Inoue Kowashi submits his 'Opinion on a constitution'. Issue of sale of Development Office property. Ueki Emori publishes 'Draft of a Japanese constitution. 1881 Political Change. Ōkuma leaves office. Imperial Instructions on establishing a parliament. Formation of Jiyūtō. Beginning of Matsukata financial policy (to 1886).

The number of samurai and others at that congress was just a few dozen people. . . . There was nobody of wealth or high rank, only one-sword singletons from the samurai who have pledged allegiance to the State. With the situation for the launch of the *Aikokusha* being like this, it is difficult to be optimistic. When headquarters were set up in Tokyo, the finance for maintaining it was poor, so that in a few years on it collapsed, and this was inevitable.

(Vol. 1, p. 160)

Such sluggish progress of 'popular rights based on samurai' continued through the re-launch congress of the Aikokusha held in Ōsaka in September 1878. Those who gathered were exclusively samurai, and they all came from areas to the west of Aichi prefecture (Kōchi, Saga, Wakayama, Kurume, Okayama, Matsuyama, Tottori, Aichi, Kumamoto and Takamatsu). There were no representatives at all from north of the Kantō, and nobody came from the peasant association.

The nature of the Aikokusha began to change from the third congress in November 1879. At that congress representatives of the association of high-ranking peasants from Fukushima and Fukui prefectures were present, and exercised influence on the direction of the movement.

The Tosa visit of Kōno Hironaka

The example of Kōno Hironaka, who attended as a representative the congresses of the Fukushima prefecture peasant association, the *Sekiyōsha* (formed in 1875 with 200 members) and the *Sanshisha* (founded in 1877, with about 80 members) is important as the beginning of self-assertion of 'peasant rights' against 'samurai rights'.

Management, 1880–1893 85

The *Sekiyōsha* sent Kōno Hironaka to Kōchi prefecture, and planned a coalition with the Tosa *Risshisha*, which was the harbinger of the Popular Rights Movement. This was in July 1878, but it was not until a full year later, in August 1879, that this plan was implemented (Shōji Kichinosuke, *Nihon seisha seitō hattatsu shi*, Ochanomizu Shobō, 1959, pp. 51–2). The 'certificate entrusted' to Kōno by a representative of the *Sekiyōsha* in June of the same year, included the statement: "In order to carry out the resolution of 24th July 1878, Kōno Hironaka is now sent with the following rights: 1, he is given full powers to confer with the *Aikoku Risshisha* and to control the revision of the resolutions of 24th July" (ibid., p. 52).

The reasons for the delay are unclear, but at the time of Kōno's visit to Kōchi in August 1879, about a thousand yen of travel expenses were given to him by the *Sanshisha*. Seen in terms of the inflated rice price situation, at the time of the previous year's resolution neither the *Sekiyōsha* nor the *Sanshisha* would have been able to afford to pay expenses at that level.

How much 1,000 yen in 1879 – over 130 years ago – would be worth today is frankly difficult to say. But two years later, in 1881, I know that *mori soba* and *kake soba* (simple noodles, cold and hot respectively) cost one sen, two rin (Katō Hidetoshi et al., *Meiji, Taishō, Shōwa sesō shi* ['History of Social Conditions in the Meiji, Taishō and Shōwa eras'], p. 84). If *kake soba* and *mori soba* today cost 500 yen, that means the price has increased 46,000-fold, so that Kōno's travel expenses would today amount to around 46,000,000 yen. Since such a figure is extremely hard to believe, when Kōno wrote in his diary "Money 50 *itsu*" (one *itsu* was 20 *ryō*, and *ryō* was used with the same meaning as *yen*) it is possible that '*itsu*' was written in error (Shōji, *Nihon seisha seitō hattatsu shi*, p. 117).

Even though we cannot be sure about this, we may speculate that the travel expenses given to Kōno were a very substantial sum. As we explained at the end of Chapter 3, Godai Tomoatsu, in his reflections on land tax reform, wrote: "When considering changes to the tax system, (we must remember that) only peasants enjoy great prosperity, and are gathering quite amazing wealth." This passage seems rather persuasive.

It is true that he received a generous allowance for travel and accommodation, but in 1879 it was only possible to travel by train between Shinbashi and Yokohama, and between Kōbe and Ōsaka, and to travel from Fukushima to Kōchi would have been difficult beyond imagining for us today.

Kōno set out from Ishikawa on 21st August, but his real journey began from the 24th. On that day he left Shirosaka at six thirty in the morning, and arrived at Akutsu on the banks of the Kinugawa river at eight in the evening. This was a 14-hour journey in the rain on his thirtieth birthday. The next morning at five he left by ship, sailed down the Kinugawa river and at three in the afternoon disembarked at Kubota, where he "immediately hired a carriage", and at eight in the evening arrived at the banks of the Edogawa river, where he embarked on a ship at nine o'clock the same evening. He spent the night on board, and at noon the next day (26th) disembarked at Nihonbashi Koamichō.

86 *Japan's Modern History*

Between five in the morning of the 25th and noon on the 26th, he had travelled a good 31 hours by ship, 'carriage' and then ship again, but far from reaching his destination of Kōchi, he had only arrived at his intermediate stage of Tokyo. This shows how bad communications were to the north of Tokyo, and at the same time reveals the passionate enthusiasm of village youth belonging to the movement to establish a 'popularly elected assembly'. There was a strong correlation between the increasing wealth of the peasantry and their enthusiasm for political participation.

Speaking of transport convenience, it was far easier to travel from Tokyo, via Ōsaka, to Kōchi. Since Kōno lodged at Tamachi, near Shinagawa in Tokyo, he took the train from Shinagawa to Yokohama, then went by steamship from Yokohama to Kōbe, and travelled thence by train from Kōbe to Ōsaka. After spending three days in Ōsaka, he returned to Kōbe by train, and took a steamship to Kōchi. There was all the difference in the world between this and his journey from Fukushima to Tokyo, by 'carriage' and river boat. As for the 'carriage' in "I hired a carriage", I need to wait for specialists in this field to tell me what kind of a vehicle this referred to. The principal theme of this chapter is 'political participation of the peasantry', but when we consider that Tōhoku and Hokuriku are rice-producing areas, then one aspect of this was political participation by residents of Kantō and Tōhoku, whose transport network was extremely underdeveloped.

Let us return to our main theme. Kōno, who arrived in Kōchi towards the end of September, held a succession of meetings with major figures from the *Risshisha*, including Itagaki Taisuke. Kōno's aims were to admit the two peasant associations from Fukushima (*Sekiyōsha* and *Sanshisha*) into the *Risshisha* as the central group of leaders from the Tōhoku and Hokuriki regions, and at the third congress of the *Aikokusha*, expected in November, to persuade the *Rishsisha* to agree with the united opinion of associations from the whole of Japan to petition the Emperor to establish a parliament. The *Risshisha* was positive about the second of these aims, but negative about the first.

It is easy to understand why the *Risshisha* was positive about the second objective. They would most likely have welcomed the fact that representatives of the peasant movement from Fukushima had travelled a great distance to ask for cooperation in the movement to set up a parliament from the *Risshisha*, a samurai association having no base of support north of Tokyo, and the *Aikokusha* (based in Ōsaka) which was a national association.

Concerning the first aim, however, the *Risshisha* had a negative opinion for two reasons. Their first reason was that as the leading force in the movement to establish a parliament, they did not want to weaken their own position. If they were to recognise Kōno and his colleagues as the core of the Tōhoku and Hokuriku associations, this might well divide the *Aikokusha* between the eastern and western parts of Japan.

Another reason was that the phenomenon of demands for political participation stemming from a rising standard of living on the part of landlords was by no means confined to Fukushima. The Deputy President of the *Aikokusha*, Nishiyama Yukizumi, informed Kōno that peasant associations in Ibaragi and Aomori

Management, 1880–1893   87

were applying to join the *Aikokusha*. The *Risshisha* itself intended to control the peasant associations that were springing up in Kantō and Tōhoku.

While Kōno was visiting Kōchi in September, the peasant associations with their proliferating membership and the power struggles taking place in the *Risshisha* and *Aikokusha*, the main home of the Popular Rights Movement, became apparent at the third congress of the *Aikokusha*.

Samurai popular rights and peasant popular rights

The most crucial issue for this congress was to organise a congress gathering together many peasant associations in March of the following year (1880), in order to "petition His Majesty to establish a parliament in our Empire". But opinion was divided over whether to petition the Emperor in the name of the *Aikokusha* at its fourth congress, or to hold a congress separate from the *Aikokusha*, simply requesting the establishment of a parliament.

It is noteworthy that the *Jikyōsha* (represented by Sugita Teiichi), of Fukui prefecture, which had a representative status similar to that of the *Sekiyōsha* of Fukushima, expressed the opinion that "[t]o make a request in the name of the *Aikokusha* alone would be favouritism. It would be disappointing if the base of support were too narrow" (Shōji, p. 103). Putting it in rather simple terms, representatives of peasant associations who had recently joined the movement, dissociated themselves from associations based on former samurai, and argued for a congress bringing a wide range of supporters together to request the establishment of a parliament in March of the following year.

Leaving aside the details here, the March congress was held separately from that of the *Aikokusha* as a congress of the *Kokkai Kisei Dōmei* (Alliance to promote a parliament), and representatives of the 72 associations throughout the nation jointly signed a "petition requesting permission to establish a parliament". Of these 72 names, 29 were clearly identified as commoners. Since it is impossible to imagine that the former samurai themselves would have been slow to identify themselves by the title of *shizoku*, meaning former samurai, if we add six more names whose status was not identified the number of commoners reaches 35, or nearly half the total. On the occasion of the March 1880 congress, they were now divided between 'samurai popular rights' and 'peasant popular rights' movements.

The emergence of 'peasant popular rights' accelerated a fundamental reform in the character of the 'assembly argument', which had existed since Bakumatsu times, and the 'constitution argument', which had been in place since 1872.

Even in advanced European countries, as the model for Japan as a modern state, the introduction of universal suffrage took place after the beginning of the twentieth century, and this was many years ahead of the foundation of the *Kokkai Kisei Dōmei*. Even more so, in Meiji Japan, which had only just begun aiming to enter the ranks of modern states, the qualifications of electors had to be strictly limited. The proposals to set up a parliament that had emerged since the Bakumatsu period had, though unspecifically, limited these qualifications to '*bushi = shizoku*'

88 *Japan's Modern History*

(warriors = former samurai). But the well-known phrase from the 'Petition to Establish a Popularly Elected Assembly' that "[t]hose people who have a duty to pay tax to the government, should be given the right to approve or reject what the government does", came to fruition with a speed exceeding the expectations of the eight former samurai who signed it.

Assuming it was not possible to confine voting rights to those having the status of former samurai (*shizoku*), there was no alternative to limiting it in terms of amount of tax paid. This would mean that electors were those who paid relatively high land tax. Since at that time no direct taxation existed apart from the land tax, it was logically inevitable that the bulk of electors would be village landlords.

At the moment that they perceived this, those within the Meiji Government arguing for a constitution, as well as those arguing for an assembly, were forced to change tack radically. Since most electors would be village landlords once a parliament was in existence, the first demand of such a parliament would be a reduction in the land tax, the burden of which fell on them alone. Assuming that the parliament was not wholly irresponsible, it would demand that government expenditure be cut back in the face of reduced land tax revenues. For those within the government promoting constitutionalism (democracy from above), it was necessary to create a system that would prevent the parliament from reducing the land tax (and thus government revenues).

The peasant movement to establish a parliament, from the Edo period into the early Meiji period, which except for occasional uprisings had not taken the road of participation in politics, at first sight was not part of our 'Age of Management', but should rather be inscribed in the 'Age of Construction'. But what had been thought of during the 'Age of Construction' stopped short at a parliament of former samurai, while a 'peasant parliament' was not envisaged. The Meiji Government was now forced to reconfigure, from a 'management' perspective, the character of 'constitution' and of 'assembly'. The sharp rise in prices following the Seinan war had caused difficulties for policies of investment and industrial development, and had forced a change towards defence against attacks on government finances. Thus 'peasant political participation' brought about a conservative mutation in thought, emphasising 'management' in its attitudes towards 'constitution' and 'assembly'.

Breakdown of the 'prosperous country' line and divisions in the constitutional system plan

The relationship between financial and constitutional arguments

While village landlords, now prosperous, were becoming active in the movement to establish a parliament, increasing the land tax might well have proved fatal for the Meiji Government. Even with the alternative plan of Ōkuma Shigenobu, who was both councillor and Finance Minister, to raise a 50,000,000 yen foreign loan in May 1880, if prices rose then tax revenue would fall. In this system based on the land tax, government revenues would continuously decline and there would be no means of repaying loans. When, in August of the same year, confidants of the Emperor came out against this bill, they were not fully aware of the mutual relationship between land tax, business conditions and government finances, but in effect they were right.

The only method of keeping the finances healthy, assuming inflationary conditions, under a land tax system in which tax revenues were falling, was for the government to create deflation. The Matsukata deflation, which lasted for over four years between 1882 and 1886, was just such a policy.

Even between Ōkuma Shigenobu, who continued Ōkubo's policies of investment and industrial development after his assassination, and Matsukata Masayoshi, whose policies of financial retrenchment were known as the 'Matsukata deflation', there were, on close examination, certain common features. For instance, if we take the liquidation of 40 million yen of inconvertible paper money issued during the Seinan war, there was not a great deal of difference between the liquidation of more than one quarter of that sum under Ōkuma's financial policy, and the amount liquidated during the period of Matsukata's financial policy.

In contrast, under the financial policies of Matsukata, who restricted government expenditure over a period of three years, the amount of paper money in circulation declined, and as a result prices fell (ibid., pp. 188–9). If we look at the rice price, which had a direct influence on real government revenues and on the incomes of rural landlords, in 1880, before the Matsukata financial regime began, the wholesale price in Tokyo was 10 yen, 59 sen per *koku*, whereas in 1884, three years after the policy began, the price had fallen to 5 yen, 29 sen. In effect the rice price had halved in three years.

As a result, medium-level landlords had become owner farmers, and owner farmers had become part owners and part tenants.

Establishing a parliament from above

The transition from Ōkuma financial policy to Matsukata financial policy created severe changes in the government finances and in the lives of farmers, but this change required well over a year to implement. Even after the withdrawal by the Emperor in August 1880 of the 50 million yen loan offer bill, in the 17 months until he was dismissed as councillor in the October 1881 political change (*seihen*) Ōkuma operated as the central leader of the Meiji Government.

Under Ōkuma's financial management after the foreign loan had been forbidden, inflation did not continue, but prices were halted at a high level. So the farmers, who had maintained their prosperity, between March 1880 and October 1881 continued to demand that a parliament be established.

In order to promote in parallel continuing inflation and a continuation of demands by rural landlords for a parliament, what Ōkuma proposed was 'the establishment of a parliament from above'. If a parliament were to be set up after Matsukata-type deflationary policies had been adopted, the rural landlords would seek to offset a fall in the rice price by demanding a reduction in land tax, so that in a newly established parliament they would continue to demand such a

90 *Japan's Modern History*

reduction. Government and parliament would continue year by year to confront each other over tax policy, and thus the transition to constitutional government would institutionalise domestic disorder. Matsukata deflation and setting up a parliament could not go together.

By contrast, under Ōkuma's financial policies of in effect halving the land tax, the rural landlords did not demand further reductions in the land tax. Advocates of 'popular rights for former samurai', such as Itagaki Taisuke, naturally had no interest in the land tax question, and those promoting 'popular rights for farmers' also did not demand reduction in land tax before the advent of Matsukata deflation. As one example, let us look at the 'Petition to establish a parliament' of 1880, by the famous farmers' association of Fukushima prefecture known as the *Sanshisha*, led by Kōno Hironaka. It contains the following statement:

> Today farmers are mostly resting and recuperating, and compared with the days of strict exaction of taxes before the feudal system was abolished, they are relaxed and strong. They may already be termed wealthy, and they may not be called poor. For if the legal system had become appropriate, even if land tax were slightly increased, this would not be a great problem for people like us. But what does 'legally appropriate' actually mean? What is needed is to establish a parliament and consult a wide range of people over matters of policy.
>
> (Kadokawa Daikichi, Gabe Masaji [eds], Meiji kenpakusho shūsei ['A Collection of Meiji Period Petitions'], Chikuma Shobō, 1987, vol. 8, p. 341)

The opinion of Godai Tomoatsu of the Meiji Government side, mentioned in Chapter 3, that the peasantry had become prosperous, was now admitted in this same year 1880 by the peasant Popular Rights Movement itself.

There are no materials suggesting that other farmers' associations agreed with the *Sanshisha* that it would be acceptable to have a land tax increase once a parliament was established. But there are a number of examples where farmers' associations were not demanding a reduction in land tax, but rather were pressing for their own right to participate in politics.

If this is the case, then the line of 'establishing a parliament from above', in other words setting up a parliament as quickly as possible as a quid pro quo for advancing the cause of 'investment and industrialisation' while maintaining a situation in which inflation persisted, could be one option for the Meiji Government. One example of this was the petition to the Emperor by Councillor Ōkuma Shigenobu through the Minister of the Left.

The core of Ōkuma's petition is clear just from the individual headings at the beginning:

1 The year and month for establishing a national parliament should be announced.
2 Cabinet members should be appointed after ascertaining the will of the people.

Management, 1880–1893   91

3   Political party officials and permanent officials should be separated.
4   A constitution should be promulgated under the name of the Emperor.
5   Deputies should be chosen by the end of 1882, and at the end of 1883 a national parliament should be established.
6   Principles of administration should be established.

(Ienaga Saburō et al. [eds], Meiji zenki no kenpō kōsō ['Constitutional Proposals in the Early Meiji Period'], Fukumura Shuppan, 1987, pp. 130–1)

There is no real need to summarise this again, but Ōkuma's proposal was for a constitution to be promulgated under the name of the Emperor within one or two years, then in two or three years for a parliament to be established, and at the same time for the party or parties with a majority in the parliament to hold power. In other words, this was a proposal for a parliamentary cabinet system.

The opinion of Ōkuma Shigenobu concerning a constitution

Even so, since the Meiji Government at that time did not have a political party, if his proposal were adhered to the government itself would have to found a party of government (*yotō*). What is important in this respect is the sixth item: "Principles of administration should be established." In his explanation, Ōkuma argued as follows:

> As I have said before, when it comes to setting up a governing structure, and in response to the wishes of the people appointing cabinet members, what we must do is to establish political parties. When it is desired to set up political parties, what we must do is to establish the principles of administration that they should maintain. For if in constructing the present cabinet it is wished to form a political party, what is most important in its construction is to establish a philosophy of administration. But for this reason, after a date for the establishment of a parliament has been announced, it is my earnest desire that the philosophy of the present cabinet should be determined. Concerning a philosophy of administration, I have my own opinion.
>
> (Ibid., p.135)

His argument that "when it is desired to set up political parties, what we must do is establish the principles of public administration that they must maintain" continues to exercise commentators even today in 2012, over 130 years later. Progress in 'politics' is extremely slow.

The question, however, does not lie here. When Ōkuma requested that the Emperor first set a date for the establishment of a parliament, and then promulgate an Imperial Constitution, he intended at the same time to organise a "political party in constructing the present cabinet".

Ōkuma had a close paternal relationship with Fukuzawa Yukichi, founder of Keiō University, and the man who drafted Ōkuma's petition to the Emperor was Fukuzawa's older disciple, senior Secretary of the Cabinet Yano Fumio. Fukuzawa and Yano were the central figures in the *Kōjunsha*, which constituted an elite

92 *Japan's Modern History*

of more than 1,600 men who had graduated from Keiō University and were active in the government bureaucracy, financial circles and the media. The 'personal constitutional draft', published by the *Kōjunsha* in the *Kōjun Zasshi* ('Kōjunsha Journal'), following the lines of Ōkuma's petition to the Emperor, unveiled in general terms the contents of the 'Imperial Constitution' that Ōkuma had in mind.

Even though, however, it had an influence within the government, in financial circles and the media, and contained a draft constitution to be implemented, a government political party could not be created on this basis alone. Ōkuma and Fukuzawa probably expected the support of the farmers' Popular Rights Movement.

As we have already explained, the Popular Rights Movement congress of March 1880 was not the fourth congress of the *Aikokusha*, representing the former samurai Popular Rights Movement, but was the first congress of the *Kokkai Kisei Dōmei*, where about half of those who signed the petition to institute a parliament, adopted at the congress, were 'commoners', meaning rural landlords. Economically, these people were reasonably satisfied and had no intention of pressing the government to reduce the land tax, even when a parliament was established. This *Kokkai Kisei Dōmei*, at its second congress, held in November 1880, decided that before its third congress a year later draft constitutions would be made and held in readiness by each association.

However much the association representatives enthusiastically wished to institute a parliament, writing a draft constitution was beyond the capacity of all of them. At this point the constitutional draft written by the Fukuzawa Yukichi group was published in the *Kōjun zasshi* and in the *Yūbin Hōchi shinbun* (May). Even though it was not possible for local leaders to reproduce it as their own drafts, it would have been generally available for reference. This was a carefully ordered constitutional draft consisting of 79 articles, made up of Chapter 1 (Rights of the Emperor), Chapter 2 (Cabinet), Chapter 3 (House of Elders = upper house), Chapter 4 (National Assembly = lower house), Chapter 5 (Judiciary), Chapter 6 (Popular Rights = freedom of belief, freedom of expression) and Chapter 7 (Amendment of the Constitution). The Great Japan Imperial Constitution promulgated eight years later, in February 1889, was the complete opposite in terms of content, but the earlier draft was a detailed document that in its form could almost be regarded as a prototype of the later constitution.

Criticism of the Ōkuma line

Strong concern about 'farmers' rights' that were beginning to be distinguished from 'the rights of former samurai', as well as about the '*Kōjunsha* private constitution' of Fukuzawa and others, was expressed by the conservative law official Inoue Kowashi (Senior Secretary of the Cabinet). Inoue, in a letter to Councillor Itō Hirobumi, wrote as follows concerning these points:

> Last year this gang of parliament petitioners (the *Kokkai Kisei Dōmei*) were making a noise but now seem to have calmed down, but this is only on the surface. Indeed, according to the reports from our local administrations in various

Management, 1880–1893 93

places, they all want to bring about change with their constitutional research, and this constitutional research has its roots in none other than the personal constitutional research of Fukuzawa, for the *Kōjunsha* of Fukuzawa is now cajoling the majority of the Japanese people. This is their best opportunity to promise political parties, their forces operate in an unstructured fashion, and they assault the brains of people in the dark. These propagandists are like those who lead a hundred thousand well-trained soldiers into an uninhabited field.

(Inoue Kowashi denki hensan iinkai, Inoue Kowashi den; shiryō hen dai 4 ['Biography of Inoue Kowashi; Materials Volume No. 4'], Kokugakuin Daigaku toshokan, 1971, p. 47)

It was possible for Councillor Ōkuma Shigenobu's proposal to establish a parliament to join up, not just with the *Kōjunsha* whose members amounted to little more than 1,600, but also with the movements of farmers' rights associations throughout the country now amalgamated into the *Kokkai Kisei Dōmei*.

The fact that Inoue Kowashi's letter was dated July 1881 had great significance. As I have already explained, at the same time Ōkuma was being challenged over his financial policies by Matsukata Masayoshi. Matsukata and Inoue may or may not have been exchanging opinions, but it is clear that they had caught him in a pincer attack over his financial and constitutional policies. As I have already mentioned on several occasions, Matsukata's deflationary policies and farmers' rights could not coexist. If the government were to accept Matsukata's financial policies, which would double the tax burden on farmers, it would be necessary to find a policy for the parliamentary and constitutional proposals. Itō Hirobumi, a central leader of the Meiji Government along with Ōkuma, was pressed to separate himself from the Ōkuma line, in financial policy towards Matsukata Masayoshi and in constitutional policy towards Inoue Kowashi.

The Senior Secretary of the Cabinet Inoue Kowashi began criticising Ōkuma's and Fukuzawa's 'cabinet within parliament' arguments and began to draft counterarguments from June 1881. Ōkuma's March petition to the Emperor, mentioned above, was addressed to the Minister of the Left, Prince Arisugawa Taruhito, but although the Prime Minister, Sanjō Sanetomi, was aware, even the Minister of the Right, Iwakura Tomomi, did not know its contents at the beginning of June. Itō Hirobumi, who had been a colleague of Ōkuma and a councillor, first knew its contents on 27th June. At the end of the copy that he transcribed, there is the following note from him: "27th June 1881, requested Prime Minister Sanjō to borrow it from His Majesty, copied in my own hand having first perused it" (*Itō Hirobumi den*, vol. 2, p. 994). Ōkuma's petition to the Emperor was delivered to the Emperor through the Minister of the Left, but it was not until June that the Minister of the Right or Itō Hirobumi were apprised of its contents.

We do not know the precise date on which Iwakura himself knew about the Ōkuma petition, but in a letter dated 14th June from Inoue Kowashi to Iwakura, he wrote: "After I had the honour to see it in the secretariat, I meditated and deliberated". It is clear that Iwakura got hold of it for the first time in June, showed it to Inoue and requested his opinion.

94 *Japan's Modern History*

However this may be, from the beginning of June 1881 the drawing up of proposals against those of Ōkuma on constitution and parliament were initiated by the hand of Iwakura and others. At this time Inoue sent to Iwakura the book *Minjō isshin* ('Renewing the Life of the People') by Fukuzawa Yukichi, which had been published two years earlier, and it is important to note that he aroused Iwakura's concern over the fact that Fukuzawa Yukichi was behind Ōkuma.

Inoue's opinions on a constitution

The developments outlined above are well known to all researchers in modern Japanese history. What I have added is the assertion that the change from the 'Age of Construction' to the 'Age of Management' took place halfway through 1881, and that the key personalities in this change were Matsukata Masayoshi in finance policy and Inoue Kowashi in constitutional policy.

Inoue's arguments about a constitution and a parliament were in contestation with those of the Ōkuma officials within the government and the *Kōjunsha* of Fukuzawa Yukichi outside the government, as well as the farmers' rights movement linked with it. Inoue argued that on the one hand cabinet should be kept separate from political parties, and on the other hand cabinet should be above the parliament. It goes without saying that this corresponded closely with Matsukata's deflationary policies.

In June 1881, Inoue presented to Iwakura, Minister of the Right, his 'Opinion on the Constitution' in three parts, and in it may already be seen the essence of the Great Japan Imperial Constitution promulgated in 1889.

In the first part of this document, the view is put forward that rather than a British-style 'cabinet within parliament' system, a German-style constitutional monarch should be adopted, in which the rights of the Emperor and the executive should be stronger than those of the parliament. It is clear that this was an extension of the ideas advanced by Kido Kōin while the Iwakura Mission was visiting Europe in 1872–3, as we have already discussed, but this was a far more refined version of it. Inoue made the criticism that the British-type constitutional monarchy being advocated by Ōkuma and Fukuzawa was in reality just a cabinet within parliament system with the monarch removed. Inoue's views were expressed as follows:

> The monarch is controlled by the interests of the parliamentary majority, and authorises policies through endorsement ceremonies for the victorious party like a flag blown to the left and to the right. For even if nominally executive power belongs to the monarch, the reality is that the heads of the executive are in fact the party bosses, and real executive power lies in the hands of the parties in parliament. Even though sovereignty is said to be split between the monarch and the parliament, in actual fact it lies with parliament alone, and the monarch merely defends his nominal position.
>
> (Inoue Kowashi denki hensan iinkai [ed.], *Inoue Kowashi den; shiryō hen dai ichi*, Kokugakuin Daigaku toshokan, p. 226).

Inoue then went on to argue that in German-style constitutionalism, relations between the monarch and parliament were the reverse of this:

> By contrast in Prussia, the monarch not only rules the people, but controls the administration, and even though legislative power is shared between the monarch and parliament, administrative power lies principally in the hands of the monarch, who does not yield it to others. The monarch, without reference to the distribution of seats among the parties, selects the prime minister and his administration (ibid., p. 226).

For ease of comprehension, this was called 'German-style constitutional monarchy', but the model being used was that of Prussia, the largest of the German provinces, as Inoue acknowledged.

Inoue wrote the constitutional article necessary to produce a system where "the monarch, without reference to the distribution of seats among the parties, selects the prime minister and his administration" in his "Opinion on the Constitution", no. 2. This boiled down to three points.

> 1. In the constitution it should be clearly stated that the Emperor selects and dismisses ministers and imperially appointed officials below them.
>
> (Ibid., p. 228)

In article 10 of the Great Japan Imperial Constitution (henceforth 'Meiji Constitution'), Inoue's proposal is realised: "The Emperor determines the organisation of the different branches of the administration, and salaries of all civil and military officers, and appoints and dismisses the same." The fact that in "civil and military officers" are also included cabinet ministers from the prime minister down is clear from the publication of Itō Hirobumi (in fact written by Inoue Kowashi), *Commentaries on the Constitution of the Empire of Japan* (Itō Miyoji trans., 2nd edn, Tokyo, 1906).

> 2. In the constitution, the responsibilities of the prime minister should be established, and collective responsibility should be separated from individual responsibility.
>
> (Ibid., p. 229)

This requirement of Inoue was incorporated as it was into the Meiji Constitution, and it became the highly notorious article 55 on the system of individual ministerial responsibility (system of irresponsibility): "The respective Ministers of State shall give their advice to the Emperor and be responsible for it" (ibid., p. 229)

The argument for maintaining the existing taxation system

As for the third point, in Inoue's draft there was an original proposal and a revised proposal, and the meaning was entirely different depending on which one was chosen. We first cite the text of the revised version:

96 *Japan's Modern History*

> 3. In the constitution we must learn from the following article in the Prussian constitution. In article 109 of the Prussian Constitution, the existing system of taxation remains in force.
>
> (Ibid., p. 229)

This provision is not in the Meiji Constitution. At the time when the Constitution was promulgated and the Diet (Parliament) established, the Meiji Government had too weak a power base to be able to establish a constitution stipulating that the 'existing taxation system' could not be changed, and this was because, on the contrary, the power of the taxpayers (farmers' rights movement), who had coalesced in the *Kokkai Kisei Dōmei* in 1880–1, remained strong.

But for the constitutional specialist Inoue Kowashi, who had come to prominence as a fellow traveller of Matsukata's policies of deflation, this was probably his real intention. This was because the rural landlords, worrying about the collapse in the price of rice, were insisting that in the parliament that was to come there should be a reduction in land tax, in other words a reduction in current taxation levels. The Meiji Constitution eight years later certainly did not incorporate Inoue's blunt assertion. His argument, however, was brought to life in the Meiji Constitution in another form.

If we put together article 33, "The Imperial Diet shall consist of two Houses, a House of Peers and a House of Representatives", and article 37, "Every law requires the consent of the Imperial Diet", the House of Representatives, consisting of representatives of the people (even though there were limits according to the tax they paid), could pass bills to reduce land tax as often as they wished, but if the House of Peers vetoed them, these bills would not become law. So since the House of Peers consisted of Court nobles and former major and minor domain lords from the Bakumatsu period as well as elder statesmen (the Ōkubo and Kido houses) and retired government officials (members chosen by the Emperor), they swallowed the government view and rejected proposals to reduce the land tax at the legislative stage. Inoue's clear hard-line argument in 1881 was transformed by Inoue's own hand eight years later into an extremely skilful system.

On the other hand, Inoue's original draft, before it was revised, had sought to limit the powers of parliament, not over the payment of tax, but over its expenditure. In his words: "When the government and parliament cannot agree on concerning budgetary expenditure, the budget of the previous year (can be implemented)." This point was inscribed in article 71 of the Meiji Constitution as the "right to implement the budget of the previous year", which has somehow become a target of attack among historians. In the next chapter I shall investigate this further, but as the American scholar of Japanese history George Akita pointed out 43 years ago, a provision making it possible to continue with the budget of the previous year was for those involved in government not an entirely advantageous provision (George Akita, *Foundations of Constitutional Government in Modern Japan, 1868–1900*, Boston MA, Harvard University Press, 1967). Today in the early twenty-first century, it is rare for a budget to have less expenditure than that of the previous year.

Management, 1880–1893   97

The parliamentary rights argument of Ueki Emori

While Iwakura Tomomi, Itō Hirobumi, Inoue Kowashi and others came out using the German autocratic constitution as a tool of opposition to a British-type 'cabinet within parliament' system being promoted by Ōkuma Shigenobu and Fukuzawa Yukichi, within the *Kokkai Kisei Dōmei*, proponents of former samurai rights against peasant rights began to arm themselves intellectually. The journals *Aikokushi rin* ('Collections of Patriotic Thought') and *Aikoku Shinshi* ('New Patriotic Journal'), in which Ueki Emori played a central role, constituted this group.

The most important characteristic of this group, in contrast to Ōkuma, Fukuzawa and others, was that they did not aim at participation in power. However, unlike the permanent opposition party status of the post-war Japan Socialist Party, Ueki and his friends aimed to win a majority in the House of Representatives and remain as the opposition. Putting it another way, since it was fine to keep parties outside the executive, political parties might as well control parliament. The *Aikoku Shinshi* of Ueki and others expressed this in the following terms:

> We should plan for a separation of rulers and ruled, not engage in posturing about mixing the people and the rulers, but we should preserve the atmosphere of ourselves the people, and maintain this principle as our most important spirit. This is the spirit of the third stage of the people against the State.
> (Aikoku Shinshi, 12th November 1880)

The former samurai rights faction, represented by the *Aikoku Shinshi* ('New Patriotic Journal'), by forming a political party and aiming to win a majority in parliament, was taking its stand on the principle of representative democracy. On this point, they clearly differed from the direct democracy of Jean-Jacques Rousseau, which had become influential through the translations of Nakae Chōmin.

If, however, we read only the part cited, Rousseau's 'assembly of all the people' is brought to mind. Even in his social contract argument, although the whole people is sovereign, the government exists separately from it, and the sovereign people, separate from the government, only meet regularly once a year, when they determine the shape of the government and say who should constitute its members (Iwanami Bunkō ban, p. 142). The assertion by the *Aikoku Shinshi* that executive power is held by the government, while the people's *representatives* (this differs from Rousseau) control parliament, clearly reflect Rousseau's influence. This is the reason why, whereas Ōkuma and Fukuzawa were called the 'British faction, and Iwakura, Itō and Inoue Kowashi were called the 'German faction', the left wing of the *Kokkai Kisei Dōmei* based on the *Aikoku Shinshi* was widely termed the 'French faction'.

Since the *Aikoku Shinshi* was the organ of Itagaki Taisuke's *Risshisha* and of the *Aikokusha*, it maintained its influence as before within the *Kokkai Kisei Dōmei*. For the sake of simplicity, I have spoken of the difference between the factions of former samurai and of farmers, but more precisely the dispute between them was a dispute between the leaders and supporters within what is broadly termed

98   *Japan's Modern History*

the 'Popular Rights Movement'. If we go on from this, the *Kōjunsha*, consisting of urban intellectuals led by Fukuzawa Yukichi, and the original Popular Rights Movement, led by Itagaki Taisuke, were fighting for support within the newly emerging farmers' rights movement over the political situation in 1881. So it was Inoue's conservative constitutionalism that entered as an intruder into the competition between these two advocates of a parliament.

Subtle differences between the conservative faction and the progressive faction

If we examine the dissension over this three-pronged constitutional proposal, the reasons for what is known as the political change of 1881, namely the defeat of Ōkuma and Fukuzawa, become clear. Among the conservative Inoue Kowashi, the progressives Itagaki Taisuke and Ueki Emori, the common factor was that they were not demanding restrictions on executive power in the constitution.

I have already described in detail how Inoue made great efforts in his constitutional proposals to guarantee the supremacy of the executive over the legislature. On the other hand, so far as the executive was concerned, in Ueki's plan, in which the Meiji Government would themselves control the legislature, neither 'cabinet within parliament' nor even the drafting of the constitution were given much emphasis. The highest priority was given to consolidating a centrist party (later to be the *Jiyūtō* – Liberal Party) and associations intended to support it (later the branches of the *Jiyūtō*), in order to win a majority in the House of Representatives. Let us examine two examples that demonstrate this.

The first example is the second congress of the *Kokkai Kisei Dōmei* held in November 1880. The fifth proposal submitted to the congress was as follows:

> In this congress, constitutional proposals should be examined and decided. Five members should be selected for a committee to make such proposals. Apart from this, ten committee members should be selected.
> (Meiji bunka zenshū; zasshi hen ['Collection of Meiji Culture: Historical Section'], p. 181)

At this congress, however, the proposal to draw up model proposals for a constitutional draft was rejected. The man who lit the fuse of the contrary argument was recorded as the 49th member, Sugita Teiichi of Fukui, and his reasoning was: "If the urgent business that we have today is to strengthen the consolidation of our local organisations, and thus build up our strength, selecting tens of people to spend days on constitutional drafts is a path to be avoided." He was insisting that strengthening the party base was more important than drafting constitutional proposals.

Using an interval in the congress of the *Kokkai Kisei Dōmei*, a meeting of the *Aikokusha* of Itagaki and others was held, and at this meeting Sugita Teiichi proposed: "The *Aikokusha* should be dissolved, and a major political party should be organised on the principles of liberalism" (ibid., p. 186).

As I have already mentioned, in July 1881 the conservative theorist Inoue Kowashi realised that the *Kokkai Kisei Dōmei* movement was feverishly drafting constitutional proposals, and that Fukuzawa Yukichi's *Kōjunsha* was replacing Itagaki's *Aikokusha* as leader of the movement. But the *Aikokusha* group within the *Kisei Dōmei*, ever since its second congress, was setting about forming "a major liberal party", so that Fukuzawa's control of the movement had not penetrated so deep as Inoue expected.

A second example demonstrates this. Since the second congress decided that the third congress would be held on 1st October 1881 in Tokyo, whether it should move in the direction of making constitutional proposals or whether it should move in the direction of forming a liberal party was debated behind the scenes by the conservatives, the centrists and the progressives.

If they were to move in the direction of making proposals for a new constitution, the power of Councillor Ōkuma Shigenobu, who was proposing that a constitution and a parliament should be rapidly instituted, would increase, and within the movement Fukuzawa's *Kōjunsha* would seize the leadership. If, on the contrary, the congress were to move in the direction of forming a liberal party, then in the government the conservatives Iwakura Tomomi (Minister of the Left), Councillor Itō Hirobumi and Inoue Kowashi (Cabinet Senior Secretary) would predominate. Within the movement Itagaki Taisuke and others of the former *Aikokusha* tendency would recover their leadership. Since the two of them were placed at the opposite left and right poles to each other, the fact that strengthening the executive and strengthening the legislature could both occur in parallel has already been pointed out.

The political change of 1881 and the formation of the Liberal Party

This subtle dividing of both the left and the right brought about the defeat of Ōkuma and Fukuzawa. On the government side, Ōkuma and the principal officials of his network were dismissed, and on the movement side, Itagaki Taisuke, who was concerned, not with a constitution, but with gaining control of parliament, was victorious. The 'Meiji political change' (12th October) and the formation of the *Jiyūtō* (18th October) were the key events.

Of these two events, much is known about the first, but the fact that the second – the formation of the *Jiyūtō* – was one reason for the defeat of Ōkuma is not well known. I want now to introduce the second example, mentioned above.

At the end of August 1881, Itagaki Taisuke of the Tosa *Risshisha* left Kōchi and went to Kōbe, and on 10th September, gathering an audience of 'over 5,000', he held a major speech meeting. Next he left Kōbe and travelled again by ship to Yokohama; on 15th September he arrived at Yokohama, and on the 16th he travelled by train to Shinbashi. As we have seen earlier, the Fukushima popular rights advocate Kōno Hironaka had gone to Kōchi, but in the opposite direction. At that precise time, the route Kōchi → Kōbe → Yokohama → Shinbashi was exceptionally convenient.

At Shinbashi station, representatives of local associations under the umbrella of the *Kokkai Kisei Dōmei* who had already come to the capital for their third congress (in fact it was not held) came out to meet him. This was not all, for

100 *Japan's Modern History*

representatives of associations following the line of Ōkuma and Fukuzawa, aiming to write a constitution and establish a parliament, and even more, urban intellectuals (those representing Tokyo journalistic circles), also met Itagaki at Shinbashi station.

Just to mention famous individuals and associations, representatives of the *Ōmeisha* of Numa Morikazu, as well as Baba Tatsui, Ōishi Masami, the *Kokuyūkai* of Suehiro Shigeyasu, the *Tokyo Keizai Zasshi* ('Tokyo Economic Journal') of Taguchi Ukichi and Fukuzawa Yukichi's *Kōjunsha* all gathered at Shinbashi station. Itagaki Taisuke, who may be called the grand old man of the Popular Rights Movement, retained his longstanding renown. These urban-style intellectuals aimed to unite Ōkuma Shigenobu, advocate of a parliament from the government side, and Itagaki Taisuke, who was outside the government, and so sweep away the conservative government leaders represented by Itō Hirobumi and Inoue Kowashi. But Itagaki rejected their demands, and in order to build up the base for the foundation of his political party went off on a tour of the Tōhoku region.

It was on 26th September that Itagaki rejected their request, and it was on 12th October that the conservatives within the government dismissed Ōkuma Shigenobu and the officials working under him. And Itagaki held the inaugural congress of the Liberal Party on 18th October. Conservatives and progressives continued to exist, but the liberals, whose views lay somewhere between them, quickly lost power within the government and within the movement. This was the famous 'Political Change of Meiji 14 (1881)'.

Rehabilitation of the 'powerful military' argument, and dispute between Japan and China

Cultivation of a pro-Japan faction in Korea

When, with 1880–1 as the turning point, finance and constitution were decoupled from each other and the 'Age of Construction' turned into the 'Age of Management', a 'management' period also began in the sphere of 'strong military'.

As I have already explained, the slogan 'strong military' in the 'Age of Revolution' meant exporting special local products and importing warships and weapons. 'Strong military' in the 'Age of Construction' discussed in the previous chapter did not mean just building up military strength as such, but rather respecting the voice of the revolutionary forces that were supporting the Meiji Restoration.

In the 1877 Seinan war, when the revolutionary forces had failed in their uprising, 'strong military' for a while disappeared from the government's slogans. In 'prosperous country and strong military' (*fukoku kyōhei*), only 'prosperous country' stood out.

Nevertheless, 'prosperous country' was also forced from the scene with the emergence of the Matsukata policies. With policies of healthy finance, in which government expenditure was being cut back and inconvertible paper money was being redeemed, budgets aimed at promoting investment and industrial development disappeared.

Management, 1880–1893 101

In this sort of situation, a change of apparel, in which 'strong military' replaced 'prosperous country', appropriately enough in an 'Age of Management', emerged once again.

This newly fitted-out 'strong military' argument was that, over a period of time, a level of preparation of the Army and the Navy equivalent to that of a current hypothetical enemy should be accomplished. The phrase 'hypothetical enemy' was perhaps too strong, but it had a much greater sense of realism about it than the 'hypothetical enemy' after the victory in the Russo-Japanese war in 1905, which we shall analyse in Chapter 5.

It goes without saying that Japan's 'hypothetical enemy' of the time was the largest and strongest power in Asia, namely Qing (Ch'ing) China. From about 1880, when the Kanghwado (Kokado) Treaty between Japan and Korea of 1876 was put into operation, the conflict of interests between the two countries over Korea became quite clear.

From about the time that, in accordance with the Kanghwado Treaty, the Wŏnsan port was opened, there were those within the Korean government who were showing interest in Japanese modernisation. The Japanese consul in Korea, Hanabusa Yoshimoto, in a memorandum in February 1881 to the Foreign Minister, Inoue Kaoru, wrote that the anti-Japanese elements in the Korean government "having received high aristocratic rank do not know what is happening outside their own circle", whereas the pro-Japanese faction "are educated and able, have not simply been granted their position, they understand something about how things work abroad . . . and wish to reform domestic politics" (Gaimushō, *Nihon gaikō bunsho*, Gaimushō, vol. 14, p. 332).

With this perception of the internal Korean situation, an outstation of the Japanese Foreign Ministry in June 1881 warmly welcomed an unofficial inspection delegation from Korea of around 60 people, and reported to the headquarters of the Ministry that it was the basis of the pro-Japan faction:

> This group should be regarded as the basis of the element in Korea wishing to open up the country, and I should like them to be treated as well as possible, using your best efforts to open their eyes.
>
> (Ibid., p. 305)

Thus Foreign Ministry officials in Korea, Fukuzawa Yukichi's Keiō Gijuku University and others were deepening their relations with young Korean officials and young people, but at the same time this aroused anxiety about Japan within China of the Qing (Ch'ing) dynasty, which had been the suzerain over Korea, as well as among the conservative leaders in Korea. The Korean conservative faction became pro-China, and the progressive faction became pro-Japan.

The China threat argument of Yamagata Aritomo

While competitive relations with Qing (Ch'ing) China were becoming evident, some in Japan were once again becoming concerned with the power of China.

102   *Japan's Modern History*

Table 4.2

Year	Meiji era year	Prime Minister	Event
1880	13		Yamagata Aritomo signals a China threat (Military preparation strategy for near neighbours). Army and Navy expansion begins.
1882	15		Imperial Rescript to soldiers and sailors. Matsukata deflation begins. Itō Hirobumi goes to Europe for research into constitutions. *Rikken kaishintō* founded. Imo Incident, in which Koreans surround Japanese Embassy in Seoul. Bank of Japan begins. Fukushima Incident.
1884	17		Land tax amendment law. Peerage establishment law. Kabasan Incident. Military coup in Korea failed. Liberal Party dissolution. Chichibu Incident. Kapsin Incident.
1885	18	Itō	Tientsin Treaty (between Japan and China; withdrawal of troops from the Korean peninsula). Ōsaka Incident. Launch of cabinet system.
1886	19		Imperial universities law. Education law. First treaty revision conference. Navy public loan issued.
1887	20		Tokutomi Sohō publishes *Kokumin no Tomo* ('The People's Friend'). Inoue presents to Prime Minister Itō a 'constitutional draft'. Petition movement over the Sandai (three big issues) Incident. *Daidō danketsu* movement of Gotō Shōjirō and others. Security law.
1888	21	Kuroda	City system and system of towns and villages inaugurated. Privy Council launched.
1889	22	Yamagata	Promulgation of the Great Japan Imperial Constitution. Imperial Household Law. Tōkaidō railway line completed between Shinbashi and Kōbe. Foreign Minister Ōkuma attacked and injured by a *Genyōsha* member. From year end economic panic begins.
1890	23		Ōi Kentarō and Nakae Chōmin found *Jiyūtō* (Liberal Party). Prefectural system and postal system inaugurated. First general election. *Rikken Jiyōtō* founded. *Genrōin* (House of Elder Statesmen) abolished. Imperial Rescript on Education issued. Imperial Diet (Parliament) opened.
1891	24	Matsukata	*Jiyūtō* changes name to *Rikken Jiyōtō* (Constitutional Liberal Party) (President Itagaki Taisuke). Ōtsu Incident. Ashio copper mine poisoning incident becomes an issue. 'Reckless courage' speech by Navy Minister Kabayama.
1892	25	Itō	Second general election (electoral interference on orders of Shinagawa, Home Minister).
1893	26		Imperial Edict on harmonious cooperation. Civil servant appointment law promulgated.
1893	27		Sino-Japanese war.

Management, 1880–1893 103

Ever since the Bakumatsu period, among Japanese leaders both in and outside the government, who had only been concerned with the threat from the Western great powers, the idea of a threat from China had been increasing.

The first person in the Meiji Government to express the view that China was a threat was perhaps the Chief of the General Staff at the time, Yamagata Aritomo. In November 1880, when he presented to the Emperor the 'Military preparation strategy for neighbouring areas' (*Rinpō heibi ryaku*), assembled by the General headquarters staff, he himself had written the address to the Throne (*jōsōbun*), whose central arguments were first, that China was powerful, and secondly that for a neighbouring country to be powerful was not something to be regarded as simply desirable; rather Japan should once again strive to create a 'strong military'.

On the first point, Yamagata maintained that between 1874, at the time of the Taiwan expedition, and now six years later, Chinese military capacity had become far greater. In his words:

> The territory of China today is large, the total area of its 18 provinces is approximately ten times that of Japan, and its population of 400 million is more than ten times that of Japan. . . . China is now urgently upgrading its military system, as well as its sea defences. . . . In Fuzhou they have established a large shipbuilding yard and are building vessels both large and small, in Guangzhou, Fuzhou, Hangzhou, Shanghai, Nanjing, Jinan, Tianjin and elsewhere new military facilities are being built, guns and ammunition are being produced, at strategic locations in Dagu, Beidang, Liaoning, Wusongjiang, Yinzhenjiang, Wuliangshan, Nanjing, Jiujiang, Hankou, Ningbo, Fuzhou and Guangzhou, they are producing guns, and Li Hong-Zhang has a home guard of 20,000 men, who are troops well trained according to British methods. . . . In 1874 they had gun batteries at Dagu, Beidang, Fuzhou and elsewhere, but since then year by year they have obtained large guns from Krupp, Armstrong and elsewhere.
>
> (Yamagata Aritomo ikensho, pp. 96–7)

For Yamagata, who was a rational military leader, this 'strong military' of China was not something to be welcomed. Rather than the fantasy of allying China and Japan against Western penetration of Asia, the reality of competing with China for control of Korea was crucial. Yamagata argued in the following way:

> The military strength of our neighbouring countries, on the one hand is something of which to rejoice, but on the other hand, something of which to be fearful. Concerning this, we may rejoice at receiving help from East Asia, but if discord breaks out, we should be concerned and prudent.
>
> (Ibid., p. 97)

Yamagata, understanding the situation in this way, believed that it was essential to change the emphasis of *fukoku kyōhei* away from 'prosperous country' (*fukoku*) to 'strong military' (*kyōhei*). In his words:

104 *Japan's Modern History*

'Prosperous country' and 'strong military' were previously given the same importance and neither was seen as either means or end. There is no room for doubt that European countries are intent on rearming. Now if we say that 'prosperous country' is the end and 'strong military' the means, then the sentiment of the people will be to resort to their own interests, ignoring the public interest, so that our weakness will increase month by month, and our indecision will become more pervasive year by year. Cleverness will become the highest morality, ostentation will become the custom of the people.

(Ibid., p. 91)

The 'strong military' argument becoming realistic

At that time, the Chief of the General Staff, in charge of both the Army and the Navy, was advocating a reconstruction of the 'prosperous country, *strong military*' argument, on the basis of anxiety about China.

As we have already explained, from the year after Yamagata's memorandum, the Japanese government had begun to try hard to foster the pro-Japan tendency within the Korean government. If we put these two things together, it was quite logical that Japan and China should engage in an arms race over the right to control Korea. It is true that the Sino-Japanese war did not break out until more than ten years later in 1894, but the first step was taken in 1880–1.

There is a reason why the first step on the road to the Sino-Japanese war was the beginning of the 'Age of Management'. First of all, this differed from the war to expel foreigners that occurred in Bakumatsu times when the Chōshū and Satsuma domains unexpectedly precipitated it. It also differed from the proposals to make war on China suddenly proposed by the Restoration revolutionary forces in 1874. Unlike either of these cases, it was accompanied by a plan for the medium term. Until Japan could build up an army and a navy to match those of the powerful nation of China, a precipitate outbreak of a Japan-China conflict was avoided.

There is no room for doubt that the Sino-Japanese war in 1894 started with aggression against Korea. The argument that unless Japan took it, China would do so was an argument between Japan and China, and had no scope to be conducted between Japan and Korea. However, Japan–China and Japan–Korea relations in the rather more than ten years up to the Sino-Japanese war of 1894 corresponded to the appellation 'Age of Management', since there was a goal, there was preparation, and restraint was effective.

The second reason for including in the 'Age of Management' the rearmament of the Army and Navy targeted on China from 1880 was that it was consistent with the Matsukata sound finance policies that had ended the developmental 'prosperous country' line.

Of course, Matsukata's financial policies which had kept the expenditure budget at a fixed level over three years, and the increase in size of the Army and Navy, were at first difficult to reconcile with each other. Nevertheless, the Ministry of Finance and the Army and Navy came to a compromise over freezing expenditure but increasing expenditure for military expansion, by supplementing it with

Management, 1880–1893 105

increased indirect taxes on *saké* and tobacco. The liquidation of paper money lasted for three years, and although it was insufficient, growth in Army and Navy expansion was carried out.

On the other hand, the *Kapsin (Kōshin)* Incident in 1884, two years after the *Imo (Jingo)* Incident in 1882, took place when the Japanese consulate and its guard forces, which had been assisting the coup d'état by Kim Ok Kyun, were attacked by Chinese forces led by Yuan Shikai and routed, being forced to return to Japan, and since this was a serious loss of face for Japan, henceforth the demands of the Army and Navy for military expansion against China reached a level that could not be satisfied by increases in direct taxation.

Happily, as the result of liquidating paper money over three years, the international value of the yen rebounded, and it became possible to issue public loans for the Navy at low rates of interest. The real income from Navy loans over the four issues between 1886 and 1889, reached 17 million yen. Expenditure on the Army and Navy from increases in indirect taxation of 7,500,000 yen was thus greatly increased. Relations between Matsukata's financial policies and military expansion for the Army and Navy, which were confrontational at the time of the *Imo* Incident of 1882, by the time of the *Kapsin* Incident of 1884 had become manageable. It is easy to regard the Sino-Japanese war of 1894–5 as an extension of this increase in the strength of the Army and Navy (*Muroyama*, ibid., pp. 191–209).

Third, the demands of the Army and Navy, from the High Command's 'Strategy for Preparedness against Neighbouring Countries' of 1880 to the loans issue for the Army and Navy of 1886, were consistent with the establishment of a conservative constitution, advocated principally by Inoue Kowashi.

If, following Ōkuma Shigenobu, a 'cabinet within parliament' system had been launched, and the *Imo* Incident or the *Kapsin* Incident had broken out, parliament would probably have rejected the military expansion budget. The idea that in times of a foreign crisis the Japanese people should unite in solidarity was a discourse that emerged when a real crisis emerged. Just because the Japanese consulate in Korea was burned down by Japanese people (*Imo* Incident), or because the Japanese consul in Korea and his force of guards had failed in his attempt to support a coup by pro-Japan elements (*Kapsin* Incident), the parliament would not have easily consented to an increase in the budget for the Army and the Navy. This is clear if we look at politics after the inauguration of the Diet in 1890, which we shall treat in the next section. Until just before the outbreak of the Sino-Japanese war in 1894, the House of Representatives rejected budgets for military expansion.

When we think about this situation, Inoue Kowashi's provision in his 'Opinion on the Constitution' for 'the right to operate the previous year's budget' becomes important. If increased expenditure for the Army and Navy had been completed before the inauguration of the Diet in 1890, then by an Inoue-type constitution that was likely to be established, it was protected against being slashed by the Diet.

In this way, the plan for rearmament of the Army and Navy that was begun in 1880 and completed in 1889 was in financial terms (Matsukata finance) an 'Age of Management', blended with what in constitutional terms was also an 'Age of Management' (Inoue Kowashi, *Kenpō iken*, Kokugakuin Daigaku toshokan, 1966).

106 *Japan's Modern History*

Promulgation of the Constitution and inauguration of the Diet

The era of bureaucracy

The 'Age of Management' was the 'Age of Bureaucracy'. Apart from the fact that the Great Japan Imperial Constitution had been inaugurated, and the righteous arguments of intellectuals out of power were no longer needed, the influence of government officials legislating and implementing various policies was increasing instead, based on narrow interpretation of the Constitution and regulations. As we shall see shortly hereafter, under the Meiji Constitution, which made the government bureaucracy supreme, this tendency stood out. In contemporary language, this was a change from political leadership to bureaucratic leadership. Three years after the Constitution was promulgated, a Home Ministry official of the time, Tsuzuki Keiroku, wrote two essays: 'Transcendentalism' and 'The Argument for Popular Politics'. From then on, the image of government officials boasting about the 'Age of Management' arose.

As for 'transcendentalism', immediately following the promulgation of the Constitution, the Prime Minister, Kuroda Kiyotaka, announced that, being unconstrained by the inclinations of the Diet and political parties, 'in transcendence' they were carrying out the policies they believed in. The essay of Tsuzuki was written to explain more accurately this philosophy. Tsuzuki wrote as follows:

> A minister of state in a constitutional nation, must always in domestic policy make national interest the aim of his administration . . . study the means of accomplishing what he believes to be the national interest, and however much it may offend the Diet or public opinion he must unbendingly petition the Emperor for what he believes right. . . . He must petition the Emperor for as many successive dissolutions of the Diet as necessary to bring it round to his way of thinking.
>
> He must neither follow the wishes of the political parties, nor follow the will of the Diet, nor indeed the opinion of the people; but rather it is up to him to formulate resolute proposals directed towards national goals, to issue orders to his *officials*, to make *specialist investigations* of the affairs of state, and thus realise the goals of the State.
>
> (Tsuzuki Keiroku, Chōzenshugi ['Transcendentalism'],
unpublished manuscript, 1892, pp. 18–19; present writer's italics)

More than 40 years ago, when I was invited to visit the home of the son of Tsuzuki Keiroku in Kamakura, and found this essay that had lain in a storeroom, I was astonished at the extremely dictatorial nature of its contents. But when I read back today over the indecisiveness that party politics continues to display, I feel that though it is anti-democratic, a single thread runs through it.

Tsuzuki's Minister could to this extent ignore the Diet and ignore public opinion because of his confidence in the goals of the State, and his pride in his policies being grounded in the 'specialist' research of 'officials'. Policies based on research and legislative drafting by specialist officials were thus superior to the

Management, 1880–1893   107

demands of parliament and public opinion supported by superficial knowledge. On this point Tsuzuki developed his argument in the following way:

> In a country with a democratic political system, public opinion is supreme; it is difficult for reason to combat the irrationality of public opinion, and because what is called public opinion takes up particular issues and changes its view from one time to another, politicians in a democratic country, trying to discover which particular argument is favoured by public opinion, really have to work assiduously from morning to night, and have to expend huge efforts to sort out what is demanded by public opinion.
>
> Politicians in a nation like this advance their careers by catering to debased human wishes, but if they fail to promote these low desires, they will be unable to keep their positions. They cannot access the specialist investigations necessary to resolve the political issues of a nation, so that they can only follow what is ordered by public opinion.
>
> (Tsuzuki Keiroku, *Minseiron* ['Popular Politics'], unpublished manuscript,
> 1892, pp. 18–19)

His criticism of the lack of 'specialist investigations' among parliamentary members, under politics guided by public opinion, was also directed against journalists.

> When we consider newspaper reporters, the bulk of them are young; they may have no other means of making a living, and if so they want to have their name in the newspaper and win fame, wishing to acquire influence in that world. Their explanations are mainly superficial and easy to understand. It is extremely rare to find in a newspaper arguments based on penetrating specialist research.
>
> (Ibid., pp. 22–3)

This criticism of newspaper articles and journalists was also extended to newspaper readers, as follows:

> Most people who read newspapers lack specialist education or experience. In addition, everyone investigates particular issues in free time from work. Worst of all, newspaper editorials read after breakfast are admired like an ancient Chinese classic. Accounts based on careful specialist research are thus treated as impenetrable by businessmen. If you want to control the thought of these people, it is necessary to write in a superficial fashion that is easy to understand. It is unfortunate that arguments put forward in newspapers and in speeches are circulated in this vulgar fashion.
>
> (Ibid., p. 23)

Readers who react against Tsuzuki's bureaucratic autocracy may perhaps pay attention to his criticism of the mediocre quality of politicians' speeches, the

108   *Japan's Modern History*

arguments of journalists and television commentators, and to the audience and readership that welcomes such mediocrity.

Incidentally, Tsuzuki, who despised politicians and newspaper reporters, in January 1882 entered Berlin University, and despite suffering from tuberculosis studied there for a full four years. After returning to Japan he joined the Foreign Ministry, but from 1888 went to study in France. In 1889, when Yamagata Aritomo, Minister of Home Affairs, went on an inspection tour of France, Italy, Great Britain, Germany, Russia, America and Canada, Tsuzuki was in charge of the interpreting, having been appointed Secretary to the Japanese consulate in France, and his linguistic abilities were impressive. He was a man who symbolised the fact that the 'Age of Management' was also the 'Age of Bureaucracy'.

The age of 'country gentlemen'

When the Matsukata deflation began in 1881, farmers were divided into parasitic landlords, working landlords, independent farmers and small farmers. 'Parasitic landlords' were large farmers who did not cultivate crops themselves, but lent out land to small farmers and exacted high rents from them. Working landlords were farmers who cultivated the fields themselves, but rented out surplus land to small farmers and took modest rent from them. It is probably unnecessary to expatiate about independent farmers and small farmers.

In fact, relations between landlords and small farmers, although they changed in certain respects, continued in similar fashion until after the defeat in 1945. With the Meiji Restoration the special rights of domain lords and samurai were abolished, but this did not affect a certain type of status system among farmers, and in the course of time this status system gradually expanded.

This system of four status levels changed greatly under Matsukata deflation. Despite the fact that as the result of deflation the rice price halved, land tax was fixed and did not change, and therefore independent farmers had to abandon their land. Farmers who had lost their land became small farmers, and the large landlords bought up their land. In the study of modern Japanese history this is known as the phenomenon of 'breaking up the farmer class'. Omitting the details and looking at the result, over the seven years between 1882 and 1889, the family registers of independent farmers show a fall of from about 930,000 households to about 650,000 households. This was around a 30 per cent drop (for details, see *Kindai Nihon no shuppatsu*, pp. 120–4).

In the electoral law for the House of Representatives put into effect after the promulgation of the Meiji Constitution, the electorate was confined to those paying 15 yen of land tax or over. Land tax was assessed as 2.5 per cent of the land value as written on the title deeds, so electors, who paid 15 yen or more in land tax, were landlords owning 600 yen or more of land.

The number of such landlords had hardly dropped during the period of Matsukata deflation. Although the number of independent farmer households had fallen by 30 per cent, the number of large landlord households was almost the same (from 880,000 to 815,000). Land owned by landlords paying 15 yen or more of land

Management, 1880–1893 109

rent increased during the Matsukata deflationary period. These large landlords (and some medium landlords) were electors in the first elections for the House of Representatives in July 1890, and their number was around 500,000. More precisely they were between 450,000 and 470,000, but for a comparison with the number of electors in later elections that increased with amendments to the electoral law, it is convenient to write 500,000.

Incidentally, in 1900 there were about 1 million electors, with the increase in the land tax during the Russo-Japanese war about 1.5 million, and following amendment of the electoral law, in 1919 there were about 3 million. With universal male suffrage introduced in 1925, the electorate grew to 12 million. From these figures it is easy to understand the extent of the change.

Revival of the argument for a cabinet within parliament

The direction of the House of Representatives, inaugurated in 1890, was controlled by the preferences of small and medium landlord electors. If they sought to retaliate against increases in land tax during the Matsukata deflation, this would lead to repeated head-on clashes, of which no resolution was in sight, between Tsuzuki-type government officials and the landlord-controlled parliament. The large landlords, during the period of the Matsukata deflation, had absorbed the land of independent farmers and increased their own land holdings. If then they were to demand, not a veto-type parliament, but a participatory parliament, it would not be the demand for a reduction in taxes, but the demand for a party cabinet, that would increase in intensity. The conflict that we saw in the previous section between the *Aikokusha* of Itagaki Taisuke and others, at the time of the movement for establishing a parliament, and the Kōjunsha of Fukuzawa Yukichi, returned with the rise of popular feeling before the constitution was promulgated.

The result was, just as in 1880–1, the defeat of the argument for a 'cabinet within parliament', and the victory of a 'veto-type parliament, of the kind favoured by Itagaki (though Itagaki himself was in the process of changing his views). The high point of the movement, however, was created by those advocating a British-style cabinet system. The new generation of intellectuals that emerged to prominence around 1887 came forward arguing that the 'former samurai rights' of the 1880–1 period were out of date. Their representative was the 25-year-old Tokutomi Sohō, editor and owner of the journal *Kokumin no Tomo* ('The People's Friend'). He criticised 'former samurai rights' in the following terms:

> These fellows are working all out on behalf of the country; what they are doing is not on their own behalf, but they are representing others. It is like someone who does not manufacture a single bottle of *saké* working hard on a petition to reduce tax on *saké*, or someone who does not own large fields working on a petition to reduce land tax, or again somebody who has no qualifications as a Diet member talking volubly about the Diet. This is even though such behaviour of expending great effort on things that do not touch them personally may be said to be a way of sincerely helping other people, of

110　*Japan's Modern History*

loving our brothers, of loving everybody. On the surface, they are admirable and respectable, but in reality because of this even the peace movement turns a little bit rough, orderly business becomes a little bit inconvenient . . . and sometimes one feels regret about the values of human freedom.

(*Kokumin no Tomo*, 3rd February 1888, p. 48)

In this way Tokutomi Sohō, who had earlier criticised 'samurai rights', thought that hopes placed on 'peasant rights' by Fukuzawa Yukichi really meant placing hopes on 'country gentlemen'. He sketched a picture of 'country gentlemen' in the following way:

The only people who are not recognised as powerful by other people, nor recognise themselves as powerful, but whose political influence has gradually increased, are the country gentlemen. Who are these country gentlemen? Such 'country gentlemen' exist in England, and they are gentlemen who have settled in the countryside. They have a certain amount of land, and because they possess land, they have the most important place among farmers who cultivate the land, and in the villages that consist of farmers. . . . Today, what sort of men are local prefectural assemblymen? If one investigates their background, it must certainly be known that most of them are men who have come from the ranks of these country gentlemen. . . . From a village, they reach a district (*gun*), from a district they reach a prefecture, and from a prefecture they spread out into the whole country. If we consider that they have power today during the formation of prefectural assemblies, we may well speculate that they will accumulate power in the future when the Diet is established.

(*Kokumin no Tomo*, 17th February 1888, pp. 87–90)

I would like to draw attention to the particular timing of these two articles by Tokutomi Sohō, published in *Kokumin no Tomo* in February 1888. A mere month and a half earlier, in December 1887, the Meiji Government had brought in a security law, and to maintain security in the capital had banished from Tokyo 541 members of the 'samurai rights faction', whom Sohō had criticised. Criticism of the radical faction by the progressive faction from within its movement coincided with suppression of the radical faction at the hands of the government.

The Daidō danketsu *movement of Gotō Shōjirō*

As a result, 1888 ushered in the full flowering of the moderate faction. This was symbolised by the tour of the Hokuriku and Tōhoku regions by Gotō Shōjirō in July and August of the same year.

In my analysis of the Bakumatsu period in Chapter 2, Gotō Shōjirō made an appearance several times as the central figure in the feudal bicameral system proposal. In the history of the early Meiji period covered in Chapter 3, he appeared as one of the signatories of the 'Petition to Establish a Popularly Elected Assembly' in 1874. But the first half of the 1880s was the period of Itagaki Taisuke,

Management, 1880–1893 111

whose movement to establish a parliament was at its height, and Gotō's name only appeared if you made an effort to find it. When because of pressure on the radical faction the need for a substitute leader emerged, he experienced a second flowering as leader of the parliamentary democracy movement.

From that time, the characteristics of what was called the *Daidō Danketsu Undō* (Unity Movement), led by Gotō, may be reduced to two. The first of these made the 'country gentlemen' of Tokutomi Sohō the target of the movement. His movement's publication *Seiron* ('Politics') wrote in relation to many of the local people who reacted to Gotō's speech tour of Tōhoku and Hokuriku: "They are rich farmers and prosperous businessmen of great wealth who are also superior to ordinary people in learning and knowledge" (*Seiron*, 21st September 1888).

The second characteristic was that Gotō and his friends, like Ōkuma Shigenobu and Fukuzawa Yukichi, sought to take power. This was not the approach of Ueki Emori, who aimed to bring about a 'veto parliament', but as was the case with Fukuzawa he wanted a system based on two major parties.

In his northern tour in July and August, Gotō himself frequently spoke of a "responsible cabinet, in other words parliamentary politics". Cabinet should be responsible to the Diet, meaning the British 'cabinet within parliament' system discussed since Fukuzawa first promoted it. The person who was most clearly in favour of this was Tokutomi Sohō, who supported Gotō in the media.

As was clear in his previously mentioned criticism of samurai rights, Tokutomi Sohō, from the Kabasan Incident of September 1884 to the Three Great Incidents Petition movement at the end of 1887, opposed movements seeking to overturn the government. (The first incident occurred when 16 men, mainly radicals from the Fukushima Liberal Party, armed with bombshells and swords, gathered on Kaba Mountain in Ibaraki prefecture, drafted a manifesto and descended the mountain, then attacked the police headquarters. The second incident took place when radicals from the former Liberal Party throughout the country gathered in Tokyo, bringing with them three demands: opposing treaty revision, obtaining freedom of expression, and reducing the land tax; the previously mentioned security law was brought in to suppress this movement.) As a counter-proposal, Tokutomi put forward a system of two major parties on the British model in the following fashion:

> Our people, currently in a party out of power, look to forming an orderly progressive party. . . . If they could possibly receive the support of the majority, then they would be in a position to control the government, and they are men who wish to run the government according to their usually held principles. . . . All that they want to achieve is to apply British-style politics to our country. This would involve having one party in government and the other out of power, this would resemble relations between parties in Great Britain, and conflict between them would be conducted in an ordered fashion. For it is desirable that many people of good will among the *farmers, artisans and merchants*, should work together.
>
> (*Kokumin no Tomo*, 20th January 1888, pp. 3–4; present writer's italics)

112   *Japan's Modern History*

It is worth noting that Tokutomi Sohō, as a supporter of a British-style two-party system, envisaged "people of good will among the farmers, artisans and merchants". From the "samurai, farmers, artisans and merchants" he wanted to exclude the samurai, who were involved in extremist movements, while those he called "country gentlemen" supported a two-party system in which the parties in power could alternate. This was Tokutomi's scenario.

Victory of the veto power-type parliament

Nevertheless, just as occurred in the Fukuzawa period, Tokutomi's expectations for 'country gentlemen' were betrayed. Rather than the *Daidō Danketsu* movement of the moderates, which had come suddenly into prominence, it was leaders of the *Aikokusha* and the former *Jiyūtō* that were respected. To simplify, compared with Gotō Shōjirō, Itagaki Taisuke enjoyed far higher name recognition.

It is possible to organise the ascent of a popular movement for a time, provided that the movement is sensitive to contemporary trends. But for a 'political party' movement to gather support in the long term throughout the country, it is necessary to construct a *jiban* (organised base of support at local level), over a long period. It was the same in the case of Socialist parties in the 'Age of Crisis' to be discussed in Chapter 6. Even though universal male suffrage was put in place in 1925, immediately afterwards the Socialist parties, lacking a *jiban*, were unable to win many seats in the House of Representatives. It was not until 1937, 12 years after universal suffrage, that the Socialists were able to take a certain number of seats.

In the same way, the *Daidō Danketsu* movement of Gotō Shōjirō, on which Tokutomi Sohō placed expectations, was unable to replace the former *Jiyūtō* (Liberal Party), which for nearly nine years from 1880 had been building up its *jiban* in local areas. This became clear when, at the time when the Meiji Constitution was promulgated, prominent imprisoned members of the former Liberal Party were released from gaol in a general amnesty. Once released from their cells, 458 convicted political criminals and those with their cases still pending resumed political activity. At the same time 451 who had been banished from Tokyo under the security law were able to operate freely.

Tokutomi Sohō, who was advocating a British-style two-party system and was criticising the idea of a veto parliament along the lines of the former *Jiyūtō*, realised that his own faction would be defeated by this general amnesty. He argued as follows:

> So far, when members of the former Jiyūtō, imprisoned because of the Fukushima Incident (an incident in which the Fukushima *Jiyūtō* was suppressed by Mishima Michitsune, the Governor of Fukushima in 1882) and the Ōsaka Incident (a failed terror attempt against a Korean VIP by a Liberal Party member in 1885), as well as other incidents, were released from prison, members of the former *Jiyūtō* who had previously hesitated to participate all went together to the *Daidō Danketsu*, and thus subjected the *Daidō Danketsu* to a certain amount of pressure, reducing the original members' influence.

Management, 1880–1893   113

Even if this had not happened, the majority of the *Daidō Danketsu* were controlled by members of the former *Jiyūtō*, who in addition are a new and formidable force. The force of the main stream (the 'country gentlemen' strategy of Gotō and others), is put under pressure by the force of its tributary (that of the former *Jiyūtō* tendency). . . . The gentlemen of the *Daidō Danketsu* since last year have had a difficult time in managing their organisation, in other words the stage which members of the original *Daidō Danketsu* have constructed has become the place on which the former *Jiyūtō* radicals exercise their skill. People are secretly worried about this.

(*Kokumin no Tomo*, 11th May 1889)

Politics for several years after the Meiji Constitution was promulgated and the Diet was convened developed along the lines of Tokutomi's prediction. The forces advocating a political system based on two major parties, like the British system (the *Rikken Kaishintō* [Constitutional Progressive Party]), ironically, far from being able to win a majority in the House of Representatives which was their major premise, could not muster more than 40 in a House totalling 300 seats. On the other hand, the former *Jiyūtō*, consistently criticised by Tokutomi Sohō, once again reconstructed as the *Jiyūtō*, managed to maintain around 130 seats out of 300. The first parliament to be set up in Japan from that day became a 'veto-type parliament'.

Promulgation of the Constitution

As we have already maintained, from around the time when the Constitution was promulgated the government clearly promoted 'transcendentalism', whereby the government ignored the trends of the majority in House of Representatives. On the other hand, 'country gentlemen', who constituted a large majority of electors in Japan's first general elections, supported the *Jiyūtō*, which promoted confrontation with the government. This was not as difficult a situation as that which we see every day, early in the twenty-first century, of the 'twisted Diet' (*nejire kokkai*), in which the two houses have opposite majorities. The government budget presented annually was annually rejected by the House of Representatives, and on the other hand bills to reduce land tax, passed every year through the House of Representatives by the 'popular parties', were nullified by the House of Peers, which consisted of former domain lords and officials who had 'descended from Heaven' (*amakudari*). The government was not able to increase its expenditure budget, while on the other hand the *Jiyūtō* and its collaborators were unable to pass bills to reduce the land tax.

One reason for this stalemate was the Great Japan Imperial Constitution.

The most notorious articles of the Meiji Constitution were article 11 (independence of the right of command) and article 55 (independent responsibility of Ministers of State). The former is known as the cause of irresponsible actions by forces in the field following the Manchurian Incident of 1931, and the latter as the reason why ministers below the Prime Minister shifted responsibility (system of

114 *Japan's Modern History*

irresponsibility) at the outbreak of war with Britain and America in 1941, and at the end of the war.

Articles 67 and 39 of the Constitution were useful to the government. The reason why article 71, seen as important, enabling a government to carry on with the budget of the previous year, was not in fact a useful weapon in the hands of the government, has already been explained. This was because by operating the previous year's budget, the raison d'être of the government came under question.

Against this, article 67 was an important provision from the government's point of view. It read: "Those already fixed expenditures based by the Constitution upon the powers appertaining to the Emperor . . . shall be neither rejected nor reduced by the Imperial Diet, without the concurrence of the government."

"Those already fixed expenditures based by the Constitution upon the powers appertaining to the Emperor" meant current administrative and military costs. So long as this article was in existence, the Diet in its budget deliberations could not reduce administrative costs. The majority parties in the House of Representatives, which had the support of rural landlords and aimed to reduce the land tax, were unable to devise measures of reducing taxation by eliminating waste.

Another weapon in the hands of the government was article 39, which read as follows:

A bill, which has been rejected by either the one or the other of the two Houses, shall not be again brought in during the same session.

The phrase here "one . . . of the two Houses" meant, as we have explained, the House of Peers, made up of former domain lords, elder statesmen and officials who had 'descended from Heaven'. And under "a bill" was included a bill to lower the land tax. In other words, demands by rural landlords to reduce land tax might well pass the House of Representatives, but then would be rejected by the House of Peers and therefore fail to become law.

Most things, however, have two sides to them. If the government wanted to *increase* administrative expenditures, or military expenditures, or expenditures on public works, article 67 only protected "fixed expenditures". Moreover, when the government decided that it needed to increase land tax, which was a crucial source of revenue, article 37 did not protect the government. Quite contrary to the situation concerning land tax reduction, the House of Peers would probably agree to a land tax increase, but in this case the House of Representatives, which also constituted "one . . . of the two Houses", would probably reject a land tax increase. So long as the government and the House of Representatives were at loggerheads, while expenditure and revenue could not be reduced, neither could they be increased.

The Japanese constitutional system, launched in 1890, over the ten years until 1900, when Itō Hirobumi, the Elder Statesman from the Restoration period, formed a grand alliance with the *Jiyūtō* (*Kenseitō*) led by Itagaki Taisuke, forming the *Rikken Seiyūkai*, was searching for a way of stabilising the constitutional system. From the perspective of the 'management' of articles in the Constitution

Management, 1880–1893   115

(that were no more than pieces of writing), both the government and the House of Representatives had continued to make operational mistakes.

Confrontation and compromise in the Diet

For more than a decade, these ten years were portrayed as the history of *Jiyūtō* corruption. The man who was almost always cited in this context was Kōtoku Shūsui, representative of Meiji socialism, contrasted with both the Popular Rights Movement and with the *Rikken Seiyūkai*, who wrote: "At that time, who would have thought it. . . . Their flowing tears and running blood have now become the only ornament of these hateful dictators" (Kōtoku Shūsui zenshū henshū iinkai [ed.], *Kōtoku Shūsui zenshū* ['Complete Works of Kōtoku Shūsui'], Meiji Bunkō, 1970, vol. 2, p. 424).

Even so, over the four years to the outbreak of the Sino-Japanese war in 1894, the *Jiyūtō* and the *Kaishintō*, advocating 'reduction of government expenditure' and 'mitigation of people's burdens', did rather well in the House of Representatives. Only in the first Diet session did the *Jiyūtō* avoid rejection of the budget and a House dissolution, by compromising (betrayal by the Tosa faction). In the second Diet session it cut the government budget and accepted dissolution of the House of Representatives.

At the time of the general elections following the dissolution (February 1892), on the government side, under orders from Shinagawa Yajirō, the Minister of Home Affairs, the police and conservative faction bullies throughout the country were mobilised to interfere in the elections. Despite this the *Jiyūtō* and the *Kaishintō* performed well. The two parties together did not attain a majority of seats, but if we add those sympathetic to the popular parties in the Independent Club and among unaffiliated members, the 'popular parties' as a whole just about managed to reach a majority.

The conflict between the government and the House of Representatives, despite efforts by the leaders of the *Jiyūtō* to bring about a compromise, came to a head in the fourth Diet session. In the background to this head-on clash was the already mentioned fact that article 67 of the Constitution pointed in two opposite directions.

In fact article 67, as we have seen, forbade the Diet to impose a reduction in important expenditures without "the concurrence of the government". But the article did not go so far as to stipulate that the draft budget could be put into operation in cases where the House of Representatives wilfully reduced the budget. In this case the only thing that the government could do was dissolve the House of Representatives on the grounds that the House had violated the Constitution. What the result would be of general elections following Diet dissolution was obvious from the previous year's elections (1892). It was clear that the reduction by the House of Representatives in items of expenditure (current administrative and military expenditures) contravened the Constitution, but there was nothing in the Constitution about what the government could do in such a situation.

Therefore, while conservatives within the government insisted that the behaviour of the House of Representatives was unconstitutional, radicals within the

116 *Japan's Modern History*

Jiyūtō and *Kaishintō* argued that the reduction of expenditure on article 67 items should be judged by the voters at the time of the general elections.

Change of direction by the Jiyūtō

At the time, however, of deliberation over the third budget, among leaders of the largest majority party, the *Jiyūtō*, there were some who began to look for a way out of repeated head-on clashes with the government. When the first Matsukata cabinet resigned in order to take responsibility for its interference in the electoral process, and Itō Hirobumi, known as a moderate in the *hanbatsu* (domain faction) government, agreed to bear the consequences of this, realists within the *Jiyūtō* announced the following policy at the Policy Affairs Research Council of the party:

> Our party does not aim to make only negative reforms. We are people who wish to manage positive projects, and ourselves to take responsibility for them. Our party wishes progressively to devise reform and development of projects in agriculture, industry and commerce, to foster the strength of our people, and thus entrench national power itself.
>
> ([*Jiyūtō*] *tōhō* ['Liberal Party Bulletin'], July 1872, p. 3)

This approach reminds us of the 'prosperous country' line of Ōkubo Toshimichi that we investigated in Chapter 3: "Age of Construction".

What, however, was being proposed here was a major change of direction for the *Jiyūtō*. If we put together "negative reforms" and "positive projects", eliminating waste would not lead to tax reduction. Rural landlords, who were the supporters of the *Jiyūtō*, were unlikely to accept this change overnight.

Moreover, whatever may have been the real intention, the demand for "negative reforms", in other words administrative retrenchment, was still alive. Of the two great Liberal Party slogans of that era – 'retrenchment of government expenditure' and 'mitigating people's burdens' – they were not going to lower the flag on the first of these. Thus it was Constitution article 67 that banned legislation to reduce waste in government expenditure, and the government was continuing to announce its 'non-consent' to expenditure reduction on article 67 items, in the 1891 and 1892 budgets. Even for Itō Hirobumi, who welcomed the movement towards a change of direction in the *Jiyūtō*, there was no question of making concessions to the House of Representatives if it meant having the current government lose face. For pragmatic leaders in the *Jiyūtō*, such as Hoshi Tōru, who was aiming at a change in direction, the situation was the same. It would perhaps be possible to obtain the support of its electors (rural landlords) for a change of policy from 'reducing land tax' to 'mitigating people's burdens' when the latter meant expanding public works.

At the time that the Diet was inaugurated, Matsukata deflation was ending, rice prices were on a rising trend, and the real tax burden on landlords was becoming less. But neither party members nor electors could easily agree to change over-

Management, 1880–1893 117

night their slogan 'retrenchment of government expenditure', meaning cutting administrative waste.

Imperial Proclamation for harmony and cooperation

Itō Hirobumi, who needed to save the face of the extremist faction within the government, as well as the Jiyūtō leadership group of Hoshi Tōru and others who were finding it difficult to gain the understanding of their supporters for the abandonment of the promise to 'retrench government spending' which was so popular, apparently as a joint action entreated the Emperor to intervene.

Concerning the pre-war Japanese Emperor, the image of a dictatorial monarchy sits side by side with the image of a figurehead. I do not believe that the Meiji Emperor exercised real power, but his authority greatly exceeded that of the (post-war) symbolic Emperor. Seen from this perspective, the Imperial Proclamation for Harmony and Co-operation of February 1893, which stemmed from the joint petition to the Emperor by the Prime Minister, Itō Hirobumi, who controlled the executive, and the President of the House of Representatives, Hoshi Tōru, who represented the legislature, had an important significance.

The petition to the Emperor was sent from the President of the House of Representatives, Hoshi Tōru. In it he explained to the Emperor, first, the situation in the House of Representatives since its inception over 'reduction of government expenditure' and 'mitigation of people's burdens'; second, he requested that the Emperor prevail on the government to make responsible explanations whereas, using article 67 as a shield, it was merely repeating its 'non-consent' to demands from the House of Representatives; and third, he explained the legality of the House of Representatives' demands, as a countermeasure, to reduce naval expansion expenditures. In addition Hoshi requested the Emperor to intervene in favour of 'harmony and cooperation' on the part of the 'legislative and executive branches'.

We have already shown that the Meiji Constitution gave to the government a high status in relation to the Diet, and was thus relatively undemocratic. But even so, it was also true that the Diet was one of the organs of state. For this reason the House of Representatives had the right to petition the Emperor to impeach the government, and when its President, Hoshi Tōru, visited the Palace bearing a petition, the Emperor permitted the visit and accepted the petition. The *Meiji tennō ki* ('Record of the Meiji Emperor'), records Hoshi's visit on 8th February in the following terms:

> The President of the House of Representatives, Hoshi Tōru, visited the Palace and presented a petition concerning a resolution of the House of Representatives made the previous day. He was given an audience with the Emperor at the Phoenix Room, and the petition was received, in order to be read carefully, as was told to him.
>
> (Kunaichō [ed.], Meiji tennō ki ['Record of the Meiji Emperor'],
> Yoshikawa Kōbunkan, 1973, vol. 8, p. 179)

118 *Japan's Modern History*

Opposing this, on the 9th February Prime Minister Itō Hirobumi, as Head of the Executive, visited the Palace and presented a petition to the Emperor criticising the House of Representatives. We shall omit its contents here, but having received petitions from the heads of the legislature and of the executive, on 10th February 1893 the Emperor issued the 'Imperial Proclamation on Harmony and Cooperation', which held an important significance for the consolidation of constitutional governance in Japan. It reads as follows:

> The items of expenditure referred to in article 67 of the Constitution already belong to the guarantees of the (constitutional) text, and today should not be cause of conflict. But we especially order ministers that every part of the administration should be reorganised with care according to necessity, conducting mature deliberations, in the expectation of no miscalculation, and we expect decisions.
>
> When it comes to military matters, one day's relaxation may lead to a hundred years of regret. We order that expenditures of the Court be cut, and that annual expenditure over six years be reduced by 300,000 yen annually, and we also order civilian and military officials, with the exception of persons in special circumstances, to pay one tenth of their salary (over a six-year period) in order to supplement the costs of building warships.
>
> We hope that the constitutional organs of the Diet and cabinet ministers will pursue the path of harmony and cooperation across each of their respective spheres of influence, and assist our great tasks, so as to produce an excellent final result.
>
> (Meiji tennō ki, vol. 8, p. 206)

The significance of the Imperial Proclamation

This Imperial Declaration contains three important points.

The first point is that, in contrast to the 'transcendentalism' of Tsuzuki Keiroku, the Diet is considered one of the "constitutional organs", alongside the government. The Constitution, promulgated in 1889, and the Diet, installed in 1890, on the occasion of the fourth Diet session had discovered a solution in the concept of 'management'. Incidentally, the term "produce an excellent final result" (*yūshū no bi o nasu*) used in the Proclamation was used again 23 years later, in 1916, by Yoshino Sakuzō, representing 'Taishō Democracy', in the phrase "explaining the basis of constitutional government, and proposing a path to complete an excellent final result" (*sono yūshū no bi o sumasu michi o ronzu*).

Second, the Proclamation argued that article 67 of the Constitution should be shelved. The government's explanation was literally correct, but it promised that on the orders of the Emperor reorganisation of "every part of the administration" should be carried out. Beginning with the next Diet session, it became impossible for the government to brandish article 67 of the Constitution and ignore the opinions of the Diet.

Third, since the Proclamation did not entirely reject the right of the Diet to reduce new expenditure for military expansion as the Palace expenses as well as salaries of civilian and military officials were to be reduced by 10 per cent, the Diet also should not insist on its own rights. If we put this together with the second point, it recommended that in reduction of expenditure the government should be allowed to defend its position nominally, but should concede on the essence, and on expenditures earmarked for expanding the Navy the same demand should be made of the Diet.

In other words, when the fourth Diet session was reached (since the third Diet session was a special session because of a Diet dissolution, deliberations over the ordinary budget took place for the third time), both the government and the Diet had in the end discovered a way of overcoming the contradictions between the letter of the Meiji Constitution and the practicalities of actually managing the Diet. The Meiji constitutional system was attaining stability as the result of 'management'.

Two roads to 'compromise between the government and the Diet'

There were two obstacles at this stage of 'stability', but they were not incapable of being overcome.

The first was the question of how to bring about politically 'harmony and cooperation', that is to say harmony and cooperation between the executive and legislative branches. Logically speaking, there were only two choices: either to create a broad coalition between the two, or to have a two-party system in which the two of them were divided vertically.

When we examine the first of these – the grand coalition – we find a good example in the post-war permanent coalition between the government bureaucracy and a single ruling party, an arrangement known as the '1955 system', or 'dominance by the Liberal Democratic Party'. If, on the contrary, we explore the second alternative, we find an example in the system based on two major parties established with the founding in 1900 of the *Rikken Seiyūkai* between government officials loyal to Itō Hirobumi and the *Jiyūtō* (*Kenseitō*) on the one hand, and on the other hand conservative Yamagata faction officials and the *Rikken Dōshikai* (the name of the party was changed frequently), successor to the *Kaishintō*.

A difficult point is that if we compare the *Rikken Dōshikai*, created in 1913 by Katsura Tarō of the conservative Yamagata faction, with the *Rikken Seiyūkai* of Hara Kei, who succeeded Itō Hirobumi and Saionji Kinmochi, the former was the more liberal. The Yamagata faction, which accepted control by military and bureaucratic cliques, ended up constructing a political party (*Rikken Dōshikai* → *Kenseikai* → *Rikken Minseitō*) that was more liberal than the liberal-inclined *Seiyūkai* led by Itō, Saionji and Hara.

Thus, when today we hear the words 'Taishō Democracy', it is a question of individual judgement whether we think of the first 'commoner prime minister' Hara Kei, or whether we think rather of Hamaguchi Osachi of the *Rikken Minseitō*, who negotiated the London naval disarmament agreement. Such great complexity

120   *Japan's Modern History*

in historical understanding still continues in relation to the political world and the commentators that lead Japan in the twenty-first century.

Among today's politicians, and among commentators that evaluate them, most completely lack awareness about whether they themselves respect the *Seiyūkai* of Hara Kei, or on the contrary whether they represent a continuation of the *Minseitō* of Hamaguchi Osachi. An example of this is that a leader of the *Minshutō*, which in 2009 overthrew the government of the Liberal Democratic Party that is often compared with the pre-war *Seiyūkai*, cited the name of Hara Kei of the *Seiyūkai* as a politician that he particularly respected.

This confusion in historical understanding explains why, compared with the 'Age of Management' that has been the subject of this chapter, the overall view of the long 'Age of Reorganisation' that followed has been the subject of so little basic agreement among historians. In Chapter 5, this writer will attempt to confront the problem in his own way.

5 Reorganisation, 1894–1924

Two issues of the 'Age of Reorganisation'

Since the 'Age of Management' was an age of bureaucrats and rural landlords, the issues of the 'Age of Reorganisation' which replaced it were clear. At the regime level, one issue was to get rid of bureaucratic cabinets and replace them with party cabinets, or in contemporary language, to establish 'political leadership'. Another issue for the 'Age of Reorganisation' was, at the level of electors who supported politics from the grass roots, that of eliminating the special rights of rural landlords and giving the vote to workers in urban commerce and industry, as well as to small farmers. In other words, normalising party government and installing universal (male) suffrage were the two issues concerned.

Of course, since party cabinets and universal suffrage were the two great questions of what was called 'Taishō Democracy' between 1912 and 1925, we may say that the 'Age of Reorganisation' was the same as 'Taishō Democracy'. But if we regard party cabinets as entailing two major parties, it was not until the final year of the Taishō era (1925) that this was accomplished, and that was also the year in which universal suffrage was introduced.

In the expression 'Taishō Democracy' is contained the nuance that democracy actually existed, but in fact it only existed at the 'movement' level, whereas in custom and system the two-party system and universal suffrage were only achieved after the beginning of the Shōwa era (the first election under universal suffrage was in 1928). Calling the period the 'Age of Reorganisation' in this chapter has the purpose of making this clear.

There is a reason specific to Japan for identifying the issue of the 'Age of Reorganisation', not just as the establishment of a party cabinet system, but rather as the 'customisation' of a two-party system (the 'customisation' of a system is a curious expression, but the meaning will become clear as the argument develops). A party cabinet itself was already established earlier, under Hara Kei, but it was a one-party dominant system, which closely resembled the regime mingling together the Liberal Democratic Party and the government bureaucracy that lasted until very recently (September 2009).

So long as the system of cooperation between these two great forces (the government bureaucracy and the major party based on rural landlords) was not

122 *Japan's Modern History*

disrupted, parties out of power had no chance to take power, and in the democratisation movement the aim of legislating universal suffrage was not realised.

Reconciliation between bureaucracy and popular parties preventing 'reorganisation'

The key factor uniting the government bureaucracy and rural landlords in pre-war Japan was the *Rikken Seiyūkai* party, created by former popular rights activists who installed as President Itō Hirobumi, a politician originating in domain politics. The principal leader in the founding of the *Rikken Seiyūkai*, having been leader of the *Jiyūtō* (*Kenseitō*), was Hoshi Tōru, but the man who turned the *Seiyūkai*, led by Hoshi, into a stable and dominant political party, was Hara Kei, the first commoner to be Prime Minister, who is wrongly credited – even today – with being a party politician representing 'Taishō Democracy'. As we shall gradually reveal below, Hara, before he met his untimely death in 1921, continued to oppose a system of two major parties, as well as universal suffrage, and was a conservative party man.

The present writer has revealed his conclusion a little too early. In the next section, I shall investigate the process leading to the formation of the *Rikken Seiyūkai* in 1900, concentrating on Hoshi Tōru, the former popular rights activist, who had been the principal leader of the *Jiyūtō*.

Positive policies and the formation of the *Rikken Seiyūkai*

Beginnings of the intimate relationship between parties and bureaucracy

A regime of intimate linkage between a conservative party and the government bureaucracy, which came to control Japanese politics for many years both before and after the Second World War, developed after the conclusion of the Sino-Japanese war in 1894–5. The *Jiyūtō*, which for several years following the establishment of the Diet in 1890 had combated the 'domain-clique' (*hanbatsu*) government, clearly set out its change of direction.

In March of the year after the Sino-Japanese war ended (1896), the *Jiyūtō* President, Itagaki Taisuke, spoke as follows at the party meeting (*kondankai*):

> When we reflect upon the condition of our country in the East Asian situation, we see that expansion of our military capacity is essential. Accordingly, we need to make expenditure from the national treasury. This means that we must aim to raise more revenue for the treasury. We must therefore raise new taxes. We must break with past negative policies of mitigating people's burdens, adopt developmental policies and embark on many different projects, thus producing greater and more widespread prosperity for the people.
>
> ([*Jiyūtō*] *tōhō* ['Jiyūtō Party Bulletin'], 11th April 1896, p. 1)

As we have already seen in the previous chapter, since before the Sino-Japanese war the leadership of the *Jiyūtō* had wanted to end the head-on clashes between the 'domain-clique' government and the House of Representatives.

Towards the Sino-Japanese war: revolt by the **Tōnghak**

Nevertheless, it required a quite major change in the situation to abandon basic policies, advocated for nearly ten years, of cutting back administrative expenditure and reducing the land tax, in favour of 'positive policies' of forgetting about taxes and extending the rail network to the local areas. The rise in nationalism occasioned by the outbreak of the Sino-Japanese war, and receipt of the indemnity paid by China following the Japanese victory (about 330,000,000 yen; annual government expenditure before the war was around 80,000,000 yen) made it possible for the *Jiyūtō* to change direction from 'mitigating people's burdens' (*minryoku kyūyō*) to 'positive policies' (*sekkyoku seisaku*).

As we have seen in Chapter 4, from the time of the *Imo* Incident in 1882, and the *Kapsin* Incident in 1884, a direct confrontation between Japan and China over control of the Korean peninsula was only a matter of time. By the terms of the Tianjin Treaty of 1885, both countries promised to pull their forces out of the peninsula together, and if they were to mobilise troops in any circumstances, they promised to "inform their counterparts", but under this temporary truce both states were working to expand their armies and navies.

What gave cause for the opening of hostilities was the so-called *Tonghak* peasant rebellion. The Korean government, unable to quell this revolt with its own forces, called upon China to send troops, and the Government of China, in accordance with the terms of the Tianjin Treaty, officially informed the Japanese government of its troop mobilisation (6th June 1894).

News of the *Tonghak* rebellion also reached the government of Japan, and four days before it received the Chinese government's official notification of its troop mobilisation the second Itō cabinet made a cabinet decision to send troops to combat this. When the notification reached the Japanese government, mobilisation of the mixed brigade, exceeding 7,000 troops, of the 5th Hiroshima division (at the brigade level artillery and other elements supplemented the infantry) was already ordered.

Despite this rapid reaction, by the time the advance party of the mixed brigade reached Kanjō (Seoul) the *Tonghak* rebellion had already been suppressed by Chinese forces. Japan had lost her raison d'être for sending troops.

Mutsu Munemitsu's argument for making war on China

Around this time, whether a raison d'être existed or not, a strong argument for going to war with China was made by the Foreign Minister, Mutsu Munemitsu. In a letter to the Prime Minister, Itō Hirobumi, he argued as follows:

> According to two telegrams on separate sheets, compared with the tough attitude of the Chinese military forces on being in Korea, the Government of China seems very keen to avoid sending more troops there. Therefore, if we are unable to avoid a final confrontation, we should not fail to seize this opportunity. From ancient times there are many examples of those who adhere to righteous reasoning and give advantage to enemy forces. In addi-

124 *Japan's Modern History*

Table 5.1

Year	Meiji era year	Prime Minister	Event
1894	27	Itō	*Tonghak* uprising. Sino-Japanese war.
1895	28		Shimonoseki peace conference. Three-power intervention by Russia, Germany and France. Subjugation of Taiwan.
1896	29	Matsukata	*Rikken Kaishintō, Rikken Kakushintō* and others unite to form *Shinpotō* (Ōkuma Shigenobu). First post-war tax rise.
1897	30		Gold standard established. Labour Union Promotion Society formed.
1898	31	Itō	*Jiyūtō–Shinpotō* coalition rejects land tax increase bill. *Jiyūtō* and *Shinpotō* combine to form
		Ōkuma	*Kenseitō*, and form first Ōkuma Cabinet (Ōkuma-Itagaki). *Kenseitō* (former *Jiyūtō*) divides into the *Kenseitō* and the *Kenseihontō* (former *Shinpotō*).
		Yamagata	Land tax law amended (land tax rise of 13.2%, since land tax value had increased from 2.5% to 3.3%).
1899	32		Revision of Civilian Officials Appointment Law. Yokoyama Gennosuke publishes "Japan's Lower Society". Treaty revision accomplished (legal rights restored.
1900	33	Itō	Security police law. Electoral law revision (suffrage to those paying over ten yen direct tax). Convention that Army and Navy ministers must be serving officers. North China Incident (mobilisation following Boxer Rebellion). *Rikken Seiyūkai* formed, with Itō Hirobumi as President.
1901	34	Katsura	Yawata steelworks begin production. Patriotic Women's Association formed. *Shakai Minshutō* (Social Democratic Party) founded, banned directly. Hoshi Tōru assassinated. Tanaka Shōzō petitions Emperor over Ashio mine pollution issue.

tion, our influence in Korea is not to be compared with the influence of China, which has been built up over a long period. At this time, using whatever pretext, we should provoke a clash with Chinese forces, somehow gain a victory, then we should bargain in our foreign policy, using tough and flexible tactics depending on the situation . . . and if in the end a conflict is unavoidable, it will be best to fight on a day when we should be victorious. . . . Tomorrow I will contact you, probably by telephone.

(Shungiku kō tsuishōkai [ed.], *Itō Hirobumi den*, Tōseisha, vol. 2, pp. 63–4)

Foreign Minister Mutsu's argument in favour of starting a war with China had already become patent at the Cabinet meeting on 15th June. At that meeting Mutsu held that the proposal of the Japanese side to conduct reform of the Korean government working together with the Government of China was a tactic to gain time before engaging in war with China. He expressed the following view:

Reorganisation, 1894–1924 125

Irrespective of how our negotiations with China progress, until we see what the results are, our forces which have now been sent to Korea should definitely not be withdrawn. And if the Chinese government does not support our proposal, the Imperial Government must independently fulfil its duty of bringing about reform of the Korean government.

(Ibid., p. 58)

The Cabinet decision versus the Emperor's opinion

The Meiji Emperor and his advisers showed great anxiety concerning Mutsu's policy of recklessly aiming for war with China, but Mutsu brushed the Emperor's concerns aside. The way this developed is clear from the following letter that he sent to the Prime Minister, Itō:

> The Head Chamberlain, Tokudaiji (Sanetsune), has just paid me a visit to deliver a message from the Emperor; he questioned me in detail concerning the recent Cabinet resolution that was conveyed to the Emperor, and I replied explaining minutely the course of the recent cabinet discussions. I was able to perceive the Emperor's anxiety about future developments, and in particular about the final part of the cabinet decisions, namely the item not to withdraw our forces from Korea until the Japan–China negotiations are finally settled, and the item that if the Chinese government were not to agree, the Imperial Government should do its best to achieve its objectives relying on its own strength alone. Munemitsu (I myself) gave my detailed opinion about relations between Japan, China and Korea, and about the future fate of the three countries, and explained that if the final two items, which constitute the core of the cabinet decisions, were to be omitted, then the whole basis would be undermined. . . . I must emphasise that if the Imperial Will were different from decisions of Cabinet, this would indeed be a most serious matter. I shall be honoured if you would visit the Court tomorrow morning, and persuade the Emperor personally.

(Ibid., pp. 59–60)

The letter from Mutsu shows graphically the complexity of Meiji Government foreign policy history. First of all, the Great Japan Imperial Constitution did not envisage situations where the 'Imperial Will' and a 'Cabinet decision' might differ. In article 55 it was written that "The respective Ministers of State shall give their advice to the Emperor and shall be responsible for it" and in Itō's *Commentaries on the Constitution*, he wrote:

> But with regard to important internal and external matters of State, the whole government is concerned, and no single Department can, therefore, be charged with the conduct of them. As to the expediency of such matters and as to the mode of carrying them out, all the Ministers of State shall take united counsel, and none of them is allowed to leave his share of the business a burden upon

126 *Japan's Modern History*

> his colleagues. In such matters, it would of course be proper for the Cabinet
> to assume joint responsibility.
>
> > (Marquis Hirobumi Ito [Tr. Baron Miyoji Ito], *Commentaries on the
> > Constitution of the Empire of Japan*, 2nd edn., Tokyo, Chuo Daigaku,
> > 1906; reprinted Westport CT, Greenwood Press, 1978, pp. 104–5)
> > [note: the word 'Cabinet' occurs in Itō Miyoji's translation, but not in
> > the original Japanese text, nor in the Meiji Constitution itself].

Since going to war with China was "an important internal and external matter of State" this was not a matter for the individual responsibility of the ministers of Foreign Affairs, Army and Navy, but one where it would be proper "for the government as a whole to assume joint responsibility". Clearly this referred to 'cabinet resolutions'. If a cabinet resolution clashed with the opinion of the Emperor, article 55 of the Constitution would become a dead letter.

Second, despite what was often thought to be the independent responsibility of each minister to the Emperor according to article 55, the practice had not become established whereby the Emperor would have summoned the Foreign Minister into his presence to hear his report on the situation. It was the Head Chamberlain, Tokudaiji Sanetsune, not the Emperor himself, who conveyed the Emperor's concerns to the Foreign Minister, Mutsu, and demanded an explanation from him. The Foreign Minister was only able to persuade the Emperor indirectly, and it was none but the Prime Minister, Itō Hirobumi, who was able to petition the Emperor, on lines in sympathy with Mutsu's opinion. Whether it was a question of 'total responsibility' concerning 'important internal and external matters of State', or the indirect petitioning of the Emperor by the Foreign Minister, the system of independent responsibility under article 55 was severely restricted (but the famous 'independent supreme command' by the Emperor in article 11, was not confined in this way. I shall re-examine this question in Chapter 6.)

In the end Itō persuaded the Emperor face to face, and on 1st August a declaration of war against China was issued in the Emperor's name.

Conclusion of the Sino-Japanese war: the Shimonoseki Treaty and the triple intervention.

The trend of events was decided a year and a half after the beginning of the war. The Japanese Army in its general attack on 15th November forced the capitulation of P'yŏngyang, and two days later, on the 17th, the Japanese Navy after a fierce struggle with the Chinese northern ocean fleet forced the two warships *Ding Yuan* and *Zhen Yuan* to flee the scene. The Army, which had increased in strength with the naval victory, marched in the direction of the Liaodong peninsula, and at the end of 1894, four months after the opening of hostilities, had occupied the greater part of the peninsula, including Lushun (Ryojun, Port Arthur) and Dalian (Dairen).

In February 1895 the Sino-Japanese war came to a de facto conclusion with the surrender of the Chinese northern ocean fleet at Weihaiwei, and on 20th

March the Chinese government plenipotentiary, Li Hong-Zhang, arrived at Shimonoseki and the peace conference began. If one reads his argument at the conference forgetting that he was a protagonist, it seems reasonable. What Li was insisting on was that the Japanese war aim had been the independence of Korea, and that therefore in this peace conference Japan should, first, guarantee Korean independence; second, at a peace treaty to end a war whose aim was 'Korean independence' it made no sense for Japan to demand of China the cession of the Liaodong peninsula; third, it also made no sense for Japan to demand from China the cession of Taiwan, which had not been occupied during the war; fourth, reparations in a war between independent nations should be limited to the 150 million yen that Japan had actually spent in the war, and there was no basis for a 300 million yen claim.

The second of these four assertions, namely the inappropriateness of the demand for China to cede the Liaodong peninsula, had been made also, over the heads of the government of Japan, to the Russian government, which was seeking to obtain the rights over the peninsula for itself. The fact that Russia appealed to Germany and France to demand the return of the Liaodong peninsula by Japan to China is famous as the 'Tripartite Intervention' (23rd April). It is known that this Tripartite Intervention became a reason for the Russo-Japanese war ten years later, but what exerted a great influence on domestic politics was the indemnity paid by China of around 300 million yen for the return of the Liaodong peninsula. For Japan, whose national expenditure before the war had been about 80 million yen per annum, it was extra revenue surpassing annual national expenditure more than fourfold. For the first time the means were available to fulfil the *fukoku kyōhei* that had been the aspiration since Bakumatsu times. The previously cited speech of the *Jiyūtō* President, Itagaki Taisuke, was aiming at a policy change by means of this revenue, from demands for reduction in the land tax (mitigating people's burdens), to railway construction, improvement in port facilities, establishment of higher educational institutions and so on, meaning expansion of public works aimed at the regions (positive policies).

As we saw in Chapter 4, the largest base of support for the *Jiyūtō* was the village landlords, and the land tax that they bore was a fixed tax paid in money. It was a system where, if the price of agricultural products, starting with rice, were to rise, the tax burden on landlords would fall. Under this system, from the middle of the Sino-Japanese war until the post-war period, as a result of prices rising sharply, and in particular the rice price continuing to rise, by 1898 the price of rice was twice what it had been before the war. The landlords, whose tax burden had halved, ceased to demand that the land tax should be reduced, as they had before the war.

Important taxpayers were not demanding tax reductions, and an indemnity had come from China amounting to four times the pre-war annual State revenues. Expectations by the *Jiyūtō* leaders, including Itagaki Taisuke, of a simultaneous fulfilment of 'prosperous country' (*fukoku*) and 'strong military' (*kyōhei*) were not unreasonable.

128 *Japan's Modern History*

Military expansion and tax rises

The *Jiyūtō* leaders, however, underestimated the urge for military expansion on the part of the armed forces of a victorious country. The extraordinary 8–10-year budget, drawn up by the 2nd Itō Cabinet under pressure from the demands of the Army and Navy, was 280 million yen, and the revenue source consisted entirely of reparations payments by China.

On the other hand, the reparations payments did not provide the revenue for 'positive policies' (chiefly costs of expanding the rail network), as had been expected by the *Jiyūtō*, and over seven years 40 million yen were raised from public loans for projects.

The figures of 280 million yen for military expenditure, and 40 million yen for public works, show just how far *kyōhei* was in the lead and *fukoku* had become subordinate, but things did not settle down into that pattern. If there was 280 million yen for military expansion as extraordinary expenditure, then operating expenditure would naturally increase as well (it would be necessary to spend on consumer goods, such as bullets, and salaries). According to calculations made by Matsukata Masayoshi as Finance Minister and his successor Watanabe Kunitake, operating costs for the Army and Navy rose annually on average by about 20 million yen.

Unlike extraordinary expenditure, the increase in operating costs could not be met by public loans. But the total income tax revenue before and after the Sino-Japanese war was about 2 million yen, and even if it were doubled that would only amount to another 2 million yen. Whether they liked it or not, increasing operating costs of the Army and Navy could only be met by increasing revenue from land tax by around 40 million yen in total.

If land tax were increased from the current 2.5 per cent to 4.0 per cent, a tax take of less than 40 million yen would rise to more than 60 million yen. This would constitute a rise in tax revenue of 20 million yen and would be sufficient to meet the operating costs of the Army and Navy.

In any period, however, an increase in taxation does not work out exactly as assumed by desktop calculations in the Ministry of Finance. It is true that as a consequence of the increasing price of rice during and after the war, rural landlords were not demanding reductions in land tax. Rather than reducing land tax, what they wanted was completion of public works, including especially expansion of the rail network. If, however, it came to an actual increase in land tax, that was a different matter, since the combination of a tax rise and rail network expansion was for rural landlords hardly different from collecting contributions in order to expand the railways.

Moreover, around the time of the Sino-Japanese war the House of Representatives itself ceased to be a monopoly of the *Jiyūtō*. Before the war, the *Rikken Kaishintō* of Ōkuma Shigenobu accounted for fewer than 50 seats out of 300, but after the war, in March 1896, it had absorbed various other parties, and had become a major party (now called *Shinpotō*) accounting for 100 seats out of 300. Incidentally, the *Jiyūtō* at this time had 109 seats, so that the relative strength of the two parties in the House of Representatives was almost even.

Reorganisation, 1894–1924   129

The party supporting village landlords who wanted railways but disapproved of tax increases now split. Those who wanted to attract railways supported the *Jiyūtō*, whereas those who opposed tax increases backed the *Shinpotō*.

Constitutional system unable to enforce tax increases

If it had been before the Sino-Japanese war, the situation of a divided House of Representatives would have usefully enabled the 'domain-clique' government, which favoured 'transcendentalism' (*chōzenshugi*, see Chapter 4), to manipulate the parties. But the problem for the domain-clique government after the war was not to prevent tax reduction demands from the House of Representatives, but rather itself to introduce into the House proposals for increased taxation. As I have pointed out in the previous chapter, according to article 37 of the Constitution, if the House of Representatives were to reject the bill, tax rises would not occur. The autocratic character of the Meiji Constitution is well known, but the House of Representatives was vouchsafed sufficient authority to bury the government's tax increase bill.

A favourable consideration for the domain-clique government was that in their view, unlike the *Shinpotō*, the leaders of the *Jiyūtō* were favourable to the realisation of 'positive policies', even if they accepted a tax increase. This is clear from the speech by Itagaki Taisuke quoted as the beginning of this chapter. Therefore, if there were no general election, the second Itō Cabinet might be able to shepherd the land tax increase bill through the House of Representatives by adding votes of the pro-government *Kokumin Kyōkai* and sundry unaffiliated members to the votes of the *Jiyūtō*.

Members of the House of Representatives, however, then as now, served for a four-year term, and the most recent election was in September 1894, right in the middle of the Sino-Japanese war. Whether or not parliamentary dissolution took place, there would be a general election during 1898.

In this situation the 2nd Matsukata Cabinet summoned the Diet on 24th December 1897, with little chance of the land tax increase bill being passed dissolved the House of Representatives the very next day, and on the same day as the dissolution (25th December) resigned en masse. Indeed, those two days showed graphically the difficulty posed by the land tax increase issue for the domain-clique government.

The only light on the horizon was that in the general elections following the dissolution, the *Jiyūtō* of Itagaki Taisuke, who had a close relationship with the next Prime Minister, Itō Hirobumi, might win an overwhelming victory. If this happened, relations between the *Jiyūtō* and Itō would resemble those of the *Rikken Seiyūkai* in September 1900. Itagaki himself publicly set out this path. In a speech delivered in Tokyo at the end of February 1898, during the electoral campaign, he spoke as follows:

> If I say whom I would choose as a politician, I think that above all it is inevitable that I should assist Marquis Itō (hear hear!). First of all, he enjoys the trust

130   *Japan's Modern History*

of His Majesty, and he is also trusted in the bureaucratic world. . . . In recent times, his political opinions and mine have been in harmony, and on the question of completing the construction of a constitutional regime, we both hold the same opinions. . . . Mr Itō is the man who today controls the power of the bureaucracy, while I run a major political party. This being the case, I think that we must maintain a strong government and save this country by means of these two great forces over the next two or three years.

([*Jiyūtō*] *Tōhō*), 1st March 1898, pp. 36–7)

The *Jiyūtō*, however, in these elections, had only won a narrow victory. The election results showed that the *Jiyūtō* had won 97 seats and the *Shinpotō* 91, out of 300.

Firmly establishing a landlord assembly

The reason why, despite having made crystal clear its position as a party in power, the *Jiyūtō* won less than one-third of the seat total was that, as before, the electorate was restricted to landlords whose number was at the least just under 500,000. Even though it was eight years since the Diet was instituted, the qualifications needed to be an elector (payment of over 15 yen in direct tax), as well as the number of electors, had not changed since the time of the first general election. Of course, the reason for dissolving the Diet was the issue of increasing land tax, and since those who paid land tax were mainly rural landlords, the *Jiyūtō*, which supported a land tax increase, was hard put to bring off a major victory. Compared with the military, the economy and society, all of which had shown enormous change at the time of the Sino-Japanese war, 'political society' was intransigently stuck in its ways.

I have already explained how after the Sino-Japanese war the build-up of the Army and Navy proceeded at breakneck speed. In the economy also, the textile industry, which consisted typically of small engineering works, moved from being import-dependent to engaging in domestic production, and following the Sino-Japanese war began exporting to the Chinese market. Also, the silk industry, which was the largest exporting industry of Meiji Japan, succeeded in mechanising itself after the war and doubled its exports. The railways, which were the largest infrastructure industry, in receipt of investment from merchants and industrialists as well as from major landlords, developed at a rapid pace.

The rapid development of the arms industry, spinning and silk manufacture made labour questions come to the fore. Newspaper journalists together with the Ministry of Agriculture and Commerce published a survey of the appalling labour conditions of workers in both traditional industries and modern engineering works (Yokoyama Gennosuke, *Nihon no kasō shakai* ['Japan's Lower Class Society'], Iwanami Bunkō, 1899, 1949; and Nōshōmushō [Ministry of Agriculture and Commerce], *Shokkō jijō* ['Conditions of Workmen'], 1901 Survey, Seikatsusha, 1947). But only political society failed to change, and in a population of 40 million, a mere 500,000 rural landlords monopolised the right to vote.

Reorganisation, 1894–1924   131

When we examine this political society, quite unchanging from the time when the Diet was inaugurated in 1890, we see that in the early Diet sessions the land tax reduction argument of the 'popular parties' became opposition to an increase in land tax, and then a change was planned to 'positive policies', implying acceptance of a land tax increase. It seems that these mutations were little more than a storm in a teacup. Similarly, the perpetual cycle of conflict and compromise between the domain-clique bureaucrats who believed in 'transcendentalism', and the village landlords who monopolised the right to vote for members of the House of Representatives, as well as the parties that represented them – *Jiyūtō* and *Shinpotō* – may be considered little more than changes conducted in a teacup.

The political parties changed their character according to what was happening in their support base. In so far as this was the case, the *Jiyūtō* and the *Shinpotō*, whether fighting or agreeing with the domain-clique bureaucrats, had as their base fewer than 500,000 rural landlords, and were basically unconnected with the 'Age of Reorganisation'.

Seen from this perspective, in 1898 the *Jiyūtō* and the *Shinpotō* returned to the position of 'popular parties' they had held before the Sino-Japanese war, and joined hands in organising Japan's first 'party cabinet' (the first Ōkuma Cabinet and the Cabinet jointly led by Ōkuma and Itagaki), while two years later, in 1900, *Kenseitō*, formed out of the former *Jiyūtō*, changed its line to one of 'positive policies' and returned to cooperating with government officials close to Itō, and formed the *Rikken Seiyūkai* with Itō as its President. This means that the politics of Japan remained stuck in the 'Age of Enforcement'. It hardly needs to be stated that the key to moving from 'enforcement' to 'reorganisation' lay in expanding the electorate, and in the attainment of universal suffrage as its fulfilment.

From grand coalition to reconciliation between bureaucracy and parties

Even so, these teacup storms were major issues for those involved in them. Precisely because a majority of the rural landlords felt that as taxpayers they had no obligation to be the only ones bearing the burden of the operating costs of the Army and Navy, Itagaki's *Jiyūtō* at the general election of March 1898 in effect tasted defeat.

Just as in any period, it is rare for a single-party line to be supported by all party members. One result of the outspoken support by the party leader, Itagaki, for the *hanbatsu* was that when at the elections victory was not achieved, the forces within the *Jiyūtō* opposed to a land tax increase grew. This was a return to the pre-war popular party position. The *Jiyūtō* and the *Shinpotō* rejected the 60 per cent tax increase proposed by the third Itō Cabinet by the overwhelming majority of 247 votes to 27. When we consider that the House of Representatives had 300 seats, the importance of these 247 contrary votes is easily understood.

Following the Sino-Japanese war, the Itō Cabinet as well as the Matsukata Cabinet accepted Army and Navy expansion, and brought in their policy of meeting the consequent increase in operating costs through an increase in land tax.

132   *Japan's Modern History*

But with the rejection of the land tax increase by the House of Representatives in June 1898, the domain-clique government found itself in a predicament. They judged that, under the Meiji Constitution, there was no way of passing the land tax increase bill.

Until the end of December 1898, when the second Yamagata government passed the bill for a compromise measure, providing for a 32.2 per cent rise in land tax over a five-year period, the policy of the domain-clique government was rather complicated.

First, the Itō Cabinet, whose land tax increase bill had been defeated by a large margin, immediately dissolved the House of Representatives and then resigned en masse. Up to this point this was just the same as what the Matsukata Cabinet had done. But before the Itō Cabinet resigned, the *genrō* (elder statesmen), who, like Itō himself, as veterans of the Meiji Restoration had been advisers to the Emperor in respect of appointing the Prime Minister, proposed that orders be given to the leaders of the two parties, which had opposed the tax increase bill, to form the successor cabinet. The proposal was to appoint Ōkuma Shigenobu of the *Shinpotō* to be Prime Minister and Itagaki Taisuke of the *Jiyūtō* to be Home Affairs Minister, and to allow them freely to construct their cabinet.

Yamagata Aritomo, who enjoyed the confidence of the Army and Navy as well as of the government bureaucracy, opposed this, but facing an overwhelming majority in the House of Representatives he could not go so far as to propose himself as prime minister. Since the 247 members of the House of Representatives who had opposed the land tax increase bill brought together the *Jiyūtō* and the *Shinpotō* to found the *Kenseitō*, it was clear that in the August elections they would increase their seat total. Thus, eight years after the Diet was established, a party cabinet was inaugurated in which all the ministers, apart from the ministers for the Army and Navy, came from the former *Shinpotō* and the former *Jiyūtō*. For the domain-clique elements, this was a situation where, in both ideological and power-struggle terms, they had suffered total loss of face.

For Itō Hirobumi, however, who for several years from the Sino-Japanese war had established good relations with the *Jiyūtō*, the scenario of a return to power was not entirely absent. If the former *Jiyūtō*, which was now merging with the *Kenseitō*, should split the party and support a land tax rise, the formation of a fourth Itō Cabinet with itself as party in power was not impossible.

Creators of harmony between bureaucracy and party

The opportunity was given by the return to Japan of a former *Jiyūtō* leader, who for over two years had served as Minister in the United States, Hoshi Tōru. As shown in Chapter 4, Hoshi, had opposed a 'popular party' alliance with the *Rikken Kaishintō* until just before the Sino-Japanese war, and without tiring of the negative view that land tax ought to be reduced was insisting, with his use of the expression 'positive policies', that local development should be pursued through the development of public works. So Hoshi returned from the United States after the coalition cabinet of *Jiyūtō* and *Shinpotō* had been formed. Concerning Hoshi's

Reorganisation, 1894–1924 133

activities after his return to Japan, the Metropolitan Police Superintendent wrote as follows to the Prime Minister, Ōkuma Shigenobu:

> Since the former *Jiyūtō*, based on its Kantō faction, is discontented, and is secretly devising strategies to split the party, and even though there are those in its central executive headquarters who are trying to bring about reconciliation, the supporters of Hoshi are working hard behind the scenes so as to stir things up. The other day at the Kantō Club in the *Kōyōkan*, Hoshi summoned to a meeting those of similar inclination from neighbouring prefectures. This was partly to demonstrate his own strength, but in the end he showed anxiety about whether it would be possible to attain his goals, proposed that he would soon gather together his sympathisers, would raise a range of difficult issues on the day of the (*Kenseitō*) Congress, and was keen to trample all over the Congress hall.
>
> > (*Waseda Daigaku toshokan shozō Ōkuma Shigenobu kankei shiryō shoshū [seitō teisatsu hōkokusho]*, unpublished materials relating to Ōkuma Shigenobu held in Waseda University library [Political Party Surveillance Reports], 19th September 1898)

The immediate occasion for the split in the *Kenseitō* into the *Kenseitō* (former *Jiyūtō*) and the *Kenseihontō* (*former Shinpotō*) was a dispute between the two factions over the succession to the Minister of Education, who had resigned, and the preparations for this had already been put in train with Hoshi Tōru as the main actor.

The second Yamagata Cabinet

The *Kenseitō* formally split on 29th October 1898, and as a result the first Ōkuma coalition Cabinet resigned on the 30th. Its successor Cabinet was a 'transcendental' cabinet, led by Yamagata Aritomo, without a single party member included, and the *Kenseitō* (former *Jiyūtō*), led by Hoshi Tōru, supported the cabinet externally.

The second Matsukata and third Itō cabinets had resigned because of the rejection of bills to increase land tax, and the *Kenseitō* of Hoshi Tōru, which had decided to support the Yamagata Cabinet from the outside, had no choice but to accept some degree of land tax increase. I shall have to omit the details of this, but the reader is referred to the present writer's *Meiji kenpō taisei no kakuritsu*, pp. 206–35 (translated into English as *The Establishment of the Japanese Constitutional System*, London and New York, Routledge, 1992, Chapter 7). But the points of compromise between the Cabinet and the *Kenseitō* were that the tax increase was for only five years, and that the Itō Cabinet's 60 per cent increase was reduced to 32 per cent. On the basis of this compromise, the land tax increase bill passed both Houses, and was promulgated at the end of December 1898.

The question is, what had the *Kenseitō* gained by this compromise? The party's leader, Hoshi Tōru, in a signed article in March 1899, argued as follows:

134   *Japan's Modern History*

First of all, we need to have great ambitions. . . . We do not need to hasten to make great achievements, and we must not miscalculate our actions through impatience and lack of care. The key is to win victories through perfection.

Secondly, to open doors means not to begrudge operating on a broad front. We need to call in all the talent we can find, and accept rival leaders. If they fashion themselves anew, we should not exclude anyone, complaining that they are elder statesmen (*genrō*).

Thirdly, we must strictly follow party rules. Our party, like the proverbial snake on the mountain, must maintain close relations between its head and its tail. If we are self-controlled, keep to the rules and consistently follow the law, we should manage our affairs all the better.

Fourthly, we must firmly maintain our local base of support. What makes a party thrive is its local base. Political victory or defeat is brought about by victory or defeat in the localities. Speaking frankly, if the proximate cause of political reform stems from meetings at Oiso, Waseda and the Imperial Hotel, victory or defeat in the localities must be regarded as a more distant cause. The most important thing is the local area.

(*Kenseitō kikanshi* ['Organ of the *Kenseitō*'], *Jinmin* ['The People'], 19th March 1899)

This article, which to later generations may seem abstract, would have had a concrete meaning to his contemporaries.

The first point required that, even though the Yamagata Cabinet was giving nothing back in return for the party's support for its tax increase policies, the party's policy of supporting that Cabinet must be understood. The second point made clear that the idea of the *genrō*, Itō Hirobumi, becoming President of the *Kenseitō* was making progress. The third point declared that former members of the *Jiyūtō*, who were continuing to waver between opposing tax increases and demanding expansion of public works, were now required to follow the party leadership.

The article set out clearly the road towards the *Rikken Seiyūkai*, formed in 1900 as the ruling structure with the *genrō* Itō Hirobumi as its President, and selected 'positive policies' (policies of development) as the flagship approach of the *Seiyūkai* over the next 30 years and more. In that sense this signed article by Hoshi Tōru had an epoch-making significance.

Positive policies and the development of the Tōhoku region

The 'positive policies' of the *Seiyūkai*, from Hoshi Tōru to Hara Kei, and then to Takahashi Korekiyo, sought to extend the railways, reconstruct harbours and expand infrastructure, but we ought not to overlook the fact that it also aimed to develop the Tōhoku region in the north. In April 1899, attending the branch meeting of the six Tōhoku prefectures at Sendai, Hoshi made a speech in the following terms:

Reorganisation, 1894–1924 135

If we ask how agricultural development in Tōhoku compares with that of south-western regions, we have to say that it lags behind. So far as the economy is concerned, manufacturing and commerce are in a similar state, while financial institutions are also retarded. . . . Since transport institutions in Tōhoku are underdeveloped by comparison with the Kansai, it is imperative to develop them. In education also, both standard and higher education are completely behind the times. . . . To raise this region up to the level of the Kansai, there is no alternative but to put in place new positive (developmental) policies

(Jinmin, 11th April 1899)

The delay in modernising Tōhoku by comparison with south-western regions was the reason for the defeat of the 28 Tōhoku domains in the Boshin war, and it was also the result of that war. It is clear that the retarded development of *fukoku kyōhei* in the Bakumatsu period was the reason for the defeat of Aizu by Satsuma, and at the same time, with the defeat in the Boshin war, and the fact that they were left behind in terms of the benefits of modernisation after the Meiji Restoration, it explains the backwardness of the Tōhoku region.

This region, left behind by modernisation, was a region full of traditional industries, and rice production was its biggest industry. Now, as I have already pointed out many times, those who held a majority in the House of Representatives since the Diet was established were the representatives of landlords in rice-producing areas. They were demanding reduction of land tax, and opposed increases in land tax. Specifically, representatives of the Tōhoku and Hokuriku regions accounted for 50 seats out of the 300, and 44 of these opposed any increase in the land tax right to the end (Banno Junji, *Meiji kenpō taisei no kakuritsu*, p. 216 [translated as *The Establishment of the Japanese Constitutional System*, pp. 180–1]). This was the character of the Tōhoku and Hokuriku regions that Hoshi was trying to turn towards 'positive policies'. At the assembly of the *Kenseitō* for the six Tōhoku prefectures at which Hoshi made his previously cited speech, it was resolved to build harbours in Tōhoku, complete the Tōhoku rail network and establish the Tōhoku Imperial University.

The support system of the Rikken Seiyūkai

As I wrote at the beginning of this chapter, what I am calling the 'Age of Reorganisation' points to the fact that the world of Hoshi Tōru, as I have been describing, was 'reorganised' with a system of universal suffrage and a system based on two major parties. But if we focus on the decade or less from the inauguration of the Diet in 1890, we see that the 'political reform' effected by Hoshi Tōru was itself a kind of 'reorganisation'.

The *Kenseitō* of which he was leader was not hostile to Itō Hirobumi, leader of the *hanbatsu*, did not demand reduction in the land tax, and even came to cease opposing a land tax increase. What Hoshi's party received as recompense was merely control of the right to decide on public works costs, and the creation of

136   *Japan's Modern History*

rock-solid local bases of support for the *Kenseitō*. Hoshi's dream did not become a reality under the name of the *Kenseitō*, but the year after his speech, in 1900, with the formation of the *Rikken Seiyūkai* (henceforth *Seiyūkai*) under Itō Hirobumi as its President, it did.

Hoshi served as Minister of Communications in the *Seiyūkai* Cabinet (fourth Itō Cabinet) that he himself had constructed, but in June 1901, just after the Cabinet's resignation, he suffered an untimely death. In politics centred on public works, the smell of corrupt dealings hung about, his strong-arm tactics created an image of arrogance, and he was assassinated by a sword-wielding former samurai.

Nevertheless, the 'positive policies' laid out by Hoshi, as well as his line of maintaining one party in power (including quasi-ruling party periods) was continued by Hara Kei, and until *his* assassination in November 1921 he continued the basic approach of the *Seiyūkai*. The age of 'reorganisation', which is the central theme of this chapter, was an age in which challenges to the dominance of the *Seiyūkai* gradually came to achieve results.

The Russo-Japanese war and expectations of political reconstruction

The Russo-Japanese war as 'all-out war'

The Russo-Japanese war in 1904–5 was, in both military and financial terms, a real case of total war. In terms of the troops involved, it was small farmers, workers and the urban middle and lower classes that bore the burden, and in financial terms it was the rural landlords that supported it. So far as the 'equality of the four classes' proclaimed after the Meiji Restoration was concerned, the only part of it that became a reality was 'equality of military service', so that the more than 250,000 men who fought in the war were distributed 'equally' among the various classes of the Japanese people.

On the other hand, since the great majority of taxpayers were rural landlords, while the immediate war expenses were paid by means of domestic and foreign loans of 1,700,000,000 yen, both the capital and interest had to be paid back mainly through the efforts of rural landlords. If we were talking about the Japanese people at the time this chapter is being written (2011), it would be easy to understand that without increasing taxation, raising domestic and foreign loans would be problematic. By special taxes raised twice during the Russo-Japanese war, the land tax rose to 1.8 times what it had been before the war, or in money terms, by 38 million yen. As might be expected, income tax and business tax were both increased, so that taken together, it is clear that the increased revenue from these taxes amounted to over 25 million yen, and it was the rise in land tax that was the biggest.

On the one hand, small farmers, workers and the urban middle and lower classes, being politically powerless, were conscripted and sent to the battlefield, while on the other hand, the rural landlords, who before the war had been almost the only source of tax revenue, experienced an 80 per cent increase in their tax burden.

Reorganisation, 1894–1924   137

If the first of these, once the war was over, demanded political equality commensurate with their equality as servicemen, control of the House of Representatives by the *Seiyūkai*, which had been supported by rural landlords, suffered a blow (with the lowering in 1900 of the tax qualification for voting in the election law revision, the bulk of voters were still rural landlords). On the other hand, if rural landlords, who once again had been made to carry the bulk of tax increase, resolved not to be bamboozled by 'positive policies' and the like, the dominant position of the *Seiyūkai* in the House of Representatives would quickly collapse, without waiting for universal suffrage to be introduced.

Universal suffrage argument of Kita Ikki

It was Kita Ikki, later to be notorious as a fascist, who in his youth fostered expectations in relation to universal suffrage. In 1906, the year following the

Table 5.2

Year	Meiji era year	Prime Minister	Events
1902	35	Katsura	Anglo-Japanese Alliance concluded.
1903	36		Saionji becomes *Seiyūkai* President. Kōtoku Shūsui, Sakai Toshihiko and others begin to publish *Heimin Shinbun*.
1904	37		Russo-Japanese war (to 1905). First Japan–Korea Agreement.
1905	38		Treaty of Portsmouth (peace treaty between Japan and Russia). Hibiya arson incident. Second Japan–Korea Agreement (establishment of the prototype of the Japanese Governor-General's office in Korea).
1906	39	Saionji	Japan Socialist Party Founded. Railway nationalisation. South Manchuria Raiway Co. founded (*Mantetsu*).
1907	40		Post-war depression. Imperial Defence Policy. Incident of a Korean secret agent at the Hague. Third Japan–Korea Agreement.
1908	41	Katsura	Boshin Imperial Edict.
1909	42		Itō Hirobumi assassinated at Harbin.
1910	43		*Rikken Kokumintō* founded (Inukai Tsuyoshi). Great Treason Incident. Incorporation of Korea into Japan, establishment of Governor-General's office in Korea (Terauchi Masatake Governor-General).
1911	44	Saionji	Restoration of tariff autonomy. Factory law promulgated. Chinese revolution of 1911.
1912	Taishō 1	Katsura	Republic of China founded. Death of Meiji Emperor. *Yūaikai* founded. Army Minister Uehara Yūsaku resigns following rejection of bill to form two army divisions (resignation of Saionji Cabinet, establishment of new Katsura Cabinet). Taishō Political Change (first constitutional protection movement – to 1913).

138 *Japan's Modern History*

Russo-Japanese war, he published at his own expense when he was only 23 years old *Kokutai ron to junsei shakaishugi* ('The National Polity and True Socialism'), which was promptly banned. In it he wrote:

> Our patriots must reply! You, as a part of the Japanese nation, have devoted yourselves with a smile to other parts of the nation in a struggle for existence. . . . When our 40 million compatriots are summoned for the cause of our country, our 40 million compatriots are indeed our country, for it is entirely unacceptable that we should consider two or three nobles or a minority class alone as the totality of the State. . . . Since being a democratic country means being the State for everybody, you our compatriots were called upon to make sacrifices in the name of patriotism. But the duty of making sacrifices means the right of all to determine goals. . . . When the people, aroused from their sleep to the voice of [the State], are returning triumphantly in blood-soaked uniform from the fields of Manchuria, and while welcoming the attacking forces are being prepared to join those very forces, can the ruling class still say that universal suffrage is too early?
>
> (Kita Ikki, *Kita Ikki chosakushū* ['Collected Works of Kita Ikki'],
> Misuzu Shobō, 1959, vol. 1, pp. 391–2)

What the 23-year-old Kita Ikki expected was that the Russo-Japanese war, being total war, entailed the duty to perform military service and also the right to participate in the affairs of state.

With the surrender of their swords by the former samurai, Kita in the second decade of Meiji (1877–87) advocated establishing a parliament, and criticised the successors of the former popular parties which had once criticised the *hanbatsu* government for its slowness in establishing a parliament. The successors (*Seiyūkai* and *Shinpotō*) to the *Jiyūtō* and *Kaishintō*, like the former *hanbatsu government*, are now rejecting universal suffrage by repeating the same word 'premature'.

> Those who were annoyed by the way the *hanbatsu* government said that the Diet was premature now proclaim that it is premature to introduce universal suffrage. Thus neither the *Seiyūkai* nor the *Shinpotō* retain the idea of democracy they held in the past. They accept the nostrums of the economic aristocracy, pay homage to the aristocrats of the *hanbatsu* and the House of Peers, and are becoming slaves.
>
> (Ibid., p. 392)

According to Matsuo Takayoshi, the pioneering researcher of the universal suffrage movement that developed from around the time of the Russo-Japanese war and through the Taishō period, advocates of universal suffrage were not confined to Kita Ikki. (Matsuo Takayoshi, *Taishō demokurashii* ['Taisho Democracy'], Iwanami Shoten, 1974). Among socialists opposed to the war (anti-war activists), and among nationalists who supported the war, were to be found numbers of those who, like Kita, linked military service with universal suffrage. If I may quote once

Reorganisation, 1894–1924 139

again from the same book, the Socialist Arahata Kanson set out his thoughts as follows:

> I made clear my position of opposition to war and support for a peace, but the government has been ignoring the will of the people both at the beginning of the war and during it, but if the people were to obtain universal suffrage and participate in national politics, it would needs obtain the right to decide between peace or war by its own will. When I explained this, I received applause indicating agreement with my position.
>
> (Matsuo, p. 32)

Matsuo, who as another example like Kita on the pro-war side linked 'military service' with 'universal suffrage', quotes the following passage by Kuga Katsunan in the journal *Nippon*:

> The people, who bear the tax burden, have the right to consult about expenditure, and herein lies the principle of constitutional government. The people, who bear the burden of military service, surprisingly do not have the right to consult about war.
>
> (Ibid., p. 14)

Mass movement without advocacy of universal suffrage: the movement against the peace settlement in the Russo-Japanese war

The linking together of 'equality of military service' and 'equality of suffrage' was not the principal aim of the mass movement following the end of the Russo-Japanese war. The greatest common denominator was opposition to giving Russia a peace without compensation, and the individual interests of the crowds of over 50,000 that participated in the movement (the number of participants in the Hibiya arson Incident alone is said to have amounted to 30,000) were literally uncountable. Matsuo writes as follows about the diversity of participants in the following terms:

> Impoverished classes who had been deprived of their land and had departed for the cities. Craftsmen who had entered a process of dissolution. The modern working class which was now on the eve of class consolidation. The urban new middle class of salaried personnel and others who along with proletarian classes feared heavy taxation and inflation. Small and medium commercial and industrial classes having strong pre-modern characteristics and prevented from accumulating capital by business tax and other onerous taxes, in conflict with big businesses receiving special benefits from government (capitalists not in receipt of special rights). Newspapers as advocates of the dissatisfaction felt by these various urban popular classes, and progressive anti-*hanbatsu* political groups excluded from the framework of established political parties, consisting of politicians, journalists, lawyers, businessmen

140 *Japan's Modern History*

and others. What these elements suddenly revealed in history was a movement against the peace settlement, and it became the starting point for the next generation.

(Ibid., pp. 35–6)

According to Matsuo, this movement against the terms of the Russo-Japanese war peace settlement lasted for a whole month, from 5th September, when it was signed, to 4th October when the peace treaty was ratified by the Privy Council.

Given the generation of the present writer, a popular mass movement of diverse composition, lasting a month between treaty signature and treaty ratification, bears comparison with the movement opposed to the revised Japan–US Security Treaty, between 19th May and 18th June 1960. The revised Security Treaty was forced through the House of Representatives by the Kishi Cabinet, which brought mobile police into the House, and one month later, at midnight on 19th June, in accordance with the Constitution, it automatically passed the House of Councillors without that House being in session. Fifty years later, I can still feel the sense of frustration of that night, in which the revised treaty was automatically passed, when 100,000 or perhaps 200,000 students were surrounding the Diet building, in pitch darkness with not a single Diet member present.

Whether it is the Russo-Japanese Peace Treaty, or the Security Treaty, a popular movement opposed to the treaty continues to grow up to the day of ratification, and then on that day it disappears like a puff of smoke. On 4th October 1905, this multifarious mass movement suddenly evaporated, and the age of the *Rikken Seiyūkai*, a conservative party with its base of support among the rural landlords, had arrived.

The development of this kind of situation was very different from Kita Ikki's appeal, when he considered the parliamentary progress of the German Social Democratic Party, to move from 'equality of military service' to 'equality of suffrage', and 'nationalisation of landlord assets, leading towards a socialist economy' (*Kita Ikki Chosakushū*, vol. 1, p. 377) The variegated and diverse forces that were outside the two major groupings of *hanbatsu* officials and rural landlords, after organising a unified movement against the uncompensated peace settlement with Russia, fragmented according to the individual class interests involved.

Hara Kei's line of reconciling officials and politicians

Regarding in a one-eyed fashion the popular movement external to the governing regime, Hara Kei, who succeeded Hoshi Tōru as leader of the *Seiyūkai*, strengthened his alliance with Katsura Tarō, who had been in charge of the government as a representative of the *hanbatsu* bureaucracy, and furthermore, he engineered a smooth transfer of power from Katsura to the *Seiyūkai*.

Hara, right in the middle of the Russo-Japanese war, expected a popular movement after the peace settlement, and on the condition that the *Seiyūkai*, a large party, should not participate, he persuaded Katsura, the Prime Minister, to admit the *Seiyūkai* as one of the governing groups. At the meeting on 6th April 1905, the two of them expressed themselves as follows:

> Hara Kei: "Suspending the war on any conditions will not satisfy the majority of the people. In this case unless we go in for a coalition with the government, the *Seiyūkai* will have no choice but to listen to the voice of the people. But for the State, this course of action would be unfavourable."
> Katsura Tarō: "Certainly, if we win peace, the people will be dissatisfied with the conditions of it. I am ready to sacrifice myself. I should like to withdraw at the time of the proposal for post-war management. At that time I promise you to pay homage to Saionji (*Seiyūkai* President)."
>
> (*Hara Kei nikki*, vol. 2, p. 131)

The agreement between the Prime Minister, Katsura, and Hara Kei, did not simply amount to a transfer of power from the bureaucratic clique to the *Seiyūkai*. Even after Itō Hirobumi, who was one pole of the *hanbatsu* forces, was embraced as President of the *Seiyūkai*, the military, the bureaucrats, the House of Peers and others did not coordinate their activities with Itō, but they treated Yamagata Aritomo, Elder Statesman from Chōshū and having equal status to that of Itō, with great respect as their commander (this represented the formation of the Yamagata clique). Between the *Hanbatsu* forces and the leading party in the House of Representatives, unity proved impossible with the creation of the *Seiyūkai*.

After the Russo-Japanese war, the enormous expenses for which were met both by domestic and foreign loans and by emergency tax rises, but for which no reparations were forthcoming, with the Yamagata clique controlling the military and the bureaucracy and the *Seiyūkai* controlling the House of Representatives, politics was destabilised. In addition, outside these two ruling forces, as had been symbolised by the Hibiya arson incident, the discontent of myriad small business interests unrelated to the rural landlords was manifest. Between the two major forces of the Yamagata clique and the *Seiyūkai*, however the issue was regarded, construction of medium-to-long-term relations of cooperation was essential. On 17th September, when the movement against the peace settlement went nationwide, Hara Kei, meeting with Itō Hirobumi, now former President of the *Seiyūkai*, spoke as follows:

> The present political situation is divided into the *Shinpotō* (*Kenseihontō*), our *Seiyūkai* and the *hanbatsu*, these two parties are unable on their own to sustain the cabinet, while the *hanbatsu* is from now on unable to govern while excluding these two parties. But if among these three elements two of them were to agree, it would be possible to manage the affairs of State. For if the *Seiyūkai* and the present rulers (Yamagata clique) were to forge a cooperative regime, this could contribute greatly to the future path of our country.
>
> (Ibid., p. 149)

142 *Japan's Modern History*

Arrival of the Katsura-Saionji era

On the one hand, while there was a demand to transfer power from Katsura Tarō to Saionji Kinmochi, on the other hand, if it were a case of "creating a cooperative regime between the *Seiyūkai* and the present ruling faction", only one answer was possible. That answer was rotation of office. If the *Seiyūkai* came to power, Katsura, in charge of the military, the bureaucracy and the House of Peers, would cooperate from outside Cabinet. By contrast, when Katsura took power, Saionji, who was in charge of the *Seiyūkai* as its President, together with Hara Kei, would support the Cabinet in the House of Representatives.

In the political world, it is rare for a scenario drawn up by the practitioners themselves to function over the long term. But over the seven years from the ending of the Russo-Japanese war in 1905 to the transition from the Meiji to the Taishō era in 1912, politics was essentially conducted according to this scenario. Tokutomi Sohō, who aimed, as an associate of Katsura, to break away from this cosy back-scratching regime, in his book *Taishō seikyoku shiron* ('History of the Taishō era Political Situation'), 1916, described the period in the following terms:

> In the ten years between 1903 and 1912, it is no exaggeration to say that Japan was the country of Katsura and Saionji. When Katsura formed a cabinet, Saionji, heading the *Seiyūkai*, gave backing to it from the House of Representatives, and when Saionji formed a cabinet, Katsura, together with the bulk of those we should call his companions in the House of Peers, gave it support. Thus, it could be expected that, when Katsura went, Saionji would inevitably come, and when Saionji went, Katsura would inevitably come. . . . In this way ten years of political peace were maintained.
>
> Even so, if this family-like mechanism is supposed to work as the norm according to this programme, there will be no difficulty in the world. Surely, if things are like this, there will be nothing easier than politics . . . and politics will become the domain of the frivolous and idle.
>
> (Ibid., p. 6)

Moreover, since there were important differences in financial and economic policy between these two forces, cooperation between them was not as stable as Tokutomi made out. Among the government officials gathered under Katsura's wing, there were many who favoured efficient financial management and were critical of the 'positive policies' of the *Seiyūkai*, which in contemporary language would be labelled 'pork barrel'.

Even so, the electorate, which had increased after the Russo-Japanese war by 1,500,000, were in the majority still rural landlords.

With the revision of the electoral law in 1900, the tax qualification was lowered from a minimum of 15 yen, paid in direct taxation, to 10 yen, and the number of electors rose to about one million, then as the result of emergency taxation during the Russo-Japanese war those paying at least 10 yen increased, and as a result the number of electors rose to 1,500,000. Compared with the first general election, the electorate had increased threefold.

Since, however, as we have noted above, the proportion of rural landlords remained as before overwhelmingly high, even though the electorate had risen in number from 500,000 to 1,500,000, the great majority of them were still rural landlords. All that had happened was that the proportion of small and medium landlords had increased.

Landlords permissive towards taxation increase

Because with the special emergency tax, land tax had doubled, it would not be unnatural for the post-war landlords to demand a reduction in taxation rather than expansion of local public works, and to be alienated from the *Seiyūkai*. But as we have repeatedly stated, when nominal tax increases are compared with increases in the price of rice, it will be seen that the two cancel out. Since the rice price, which was 12 yen per *koku* before the Russo-Japanese war, had become 15 yen after the war, even if this did not cancel out the burden of land tax, which in fact had increased with the special emergency tax, had not increased twofold, but by 1.6 times. The rate of rice price increases, if we exclude 1909 and 1910, was consistent, so that in the final year of Meiji (1912), the real tax increase was no more than 1.2 times. The rural landlords, compensating for a modest rise in land tax, were able to rest their expectations on the 'positive policies' of the *Seiyūkai*.

The 'positive policies' of the *Seiyūkai* were brought out in the promulgation of railway nationalisation law of the first Saionji (*Seiyūkai*) Cabinet. In the first Diet session that the Cabinet experienced at the outset of 1906, a bill was promulgated for the State to buy up 17 private railways using public loans as capital.

The idea that as the result of nationalising private railways on grounds of poor management, there would right away be more trains on local railways, was incorrect. But when the *Seiyūkai* took over the government, and controlled the posts of Communications Minister and Railway Authority President, it was a different story. Which of the former private railways, now nationalised, would be given developmental priority, came to be linked directly with the interests of each region.

Given rice price increases and railway nationalisation, the *Seiyūkai* in both the 1908 and 1912 general elections overwhelmed the other parties. In the seven years between the end of the Russo-Japanese war and the final year of Meiji (1912), the *Seiyūkai* was in power for less than three years, and during the other four years it was the Yamagata clique of Katsura Tarō that controlled the cabinet. But the only two general elections in this period both occurred under a *Seiyūkai* cabinet. Going into an election as the party in power for the first time imparted persuasive power to 'positive policies' of development.

The Achilles heel of the 'regime combining bureaucracy and party'

Nevertheless, in the context of this political control by the *Seiyūkai* through its semi-permanent ruling party status and by 'positive policies', three land mines lay concealed.

144 *Japan's Modern History*

The first of these was the repeat of the Hibiya arson incident. As I have already explained, the class composition and occupations of those, exceeding 100,000 in number, who participated in this popular movement were multifarious, but the common characteristic of all the participants was disillusion with both the *hanbatsu* and the *Seiyūkai*. When we look for the one common slogan of this popular movement, replacing "oppose a peace settlement without compensation", we find that its energy had the potential even to destroy the system of cooperation between the *hanbatsu* and the *Seiyūkai*. The movement that occurred in 1912 and 1913 proclaiming "Get rid of the bureaucratic clique, defend the Constitution" (the first Constitution defence movement) had just such potential. I shall investigate this movement in the next section.

The second land mine was the alienation of the rural landlords. I earlier explained that the price of rice continued to rise following the Russo-Japanese war, except for the years 1909 and 1910. Putting it differently, over just those two years, the rice price fell by 20 per cent.

With the rice price falling, the burden of the emergency special tax that continued after the war was acutely felt by the rural landlords. When the second year of falling rice prices began, demands for a reduction in land tax intensified, and not only within the opposition *Kenseihontō*, but also within the *Seiyūkai*, the government party, calls for land tax to be reduced made themselves felt, while the second Katsura Cabinet was forced to accept a 14 per cent decrease in the tax.

For two reasons, this engendered a split in the cooperative relations between the bureaucratic clique and the *Seiyūkai*.

The first split was brought about by an attack on the *Seiyūkai* by urban businessmen. On the occasion of the post-war financial panic at the end of 1907, they put pressure on the *Seiyūkai* to resuscitate the financial system and to reduce business tax. The Alliance of Chambers of Commerce, a blanket organisation of small and medium enterprises, held an extraordinary general congress in January 1908, and while opposing the Saionji Cabinet's increases in indirect taxation and introduction of new taxes (tax on *saké*, sugar consumption tax, oil consumption tax), it made a proposal to the government demanding total abolition of the consumption tax on textiles, and an easing of business tax – matters that affected its own interests. This was the expression of dissatisfaction on the part of urban businessmen towards the Seiyūkai, which was only representing the interests of rural landlords.

Such dissatisfaction on the part of urban businessmen was later to strengthen with the aforementioned 14 per cent reduction in land tax (the land tax rate went from 5.5 per cent to 4.7 per cent [an 8 rin reduction]), and even within the *Seiyūkai* there were now those who paid attention to urban trends.

This situation made the bureaucratic clique, which was forced to cooperate with the *Seiyūkai*, consider options different from this.

The second split came to the surface over its flagship policies. Matsuda Masahisa, a *Seiyūkai* leader alongside Hara Kei, was becoming critical of 'positive policies' of development. The farmers were increasing their tax reduction demands, while in opposition to them the demands of urban businessmen for reduction of

Reorganisation, 1894–1924 145

business tax was also rising, and in the midst of this even the *Seiyūkai* was becoming unable to solve its internal problems simply by expanding public works.

The strengthening of demands both from farmers and from businessmen to reduce taxation led the *Seiyūkai* to rethink its approach of remaining semipermanently in government. If it emphasised expansion of public works, the party would have further to entrench its policies of railway network expansion and other public works. But if it placed the emphasis on tax reduction – whether of land tax or business tax – it would need to discover new flagship policies to replace positive developmental policies. It goes without saying that policies accompanying tax reduction would have to involve administrative retrenchment and control of expenditure, or in a word 'negativism'. The second Saionji Cabinet of the *Seiyūkai*, inaugurated at the end of August 1911, reveals the conversion of that party from positive to negative policies, and this also reveals the decline in influence of Hara Kei within his party.

Desire for military build-up continuing to increase

The third land mine was the demand for a military build-up on the part of the Army and Navy, buoyed by their victory in war. In the military expansion that took place after the Sino-Japanese war, there was the factor of Russia, Japan's real rival for control over Korea, but also revenues from the 330,000,000 yen in reparations. By contrast, the military build-up after the Russo-Japanese war was not motivated by a serious external threat, and internally there was no unusual income coming in from reparations, but rather it developed out of an abstract goal of becoming a major military power ranking alongside the major powers of Europe and America. This was graphically indicated in the 'Imperial Defence Policy' issued in April 1907 by the use of the term "hypothetical enemy", in the phrase "The defence of the Empire [requires] preparation against hypothetical enemies, which may be ranked in the order: Russia, America, France" (Kadota Jun, *Manshū mondai to kokubō hōshin* ['The Manchurian Question and National Defence Policy'], Hara Shobō, 1967, p. 705).

To call Russia, defeated a mere year and a half earlier, a 'hypothetical enemy' was fairly reckless, but to call America a hypothetical enemy after it had brokered peace with Russia was an extraordinary statement going beyond recklessness. Naturally, while the Army saw Russia as a hypothetical enemy, the Navy saw America similarly.

What was being celebrated in this defence policy that, with no apparent basis, was directed against 'hypothetical enemies' was the Army build-up to eight divisions, and the continental naval expansion including the construction of 12 warships and 8 cruisers, which together with 4 warships already under construction, added up to 16 warships and 8 cruisers, or a fleet of 8 – 8 – 8 (ibid., p. 717).

Under this medium-term plan, the cost of the Army and Navy, following the Russo-Japanese war, increased from around 100,000,000 yen before the war to around 200,000,000 yen after it. To what point the people would tolerate the burden of military expenditure, and when toleration had reached its limit whether

146   *Japan's Modern History*

conflict between the Army and Navy over military expansion priorities could be overcome, was our third land mine.

The Taishō political change

Eruption of demands for pluralism

During the final year of the Meiji era (1912), the three land mines of which we have spoken had arrived nearly at the point of explosion. Rural landlords were divided into a railway faction and a tax-cutting faction, and in addition to cutting taxation impacting on rural landlords, city businessmen and middle-to-lower classes concerned about indirect taxation were building up their criticism of the *Seiyūkai*. The Army, which had already succeeded in increasing its strength to six divisions between the wartime and the post-war period, in 1910 on the occasion of the assimilation of Korea pressed home its demand for an extra two divisions, namely the remaining two divisions expected to be stationed in the new colony. Meanwhile the Navy, taking advantage of the formation of the second Saionji *Seiyūkai* Cabinet in 1911, pressed for acceptance of immediate vessel construction costs, followed by an eight-year shipbuilding programme, totalling 370,000,000 yen. A general magazine of the period evaluated as follows the divisive situation of these demands that were impossible to manage:

> Speaking frankly, I am amazed at the selfishness of present day society. All 60 million Japanese surely understand the difficult state of Imperial finances. . . . But recognising the parlous state of the finances, officials are each struggling to develop their own projects. At the moment the Army strongly demands an increase in the number of its divisions, while the Navy demands that more ships be built. If we think that bankers demand repayment of national debt, businessmen demand revival of their enterprises, and if we think that the people demand reduction of their tax burden, the bulk of the people's representatives (*Seiyūkai*) are concerned with local issues of advantage, thus they are hoping for new railways, or they demand new works in harbours and rivers. While understanding that it is impossible to achieve their demands simultaneously, everyone hopes for impossible projects. This is the present situation.
>
> (*Nihon oyobi Nihonjin*, 15th November 1911, p. 7)

At that time, the day magazines were on sale was earlier than the official day of publication, so readers of this magazine would have seen it around 10th November. Less than a month later, on 5th December, the unilateral resignation of the Army Minister Uehara Yūsaku, who was demanding an increase in two divisions for Korea, forced the resignation of the second Saionji Cabinet. This precipitated the 'Taishō political change', and the beginning of the first constitutional defence movement.

Rights of Manchuria and Mongolia and increase of two divisions for the Army

As is clear from the magazine article of the time cited above, the 'Taishō political change' took place with overlapping conflicts of interest between the Army, the Navy, the *Seiyūkai*, the financial world and the business world, as well as middle and lower classes in the cities. Just with cooperation between the *hanbatsu* forces, which controlled the Army, the bureaucracy and the House of Peers, and the *Seiyūkai*, proclaiming 'positive policies' and friendly to the rural landlords, it had become impossible to coordinate these various interests. The age of 'reorganisation', which gives this chapter its title, had at last begun.

And yet, the outset of the affair lay in the insistence of the Army that it should have two extra divisions. The remote cause of this insistence was the Imperial Defence Policy of 1907, mentioned above, and the proximate cause was the assimilation of Korea in 1910 and the Chinese revolution the following year.

As we have already explained, the 'Imperial Defence Policy' had dubbed Russia a 'hypothetical enemy' shortly after defeating that country, but in a 'personal proposal' put out by the *genrō* Yamagata Aritomo in 1906, the other hypothetical enemy, second only to Russia, was not France or Germany, but China. In his words:

> In our strategic plan, the State we regard as the principal enemy is Russia, but whereas it is not necessary to prepare against other great European powers as our enemies, we must never forget the existence of China as an enemy secondary only to Russia.
>
> (*Yamagata Aritomo ikensho* ['Statements of Opinion by Yamagata Aritomo'], Hara Shobō, 1966, p. 294)

The idea of preparing against revengeful action by Russia and China, both of which Japan had defeated, has a certain persuasive power. But for Japan, which had been victorious in the war against Russia, it would have hardly been possible for China, defeated by Japan ten years earlier, to attempt retaliation, and this 'personal opinion' was submitted to the Emperor just one year after Japan's victory over Russia. In this situation, it seems hard to believe that to call for preparations against retaliation from Russia was a carefully thought-out position.

From a different point of view, however, when we consider that Japan, rather than fearing retaliation from Russia and China, was aiming to expand both militarily and politically into the sphere of influence and border areas of those two countries, the attitudes of the Japanese Army shown in the Imperial Defence Policy, the assimilation of Korea, the Japanese plan to use the 1911 revolution in China to make Manchuria and Mongolia independent, and the 21 demands to China in 1915 showed remarkable consistency. 'Hypothetical enemies' in the Imperial Defence Policy meant that Russia and China were likely to resist Japanese policies towards Korea and Manchuria.

When we look at the matter from this point of view, the reason that the Japanese Army made the government act to make Korea officially a colony becomes clear.

148 *Japan's Modern History*

But if the purpose was only to make Korea a dependency of Japan, victory in the Sino-Japanese and Russo-Japanese wars should have been sufficient. China and Russia, after all, possessed neither the strength nor the will to interfere in Japanese control of the Korean peninsula. Now that the beginning of the twentieth century had been reached, it was difficult to find a rational reason to become an Empire in possession of colonies. But if the Japanese Army's goal was the southern part of Manchuria, contiguous with the Korean peninsula, it was necessary for them to make Korea into a full colony.

In addition, in 1911, revolution took place in China, proclaiming 'expel Manchurians, support the Han Chinese', and in February 1912 the Qing (Ch'ing) dynasty disappeared. Manchurian control over the Chinese people ended, and at a time when the Army judged that the new Chinese regime would not seriously oppose Japan's incursion into Manchuria, its demand that two divisions should be stationed in Korea became stronger.

The first constitutional support movement

As is clear, however, from the previously cited article in *Nihon oyobi Nihonjin*, in Japan at that time forces other than the Army were each raising their voices to demand that their respective demands be met. Since, at a time like this, the Army insisting on its arms expansion policies made the Army Minister resign and thus overthrew the Saionji Cabinet, several other groups found a rallying point in criticising the Army. This was the emergence of the constitutional support movement.

The Army Minister insisted on two extra divisions, and the second Saionji Cabinet was forced to resign, so that when the third Cabinet of Katsura Tarō was formed (5–17th December 1912), the Hibiya arson incident that had occurred just after the Russo-Japanese war was repeated.

The movement that had taken place seven years previously opposed the peace settlement with Russia devoid of any compensation, but its slogans were: 'Overthrow the clique of bureaucrats, support the constitutional system.' It was very different in flavour from either a nationalistic mass movement or a democratic movement, but its participants and the ways of operating were surprisingly similar. It supported those Diet members of the *Seiyūkai* and the *Kokumintō* (successor to the *Kenseihontō*) who were trying to bring about a motion of no-confidence in the Katsura Government, and a large crowd surrounded the Diet building. When Katsura ordered a three-day suspension of the session, the crowd threw rocks at the newspaper companies supporting the Katsura Cabinet, and at police boxes within the city of Tokyo, and also set fire to them. The bulk of those who were arrested by the Police Department were from various occupations in Tokyo city (*sushi* makers, pawnbrokers, innkeepers, *sake* shop owners, carpenters and so on), and many of them were 17- and 18-year-old adolescents. This brings to mind the anti-peace settlement of seven years earlier (Yamamoto Shirō, *Taishō seihen no kisoteki kenkyū* ['Basic Research on the Taishō Political Change'], Ochanomizu Shobō, 1970, pp. 599–602).

Reorganisation, 1894–1924   149

These city businessmen gave blanket support to the Saionji Cabinet which, through administrative retrenchment, was combating Army expansion. Moreover, influential newspaper and magazine journalists, except for four companies – *Kokumin*, *Yamato*, *Yomiuri* and *Niroku* (newspapers) – formed a National Journalists Alliance, which made the case for getting rid of the bureaucratic clique.

Negative aspects of **Seiyūkai** *participation*

In this movement, which on so many points was reminiscent of the earlier anti-peace settlement movement, the one difference was the participation of the *Seiyūkai*. In the September 1905 movement, under the leadership of Saionji and Hara, the *Seiyūkai* turned its back on the mass movement and maintained a position of support for the peace settlement. The clique of bureaucrats and the constitutionalists joined forces to shut out the opposition parties and the mass movement.

By contrast, in 1912 and 1913, because the *Seiyūkai* participated in the movement, the bureaucratic clique and the constitutionalists were diametrically opposed to each other. Together with Inukai Tsuyoshi of the opposition *Kokumintō*, Ozaki Yukio of the *Seiyūkai* (party in power), seen as the God of constitutionalism, attracted the respect of the masses. This difference meant that there was both an internal and an external movement, which doubled its efficacy. Large numbers of people massed externally to support a motion of no-confidence in the Katsura Cabinet which the House of Representatives aspired to pass. For instance, on the day before 10th February 1913, when the no-confidence motion was put, there were said to be 20,000 participants in a speech meeting organised at the National Sports Hall in Ryōgoku by the *Seiyūkai* and the *Kokumintō*.

There was, however, a negative aspect to the participation of the *Seiyūkai*, in that the radical nature of the movement was attenuated. Over the seven years until Uehara unilaterally resigned as Minister of Defence, the *Seiyūkai* was proclaiming 'positive policies' of development and continued to cooperate with the bureaucratic clique. It may even be said that the principal culprit for the financial crisis in 1912 was the public works spending of the *Seiyūkai* rather than actions of the Army. Hara Kei, who served both as Minister of Home Affairs and as President of the Railway Bureau in the second Saionji Cabinet, wrote in his diary:

> I have exchanged opinions with the Prime Minister at the Cabinet meeting over railway building improvement. My main point is that if three or four hundred million yen from foreign loans are spent over a ten-year period, the main lines of our railways can be built, and necessary improvements can be made, thus Japan's transport institutions will be able to earn a rest.
>
> (25th October 1912)

The redemption of foreign loans taken out during the Russo-Japanese war exceeded in total 600 million yen in 1912. In addition, there was the intention to raise an extra 300 or 400 million in a foreign loan for the railways. One reason for

150   *Japan's Modern History*

the worsening of the balance of payments in 1912 (in the five years to 1911 this meant an outflow of specie amounting to 1,000 million yen) and for the worsening of the financial situation, was the positive policies of the *Seiyūkai*.

The *Seiyūkai*, which for years had alternated in power with Katsura Tarō who represented the 'bureaucratic clique', indeed this same Seiyūkai that should have borne responsibility for the worsening of financial conditions as much as the Army and the Navy, changed overnight into promoters of the slogan "overthrow the bureaucratic clique, defend constitutionalism". The fact that what needed to be reformed had come about as the result of the very movement that now stood at the head of the reform agenda meant that what could be done was limited from the outset.

The fact that the *Seiyūkai* was now in the van of the 'anti-bureaucracy' movement dealt a blow to the opposition *Kenseihontō*, which aspired to replace the *Seiyūkai* in power. The mainstream of that party, known as the 'reform faction' and exhibiting a strong ambition for power, just as the *Jiyūtō* had amalgamated with the *hanbatsu* to form the *Seiyūkai*, hastened to join the New Party (later *Rikken Dōshikai*) of the bureaucratic Katsura Tarō, which was becoming the focus of national criticism.

Without being able to overthrow the 'bureaucratic clique' and take over from the *Seiyūkai*, its policy of joining with the bureaucrats and attacking the *Seiyūkai* was unlikely to succeed right in the middle of the constitutional defence movement, so that this group was forced to remain in obscurity for nearly a year.

Short lifespan of the constitutional defence movement

Whether it was the *Seiyūkai*, whether it was Katsura's bureaucratic New Party, or whether it was opinion leaders wishing to 'overthrow the bureaucrats and defend the Constitution', none of them was able to reform the Diet in any fundamental way. Nobody was advocating universal suffrage to increase the electorate from less than 1,500,000 to 12,000,000. It is worth noting that in his previously cited *Taishō Democracy*, Matsuo Takayoshi touched on the universal suffrage argument put forward by Miura Tetsutarō, published in *Tōyō Keizai Shinpō* ('Eastern Economic News'):

> What is generally advanced as means of reforming the system to bring about 'defence of the Constitution and overthrow of the bureaucratic clique' is revision of the requirement for the service ministers to be military officers, and of the civilian officials employment law, but there is very little reference to electoral rights, and when it comes to universal suffrage, so far as I have checked, none except what the *Shinpō* has referred to.
> (Matsuo Takayoshi, *Taishō Demokurashii* ['Taisho Democracy'],
> Iwanami Shoten, 1974, p. 85)

The 'Age of Reorganisation', which gives this chapter its title, consisted of a combination of universal suffrage, meaning 'equality' of political representation,

Reorganisation, 1894–1924   151

and a political system based on two major parties. Of these, it was only the *Tōyō Keizai Shinpō* that advocated universal suffrage.

So what about the question of freedom of political choice? As already mentioned, a desire to take over the government in place of the *Seiyūkai* existed within the mainstream of the *Kokumintō*. Even so, the *Rikken Dōshikai* that they founded had Katsura Tarō, the target of the slogan "overthrow the bureaucratic clique", as its President, and for the time being no possibility existed of winning against the *Seiyūkai* in a general election. In the political movements of the early Taishō years (1912–13), which may be called the 'Taishō political change' or the 'first constitutional defence movement', the curtain had yet to be raised for the 'Age of Reorganisation'.

Emergence of *Minponshugi*

A Navy cabinet and the Siemens Incident

The first constitutional defence movement subsided after two months without realising any of its goals. In place of Katsura Tarō, who represented the Army from the Chōshū domain, Yamamoto Gonbei, boss of the Navy and from the Satsuma domain, took over the government, and the *Seiyūkai*, out of power for a mere two months, once again returned to its position of party in power.

The Yamamoto Government, formed in February 1913, meant the return of the second Saionji Cabinet, which had been overthrown by the Army three months earlier. With the exception of the Prime Minister, Foreign Minister, Army Minister and Navy Minister, all cabinet ministers were chosen from the *Seiyūkai*, and moreover Hara Kei, who had made his party a long-term ruling party by policies of expanding public works, returned to the Cabinet as Minister of Home Affairs, being the third President of the party. In addition, from this time on, Takahashi Korekiyo, who as a financial pro supported Hara's positive policies of development, was appointed Minister of Finance.

The return of the political world to its previous situation corresponded with the retreat of the mass movement. The journal *Nihon oyobi Nihonjin* ('Japan and the Japanese') regretted the over-rapid decline of the movement in the following terms: "Has the people's voice, defending the Constitution and overthrowing the *hanbatsu*, gone silent? Why ever have those who were previously so passionate now become like a flame that sputters and is extinguished?" (*Nihon oyobi Nihonjin*, 15th March 1913).

The Yamamoto Cabinet, controlling the rural landlords through the *Seiyūkai* which commanded a majority in the House of Representatives, promised to reduce business tax by administrative retrenchment, and thus gained the support of city businessmen. In July the Tokyo Chamber of Commerce invited the Prime Minister, Yamamoto, to a luncheon party, where the President, Nakano Buei, made an enthusiastic speech of welcome.

Between the Army and the *Dōshikai*, which had made common cause with the third Katsura Cabinet, discussion took place about whether to found a new

152   Japan's Modern History

Table 5.3

Year	Taishō era year	Prime Minister	Events
1913	2	Katsura Yamamoto	First constitutional defence movement (from 1912). Prime Minister Katsura forms *Rikken Dōshikai*. Removal of requirement for service ministers to be *serving* officers. Revision of public officials employment law (path opened to employment of officials by Imperial decree).
1914	3	Ōkuma	Siemens affair. House of Peers rejects naval expansion budget, leading to Yamamoto Cabinet resignation. Kiyoura Cabinet aborted. Hara Kei becomes *Seiyūkai* President. First World War breaks out; lasts until 1918.
1915	4		Twelfth general election (*Dōshikai* becomes largest party). Twenty-one demands to China.
1916	5	Terauchi	Yoshino Sakuzō proposes *minponshugi* in his essay *Kensei no hongi o toite sono yūshū no bi o sumasu no michi o ronzu* ('Explaining the basis of the Constitution and the Way to Save its Crowning Glory'). Great War boom begins. Terauchi transcendental Cabinet established. *Kenseikai* founded (Katō Takaaki).
1917	6		13th general election (*Seiyūkai* becomes largest party). Ban on gold export. Ishii – Lansing agreement. Russian revolution.
1918	7	Hara	Siberian expedition. Rice riots. Hara Cabinet begins. *Shinjinkai* founded at Tokyo Imperial University.
1919	8		3/1 independence movement in Korea. Election law revision (3 yen or more tax qualification). 5/4 movement in China. Versailles Treaty.
1920	9		League of Nations founded; Japan joins. Demonstration movement in Tokyo for universal suffrage. Post-war depression begins. New Women Association launched. Fourteenth general election (*Seiyūkai* wins absolute majority). *Nihon Shakaishugi Dōmei* (Japan Socialist Alliance).
1921	10	Takahashi	*Yūaikai* changes its name to *Nihon Rōdō Sōdomei* Hara shot dead at Tokyo station. At Washington Conference (to 1922), Four Nation Treaty signed.
1922	11	Katō Tomosaburō	Nine-power Treaty, Naval Disarmament Treaty. National *Suiheisha* (Levellers Association), Japan Farmers Union, Communist Party (first version) founded.
1923	12	Yamamoto	Great Kantō earthquake and fire. Toranomon Incident.
1924	13	Kiyoura / Katō Kōmei	*Seiyūkai* splits. *Seiyūhontō* formed (Tokonami Takejirō). Second constitutional defence movement. Three-faction constitutional defence Cabinet (*Kenseikai, Seiyūkai, Kakushin Club*).

Reorganisation, 1894–1924 153

party, appointing as its President Ōkuma Shigenobu, who had consistently fostered parties opposed to the *Jiyūtō = Seiyūkai*. But the Yamamoto Cabinet, which was backed by both rural landlords and city businessmen, reinforced reform to strengthen control over the military and the bureaucracy (removing the requirement that the Army and Navy ministers be *serving* military generals or admirals, reforming the civilian officials employment law and broadening the scope of political employment), which brought results for what in contemporary language should be termed 'political leadership'. Until in 1914 the Navy corruption affair known as the Siemens scandal occurred, there was no room for the opposition forces to find weak points to attack this Cabinet.

The corruption affair that forced the resignation of the Yamamoto Cabinet began with the leakage of information from within the German firm of Siemens – Schukkelt, but the substantive corruption scandal was between the British firm of Vickers and the naval base in the port of Kure over the order for the cruiser *Kongō* ('Diamond'). It was discovered that Matsumoto Yawara, who had served the chief of the naval warship headquarters at the time of the Yamamoto Cabinet, had corruptly accepted 400,000 yen through Mitsui Bussan at the time when, four years previously, he had been chief of the Kure base.

The press and the urban masses, which one year earlier had made a clandestine transition from attacking the bureaucratic clique and defending constitutionalism, were unlikely to overlook corruption in the import of warships for the Imperial Navy, which they seem to have regarded as sacred. Moreover the Navy, having received the support of the *Seiyūkai*, had presented to the House of Representatives in the context of the 1914 budget a request for a supplementary 70 million yen for additional warship building, in addition to the regular 90 million yen it was receiving. It was natural that public opinion should have been angry that when the Navy was using the people's taxes to order warships and cruisers from abroad, senior naval officers should receive kickbacks from the suppliers. A crowd estimated at between 30,000 and 100,000 gathered in the vicinity of the Diet, to observe whether a petition to the Emperor for the impeachment of the Cabinet, presented by the *Rikken Dōshikai* and other opposition parties, would pass or not. Strangely enough, one year earlier on 10th February, a mass movement had overthrown the Katsura Cabinet.

The House of Peers and the mass movement

Nevertheless, Hara Kei, who as President of the *Seiyūkai* controlled a majority in the House of Representatives, and as Home Minister was in charge of the police, not only rejected in the Diet the motion for a petition to the Emperor to censure the Cabinet, proposed by the opposition parties, but violently dispersed the crowd outside the Diet.

Facing Hara, who by force of numbers and with the power of the police was prepared to leave the issue of naval corruption unresolved, stood an unexpected organisation. This was the House of Peers.

Since the formation of the Diet in 1890, the House of Peers had never overthrown a cabinet. This same House of Peers now rejected the naval budget that

154 *Japan's Modern History*

had been passed by the House of Representatives, and forced the resignation of the Yamamoto Cabinet.

It was not only the rejection of the budget by the House of Peers that was unprecedented. This was also the first time that the House of Peers, which continuously for 23 years had played a role as bulwark of *hanbatsu* governments, had acted in accordance with the expectations of the press and the people. Den Kenjirō, a member of the House of Peers, in his diary entry for 28th February, when the *Kenkyūkai* and the *Sawa Club*, being the mainstream of the House of Peers, had resolved totally to reject the 70 million yen in supplementary expenses that the House of Representatives had passed, wrote the following:

> The discovery of this naval corruption affair has suddenly exacerbated the political situation and caused anger, creating a great commotion throughout the capital, and enormous unrest in the Lower House. All the newspaper companies have banded together and the general public are terrified, while public opinion is seething beyond exaggeration. All of them look up and anticipate respectfully the attitude of the Upper House. The positions of each faction in the Upper House are now being settled, and they are about to act fair and square to wield a great axe against the government. What measures the government will deploy in response to this I am about to watch with keen interest. [The original is written in Japanese style *kanbun* (Chinese grammar).]

Since the House of Representatives and the House of Peers had come to differing conclusions concerning the budget, a council of both houses was held; but it failed to reach a compromise, so on 23rd March a plenary session of the House of Peers rejected the decision of the House of Representatives by an overwhelming majority, and the 1914 budget failed to be approved. On the 24th the Yamamoto Cabinet resigned.

Formation of the second Ōkuma Cabinet

Following the resignation of the Yamamoto Cabinet, selection of its successor by the Council of Elder Statesmen (*genrō kaigi*) proved difficult, but in the end on 13th April the Imperial Command was received by Ōkuma Shignobu to form a government.

The formation of this Cabinet heralded in three senses the coming of the 'Age of Reorganisation'.

First of all, it meant the collapse of the power of Hara Kei. Ever since Hara had succeeded Hoshi Tōru in 1901, he had consistently placed the *Seiyūkai* in the position of government party, or quasi-government party. We have repeatedly emphasised that this was assured by alternation in power between Katsura, representing the forces of the *hanbatsu*, and Saionji, President of Hara's own party. The essence of this cooperative line between the bureaucrats and the *Seiyūkai*, which at times could be termed a pseudo-two-party system, was to prevent parties other than the *Seiyūkai* from acceding to power, so that it was more like a pseudo-dominant-party system, and thus the historical forerunner of the dominance in the post-war period of the single Liberal Democratic Party.

As the result, however, of being placed on the front line of the Siemens affair as the government party of the Yamamoto government, Hara's pseudo-dominant-party system was dealt a fatal blow.

Second, corresponding to the defeat of Hara, an opposition party based on the *Rikken Dōshikai* was founded under Ōkuma Shigenobu (consolidated into the *Kenseikai* in 1916). If Hara had succeeded to the tradition of the *Jiyūtō* founded in 1881, Ōkuma had been President of the *Rikken Kaishintō*, founded the next year in 1882 in conflict with the *Jiyūtō*, and was leading the *Shinpotō*, which was its successor. In 1898 he became Prime Minister of the first party cabinet in Japanese history. As a party leader matching Hara of the *Seiyūkai*, nobody more suitable than Ōkuma actually existed. With Katō Takaaki, who became leader of the *Rikken Dōshikai* in succession to Katsura, and who a year earlier had been the butt of the slogan 'overthrow the bureaucratic clique', in terms of both his career background and his popularity he was thought to be insufficiently powerful to chase Hara's *Seiyūkai* from power.

Third, Yoshino Sakuzō, who the previous year (1913) had returned to Japan after about three years of study in Europe and America, while the second Ōkuma government was being formed, envisaged the arrival of a two-major-party system along British lines, and expressed the hope that the Cabinet would bring about universal suffrage, which he had become confident about during his stay in Europe and America.

Views of Yoshino Sakuzō on universal suffrage and a two-major-party system

It is quite unusual for a single thinker to exert a major impact on real politics. But there are cases when the power of such thought, in its content and its timing, matches that of the President of a major party.

In the full three years that he spent in Europe between June 1910 and July 1913, on the one hand, although he did not go so far as to participate in demonstrations demanding universal suffrage by socialists and radical liberals, he studied them at close quarters. He had the capacity to make comparisons with the significance and failings of the two mass movements that took place in Japan while he was abroad. Before bringing up for discussion, as an expert on Europe and America, the failings of mass movements in Japan, he first of all affirmed them. In his words: "When we take an overall view of the development of constitutional government in Japan, we see reasons for believing that the phenomenon of this kind of threatening mass movement is something to be welcomed" (Yoshino Sakuzō, *Gendai no seiji* ('Contemporary Politics'), Jitusgyō no Nihon sha, November 1915, pp. 3–4). Why it was "to be welcomed" he explained in the following way:

> As far as this is concerned, in the sense of giving to the judgement of the people final decisions on interpretation of political matters and transfer of

156 *Japan's Modern History*

political power, and also in the sense of according major political significance to the judgement of the people, I believe that this is a phenomenon to be welcomed.

(Ibid., p. 4)

This Professor of the Faculty of Law of Tokyo Imperial University expressed on a public platform the view that the emergence of a mass violent movement was "a phenomenon to be welcomed", and then made clear his goal that the people should participate in policy decision making and choice of government.

The only way of guaranteeing popular participation in policy decision making was a system of universal suffrage, and to guarantee popular participation in choice of government required a cabinet system within parliament. In *Chūō Kōron* immediately after the first Yamamoto Cabinet resigned, Yoshino argued that it was time to implement two things – universal suffrage and a cabinet system within parliament (April 1914).

This was the result of his three-year stay in Europe and America, during which he had both observed in the streets and conducted desktop research. Mr Iida Yasuzō, who has reproduced Yoshino's diary during the period he spent in Europe and America, in his commentary on it distinguished five categories of Yoshino's 'overseas study methods', but if we boil these down in a rather imprecise manner, we may divide them into the studies he conducted when out and about, and the studies he conducted at his desk.

The fact that Yoshino during his overseas study frequently went out to see what was going on is clear from his writings after his return to Japan, but his desktop study is Iida's discovery, and since it is closely linked with Yoshino's two-major-party argument that we are about to discuss, I wish to cite a key passage. Mr Iida writes as follows:

> Well, as for the fifth (study) approach, it was what we may call the efforts that he made purely on his own, obtaining information from his reading of books and newspapers, and having the experience of going out himself to places such as bookshops. In Paris he fished out books in second-hand book markets, in Leipzig bookshop Fokks and the Times bookshop in London he collected books on politics in various countries and on theories of socialism, and frequently he was so absorbed in his books that he had to treat the tiredness of his eyes by going for walks. . . . Also, apart from newspapers of the place where he was, he subscribed to the Echo and the Times as a regular reader . . . he read about long-term trends in the labour movement at various locations, and about 'emancipation'.
>
> (*Yoshino Sakuzō senshū* ['Selected Writings of Yoshino Sakuzō'], Iwanami Shoten, 1996, vol. 13, p. 435)

This extract explains why Yoshino, who had spent the greater part of his overseas study time on the European continent, and had mainly witnessed a realistic kind of socialist movement, immediately after the Siemens affair put the case, not only for universal suffrage, but also for the introduction of a two-major-party system along British lines.

Yoshino's article in *Chūō Kōron* for April 1914, entitled *Minshūteki jii undō o ronzu* ('Argument for a violent mass movement'), is well known. We should also not overlook his article in the journal *Taiyō* for May, which is a broad-based political analysis of the fall of the Yamamoto Gonbei Cabinet and the establishment of the second Ōkuma Cabinet. In this article Yoshino emphasises, not a system of cabinet within parliament in general, but the need for a two-major-party system.

In post-war Japan, the system of cabinet within parliament established in the Constitution has never been violated. But over the 54 years between 1955 and 2009, there was not a single instance of any party other than the Liberal Democratic Party winning power through a general election. A parliamentary cabinet system without transfers of power (apart from one short period) lasted for 54 years. If we think about it, it goes without saying that a parliamentary cabinet system in general and a system of two major parties are not the same thing.

In his May 1914 article in *Taiyō*, Yoshino insists that a party cabinet system will not work effectively unless there is a two-major-party system. In his words: "In order for a party cabinet system to work properly, there must be confrontation between two major parties. It is common for cabinets to be formed on a party basis where there are divisions between small parties, but unless there is confrontation between two major parties, the full potential of a party cabinet cannot be realised" (Yoshino, *Gendai no seiji* ['Contemporary Politics'], p. 71).

This conclusion does not seem to have sprung from the politics of continental Europe, where he spent most of his time abroad. In the words of Iida Taizō, interpreter of Yoshino's diaries, it was something that he derived "as one might say, purely on his own", and it was from the history and current circumstances of British politics that he arrived at this conclusion.

Yoshino's support for the Ōkuma Cabinet

It was at the time when Yoshino, with the politics of Japan before his eyes, regarded positively the transfer of power from the Yamamoto Cabinet, based on the *Seiyūkai*, to the second Ōkuma Cabinet, based on an alliance of small factions, that the real nature of the 'Age of Reorganisation' became clear.

The Ōkuma Cabinet was dogged by the image of the return of the third Katsura Cabinet that had been felled a year earlier by a mass movement. The journal *Nihon oyobi Nihonjin* wrote: "Public opinion regards the Ōkuma Cabinet as a bureaucratic cabinet, and criticises it as being out of touch with the demands of the time" (15 May 1914, p. 65). Yoshino, the Tokyo Imperial University Professor newly returned home from Europe and America, wrote decisively of the Ōkuma Cabinet: "I welcome the formation of the Ōkuma Cabinet, for the sake of Japanese constitutional development". This counter-posed high expectations for the Ōkuma Cabinet against criticism of it stemming from recent past experiences.

158 *Japan's Modern History*

The first element in his hopeful assessment was the maintenance of a party coalition having sufficient numbers to counter the *Seiyūkai* of Hara Kei. Yoshino argued as follows:

> I am concerned that the three so-called non-*Seiyūkai* factions gathered under the umbrella of the Ōkuma Cabinet should so far as possible clear their minds and continue to consolidate their alliance. If they should fail in this, they will immediately split the government, losing control of one side of it, and this poses a considerable risk of returning government to the *Seiyūkai* and the bureaucracy.
> (Yoahino Sakuzō, *Gendai no seiji* ['Contemporary Politics'], p. 77).

His second expectation was that with the introduction of universal suffrage, the *Seiyūkai* – party of landlords – could be outstripped in influence. He expressed this hope in the following way:

> I should like to recommend to the new government party that it open up a new base of support separate from that of the *Seiyūkai*. In other words, I should like to recommend that by resolutely bringing in universal suffrage, which is desired by a majority of the people, support should be cultivated among those who are newly enfranchised. By leaving the electoral law as it is, and contesting the same ground as the *Seiyūkai*, it will no doubt prove difficult to overtake that party.
> (Ibid., p. 79)

This thinker of the 'Age of Reorganisation' did not clothe himself in political neutrality. Yoshino was publicly advocating bringing to an end political dominance by the landlord-backed *Seiyūkai* by means of conflict between two major parties, and through universal suffrage,

In his two texts written around the time when the Ōkuma Cabinet was inaugurated, Yoshino did not yet use the word 'people-based politics' (*minponshugi*). Yoshino's 'people-based politics' encompassed not only universal suffrage and politics based on two major parties. The fact that social democratic elements were also included is explained in the present writer's earlier work, Banno Junji, *Nihon kenseishi* ('A History of Japanese Constitutionalism'), Tokyo Daigaku shuppankai, 2008.

In a nutshell, *minponshugi* was above all a doctrine concerning 'the goals of politics', and insisted that politics should work for the interests of the people as a whole. At the same time, *minponshugi* concerned 'the conduct of politics', and also insisted that politics should be based on the intentions of the people as a whole. The first of these was a socialist argument, while the second was an argument for political equality (universal suffrage), and for freedom of political choice (two-major-party system). 'People-based politics' (*minponshugi*) brought together these three points, and in terms of post-war political discourse was an argument not dissimilar to that of the social democracy seen widely in Western Europe (Yoshino Sakuzō, *Yoshino Sakuzō senshū*, vol. 2, pp. 35–6).

Even so, among the three elements in *minponshugi* (social equality, political equality, freedom of political choice), those that seemed realistic in Japanese politics of the early Taishō period were the last two, namely universal suffrage and a two-major-party system. Yoshino held out hope that these might be realised by the second Ōkuma Cabinet.

The 'regular procedures of constitutional government' (*kensei no jōdō*) and 'the decade of fidelity in adversity' (*kusetsu jūnen*)

Outbreak of the First World War

Among the two expectations entertained by Yoshino, the original form of the two-party system came into being at the 12th general elections held in March 1915. The three factions of the Ōkuma Cabinet (*Rikken Dōshikai, Mushozoku dan, Chūseikai*), between them won 244 seats out of 381, whereas the *Seiyūkai* lost 80 seats, being reduced to the status of a small party controlling a mere 27 per cent of the seats in the House of Representatives. For the *Seiyūkai*, this was the first time in the 15 years since it was established in 1900 that it had suffered such a reverse.

Nevertheless, the original form of a two-major-party system did not last long. The outbreak of the First World War in August 1914 gradually created conditions favourable for a revival of the *Seiyūkai*.

When it first broke out, the war worked in favour of the Ōkuma Cabinet. As we have already seen, the political turmoil at the outset of the Taishō period meant that the outpouring of demands to satisfy the interests of various political forces came up against a wall of financial constraint. But Japan of course was not a major belligerent power; the outbreak of war alleviated rivalry between the Army and the Navy, and it applied the brakes to demands by rural landlords and city businessmen. Inter-service rivalries were sorted out with the formation, a month before the outbreak of war, of the Military Affairs Council (*bōmu kaigi*), consisting of the Prime Minister, Foreign Minister, Finance Minister, Army Minister, Navy Minister, Chief of the Army General Staff and Chief of the Navy General Staff.

In meetings that had taken place before the war, conflict continued as before between the Army, Navy and Finance ministries, but after the outbreak of war the Minister of Finance, Wakatsuki Reijirō, resisted demands for tax reductions from city Chambers of Commerce, and expressed his agreement with expansionary demands from the Army and Navy. Den Kanjirō, a member of the House of Peers, recorded in his diary the following statement by the Finance Minister, Wakatsuki:

> Even though the present Cabinet, when it produced its first political platform, applied policies both of tax reduction and a national defence plan, yet influenced by the turbulence of the World War, it is in financial and economic difficulties, and its plan to reduce taxation has no chance of bearing fruit. The plan to increase the size of the Army by two divisions and also to augment

160   *Japan's Modern History*

the Navy has already been pending for several years, and postponing it is not good for the State. Not only will it not go through discussion in Cabinet, but when it comes to a decision of the Defence Council, that will not disagree with a decision of Cabinet.

> (*Den Kanjirō nikki* ['Den Kanjirō Diary'], microfilm in the
> *kensei shiryōshitsu* of the National Diet Library, 8th October 1914.
> The original is in Chinese-style *kanbun.*)

Given that because of the outbreak of the First World War he had had to abandon his party platform pledge to reduce business tax, and at the same time accept Army and Navy expansion, the developmental policies of the rival *Seiyūkai* were quite naturally ignored. It was unfortunate for the opposition *Seiyūkai*, which later attained a majority in the House of Representatives, that they were unable to support the bill to increase the size of the Army by two divisions, which they had rejected two years before during their own Cabinet (second Saionji Cabinet). Even Hara Kei recognised that the outbreak of the First World War meant that the hostile mood to military build-up was diminishing. However, even if the party had actually been in power, as an opposition party it could not make a 180-degree turn in its policies of two years earlier. The *Seiyūkai*, which in the House of Representatives had rejected a two-division increase in the size of the Army while the mood was warlike, suffered a humiliating defeat in the elections following Diet dissolution, as we have already related.

In China policy also, the Ōkuma Cabinet came to align itself with the Army. What the Army wanted was for rights over Manchuria and Mongolia, won during the Russo-Japanese war, to be made permanent, and the 21 demands that the second Ōkuma Cabinet imposed on China in 1915, up to its final notification, stipulated in its second item (sixth article in the notification): "The two Contracting Parties agree that the lease of Lushun [Ryojun, Port Arthur] and Dalian [Dairen], as well as the two railways of South Manchuria and Anfeng, shall each be extended to 99 years" (Gaimushō, *Nihon gaikō nenpyō narabini shuyō bunsho* ['Chronological Table of Japanese Foreign Policy and Important Documents'], Hara Shobō, 1965, vol. 1, p. 383).

Katō Takaaki, Foreign Minister when this treaty was signed, continued to insist on the legitimacy of this treaty of 21 items right up to the formation of the Cabinet of three pro-Constitution factions nine years later in 1924. In the background was probably the mainstream view of the Foreign Ministry at the time he was Foreign Minister, which aimed to coordinate with European imperialist policies of Russia, Great Britain and elsewhere. They did not believe that the foreign policy of America, which lacked colonies, would become the mainstream after the war. While a treaty based on the 21 demands was under negotiation, the Army Deputy Chief of Staff Akashi Motojirō made this clear in a letter he wrote to Terauchi Masatake, Governor of Korea. In his words: "In the view of the Foreign Ministry, Russia has no objection and should rather express warm support for it . . . and Britain has no reason to oppose it. Everybody agrees that whatever the US says is unimportant" (*Terauchi Masatake kankei bunsho*

Reorganisation, 1894–1924 161

['Material relating to Terauchi Masatake'], *kensei shiryōshitsu* of the National Diet Library, 6/44, 3rd February 1915).

The Terauchi Cabinet and the return to office of the Seiyūkai: *arrival of the Great War boom*

The reason why the Army, which with the two-division expansion and the 21 demands against China had become closely aligned with the Ōkuma Cabinet, should have become alienated from that Cabinet and reconciled with the *Seiyūkai* of Hara Kei was also to be found in the First World War. The war brought about two contrasting results: in the earlier period it had the effect of augmenting financial burdens, whereas in the later period both finances and the business economy took a turn for the better. In other words the First World War boom had arrived.

While the European great powers – Great Britain, France, Russia, Germany and so on – were forced into an all-out war, Japan, being only a token participant in the war, saw its exports rapidly increase from around 1916. The total value of exports when the war broke out (and the second Ōkuma Cabinet was formed) was just over 600,000,000 yen, whereas two years later in 1916 (towards the end of the Ōkuma Cabinet) it had nearly doubled to a little less than 1,200,000,000 yen. The increase in exports meant the expansion of private business, and as a result government revenues, principally from income tax, rose rapidly. As a result of the increase in income tax revenue from 1916, income tax in 1917 exceeded land tax for the first time in Japanese modern history.

The Great War boom also made rural landlords rich. Since, as we have pointed out on several occasions, land tax was a tax having a fixed monetary rate and not affected by price changes, rural landlords became prosperous depending on how far the price of agricultural produce rose. As seen in the price of rice, the central agricultural product, the rice price, which at the outbreak of war had been around 16 yen per *koku* (Tokyo wholesale price), from two years later in 1917 had begun to shoot upwards, and in 1918 (when the Hara Government was formed – see later) the price had doubled to around 32 yen.

When rural landlords became prosperous in an economic boom, this was a chance for the *Seiyūkai*. In October 1916 the Elder Statesman (*genrō*) Yamagata Aritomo pressed Ōkuma to resign, and brought about the formation of a successor Cabinet under Terauchi Masatake, who was both Governor of Korea and Doyen of the Army. It is not established how far he was expecting the Great War boom and the *Seiyūkai* resurgence. He did, however, select Hara Kei as his coalition counterpart, and in the thirteenth general election held in April 1917, the *Seiyūkai* increased its seat total by 48 (111 to 159), and the *Kenseikai*, which had held a majority in the House of Representatives at the time of dissolution, lost 76 seats, being reduced to the status of second party.

The term 'regular procedures of constitutional government' (*kensei no jōdō*), still used occasionally in the mass media in the twenty-first century, was first employed, before the Diet was dissolved, by Katō Takaaki, President of the

162   *Japan's Modern History*

Kenseikai, which controlled a majority in the House of Representatives but as an opposition party. In November 1916, in a speech given in Yamagata City, Katō spoke in the following way:

> Of course, there is no provision in the Constitution insisting that it should be the leader of a political party that forms a cabinet, but in terms of the real intentions of the Constitution it is natural that a party leader should form a cabinet. . . . In present circumstances our party, within what the law permits, must work strenuously to turn our management of constitutional government into a regular procedure (*kensei no unyō o sono jōdō ni kaes[u]*).
> (Itō Masatoku, (ed.), *Katō Takaaki*, Hōbunkan, 1929, vol. 2, pp. 241–2)

The phrase "to turn our management of constitutional government into a regular procedure" is almost certainly the origin of the expression 'regular procedures of constitutional government' (*kensei no jōdō*).

When the *Kenseikai* was formed in October 1916, it actually held a majority of seats in the House of Representatives (199 out of 381). To say that the majority party ought to form the cabinet was an assertion following in general terms the principle of *kensei no jōdo*. That party was formed, however, the day after the transcendental cabinet of Terauchi Masatake was inaugurated, in which the *Seiyūkai* (in opposition to the *Kenseikai*) was a quasi-government party.

Kensei no jōdō in the true meaning of the term would first become a reality if the Terauchi Cabinet were to dissolve the Diet and the *Kenseikai* won a majority at subsequent general elections. But as we have already seen, at general elections held the next year the *Kenseikai* was soundly defeated. The term *kensei no jōdō* was invented in 1916, but it took until June 1924 for it to become established in actual politics, with the formation of the three-faction pro-Constitution Cabinet of Katō Takaaki. The eight years that it took from defeat in the 1916 general elections and consequent minority party status, to its return to power as the number one party in the 1924 general elections, were later called by the *Kenseikai* "the decade of fidelity in adversity"(*kusetsu jūnen*).

Confrontation between the Hara Cabinet and *Minponshugi*

Pro-US line of the Terauchi Cabinet

Even during the third Katsura Cabinet, which was forced out of power after a mere 61 days by a popular movement, a model was created for the *Kenseikai* later to advocate *kensei no jōdō*. By contrast the Cabinet led by the Army Elder Statesman Terauchi Masatake, which resigned less than two years after it began because of the Siberian expedition failure and the rice riots, was a transcendental Cabinet conspicuous only by its incompetence. But this Cabinet, in fact, in preparing to deal with the transformation of the international order following the First World War, and in setting the stage for the first cabinet to be led by a commoner, Hara Kei, was a cabinet that should be given some credit.

Reorganisation, 1894–1924 163

As we have already indicated, when the Ōkuma Cabinet forced its 21 demands upon China, it counted on the acceptance of this by the colonial powers Great Britain, France and Russia. Brushing aside the anti-colonialism of America, which was becoming the world's biggest military and economic power (*fukoku kyōhei*), it had expanded its strategy towards China.

The idea that the outdated imperialist foreign policies pursued by the new *Kenseikai* President, Katō Takaaki, in his time as Foreign Minister, were reversed by a transcendental cabinet having the Elder Statesman Terauchi Masatake as Prime Minister, may seem paradoxical. But in October 1916, when Terauchi was sworn in as Prime Minister, more than two years had passed since the outbreak of war, and a change in the fortunes of the war created by American participation was imminent. For Japan also, the time had come when it was no longer feasible to continue policies towards China like a looter at the scene of a fire.

Unlike politicians, government officials are not bound by previous statements. Unlike Katō Takaaki, President of the *Kenseikai*, who continued time and again to insist on the legitimacy of the 21 demands from his time as Foreign Minister, the Vice-Minister for Foreign Affairs, Shidehara Kijūrō, was changing course towards policies centring on the United States and away from Great Britain and France. The same was true within the Army. Of the two Deputy Chiefs of Staff (Akashi Motojirō and Tanaka Giichi) who, from the 21 demands to the strategy of rejecting Yuan Shikai, had supported the second Ōkuma Cabinet's policies of interfering in Chinese affairs, Tanaka softened his position and adopted the line of non-interference in China, and of taking the United States seriously. Politicians find it hard to change, whereas government officials adapt more nimbly.

Gotō Shinpei, who had appointed himself to the task of constructing the Terauchi Cabinet, from this perspective was a politician, not a bureaucrat. He believed that responsibility for policies of interfering in China lay not with the Prime Minister, Ōkuma, alone, but also with the Foreign Minister, Katō Takaaki, Vice-Minister Shidehara Kijūrō and Tanaka Giichi, Deputy Chief of the General Staff, and he pressed Terauchi to punish them as equally to blame (*Terauchi Masatake kankei bunsho*, 27/50, 3rd May 1916, Gotō to Terauchi). Terauchi, however, did not accept this, and retained both of them in their posts. During the Hara Cabinet that followed, Shidehara and Tanaka both became strong supporters of Hara's policies of emphasising relations with the United States. Thus, under the Terauchi Cabinet, which has a bad reputation in historical research as a military clique cabinet or a transcendental cabinet, the foundations were laid for the foreign policy line of Hara Kei, who was later to become famous for accepting the 'Washington system'.

The Siberian expedition and the rice riots

The Terauchi Cabinet, which laid the foundation stone of the policy of improving relations with the United States, is famous for one policy failure, namely its expedition against revolutionary Russia, in other words the Soviet Union. This was the episode whereby, in order to defend the troops of Czechoslovakia in

164   *Japan's Modern History*

Siberia against the Russian revolution, an expedition was sent along with those of America, Britain and France. It is, however, a rather harsh judgement to regard the expedition as a failure in the foreign policy of the Terauchi Government. The expedition sent by this government was in accordance with an American proposal, to which Britain and France also acceded. Moreover, it was not the responsibility of the Terauchi Cabinet that Japanese troops remained in Siberia even after European and American troops had been withdrawn. The Terauchi Cabinet tendered its resignation less than two months after the expedition was sent, and since Terauchi was succeeded by Hara Kei, famous as the first commoner Prime Minister, who inherited the consequences, responsibility for the troops remaining in Siberia for the long term lay not with Terauchi but with Hara.

On the other hand, the announcement of the Siberian expedition at the beginning of August 1918 was a reason for the nationwide uprising known as the rice riots, and this forced the resignation of the Terauchi Cabinet.

When the United States appealed to Japan to participate in a joint expedition on 8th July, rice merchants, concerned that Japan was, for the first time during the Great War, going to be involved in real warfare, bought up rice and were reluctant to sell it, so that the rice price increased rapidly day by day. So the day after the expedition was announced, a demonstration calling for rice deliveries broke out among fishermen's wives at Nishimizubashi town in Niikawa county, Toyama prefecture. This incident, famous as the 'Toyama women's riot', spread in no time throughout the country, included big cities such as Tokyo and Osaka, and in 38 cities, 153 towns and 177 villages movements of underprivileged people demanding sales of cheap rice turned into mob violence. The Terauchi Cabinet suppressed the movement, by not only using the police but also deploying the army, but on 21st September, after the uprising had been calmed, it resigned, and on the 29th a *Seiyukai* Cabinet, headed by Hara Kei, famous for being a commoner, was established.

Commoner Prime Minister opposed to universal suffrage

If we were to conduct a public opinion poll asking which single individual comes to mind in connection with the term 'Taishō Democracy', probably Hara Kei would be chosen in the top spot. But if we define 'Taishō Democracy' as incorporating universal suffrage and a two-major-party system, the fact is that Hara was opposed to both of them. The popularity of Hara in post-war historical research was not connected with 'Taishō Democracy'.

As I have already pointed out, universal suffrage and a system based on two major parties were the principal elements in Yoshino's *minponshugi*. Yoshino hated Hara, who rejected both these elements. In the column titled 'contemporary issues and trends of thought' (*jiron shichō*) of the journal *Chūō Kōron* for April 1920, Yoshino judged Hara harshly as "[a]n incomparably deformed politician without parallel in the world, who separates politics from both philosophy and science, and seems to operate in a totally haphazard manner".

The three years between September 1918, when he became Prime Minister, and November 1921, when he was assassinated, were the age of Hara Kei.

Reorganisation, 1894–1924 165

Since the Hara Cabinet was formed at the end of September 1918, it was impossible to make drastic changes to the budget for 1919, drafted by the Terauchi Cabinet, since the budget outline had been fixed at the end of August.

Therefore, the developmental policies of 'positive finance' which were the longstanding financial policies of Hara's *Seiyūkai* were put into effect in the budget for 1920. The content of the positive budget, explained by the Minister of Finance, Takahashi Korekiyo, in the 42nd Diet session, is concisely summarised by Yamamoto Shirō in *Hyōden: Hara Kei* ('An Argumentative Biography of Hara Kei'), Tokyo Sōgensha, vol. 2, p. 346. According to him, this meant 1,350,000,000 yen as special continuing expenditure for the Army (over 14 years) and the Navy (over 8 years), a little less than 340,000,000 yen as continuing expenditure to expand the telephone network, and 170,000,000 yen for railway extension and repair (telephone and railways combined = 510,000,000 yen). While expenditure on railways was as before, improvement of communication systems was emphasised. This was combined with expenditure to improve higher educational facilities begun in the previous year, but together these were the four great policy planks of the Hara Cabinet (improving national defence, developing education, encouraging industry, preparing transport facilities).

The Hara Cabinet, in the context of a world boom that followed the ending of the Great War, sought the opportunity to dissolve the Diet and hold general elections on the issue of 'positive policies'. As we have already explained, in the general elections of April 1917 conducted while the Terauchi Cabinet was still in office, the *Seiyūkai* regained its position of largest political party, but was far from attaining an overall majority (it won 160 seats out of 381).

The Hara Cabinet saw in the bill for universal suffrage proposed as a private member's bill by the opposition *Kenseikai*, *Kokumintō* and others, an excuse for it to dissolve the Diet. In February 1920, the *Kenseikai*, the *Kokumintō* and the Society for the Promotion of Universal Suffrage (*fusen jikkōkai*) each produced separate universal suffrage bills, but even if all three had united as one, counting the seats of small conservative factions together with the 160 Seiyūkai seats it would have been possible to defeat the bills by a margin of about 20 seats. But even so, Hara decided to dissolve the House of Representatives.

Rather than bury the universal suffrage bills in the House of Representatives by force of numbers, dissolving the Diet and appealing directly to the people sounds democratic. But if by dissolving the Diet and holding general elections the *Seiyūkai* were to win a victory, then in the four years up to the next general elections that party would continue to insist that majority opinion regarded universal suffrage as premature. Rather than a rejection by the House of Representatives lasting a year, they chose dissolution and general elections to make the rejection effective for four years.

Moreover, even if the reason for the dissolution was to sound out the people on universal suffrage, the points at issue in a general election would not be confined to universal suffrage. As we have seen already, issues of railway expansion, building new high schools and universities, expanding the telephone network and so on, being the four planks of the Hara Cabinet's platform, would be sure to influence the voting behaviour of electors. Now electors paid at least three yen in national taxation

166   *Japan's Modern History*

(1919 electoral law revision), and the electorate had thus increased to about 3,000,000, but this was no more than a quarter of what the electorate would be under universal suffrage, and moreover the majority of them were rural landlords. In relation to exemption from income tax, even though the tax qualification had fallen from 10 yen or more to 3 yen or more, the numbers of those paying income tax within these limits had not increased (Narusawa Hikaru, "Hara naikaku to dai ichiji sekai taisen go no kokunai jōkyō [2]" ('The Hara Cabinet and the Domestic Situation after the First World War [2]'), *Hōgaku Shirin*, 1969, p. 66).

If in 1920, the final year of the Great War boom, the majority of the 3 million electors voted for the *Seiyūkai* and its positive policies, the idea that it would also express public opinion opposed to universal suffrage (or believing it to be premature), was a political trick transcending the word 'ingenuity'. My biggest reason for regarding Hara, the commoner Prime Minister, as the enemy of 'Taishō Democracy', is here.

The elections resulted in an overwhelming victory for the *Seiyūkai*. At the time of the February dissolution and the May elections, the total number of seats had increased from 381 to 464, so rather than making a simple comparison of seat numbers, we should compare the proportion of seats won by each party. Following this method, the *Seiyūkai* increased its proportion of seats from 42 per cent to about 60 per cent, the opposition *Kenseikai* fell from around 31 per cent to around 21 per cent. The ruling party scoring 60 per cent and the largest opposition only reaching 21 per cent, symbolised the arrival of the *Seiyūkai* age and the failure of the universal suffrage movement.

Commoner Prime Minister refusing a two-major-party system

Moreover, Hara of the *Seiyūkai* had avoided transferring power between political parties consistently ever since the ending of the Russo-Japanese war in 1905, and when leaving office had transferred the Cabinet to the military clique controlled by Yamagata Aritomo, as well as the bureaucratic clique. Power was not transferred to the principal opposition party, the *Kenseikai*. Even in 1921, Hara held firmly to this position. In his diary for April of the same year, after a meeting with Yamagata, Hara wrote as follows:

> I went from Koshigoe to visit Yamagata who lives in Odawara. The gist of our conversation is as follows . . . :
> I told him that, assuming that I shall not be leading the Cabinet for ever, even if we do not need to think about it too much, we must at least consider it. Yamagata replied that he disapproved of this, for nobody would succeed the present Cabinet . . . and it was necessary to go ahead resolutely. In response, I said that it was not so simple, and that if I had to resign, then there should be somebody to replace me. Even though we might consider Katō Takaaki to some extent, I was afraid that he was always influenced by others. Yamagata replied firmly that if Katō came to power and decided to bring in universal suffrage, he himself would have to act to bolster the *Seiyūkai*.
>
> (Hara Keiichirō [ed.], *Hara Kei nikki*, Fukumura Shuppan, 4th April 1921, vol. 5, p. 369)

There are unlikely to be people who would read the latter part of this to mean that Hara was proposing Katō as his successor, and that Yamagata, who hated the idea of universal suffrage, was opposing this. However one reads this passage, it can only be understood to mean that Hara decided to take from Yamagata his essential meaning that Katō Takaaki was no good. In this meeting Hara was saying that the next government would not rotate to the *Kenseikai*, that it would be transferred either to the military clique under Yamagata or to the bureaucratic clique, and that Yamagata wanted him to remain in office for a while longer.

The fact that the universal suffrage bill had been destroyed, and a two-major-party system denied, by Hara, meant the total defeat of Yoshino's *minponshugi*. In fact, the national assembly of 34 prefectures (3 *fu* and 31 *ken*), which had met 144 times demanding the urgent establishment of universal suffrage, now rapidly faded from the scene (Matsuo Takayoshi, *Futsū senkyo seido seiritsu shi no kenkyū* ['A Study of the History of the Establishment of the universal suffrage system'], Iwanami Shoten, 1989, p. 191).

Rise and fall of the popularity of Yoshino Sakuzō

Putting this in reverse, in 1916 and up to 1920, it was the age of Yoshino Sakuzō and his advocacy of *minponshugi*. This is shown graphically from the size of his side income. According to the analysis of Matsuo Takayoshi, who has written a commentary on his diary from that period, between 1915 and 1922 Yoshino's income "from manuscript fees and other publications alone was about the same as his salary from Tokyo University, and when payment for public lectures and so on is added, it reaches two or three times his university salary" (Matsuo Takayoshi, *Yoshino Sakuzō senshū*, vol. 14, p. 395).

Since we only have a detailed record of Yoshino's income up to 1922, we are ignorant of how far his side earnings fell with the fading of the universal suffrage movement. But in the eight years from 1914 when he first began giving public lectures, until 1922 (the years 1914, 1916, 1920 and 1921 are not entirely clear, but we may assume that they were substantially the same as the others), the sheer amount of his side income clearly testifies to the great popularity of his *minponshugi*.

It is not possible to be exactly sure when the popularity of *minponshugi* came to an end. There is, however, material that shows that by 1924, at the end of the Taishō era, its popularity had completely collapsed. Rōyama Masamichi, who in his student days at Tokyo Imperial University had joined the Yoshino-influenced *Shinjinkai* (New Man Society), in his account of January 1925 wrote as follows:

> It is still fresh in our memories that the doctrines of *demokurashii* (democracy) were previously proclaimed by Dr. Yoshino and progressive men, and dominated the intellectual world. . . . Lately, public opinion has shown interest in socialist argument, while books on democracy are only to be found, covered in dust, in some corner of a second-hand bookshop, or on the shelf of a street stall for people going by.
>
> (Rōyama Masamichi, *Nihon seiji dōkō ron* ['Directions of Japanese Politics'], Kōyō Shoin, pp. 86–7)

168 *Japan's Modern History*

According to Matsuo's analysis, Yoshino's side income for 1922 was 73 per cent of his total income, whereas his university salary was only 27 per cent. In other words, neither his published works nor his theories, right up to 1922, were to be found in second-hand bookshops or street stalls. But in January 1925, just over two years later, they were only to be found "in the corners of second-hand bookshops" or "the shelves of street stalls".

One reason why the movement of Yoshino and others advocating what he now frankly called *demokurashii* (democracy) (having abandoned the limited term *minponshugi*) was losing popularity is revealed in the extract from Rōyama's writings quoted above: "Lately public opinion has shown interest in socialist argument."

From universal suffrage movement to socialist movement

Both the beginning and the end of Yoshino's popularity were governed by trends among students influenced by the new age following the conclusion of the First World War. Its beginning was marked by a speech meeting for rival candidates in November 1818 with representatives of the right-wing group *Rōninkai* (Itō Matsuo, Ogawa Unpei, Sasaki Yasugorō and Tanaka Tonemi). Yoshino himself described the atmosphere briefly in his diary:

> The speech meeting began at six o'clock. Itō, Ogawa, Sasaki and Tanaka stood up, and each in turn responded to questions. Their arguments were comprehensively challenged and demolished. At ten o'clock we made a triumphal exit. Outside there were a thousand several hundred sympathisers, so that it was impossible to move. With the help of a policeman I just managed to get onto a tram and go home. But I lost my coat and hat.
> (*Yoshino Sakuzō senshū*, vol. 14, p. 168)

The next day students of Tokyo Imperial University Faculty of Law who had supported this speech meeting founded the discussion group called *Shinjinkai* (New Man Society).

The thought, however, representative of the new age following the First World War was not confined to 'democracy'. Young students and recent graduates gradually came to look for the image of the new society in the Russian revolution, which had established a Socialist State. The official journal of the *Shinjinkai* changed its name from *Demokurashii* to *Senku* ('Pioneer'), and then to *Dōhō* ('Compatriots') and *Narod* ('Russian for "The People"'). This showed that radical students had shifted their interest from the movement for universal suffrage to socialist revolution (see Henry Dewitt Smith II, *Japan's First Student Radicals*, Cambridge MA, Harvard University Press, 1972).

Yoshino's line of first stimulating a popular movement, then using its strength to have a universal suffrage bill passed by the House of Representatives, and finally to ensure a victory for democratic parties in general elections, would take time and effort. Moreover, in reality, the *Seiyūkai*, which ignored a universal suffrage demonstration in February 1920 involving several tens of thousands, dissolved

Reorganisation, 1894–1924   169

the House of Representatives and in May won an overwhelming victory in general elections. Even with time and effort universal suffrage might be impossible to achieve.

Against this approach, the methods of the Russian revolution, whereby workers and peasants arm themselves and overthrow the ruling class, if it succeeded, would not require multi-stage procedures. Then again, unlike the mundane activity of walking to a polling booth and casting a vote, it was Russia that struck the hearts of young people with the word 'revolution'. And in Japan of those days, Yamakawa Hitoshi, planning to found the Communist Party, interpreted universal suffrage as a plot by the ruling class to blunt the revolutionary consciousness of the workers.

In post-war studies of modern Japanese history the view of Yamakawa as the most flexible and realistic of socialists has become entrenched. But this same Yamakawa, in an article published in *Zen'ei* (Vanguard), for February 1922, uncompromisingly opposed universal suffrage:

> Universal suffrage may possibly be realised in the near future. Perhaps it will come about. But today, even if the gates of the Diet are opened to the working class, the power does not exist to entice the mainstream of the workers' movement into the safety valve of the House. . . . But the danger of universal suffrage – the danger that the proletarian movement will be emasculated by parliamentarianism – has not really disappeared. It certainly has not. In any case today, the gates of the Diet are firmly locked against the working class. If those gates should ever be opened, there is no doubt that a part of the working class would inevitably choose the easy path to follow.

In 2011, while this book is being written, hardly anyone in the Social Democratic and Communist parties is warning of "the danger that the proletarian movement will be emasculated by parliamentarianism". This though is more or less true of the past 20 years, but up to the 1980s socialists and labour union leaders aimed at a Soviet-style socialism and favoured general strikes at the annual spring struggle over general elections. In this sense the Taishō period socialist Yamakawa Hitoshi, who shouted his opposition to universal suffrage, may be said to have created the template of the anti-parliamentary socialist movement in post-war Japan.

When university students passionate about 'democracy' turned to direct action socialism, the universal suffrage movement and Yoshino's *minponshugi* lost its support from the 'Left'. On the other hand, at the level of the Cabinet and the Diet, the *Seiyūkai*, which had convincingly won the general elections of May 1920 on a platform of opposition to universal suffrage, was in control. In 1921 Hara was assassinated, and in 1922 Takahashi Korekiyo, the fourth-generation President of the *Seiyūkai*, yielded power to Admiral Katō Tomosaburō, following the traditional approach of that party, with an unwritten promise requiring power to be returned before the general elections which would be held four years later (1924).

170   *Japan's Modern History*

Takahashi Korekiyo's view that the General Staff Office should be abolished

Takahashi, however, who became *Seiyūkai* President after Hara's death, did not enjoy the confidence of the elder statesmen. Ishigami Ryōhei, in his book *Hara Kei botsugo* ('After the Death of Hara Kei'), writes as follows of the succession to Katō Tomosaburō (who died of illness in August 1923):

> I do not know which month and which day it was, but when Okazaki (Kunisuke) visited Saionji, Saionji said twice that 'there is nobody at all among the *genrō* and *jūshin* who endorses Takahashi'.
>
> (Ishigami Ryōhei, *Hara Kei botsugo* ['After the Death of Hara Kei'], Chūō Kōronsha 1960, p. 59)

In defence of the reputation of Takahashi, who was a representative financier of pre-war Japan, the reason he was unpopular among the *genrō* was perhaps his proposal to abolish the General Staff Office. This was published while he was Finance Minister in the Hara Cabinet, but after a warning from Hara and Tanaka Giichi (Defence Minister), its distribution was blocked. In his *Naigai kokusaku shiron* (Domestic and Foreign Policy Opinion), published in September 1920, Takahashi expressed his real views in the following forthright terms:

> The thing that gives foreigners the strongest impression of militarism in our country's system is the General Staff Office. It was copied in the pre-war period (before the Great War) from the system of the German Empire, it is a military organisation separate from Cabinet, it is not under the jurisdiction of the Army Minister, who is the administrative authority, it is placed outside the sphere of national politics and occupies a place of independence and lack of constraint, though not only in military matters but also in foreign policy, it is a rather special body. . . . But according to a recent actual example from the German Empire, a military plan established with routine research . . . became a secret known to the enemy over a long period of the war, and hardly any new plan failed to be discovered. . . . With a cruel defeat, 50 years of plans evaporated in a single morning. There is no reason to have an independent organisation such as the General Staff Office drawing up military plans. . . . It should rather be abolished, Army administration should be unified, and we should expect a renewal of our foreign policy.
>
> (*Ogawa Heikichi kankei bunsho* ['Material Relating to Ogawa Heikichi), vol. 2, pp. 140–1)

Among liberal-minded scholars of that period, the only person who would have published such a forthright opinion would perhaps have been Yoshino Sakuzō. The famous organ theory of the Emperor by Minobe Tatsukichi recognised the 'independent command' of the Army General Staff Office and the Naval War Office, and went no further than proposing that the right of the Military to draw up disarmament treaties and so on should be brought together under the Cabinet (see Chapter 6).

Hara Kei wrote in his diary that Takahashi accepted his warning and that of Tanaka, and agreed that he would "postpone distributing (the pamphlet)" (*Hara Kei nikki*, vol. 5, p. 297). But it was included in the documents of Ogawa Heikichi, who was only a middle-ranking leader of the *Seiyūkai*, showing that Takahashi distributed his pamphlet relatively widely.

By contrast with the criticism of scholars and commentators, this was a publication by Takahashi, who within a year had succeeded Hara as President of the great *Seiyūkai* and taken over the Cabinet. It was perhaps natural then that Takahashi, who insisted that the reason for Germany's defeat in the First World War was the independent command exercised by its General Staff Bureau, was unable to succeed to power a second time.

The Council of Elder Statesmen, however, not only would not appoint as Prime Minister the President of the *Seiyūkai*, which controlled about 60 per cent of the House of Representatives; it was also impossible for them to transfer power to the President of the *Kenseikai*, which held a mere 22 per cent of the seats. Not only was Takahashi reappointed Prime Minister, but neither was Katō Takaaki given the prime ministerial post.

If the position of Prime Minister was not transferred to either of the major political parties, there was no alternative to building a transcendental Cabinet. This is why, after the Takahashi Cabinet left the scene in June 1922, non-party cabinets – two under an Admiral and one under the President of the Privy Council – succeeded it.

Change of line by the Seiyūkai *under Takahashi: second constitutional defence movement*

Once the alternation of power with the bureaucratic clique that had continued ever since the ending of the Russo-Japanese war in 1905 became untenable, it was necessary for the *Seiyūkai* under Takahashi to search for a different way to proceed. From this position, if the past were simply repeated, the precedent could be found of Hara Kei once overthrowing a bureaucratic cabinet by means of an interparty alliance. This was the first constitutional defence movement that forced the resignation of the third Katsura Cabinet using the slogan 'Overthrow the bureaucratic clique, defend the Constitution'. Takahashi Korekiyo, as *Seiyūkai* President, resolved to participate in the second constitutional defence movement.

The origin of the matter came at the end of December 1923, when the anarchist Nanba Taisuke aimed bullets from a gun concealed in a cane at the horse carriage of the Prince Regent (later the Shōwa Emperor) as he was approaching Toranomon to preside at the opening ceremony of the Diet. The Yamamoto Gonbei Cabinet, which took responsibility for this 'Toranomon Incident', resigned at the end of the year, but the reason for its resignation was not confined to this particular incident.

Yamamoto Gonbei, who had succeeded to the leadership after the death from illness of Katō Tomosaburō, was confirmed in his post on 26th August, but only

172   *Japan's Modern History*

completed the formation of his cabinet on 2nd September. On 1st September the Great Kantō Earthquake occurred. Deaths amounted to around 100,000, there were about 43,000 missing, houses totally or partially destroyed amounted to some 250,000, and huge destruction centred on Tokyo and Yokohama, but extended to Chiba, Shizuoka, Yamanashi, Saitama, and then to Nagano, Gunma and part of Tochigi. It was an enormous quake of magnitude 7.9 (also recorded as 8.2), and its intensity in the central areas was 6 (at that time the highest degree of intensity was 6). There was no serious tsunami, and of course no nuclear power stations, but in the city areas fires were intense, and the greater number of deaths in Tokyo were caused by burns.

On 16th September the Imperial Reconstruction Organisation was set up, famous together with the name of Gotō Shinpei, and under the Yamamoto Gonbei Cabinet, which both Takahashi Korekiyo of the *Seiyūkai* and Katō Takaaki of the *Kenseikai* refused to join, a reconstruction plan based on financing from more than 400,000,000 yen of public loans was passed by the Diet, but no target date for the 1924 budget itself was put in place.

Kiyoura Keigo, President of the Privy Council, who succeeded the Yamamoto Cabinet which had resigned over the Toranomon Incident, reflected on these events as follows:

> At the time of resignation of the Yamamoto Cabinet, I gave advice to Yamamoto to stay in power, saying that the horrible events that have taken place are truly unbearably frightening, but the situation would be really serious if it allowed your resignation. But he is a type not to go back on what he has resolved to do, and he has finally decided to resign.
>
> (Inoue Masaaki [ed.], *Hakushaku Kiyoura Keigo Den* ['Biography of Count Kiyoura Keigo'], Hakushaku Kiyoura Keigo den hankōkai, vol. 2, pp. 259–60)

These reflections of Kiyoura suggest that, because it was less than four months after the Great Kantō Earthquake, and because the 1924 budget bill had just been presented to the Diet, despite the Toranomon Incident the Yamamoto Cabinet could have continued. The real reason for the resignation of the Yamamoto Cabinet was that it was not confident of passing the 1924 budget, given that it was facing collaboration between the *Seiyūkai* and *Kenseikai* against this bureaucratic cabinet.

If this is the case, would Kiyoura Keigo, whose support group was the House of Peers, have accepted the leadership whatever his calculations of success? If we compare the seat totals of each party at the time of dissolution in January 1924, his reasoning can be easily surmised. The *Seiyūhontō* had 149 seats, the *Seiyūkai* 129, the *Kenseikai* 103, the *Kakushin Club* (Progressive Club) 43, others 37, vacant 3, making a total of 464. The *Seiyūkai*, which used to have 278 seats in the House of Representatives, split into the *Seiyūhontō* and the *Seiyūkai*, and the majority *Seiyūhontō* was the quasi-ruling party of the Kiyoura Cabinet.

Reorganisation, 1894–1924 173

Birth of the three-faction Cabinet

On 18th January of the same year, the three party leaders Katō Takaaki, Takahashi Korekiyo and Inukai Tsuyoshi (*Kakushin Club*) agreed to form a party Cabinet opposed to the Cabinet of Kiyoura, so that the majority party in the House of Representatives was no longer the *Seiyūhontō*, but the three factions defending the Constitution (255 seats out of 464). If in the May general elections the three pro-Constitution factions were to beat the *Seiyūhontō*, then a cabinet based on these three factions would be formed.

The election results followed this pattern. The three factions increased their seat total, winning between them 285 seats; the *Seiyūhontō* lost 34 seats, and surrendered its position as largest party to the *Kenseikai* (*Kenseikai* 155, *Seiyūhontō* 115, *Seiyūkai* 101, *Chōsei Club* 42). Naturally, the Prime Minister of this three-party constitutionalist Cabinet was Katō Takaaki, President of the largest party the *Kenseikai*. For Katō and the *Kenseikai*, this was the coming about of *kensei no jōdō* (normal constitutional procedures). It was also the end of a decade (actually eight years) of 'fidelity in adversity' (*kusetsu jūnen*).

The 'Age of Reorganisation', however, did not end with *kensei no jōdō*. Combined first of all with universal suffrage, the second constitutional defence movement clearly differed from the first such movement.

On this point the *Seiyūkai* would not make concessions. Even in the leaders' meetings of the *Kenseitō* and *Seiyūkai* held after the Diet was dissolved the *Seiyūkai* unconditionally opposed universal suffrage (Ishigami Ryōhei, *Hara Kei botsugo*, p. 153). But the issue for the second constitutional defence movement from the perspective of the press was universal suffrage. A meeting of concerned journalists held at the Matsumoto Tower in Hibiya Park on 2nd January made the following appeal: "We demand a Cabinet that will speed up the introduction of universal suffrage, and we oppose the formation of any cabinet that will not pursue this goal" (ibid., p. 102). Having broken away from the *Seiyūhontō* and participating in the constitutionalist three-faction alliance, there was no choice left for the Takahashi *Seiyūkai* other than to support universal suffrage.

In June 1924, when Katō Takaaki of the *Kenseikai* established the three-faction government, the simultaneous realisation of universal suffrage and a system based on two major parties was only a matter of time. This was the end of the 'Age of Reorganisation'.

6 Crisis, 1925–1937

Bifurcation of domestic politics and foreign policy

Kenseikai *persists with the 21 demands: Washington Conference*

In May 1925 universal male suffrage was put in place, in August a single-party Cabinet (the second Katō Takaaki Cabinet) of the *Kenseikai* was organised and the *Seiyūkai*, with the Army General Tanaka Giichi as its new President, left the government. Universal suffrage and a two-major-party system began. The 'Age of Reorganisation' was at an end.

The defection of the *Seiyūkai* from the government meant the collapse of the liberal coalition government that had earlier been formed out of three pro-Constitution factions. From August 1925 the *Kenseikai* (which from 1927 would become the *Rikken Minseitō* – henceforth *Minseitō*) changed tack towards a peace line, whereas the *Seiyūkai* under Tanaka Giichi moved decisively in a conservative direction.

In the five years between the dissolution over universal suffrage in 1920 and the departure of the *Seiyūkai* from government in 1925, if we combine domestic and foreign policy, the *Seiyūkai* and the *Kenseikai* were in a kind of 50/50 relationship. As we have already seen in the previous chapter, the *Seiyūkai* of Hara and Takahashi in domestic politics was evidently anti-democratic, whereas the *Kenseikai* directed by Katō Takaaki consistently advocated universal suffrage and in this sense was a democratic party.

When, however, we move to foreign policy, the relationship between them was reversed. The *Seiyūkai* was the more peace-inclined, while the *Kenseikai* tended towards a hard-line foreign policy. When we consider that post-war socialists and democrats valued 'peace' above all, the high reputation of Hara Kei, who opposed universal suffrage but was a peace policy man in foreign policy, is not impossible to understand.

As we have already explained in the previous chapter, Japanese foreign policy during the First World War moved fitfully from colonial imperialism to non-colonial imperialism. What determined this shift was the Washington Conference held from late in 1921 to early in 1922.

First of all, according to the terms of the Four Nation Treaty (Britain, US, France, Japan) signed in December 1921, dissolution of the Anglo-Japanese

Crisis, 1925–1937   175

Table 6.1

Year	Era name and year	Prime Minister	Events
1921	Taishō 10	Hara, Takahashi	Washington Conference (to 1922), at which the Four-Power Treaty signed.
1922	11	Katō Tomosaburō	Nine Nation Treaty, Naval Disarmament Treaty. Shandong Peninsula lease returned to China. Fascist regime established in Italy.
1924	13	Yamamoto, Kiyoura, Katō Takaaki	Cabinet of three constitutionalist factions. Shidehara foreign policy (consensus diplomacy) pursued.
1925	14	Katō Takaaki	Japan–Soviet Basic Treaty. Peace Preservation Law. Universal Suffrage Law.
1926	15	Wakatsuki	Chiang Kai-shek's Northern Expedition begins (to 1928). Death of Taishō Emperor.
1927	Shōwa 2	Tanaka	Financial panic (bankruptcy of *Suzuki Shōten*, Bank of Taiwan suspends operations). Tanaka Giichi *Seiyūkai* Cabinet established (Tanaka diplomacy). *Kenseikai* and *Kenseihontō* merge, forming *Rikken Minseitō*. Eastern Conference. Kwantung Army expedition into Shandong (to 1928).
1928	3		Universal suffrage implemented. 3/15 Incident. Seinan Incident. Chiang Tso-Lin assassinated. Paris Anti-War Treaty.
1929	4	Hamaguchi	*Minseitō* Cabinet under Hamaguchi Osachi begins. World Depression.
1930	5		Ban on gold exports lifted (return to gold standard). Second general election under universal suffrage (*Minseitō* wins majority). London Naval Disarmament Conference. London Treaty signed.

Alliance (signed in 1902), which had acted as a guarantee of the kind of colonialism embodied in the 21 demands, became inevitable. Second, according to the Nine Nation Treaty signed in February 1922 by the US, the UK, France, Italy, the Netherlands, Japan, Belgium, Portugal and China, maintenance of Chinese sovereignty and territory, as well as non-interference in her internal politics, was guaranteed. With these two treaties a major change was brought about in Japan's pre-war and wartime China policy. The first step in this process was revealed in the return to China of the leasehold rights over the Shandong Peninsula, which had been demanded in the 21 demands (Treaty to resolve the Shandong issue, 1922). Within this, all that was left of Japanese rights in China were the railway in Manchuria and Mongolia, and the right of the *Kantōgun* to be garrisoned near to the mines and the railway.

The *Kenseikai*, which had appointed as its President Katō Takaaki, who had been Foreign Minister at the time of the 21 demands, strongly opposed this treaty involving the return of Shandong. In his party's Diet report in April 1922, the following passage occurs:

176   *Japan's Modern History*

The issue of measures relating to Shandong was resolved in the so-called Japan–China Agreement during the Ōkuma Cabinet, and was also resolved internationally by articles 156 to 158 of the Paris Peace Treaty. Even though interference is not permitted, on the principle that the Washington Conference kept issues between specific countries outside its scope . . . we have had to make concession after concession, and everything has been decided according to Chinese wishes.

(Kensei, vol. 5, no. 3, p. 6)

Conciliatory foreign policy of the Seiyūkai

By contrast the *Seiyūkai*, even after Hara's death, continued to give total support to the Washington system. In its report to the Diet of April 1923, that party made clear that "the age of imperialism, in which we consider only the furtherance of our country's interests and have no concern for the interests of others, has already passed", and from this perspective endorsed the return of Shandong to China (*Seiyū*, no. 272, p. 14). While the *Kenseikai* was pursuing the pre-war imperialistic policies, the *Seiyūkai* was advocating policies of peace and national self-determination led by America.

Incidentally, another issue of the Washington Conference was naval disarmament. The Conference determined that the proportions of major warships between the great powers should be: US and UK ten each, Japan six, France and Italy three each. At the time this did not occasion serious opposition even in the Japanese Navy. I will omit the details here.

If we compare the differences between the *Kenseikai* and the *Seiyūkai* in foreign policy with those discussed in the previous chapter over universal suffrage, it becomes clear that the *Kenseikai* was conciliatory over democratisation while the *Seiyūkai* was prepared to compromise over foreign policy. Leaving aside detailed reservations and simplifying the matter, the two parties were divided from each other over 'peace and democracy'.

In these circumstances when a two-party system was set up, this did not lead to an 'Age of Crisis'. Whether it were the *Seiyūkai* or the *Kenseitō* that came to power, the two-party system, supposed to guarantee either peace or democracy, though it might not be superficially dramatic, at least did not lead to extreme rightist tendencies.

Kenseikai *change of line: Shidehara diplomacy*

When, however, the government of three constitutional factions was formed in 1924, the *Kenseikai* shifted policy to combine international cooperation and non-interference in the domestic affairs of China. This was the beginning of the famous 'Shidehara diplomacy'. For Shidehara Kijūrō, this was merely his own position that he had advocated since the days of the Hara Cabinet, but for the *Kenseikai* of Katō Takaaki, it was a big turning point in foreign policy.

Even so, Shidehara took on board this great change and dealt with it simply as "continuity of foreign policy". Indeed, he wrote: "A promise given by a government

Crisis, 1925–1937   177

officially to a foreign power, irrespective of whether it is or is not contained in a treaty, and whether or not the government or the cabinet is replaced, must not be altered because of such changes" (Shidehara Kijūrō heiwa zaidan [ed.], *Shidehara Kijūrō*, Shidehara Kijūrō heiwa zaidan, 1955, p. 263).

This declaration of Shidehara, whether we are talking about that period or about the early twenty-first century, may be regarded as extremely important. In Japan, which in 1924 was beginning a period of politics based on two major parties, if there were a switch between imperialist foreign policy and foreign policy based on the Washington system every time the government changed, then allied countries would be unable to maintain consistent policies towards Japan. This is also the same today.

Sometimes the basis of foreign policy is forced to change. For instance, over the course of the First World War and the post-war period, the world order itself underwent change, and therefore it was natural that the basis of Japanese foreign policy should change to reflect this.

On the other hand, in the incipient period of politics based on two major parties, *Kenseikai* and *Seiyūkai*, if the basis of foreign policy were to change every two or three years with a change of government this would destroy trust in Japanese foreign policy. The importance of Shidehara's statement about "the continuity of foreign policy" can be readily understood by us by reference to the failure of the Cabinet of Hatoyama Yukio, established in 2009.

Change of direction by the Tanaka Seiyūkai

Nevertheless, Shidehara's "continuity of foreign policy" even in a system of two major parties was incapable of being maintained. When the Cabinet of Katō Takaaki and Wakatsuki Reijirō resigned, the new *Seiyūkai* Cabinet of Tanaka Giichi (set up in April 1927) completely ignored the principle of "foreign policy continuity". Not only did the new Cabinet reject Shidehara diplomacy, but it even changed the foreign policy line of the *Seiyūkai* from the Hara Kei period.

The person who most clearly expressed the foreign policy of the *Seiyūkai* in the Hara Kei period was the Finance Minister, Takahashi Korekiyo, who had advocated abolishing the Staff Headquarters, as explained in the previous chapter. In his "Opinion concerning the build-up of economic strength in East Asia", published and distributed in May 1921, while Hara was still alive, Takahashi argued as follows:

> Successive governments speak in an abstract fashion about friendship (between China and Japan), but judging by past results, in China obviously, but also by the great powers, this is considered as territorial, strategic and exclusive, and is seen as a way of attaining private interests, or is admitted to involve interference in domestic affairs. As a result, foreign policy towards China lacks harmony, it causes trouble from one direction or the other, and easily becomes hard to manage.
> (Ogawa Heikichi bunka kenkyūkai [ed.], *Ogawa Heikichi kankei bunsho* ['Materials Relating to Ogawa Heikichi'], Misuzu Shobō, vol. 2, p. 146)

178   Japan's Modern History

Following on from his reflections on past Japanese policy towards China, Takahashi advocated withdrawal of Japanese forces stationed in China, including the *Kantōgun Army*. In his words:

> The essence of this fundamental change is that troop garrisons, which lead to misunderstanding on the part of China and the great powers, should be withdrawn quickly on the basis of an understanding with China, moreover military installations wherever they may be should also quickly be withdrawn, and in Shandong, as well as in Manchuria and Mongolia, policies and facilities that are misunderstood to be the starting point for territorial and strategic ambition, should be decisively and urgently revised.
>
> (Ibid., pp. 146–7)

It was Takahashi, Finance Minister in the Hara Cabinet, who succeeded Hara after his death. Moreover, between the final year of Meiji and his untimely death in 1936, Takahashi had been one of the most famous specialists concerning Japanese finance and economy. These articles by Takahashi were in no way the fantasies of a commentator seeking publicity by publishing extreme arguments. He perceived that Japanese levels of finance and technology made policies towards China possible that did not require military strength (ibid., p. 146).

When we compare this article with the arguments of Tanaka Giichi, who became *Seiyūkai* President five years later (in 1926), of Japan as an 'industrial power', it is clear that foreign policy under the *Seiyūkai* experienced a major change. What Tanaka meant by 'industrial power' was that Japan should protect "the special zone of Manchuria and Mongolia" in order to secure resources, and this represented a 180 degree shift from the *Seiyūkai* foreign policies of the Hara and Takahashi eras (*Seiyū*, No. 310, p. 3: Tanaka's speech to the local congress of November 1926).

The result of this was the Eastern Congress (*Tōhō kaigi*) held in June 1927, after Tanaka had taken office, and preceding that the first Shandong expedition by the *Kantōgun* in May.

The Eastern Congress was held under the auspices of the Ministry of Foreign Affairs, and included the Ministers of Army and Navy, the Minister of Finance, the Japanese Minister, as well as the Consul-General, in China, and in addition representatives of the Guandong Agency and the Governor-General's office in Korea. The Congress decided to protect by force Japan's special rights in relation to Japanese residents in China on account of the Northern Expedition of Chiang Kai-shek (his attack on the northern warlords designed to unify China). The Shandong expedition anticipated the decisions of the Eastern Congress and was the first step of military intervention in Chinese military affairs, intended to use the Shandong Ministry to stop the Northern Expedition in order to protect Japanese rights in Manchuria and Mongolia.

The *Seiyūkai* change of direction since the Hara and Takahashi period was also evident in internal politics. As we showed in the previous chapter, the party during the Hara and Takahashi period continued to oppose universal suffrage. On the other hand, as seen in Takahashi's argument in favour of abolishing the General Staff Headquarters, he was negative towards convergence between the Emperor and the military. Hara himself in his diary even advocated a symbolic Emperor system. In his words: "If the Emperor is not to be involved in the business of governing, but in charitable work and honours, we shall have peace" (vol. 5, p. 276, 2nd September 1920).

By contrast, the *Seiyūkai* in the Tanaka period proclaimed "Emperor-centrism". Suzuki Kisaburō, while he was Home Minister in the Tanaka Cabinet, criticised the Diet-centrism of the *Minseitō*, and insisted: "The government of our Empire must be superintended by the Emperor, so that it is very clear that it is politics centred on the Emperor. Thought centred on the Diet represents the mainstream of democracy powered by Britain and America, and is incompatible with our national polity (*kokutai*)" (cited from the criticised *Minseitō* organ *Minsei*, vol. 2, no. 3, p. 36, March 1928). If Hara Kei had read this piece, he would have passed out.

'Peace and democracy' of the Kenseikai

Against the *Seiyūkai*, whose rightward trend in both foreign and domestic policy had become manifest, the *Kenseikai* (*Minseitō*), as well as its Shidehara diplomacy, insisted on democratisation in domestic politics. The *Kenseikai* organ *Kensei kōron*, maintaining its inheritance of the *minponshugi* earlier advocated by Yoshino Sakuzō, argued as follows:

> Speaking boldly and frankly, we believe that the whole purpose of politics is to reduce the standard of living of the minority propertied and privileged classes, and raise that of the majority classes who are poor.
>
> (*Kensei kōron*, December 1926, p. 38)

As is clear from the above, from the end of July 1925, when the *Seiyūkai* pulled out of the three-faction constitutional Cabinet, the points of difference between the *Kenseikai* (*Minseitō*) and the *Seiyūkai* were evident in both foreign policy and domestic politics. To be completely accurate we would need to include some reservations here, but in broad terms a two-major-party system had been launched, between the *Kenseikai* (*Minseitō*) pursuing 'peace and democracy', and the *Seiyūkai* advocating 'aggression and 'Emperor-centrism'.

Two-major-party system and policy gap

In general it is impossible to establish definitively whether it was better that the differences between the two major parties should be vague or better that they should be clear. In 1879 Fukuzawa Yukichi identified the differences between the Conservative Party and the Liberal Party in the British two-party system as small (see Fukuzawa Yukichi, *Minjō isshin* ['Renewing the Life of the People'], Jōshō shoten, 1947). But in this two-party system in which the difference between the major parties is small, since government changed from one party to the other there

180 *Japan's Modern History*

was no way of knowing whether it was financiers, labourers, farmers or the unemployed that gained advantage from it. Although what he said is comprehensible, at the same time we cannot deny a certain dreariness about it. The problem indeed cannot be resolved at a general level, but has to be investigated in concrete terms.

Over the ten years and more of politics between the end of the First World War and the May 15th Incident of 1932, it was the first half of the 1920s, in which the *Seiyūkai* and the *Kenseikai* (*Minseitō*) showed their good points and their shortcomings in both domestic and foreign policy, that contributed to political stability and progress. This was true whichever party happened to win. Either peace or democracy – one or the other – was guaranteed. By contrast, the two-party system between 1925 and 1932, with 'peace and democracy' when the *Kenseikai* (*Minseitō*) won, but 'aggression and Emperor-centrism' when victory went to the *Seiyūkai*, was one factor leading to the 'Age of Crisis', not only in Japanese politics, but in the Japanese State itself.

Case for territorial conquest in Manchuria and Mongolia by middle-ranking Army officers

The political situation after 1925, when one wing of the two-party system approved of armed incursions into China, was good news for the hard-liners on Manchuria and Mongolia within the Army. The *Seiyūkai* Cabinet of Tanaka Giichi organised the Eastern Congress, and between 1927 and 1928 those of field officer class (colonels, lieutenant colonels, majors), centred on Colonel Nagata Tetsuzan, Lieutenant-Colonel Tōjō Hideki and Major Ishiwara Kanji, founded a group called the *Mokuyōkai* (Thursday Society). At its third meeting held in January 1928, at which Nagata Tetsuzan was present, Ishiwara Kanji gave his famous address on the topic: "The World's Final War". According to the Reports of the *Mokuyōkai* held by one important member of this group, Major Suzuki Teiichi, Ishiwara's address went as follows:

> Our Defence Policy, Major Ishiwara. . . . Expectations for future wars. Not a war of attrition involving universal national mobilisation, but so as to avoid complaints from politicians, sudden and total annihilation of the enemy. This will be an air war.
>
> The final war. Japan and America as the two *sumō* champions (*yokozuna*), rank and file will follow them, when victory or defeat quickly determined by aircraft, the final war, henceforth the most powerful will become the world's policeman. At that point, (1) aircraft conquer the world. (2) Western civilisation moves entirely to America, the special civilisation of Japan perfected in Japan. . . .
>
> (Kido nikki kenkyūkai, Nihon kindai shiryō kenkyūkai eds,
> *Suzuki Teiichi shi danwa sokkiroku* ['Suzuki Teiichi Lecture Notes'],
> Nihon kindai shiryō kenkyūkai, vol. 2, pp. 368–9)

In fact, the Japan–China war from 1937 to 1945, and the Great Pacific War, was precisely a "war of attrition involving universal national mobilisation", and the air

Crisis, 1925–1937 181

war between Japan and the US merely decorated the end of it. Ishiwara's forecasting was merely an exercise in science fiction.

Nevertheless, even if we read it as a story belonging to the world of science fiction, Ishiwara's argument about the world's final war was quite impressive. B-29s did not fly right around the world, but their flying range was 6,500 km. If the earth's radius is 6,400 km that meant that they could fly a little less than one-sixth of the circumference of the earth. Moreover, the fact that after the US victory in the Japan–US war America became global policeman confirmed Ishiwara's forecast.

On the other hand, the interest of the Army field officers, who had seen the *Seiyūkai* send three successive expeditions to the Shandong Peninsula, was not confined to science fiction. At their fifth meeting in March 1928, a proposal "to establish complete political control over Manchuria and Mongolia" was put forward by Lieutenant-Colonel Tōjō Hideki, and was adopted. It read: "For the survival of our Empire, we must establish total political control over Manchuria and Mongolia. Therefore, preparation for war by our nation's forces should be based on war against Russia, while preparation for war against China need not concern us so much. But in this war we need to be concerned with the possibility that the United States might join the war, and take defensive measures against this" (ibid., pp. 378–9).

Among the members, Nagata was Commander of the third infantry regiment, Tōjō was section head of the War Ministry equipment bureau, Ishiwara was an instructor at the Army College, Suzuki Teiichi was head of the strategy section at General Staff Headquarters, Suzuki Shōsaku was a member of General Staff Headquarters, Nemoto Hiroshi was a member of the China group in the Military Administration Bureau, Banzai Ichirō was an instructor at the Army College, Yokoyama Shizuo was a member of General Staff Headquarters, Tsuchihashi Ichiji was a military adviser to the Chinese government, and Takashima Tatsuo was a section member of the Military Administration Bureau of the War Ministry. The fact that such a group should have had as its aim the "establishment of total military control over Manchuria and Mongolia" had great significance. At a time when the conservative *Seiyūkai* Government advocated protection by force of the rights of Manchuria and Mongolia, middle-ranking officers right across the Army administration went one step further, aiming to take possession of Manchuria and Mongolia.

Minseitō *arguing for cooperation with China*

Whereas the rightward trend in the *Seiyūkai* Cabinet was contributing to the argument of middle-ranking field officers that Manchuria and Mongolia should be taken over, the *Minseitō*, from what we may call a 'left wing' position, was criticising the Shandong expedition of the Tanaka Cabinet. The Party President, Hamaguchi Osachi, in the party organ *Minsei*, argued as follows:

> After the (Tanaka) Cabinet was formed, to some extent the momentum of the Chinese disturbances has tended to encompass Shandong, and the (present)

182 *Japan's Modern History*

government . . . is mistaken in its judgement over the development of this matter; in its confusion it has sent troops to Shandong and is having them advance to Jinan. Even though, considering the subsequent development of events in neighbouring areas, it has become increasingly clear that there was no need to send troops . . . because of procrastination the Emperor's brave and loyal troops have been needlessly left in a foreign land for three months. This has invited doubts at home and abroad about the official attitudes of our Empire. It has thrown a shadow onto the future of our foreign relations, and is extremely regrettable.

(*Minsei*, vol. 2, part 2, February 1928)

Ever since the formation of the Cabinet of Katō Takaaki in August 1925, alternation in office by the two major Japanese parties was assured, and thus if the next Cabinet was to be a *Minseitō* Cabinet, policy towards China could be expected to change drastically. In concrete terms, with the *Seiyūkai* Cabinet a policy of 'protecting local people', in other words defending Japanese expatriates by sending troops to China, was pursued, but with the *Minseitō* Cabinet that followed it, on the principle of non-interference in Chinese domestic affairs, it was not the despatch of troops but rather the temporary withdrawal of expatriates that was conducted.

Concerning the great changes in China policy occasioned by changes of party in power, the middle-ranking field officers previously mentioned expressed strong concern. The leading specialist in the history of Japanese foreign policy, Inoue Juichi, in his recent work *Senzen Nihon no gurobarizumu* ['Globalism in pre-war Japan'], introduces the following reflections made by Major Suzuki Teiichi, of the *Mokuyōkai*:

Lack of trust in political parties stems from corruption scandals and the like, but not only do the *Minseitō* and the *Seiyūkai* fight in elections with opposing points of view, but this creates a situation of division, and seen from the eyes of military men concerned with national security, this is intolerable.

(Inoue Juichi, *Senzen Nihon no gurobarizumu*
['Globalism in pre-war Japan'], Shinchōsha, 2011, p. 37)

London naval disarmament and independence of the right of command

The influence of the two-party system on national security that Suzuki was concerned about became even more clear with the confrontation between the *Minseitō* and the *Seiyūkai* over the London naval disarmament issue in 1930. Moreover, this question was not confined to the rights and wrongs of naval disarmament from the perspective of security, but as we have already indicated was linked with the dispute between the two parties over the Emperor system. We may possibly say that the latter was a more important issue than the former. This was the so-called issue of infringement of the right of command.

Opposing the Hamaguchi Cabinet's intention to sign the London Treaty, because it was not possible to maintain the 70 per cent ratio of large cruisers to that of the United

States, Katō Hiroharu, the Head of Military Command, attempted to petition the Emperor directly to express his disagreement, but was prevented from doing so by members of the Emperor's staff, and then the Cabinet, without waiting for this petition, sent the command to sign the Treaty to the plenipotentiaries in London. This was the so-called issue of infringement of the right of command.

The right of the Chief of the General Staff and the Chief of the Naval Command to petition the Emperor directly without having to go through the Prime Minister or the Army and Navy ministers was called at the time 'direct appeal to the Throne by the military' (*iaku jōsō*). The fact that the government, without waiting for this power to be used, or simply ignoring it, had signed the Naval Disarmament Treaty was said to have infringed the 'right of command' (*tōsuiken*) of the Chief of the Naval Command. It is now generally agreed among scholars that the person who taught the Navy and the far Right how to attack the government using the term 'infringement of the right of command' (*tōsuiken no kanpan*) was the leading theorist of Japanese fascism, Kita Ikki.

Even so, a famous commentator of the time, Baba Tsunego, wrote that the first use of the term *tōsuiken no kanpan* was by the *Seiyūkai*. In an article in the journal *Chūō Kōron* about three years after the signature of the Naval Disarmament Treaty, Baba wrote the following:

> As is well known, one of the reasons for the rise of fascism is connected with the London Treaty. These people think that Japan made unjustifiable concessions at the disarmament conference. Moreover, at the time the Disarmament Treaty was signed, they say that the actions of Prime Minister Hamaguchi of the *Minseitō* Cabinet infringed the Emperor's prerogative concerning decisions over military strength. This later developed into a slogan used by the fascist forces, but at the time it was mainly the *Seiyūkai* that was using it.
>
> (*Chūō* Kōron, August 1933, pp. 71–2)

Following Baba's argument, let us examine the parliamentary question put by Hatoyama Ichirō of the *Seiyūkai* three days after the treaty was signed. Since today the idea that it was Hatoyama who was primarily responsible is widely known, I should like to draw attention to the high quality of his constitutional interpretation:

> According to the Navy General Staff regulations . . . the Chief of Naval Command is directly subordinate to the Emperor, has the right of direct access to the Emperor, plans matters of strategy and national defence, and after the Emperor has himself decided, he hands over the matter to the Minister of the Navy. In other words, *there is absolutely no distinction between strategy and national defence*, and nobody can disagree with the view that in both cases these matters can be entrusted to military specialists (applause). . . . On general political matters the cabinet has responsibility concerning the Emperor's prerogative, but concerning the military right of command all would agree today that the organ advising the Emperor is not Cabinet, but the Chiefs of the General Staff of the Army and of the Navy, who have direct access as advisers

184 *Japan's Modern History*

to the Emperor. . . . And indeed, for the government to oppose the opinions of the Chief of the Navy General Staff, or to ignore them, and to make changes in the military plans, is a tremendously audacious step (applause).

(*Teikoku gikai shūgiin giji sokkiroku* ['Proceedings of the House of Representatives of the Imperial Diet'], vol. 54, 25th April 1930; present writer's italics)

The Minobe school of constitutional interpretation and Navy General Staff regulations

In 1927, when *Chikujō kenpō seigi* ('The Constitution Analysed Article by Article') was published, Minobe had already realised that on the basis of the regulations of the Navy General Staff, set out in the Emperor's military ordinance in 1914, the kind of doctrine of 'infringement of the right of command' discussed by Hatoyama had been put in place. He distinguished the 'right of command' in article 11 of the Meiji Constitution, and the 'right of organisation' in article 12, arguing that matters of 'national defence', of the kind involved in disarmament treaties, were the responsibility of Cabinet, whereas the right of command (*tōsuiken*) applied to 'strategy and tactics'. But he anticipated that the 'Navy General Staff regulations' would frustrate his constitutional interpretation.

Here Minobe was developing the argument that 'military ordinances' (*gunrei*) were no more than rules for use within the armed forces, and 'national' level issues should be dealt with by 'Imperial ordinances' (*chokurei*) conditional on the countersignature of a minister (*chikujō kenpō seigi*, p. 261).

The problem was that whether they were *gunrei* or *chokurei*, they were issued with the personal approval of the Emperor. When *gunrei* and *chokurei* had received the Emperor's personal approval but were incompatible with each other, then the will of the Emperor itself was divided. Here Minobe published an acrobatic interpretation, namely that the Emperor, as Supreme Commander, issuing a *gunrei*, and the Emperor as Head of State, issuing a *chokurei*, were different entities, and that the Emperor in the first case should obey the Emperor in the second case (Minobe Tatsukichi, *Gikai seiji no kentō* ['A Study of Diet Politics'], Nihon Hyōronsha, 1934, p. 134).

Such an interpretation might pass in scholarly argument, but it was unlikely to work in the world of politics. For a non-specialist it would seem incontrovertible that when in 1914 the regulations of the Navy General Staff had been issued as a *gunrei*, the Meiji Constitution already existed, and therefore this *gunrei* had already been recognised by the Constitution. Hatoyama's interpretation was effective in the world of politics, whereas Minobe's idea of splitting the Emperor into 'Supreme Commander' and 'Head of State' was impracticable in the context of actual politics.

Self-restraint on the part of the Supreme Command

Moreover, the idea that the London Disarmament Treaty, in which Japan was added to the UK, the US, France and Italy, was a matter for the 'constitutional world', was only heard within Japan. Internationally, it was obviously an issue for a 'political world'. Within Japan, the person who best understood this was the Chief of General Staff, Katō Hiroharu, who opposed the signature of the treaty. Countering Tōyama Mitsuru, the right-wing luminary who enthusiastically encouraged defence of 'independent right of command', Katō presented the following argument:

> I, Katō, am performing my duty and making clear my opinion. Not conferring with anybody. Not listening to anyone. But what I most earnestly hope for is that this matter should not be seen merely as an important defence issue, but should be regarded as a crucial issue of foreign policy. I fear that if it is not treated cautiously, this will bring harm to the Emperor.
>
> (Itō Takashi et al., *Zoku: gendai shi shiryō 5; kaigun,*
> *Katō Hiroharu nikki* ['Second series: Modern Materials Section 5;
> Diary of Katō Hiroharu of the Navy'], Misuzu Shobō, p. 94)

The Chief of Navy General Staff of the time was telling Tōyama that the unhappiness of the Japanese Navy General Staff with this five nation treaty including the UK, the US, Japan, France and Italy, was not a sufficient reason for rescinding the treaty itself. Of course, Katō's position was that "[t]he Navy General Staff, as responsible for national defence and strategy, finds it difficult to agree in planning with the figures that are the essence of the American proposal" (ibid.). Even so, the government had already sent instructions to its plenipotentiaries to sign the Treaty, and for the Military High Command to frustrate the disarmament conference merely on the basis of Japanese domestic circumstances relating to 'infringement of the right of command' was impermissible.

Katō's position that the constitutional issue was confined within Japan, but that the Disarmament Treaty was also an international and foreign policy issue, is readily demonstrable. Looking askance at the self-disciplined tough arguments put forward by Katō, the two major parties under the two-party system pursued their controversies over constitutional interpretation with fervent enthusiasm.

Minobe's overstepping of the mark

This was not simply the result of Hatoyama alone. The Prime Minister, Hamaguchi Osachi, of the *Minseitō*, took responsibility for having signed the Disarmament Treaty, but hammered home the point that "academic arguments about such and such an article of the Constitution should be consigned to research on those articles, since we do not have time to do that" (*Minsei*, vol. 4, no. 6, p. 3, June 1930). But the opposition *Seiyūkai*, as we have seen, launched a constitutional dispute in the House of Representatives, and the constitutional interpretation that Hamaguchi was intent on avoiding came from Minobe Tatsukichi, the constitutional scholar who was acting as a proxy for the Cabinet. He spectacularly developed his constitutional arguments critical of the military in newspapers and magazines.

186 *Japan's Modern History*

As we shall see in the following, Minobe's opinions were sound. But on the rights and wrongs of the five-power Disarmament Treaty his arguments were rather wide of the mark. Let me introduce some elements of his argument.

> The functions of the Navy General Staff and the Military Council concerning national defence only exist in terms of the right to propose plans about the military. . . . This is similar to designs drawn up by engineers, and it does not go beyond individual proposals to the State.
>
> (*Teikoku Daigaku Shinbun*, 21st April 1930)

Up to this point the Navy General Staff, and also most naval officers, reacted against his arguments, but he further broadened the discourse:

> Since the military authorities are the actors having responsibility for waging war, whether they like it or not, there is a natural tendency for them to strive to strengthen war making capacity, and it is difficult for them to avoid poverty of thought concerning trends in thought over foreign policy, finance, economics and world affairs. If the State puts an absolute value on their judgement there is a danger that it will fall into the evils of militarism.
>
> (*Tokyo Asahi Shinbun*, 4th May)

This is a rather generalised argument. The idea that the Navy General Staff had poor knowledge of "foreign policy, finance, economics and world thought" was Minobe's private opinion, for which he produced no evidence. Strictly speaking, he did not write that they were poor "in knowledge" but that they were "poor in their degree of understanding", but the impression on reading it is the same.

Moreover, it is true that the Navy General Staff agreed on a 70 per cent ratio of cruisers to the level of the United States, and that the government had conceded on the earlier 60 per cent, but for Minobe to go straight into his statement that "there is a danger that the State will fall into the evils of militarism" was a jump too far. Within his insistence that "[t]he various arguments concerning the London Treaty essentially boil down to a confrontation between pacifism and militarism . . . for the military power to attempt to stand above the political power is the most dangerous thing for our country" (*Teikoku Daigaku Shinbun*, 8th September 1930), we may even feel his arrogance in relation to 'peace and democracy'. Irrespective of the rights and wrongs of the issue, it was rather the Navy General Staff that was made to shed tears over the London disarmament question. Rather than the 'military power' standing above the 'political power', it was the political power that had overwhelmed the military power.

Minobe's most extreme provocative reprimand to the Navy was a call for the Army and Navy ministers to be civilians. In the June 1930 edition of *Kaizō*, on sale from around 20th May, he published the following sweeping assertion:

> From a political perspective of genuine government independence, the only way to do it in order to determine the strength of the armed forces in the face of military opinion is to get rid of the system of military officers serving as

Crisis, 1925–1937   187

ministers. . . . Indeed, only by adopting a system of civilian ministers will it become possible to make relations between the military and the government transparent and smooth-running.

(Minobe Tatsukichi, *Gikai seiji no kentō* ['A Study of Parliamentary Politics'], Nihon Hyōronsha, 1934, p. 138)

Reaction from young naval officers

It was inevitable that young naval officers, not only having to swallow a limit on the number of cruisers at 60 per cent of the US number, but also facing pressure for civilianisation of the Army and Navy ministers, should have reacted with anger. Of course, Minobe had expressed his opinion independently of the *Minseitō*, and merely as a constitutional scholar. However, First Lieutenant Fujii Hitoshi, who had leadership status among the young naval officers, understood the attitude of the Hamaguchi *Minseitō* Cabinet towards the military as indistinguishable from what Minobe was saying in a series of presentations. In a letter to a Kyūshū colleague, dated 8th May 1930, Fujii wrote as follows:

Democrats centred on the Diet are clearly standing for office. The party government, whose power is controlled by the *zaibatsu*, says that it will bear responsibility for national defence before the Diet, but Hamaguchi plans to abolish the High Command and the General Staff, as well as taking over the power of independent access to the Throne (*iaku jōsō*), making the Army and Navy ministers civilians (thus transferring the power over military matters to the Cabinet, that is, to the political parties), and abolishing the highest military post. Now power is to be taken out of the hands of the Emperor, and they want to rob him of this final element of power over the military.

(*Gendai shi shiryō* (Materials on Modern History 4), *Kokkashugi undō* (The Nationalist Movement), 1, p. 53

Hamaguchi and the leaders of the *Minseitō* would not have read the materials incorporating Fujii's outspoken statements that we have summarised here. But if we consider Minobe's opinions as representative of the position of the *Minseitō* Government, Fujii's summary was astonishingly accurate. The Hamaguchi *Minseitō* Government ignored the Naval High Command and signed the London Treaty. It also succeeded in ratifying the Treaty, brushing off opposition from the Conference of Naval Military Councillors and from the Privy Council (22nd April, 2nd May). In these circumstances, not only among young Navy officers but also among young Army officers, movement towards a military coup d'état gathered momentum.

Convergence between young officers of the Army and Navy

While omitting the detailed circumstances, let us examine trends in the young officers' movement through the diary of Fujii Hitoshi in January 1931. But since it

188 *Japan's Modern History*

would be cumbersome to read the text of the diary, which with annotations would become even harder to read, I shall take the half page covering a single day and introduce the protagonists taken in the order in which they were written:

- Araki Sadao, Army Lieutenant-General, Commander of Sixth Division (Kumamoto). Later a central figure in the Imperial Way faction (*Kōdō ha*).
- Suganami Saburō. Army First Lieutenant. Fujii's most trusted young army officer. Later, in the May 15th Incident, he visited the Army Headquarters and pressed the Army Minister, Araki, to stand up against it.
- Kurihara Yasuhide. Army Second Lieutenant. In July 1936 executed for his complicity in the February 26th Incident.
- Yotsumoto Yoshitaka. Influenced by Inoue Nisshō, and in his period at the Seventh Higher School in Kagoshima organised the Society to Revere the Emperor (*Keitenkai*). After entering the Law Faculty of Tokyo University, he became a disciple of Uesugi Shinkichi, but after Uesugi's death he entered the Golden Pheasant Hostel (*Kinkeiryō*) of Yasuoka Masahiro, where Inoue was living.
- Inoue Nisshō. Left without graduating from the Eastern Association Special School (*Tōyō Kyōkai Senmon Gakkō*). Lived in China for nine years from 1910. After his return he converted to Nichiren Buddhism and established the *Risshō Gokokudō* in Ibaraki Prefecture, aiming to reform both the local youth and the State. In 1930, he became acquainted with Fujii Hitoshi who, like him, was seeking to reform the State in the Kasumigaura Flying School, and thenceforth they worked together. Before the May 15th Incident he participated in the League of Blood (*Ketsumeidan*) Incident, and was sentenced to an indefinite period of imprisonment.
- Gondō Seikyō. In his youth travelled in Korea, China and Russia, and engaged in extensive interactions with Chinese revolutionaries. In 1927 he wrote *Jichi minpan* ('Model for People's Self-Government'), and seeking national reform that would support a tradition of agricultural self-governance combining land and cereal crops, he became a mentor to Inoue, Fujii and others.
- Yoyogi. Designated Nishida Mitsugu. While at the Army Youth School he came under the influence of Kita Ikki, and in 1925 became a reservist, after which he was a kind of proxy for Kita, and a leader of the Army youth officer movement.

Bearing in mind these participants in the Blood League Incident, the May 15th Incident and the February 26th Incident, let us have a look at Fujii's diary for 10th January 1931:

> Araki Rokushi is sufficiently prepared. Second Lieutenant Kurihara in Kagoshima, serving under Suganami is OK. Suganami, by acting locally, has thoughts of arousing actions at central level, perceives that from now on the centre is going to be crucial, and regrets his slowness in communicating and getting started. Kitahara, serving under Yotsumoto, is in the first year of the

Seventh Higher School, but he is now controlling the *Keitenkai*, and is becoming a warrior. . . . Inoue's plan is to overthrow the established political parties, helping Ugaki (Kazushige), through the *Sokōkai* and the *Seigidan*, and then overthrow the Ugaki Cabinet. This is reported by Hama (Yūji). Meeting old man Gondō I was astonished at his learning. Yoyogi has come out of hospital and is brimming with health, and is plotting to destroy the *Minseitō* Cabinet and put the *Seiyūkai* in its place. But there is a danger that the *Minseitō* will reorganise, because of the inactivity of both left and right wing factions.

(Hara Hideo et al., *Kensatsu hiroku: go ichigo jiken* ['Secret Prosecution Record: May 5th Incident'], Kadokawa Shoten, 1989–90, vol. 3, p. 655)

The *Seiyūkai* pursued the *Minseitō* Cabinet for 'infringement of the right of command', and while Minobe Tatsukichi, speaking on behalf of the *Minseitō*, was proposing 'civilianisation' of the Army and Navy ministers, 'fascist' forces that sought to demolish control by the two major parties as such were beginning to plan a horizontal alliance between the Army, the Navy and the civilian right wing.

'Meiji Restoration' and 'Shōwa Restoration'

The horizontal alliance between young Army and Navy officers and the civilian right wing closely resembled in form the horizontal alliance, discussed in Chapter 1, between lower-ranking samurai of the three domains of Satsuma, Chōshū and Tosa, and leaderless samurai that had quit their domains. But a result leading to 'inferiors overwhelming superiors' (*gekokujō*) was quite different depending on whether the country was in a process of ascent or was experiencing decline. If I may use an old-fashioned expression, the Meiji Restoration was a 'revolution', whereas the 'Shōwa Restoration' was a 'counter-revolution'.

Distinguishing 'revolution' from 'counter-revolution' is not a question of the Emperor system. Despite the confrontation in the Bakumatsu period between 'opening the country' (*kaikoku*) and 'expelling the foreigner (*jōi*), the revolutionary forces moving things forward to the Meiji Restoration all agreed on one thing: 'revering the Emperor' (*sonnō*). On this issue there is no obvious difference between the Meiji Restoration and the Shōwa Restoration.

The big difference between the two concerned the quality of the opposing elite. In a situation of ascent, the top intellectuals of the time would assist the 'opposing elite'. As we have already explained in Chapter 1, Under Shimazu Nariakira in the *Bakumatsu* period, not only the major domain lords, but also top-level scholars of Western learning in the central government of the time (the *Bakufu*), flocked to his side. Even Saigō Takamori, who inherited the intellectual legacy of Nariakira, through the good offices of Katsu Kaishū, absorbed the latest knowledge of the *Bakufu* intellectuals Yokoi Shōnan, Ōkubo Ichiō and others. Under the slogan 'Revere the Emperor, Expel the Foreigner', the famous *Bakumatsu* period samurai, in reality, were racing to set the trend for 'opening the country in a spirit of enterprise'.

By contrast with this, the horizontal alliance that started with the London Disarmament Treaty was exactly 'Revere the Emperor, Expel the Foreigner', and they

190 *Japan's Modern History*

mostly used the word 'Emperor' rather than 'King', which is the word used in the original. They did not wish to refer to the Emperor, in a "lineal succession unbroken for ages eternal" (*bansei ikkei*), as one would just an ordinary 'king'.

It is one of the ironies of history that Kita Ikki, in 1906, shortly after the Russo-Japanese war, who scathingly criticised the 'National Polity' (*kokutai*) argument based on a 'lineal succession unbroken for ages eternal', should have become the high priest of the young Army officers advocating direct rule by the Emperor. But in the 25 years after the Russo-Japanese war, there was no trace of him having deepened the research into Western socialism that so stimulated him in his youth. What he had studied in the meantime was the Chinese revolution, and going on from that, the collapse of the Sun Yat-sen revolution, which had lacked military support. Kita, who had come to believe that it was only by military force that the West could be combated, had none of Saigō's understanding of Europe and America, nor any of the broad-based network, ranging from those who wanted to open the country to those who wanted to expel the foreigner, that Saigō had cultivated in the Bakumatsu period.

For Kita, however, and also for Gondō Seikyō, who believed in an idealised society of ancient Japan, there was only the argument of an expansionary Asian continent. What Gondō, who sought to create agricultural communities combining land and cereals, and Fujii whom he revered as his master, and other young naval officers were aiming at, seemed at first sight to differ from the proposals to occupy Manchuria and Mongolia by the Army field officer class discussed above. But in Fujii's diary for 7th August 1931, the following argument by Gondō in favour of great exploits on the continent of Asia may be found:

> A pamphlet, entitled *Hachirin tsūkō* ('A Thorough Consideration of Eight Neighbouring Countries') came from Mr Gondō. I am reading it voraciously. In order to resolve the continental question it is first necessary to investigate its history. My conclusion is that our brave and enterprising young soldiers should be led onto the Continent, and should settle into garrison life there. This increasingly grave problem leading to our people's struggle cannot be resolved merely through the wars that have occurred between Japan and China, and between Japan and Russia. Land and cereal crops should be opened to all mankind. The exclusion of Japan by the selfish nationalism of China runs counter to the spirit of the Heavenly Path. By garrisoning our men, we wish first of all to make the lives of Koreans secure, and to construct a paradise to ensure the future of Japanese on the Continent. After the reconstruction of the Japanese State, our pent up dynamism as revolutionaries should be directed towards the Continent, so that our discontents may be overcome.
>
> (Hara Hideo et al., *Kensatsu hiroku, go ichigo jiken*, vol. 3, p. 695)

Fujii, having read through Gondō's arguments, mused that "Our ancestors had unlimited yearning to carry out magnificent deeds interacting with the Continent", and wrote the following *tanka* poem:

Accompanying a million young men from the Land of the Sun, let us expand our nation to the Continent?" (*Hi no moto no hyakuman no danji uchitsurete, ware tairiku ni hirakemu ka*).

With this, the Manchurian Incident of 18th September 1931 and the May 15th Incident carried out by young naval officers were brought together as one and the same thing.

Moreover, despite the previously discussed differences between the Meiji Restoration and the Shōwa Restoration, they had in common that both controlled the military. While the two major political parties were becoming increasingly polarised, not only over the issue of rearmament, but also over constitutional questions, they were coming face to face with unanticipated attacks from a third force.

Economic policy creating a split between the two major parties: return to the gold standard and secession from it

Confusion in economic policy was brought about by alternation in power between the two major parties. In July 1929 the Hamaguchi *Minseitō* Cabinet was formed, and in November it was officially announced by the Ministry of Finance that Japan would return to the gold standard (implemented in January 1930). And then, only two years and one month later, in December 1931, now under the *Seiyūkai* Cabinet of Inukai Tsuyoshi, once again by means of an official proclamation by the Finance Ministry it was announced that Japan was going to leave the gold standard.

Since, under the gold standard, settlement of overseas balances was conducted by the transport of gold, if an exodus of gold were to be stemmed, then mainstream currency policy had to be a policy of conservative finance. But because of the need for huge war expenditures during the First World War, the belligerent states were obliged to abolish the gold standard, and indeed Japan in 1917 abandoned it. When the war was over, however, the United States returned to the gold standard (in 1919), and the United Kingdom followed the US in 1925.

Only in the case of Japan did it take a long time to return to the gold standard. One reason for this, as already explained, was the Great Kantō earthquake of September 1923, but another reason was the dislike of financial retrenchment on the part of the *Seiyūkai* because of its traditional 'positive' policies of development.

Opposing the *Seiyūkai* and privileging healthy (conservative) finance were the *Kenseikai* cabinets of Katō Takaaki and Wakatsuki Reijirō, which favoured return to the gold standard. Even so, if Japan were to plan such a move at a time when major states had already returned to the gold standard, the value of the Japanese currency would be high. In contemporary terms, a rising yen started from the level of rumour, Japanese exports became sluggish, the prices of cotton, silk and other exports collapsed. The fact that the yen–dollar ratio in 1925 was 41 dollars to 100 yen, but in 1926 it had risen to 49 dollars, the fact that over the same period exports had fallen by 20 per cent, and also that over the two years between 1925

192 *Japan's Modern History*

and 1927 the price of silk had fallen by about 33 per cent and the price of cotton by about 48 per cent, demonstrates this clearly (Takahashi Kamekichi, *Taishō Shōwa zaikai hendō shi* ['History of Changes in the Financial World of the Taishō and Shōwa periods'], Tōyō keizai shinpōsha, 1955, vol. 2, pp. 557–62).

The fact that the *Kenseikai* Cabinet (Finance Minister Kataoka Naoharu) had indicated the intention of returning to the gold standard caused the financial panic of 1927, which is known for the bankruptcy of the Suzuki General Trading Company and the suspension of operations by the Taiwan Bank.

Since the Tanaka Giichi *Seiyūkai* Cabinet that succeeded it changed the name of its traditional 'positive policies' to 'creating an industrial nation', and promoted such policies, a return to the gold standard under that government was avoided.

Nevertheless, when the *Minseitō* (successor to the *Kenseikai*), returned to power in July 1929, once again a return to the gold standard was envisaged. Even so, the decisive timing of the Finance Minister, Inoue Junnosuke, was eccentric. 'Black Thursday', which is remembered even today, was 24th October 1929, yet the Ministry of Finance issued its announcement of a return to the gold standard a mere month later, on 21st November.

Even though it was unreasonable to expect that from the collapse of the New York stock exchange it would have been possible to predict the outbreak of the Great Depression, the Finance Ministry no doubt understood that the collapse of American stocks would deal a blow to Japanese exports to the United States. On the other hand, if Japan returned to the gold standard, this would mean a rise in the yen against the dollar, and it is unlikely that the Finance Ministry did not understand that this would also adversely affect Japanese exports to the US. Until the future of the American economy became clear, postponing a return to the gold standard, which would mean forcing the yen upwards, should surely have been the natural thing to do for those in charge of financial and economic affairs.

Despite this, unlike confrontation between the two major parties early in the twenty-first century, in such confrontation during the 1920s and 1930s, the points of difference between the two major parties were both clear and firmly maintained, not only in matters of foreign policy and the Constitution, but also in economic policy. When the *Seiyūkai* came to power, positive policies of development would be pursued, and when the *Kenseikai* (*Minseitō*) formed the Cabinet, conservative financial policies would be the order of the day. Such policy changes took place every two years.

The 1930 general elections

Business depression resulting from the return to the gold standard, and the same thing stemming from the great American financial panic, reinforced each other, and their social impact was incalculable. At first, however, not only financial circles but also ordinary people believed that with orthodox financial policies economic performance would be sharpened and the economic climate would improve in the near future. Proof of this was to be found in the victory of the *Minseitō* at the general elections of February 1930. The ruling *Minseitō*, which at dissolution of the House of Representatives held about 37 per cent of the seats, won 58.2 per cent of the seats in the subsequent general elections. Even the *Minseitō* journal after the elections could not conceal its astonishment at the victory of conservative financial policies in the elections:

> Seen from the local areas what was probably most obvious was the cancellation of irrigation projects and the postponement of road and harbour projects, and therefore it looked as though our party would shrink to some extent. When we were trying to anticipate the results of the elections, the fact that the party of our opponents was stirring up the people and that our party was in an unfavourable situation at the local level, meant that the prospects of winning these elections did not look promising.
>
> (*Minsei*, March 1930, p. 12)

The fact that this article twice emphasised the unfavourable 'local' conditions shows how widespread within the party was anxiety about appeals to local interest being made by their rivals the *Seiyūkai*, and about whether they could win the elections when they were returning Japan to the gold standard and pursuing policies of financial retrenchment. Even so, the *Seiyūkai* was soundly defeated at local level, and their seat total fell from 50.9 per cent to 37.0 per cent. The bulk of the farming population believed that with a return to the gold standard the economy would recover.

Disappointing performance by Socialist parties

One feature of these general elections was that, even though these were the second general elections contested under universal male suffrage, the number of seats won by legal Socialist parties actually fell. Moreover, whereas in the previous elections the Socialist People's Party (*Shakai Minshūtō*) – the most moderate of the Socialist parties – won four out of the eight Socialist seats, this time it only won two seats.

According to the Peace Preservation Law (*chian iji hō*) passed in 1925, and especially in its revised form in June 1928, legal activity by the Communist Party, which opposed the Emperor system and capitalism, was becoming impossible. Leaders of political formations aiming to change the 'National Polity' (*kokutai*) were subject to "the death penalty or indefinite imprisonment or five years' imprisonment or house arrest"; those who "knowingly joined such a formation" or engaged in "activities intended to carry out the aims of such a formation" were subject to "more than two years of imprisonment". For the political activities of socialists, the final item, designed to punish "activities intended to carry out the aims of such a formation", was the most important. Since judgement of what kind of activities corresponded to this was left to the discretion of the Home Ministry and the Police, electoral activities of candidates close to the Communist Party were extraordinarily tightly restricted.

For the anti-Communist Socialist Masses Party, this was a very useful situation. But this party, even under such favourable conditions, lost half its seats.

194 *Japan's Modern History*

One reason for this was that the Japanese Federation of Labour (*Nihon Rōdō Kumiai Sōdōmei* – henceforth *Sōdōmei*), which was the largest support base for the Socialist Masses Party, was supporting the social policies of the *Minseitō* Cabinet, and in particular its movement to legalise unions. The *Sōdōmei*, at the time of the formation of the *Minseitō* Cabinet in July 1929, wrote officially in its journal: "The *Minseitō*'s good influence over our national labour union movement, even though it may not be fully substantive, is something that we should frankly acknowledge" (*Rōdō*, August 1929, p. 4).

The top leader of *Sōdōmei* was Matsuoka Komakichi. Matsuoka stood as a candidate for the Socialist Masses Party in the general elections of February 1930 for Tokyo No. 5 district, but lost, perhaps inevitably. For this five-member district, three candidates stood from the *Minseitō*, another two from the conservative *Seiyūkai*, and one (Ōyama Ikuo) from the far-left-wing former Labour Farmer Party (*Rōdō Nōmintō*). While the *Minseitō* was proclaiming the importance of social policy, the Socialist Masses Party was buried between the conservatives and the Left.

When, however, the global financial panic that attained its apogee in the United States was made far worse because of the maintenance of the gold standard by the *Minseitō* Cabinet, confrontation deepened within the Cabinet between the Finance Minister, Inoue Junnosuke, who was dependent on financial circles, and the Home Minister, Adachi Kenzō, much involved in social policy, and gradually the former gained the advantage. As a result, it became difficult to bring in a labour union law, and on the other hand, in the cities workers were dismissed from their jobs in increasing numbers, while in the countryside the price of rice and silk cocoons collapsed. In 1931 the unemployment rate came close to 6 per cent, and the rice price fell to some 60 per cent of its 1929 price, while the price of silk cocoons fell to below 40 per cent.

In these circumstances, labour disputes and tenancy disputes rapidly increased in number, and the fall in the price of rice even caused difficulty for rural landlords. According to Nishida Yoshiaki (*Senzen Nihon ni okeru rōdō undō, nōmin undō no seishitsu* ['The Character of the Labour Movement and the Farmers Movement in Pre-war Japan'], Tokyo Daigaku shuppankai, 1991), labour disputes increased by 70 per cent over the two years between 1929 and 1931, while tenancy disputes had increased by 43 per cent. Labour disputes, however, touched their peak in 1931 and then began to reduce in number, whereas in the villages, which were plunged into a long recession, the number of disputes continued to rise even past 1931, and in 1936 they had reached a level more than four times that of 1929 (Tokyo Daigaku Shakaigaku Kenkyūjo, *Gendai Nihon shakai 4: rekishiteki zentei* ['Modern Japanese Society 4: Historical Preconditions'], Tokyo Daigaku shuppankai, 1991, pp. 286–7).

As we have explained earlier, the ballooning of disputes between the *Minseitō* and the *Seiyūkai*, which reached their height over the London Disarmament Conference in 1930 over three issues – foreign policy, constitutional policy and economic policy – developed beyond the framework of party disputes and linked up with the Navy, the Army, the national reform movement of the far Right, the labour movement and the farmers' movement.

Clear emergence of crisis and decline of parties: from the Manchurian Incident to the May 15th Incident

Over the eight months between the Manchurian Incident of September 1931 and the May 15th Incident of 1932, Japan was in a vortex of crisis. It was confronted with three perplexing issues: an external crisis, a military coup d'état, and an economic crisis.

Ishiwara Kanji, who had proposed at the Thursday Society in January 1928 (mentioned above) a final world war, was taken on in October by the High Command of the *Kantōgun*, and from then it was only a matter of time before the Society's vision of occupying Manchuria and Mongolia was converted into reality.

Crisis of coup d'état

Domestically, the movement to reform the State began to acquire a whiff of realism around the time on 26th August 1931 when young Army and Navy officers and members of the civilian far right held a joint conference under the name of *Gōshikai*. This was about three weeks before the Manchurian Incident took place. Let us examine the diary of Fujii Hitoshi, who was present, for his description of the atmosphere at the conference:

> Afternoon, at the Japan Youth Assembly Hall in the Outer Gardens of the Ise Shrine, met under the name of *Gōshikai*. Army comrades, Navy comrades – Ōgishi (Raikō) from Tōhoku; others include Azuma (Noboru), the only Kyūshū representative, Mr Inoue's comrades, Suganami, Noda (Matao), Mr Tachibana Kōsaburō, Koga Kiyoshi, Takahashi Kitao, Shibusawa Zensuke; met for the first time Tsushima, Takahashi and Second Lieutenant Kaneko Nobutaka of the Akita Regiment and four others.
>
> Here we are constructing our organisation, and are setting up Central Headquarters in Yoyogi, Nishida (Mitsugu) is in charge, and Inoue is helping him, while Inoue's group is involved as guerrillas. This is coming together as a group of more than 30 progressive revolutionaries. We went to Shinjuku drinking *saké* and chatting, at times beating our breasts in unison.
>
> (*Kensatsu hiroku: 5.15 jiken*, vol. 3, p. 701)

For the Army national reconstruction movement, the *Sakurakai* had been formed in October of the previous year, bringing together officers of Lieutenant-Colonel rank and below, and before the young Army and Navy officers came together as the *Gōshikai*, they met as the principal figures in the *Sakurakai*.

At his meeting around this time with Hashimoto Kingorō, Fujii Hitoshi realised that in the *Sakurakai* there was no intention to mount a coup d'état, and began to distance himself from it. This protected the young Army and Navy officers after the failed coup attempt of 17th October (the October Incident), but putting it the other way round, it came to create the basis for the May 15th Incident of 1932.

196   *Japan's Modern History*

Table 6.2

Date	Shōwa era year	Prime Minister	Events
1931	6	Hamaguchi Wakatsuki Inukai	Manchurian Incident occurs (Liutiaohu Incident). October Incident (failed coup by the *Sakurakai*). Ban on gold exports (secession from the gold standard).
1932	7	Saitō	Shanghai Incident. League of Nations Lytton Commission. Blood League Incident (Inoue Junnosuke and Dan Takuma assassinated). Eighteenth general election (minority *Seiyūkai* victorious). Founding of the State of Manchukuo. May 15th Incident (Inukai Tsuyoshi assassinated). Saitō Makoto (national unity cabinet). Socialist Masses Party founded. Japan–Manchukuo Protocol signed. Economic crisis easing.
1933	8		Nazi regime established in Germany. New Deal policies launched in the US. Japan leaves League of Nations. Takigawa Incident. Tang gu ceasefire agreement.
1934	9	Okada	Manchukuo Emperor system established. Okada Keisuke Cabinet begins. Young Army officers carry out November Incident.
1935	10		Minobe Tatsukichi's organ theory of the Emperor seen as controversial. Cabinet commissions and Cabinet Research Bureau set up. National Polity clarification declaration. Army Military Bureau Chief, Nagata Tetsuzan, stabbed to death.
1936	11	Hirota	Nineteenth general election (*Minseitō* victorious, *Seiyūkai* badly defeated, Socialist Masses Party advances. February 26th Incident (Saitō Makoto, Takahashi Korekiyo and others assassinated). Hirota Kōki Cabinet formed. Washington and London treaties lapse.
1937	12	Hayashi	*Kappuku* Debate. Cabinet of Ugaki Kazushige stillborn. Hayashi Senjūrō Cabinet begins. Twentieth general elections (*Minseitō* and *Seiyūkai* level-pegging; Socialist Masses Party advances). First Konoe Fumimaro Cabinet formed. Japan–China war breaks out (Marco Polo Bridge Incident). Anti-Communist Pact between Japan, Germany and Italy. Imperial Headquarters established.

Manchurian Incident

For the second Wakatsuki Cabinet, however, the October Incident, together with the Manchurian Incident of the previous month, endangered its existence.

The crisis was provoked by the *Kantōgun* (also known as the Kwantung Army, or Guandong Army). On 18th September 1931, it was reported to the General Staff that the Chinese Army had blown up the Manchurian Railway and occupied the main cities alongside the railway.

Crisis, 1925–1937 197

Not only for the Cabinet, but also for the General Staff, this event was a bolt from the blue. Even so, until the end of November, Shidehara diplomacy succeeded in restraining the reckless actions of the *Kantōgun*. Not only the Foreign Minister, but also the Army Minister (Minami Jirō) and the Chief of the General Staff (Kanaya Hanzō), made determined efforts both to restrain the *Kantōgun* and to dissipate the distrust of the American Government. To the *Kantōgun*, which intended to advance, not only to Qiqihaer (Tsitsihar) in the north-east, but to the key Chinese base in Jilin province the north of the Great Wall, the representative of the Deputy Chief of the General Staff issued the following order:

> Rumours that the *Kantōgun* intends to use its forces in Jilin province have recently been circulating. Because among foreigners and Japanese intellectuals this is regarded as a premise for the direct use of force by the Japanese forces, caution is essential. Policy towards Jilin province must shortly be decided in light of the general situation by the Army General Staff, and from the Commander in Chief downwards thorough concern about the actions as well as all policy making by the *Kantōgun* must be made on the basis of this policy. Based on the order.
>
> (Kobayashi Tatsuo et al., *Gendai shi shiryō7: Manshū jihen* ['Materials on Modern History 7: Manchurian Incident'], Misuzu Shobō, 1964, p. 278)

This was a telegram sent on 22nd November by the representative of the Deputy Chief of the General Staff, on the orders of the Chief of the General Staff, to the Deputy Staff Officer at Mukden, Ninomiya Harushige, and the important part of it is the section beginning "foreigners . . ." On 23rd November, the US Secretary of State, Henry Stimson, through the American Ambassador in Japan, handed a strong warning to the Foreign Minister, Shidehara, concerning the attack on Jilin province by the *Kntōgun*:

> On the 23rd, Secretary of State Stimson, having received a report that there was a danger Japanese forces would attack Jilin province, sent a message that if this turned out to be the case, the patience of the American Government would reach its limit.
>
> (Evening editions of all Japanese newspapers, reporting a *Rengō* despatch from Washington on 27th)

To this warning from the American Secretary of State, Shidehara was able to give a confident reply, since, as we have seen, a day and a half before, an order had gone out in the name of the Chief of the General Staff to refrain from attacking Jilin province. Shidehara, through the American Ambassador, sent the following reply on the 24th to the Secretary of State:

> Japan has no intention of advancing in the direction of Jilin province. . . . The Japanese Government has already sent orders to this effect to the Japanese forces High Command (High Command of the *Kantōgun*).
>
> (Ibid.)

198 *Japan's Modern History*

If things had ended like this, it would probably have meant total victory for 'Shidehara diplomacy', since Shidehara, who believed in cooperation with the United States, had persuaded not only the Army Minister, but even the Chief of the General Staff, to send orders to the *Kantōgun* to refrain from attacking Jilin province.

Defeat of Shidehara diplomacy

Things, however, were completely turned on their head. The *Kantōgun* ignored the order to cease from the Chief of the General Staff, and went on to attack Jilin province, and when the Chief of the General Staff, angry that his orders had been ignored, repeated three times his cessation order, this made the US Secretary of State explode with indignation. Meanwhile, the explanatory statement that Stimson made in response to the view that he was attacking the Japanese Foreign Ministry, spelled the defeat of Shidehara diplomacy and a widening of activities by the *Kantōgun*.

Stimson held press conferences on 27th and 28th, and in the latter declared: "Through Ambassador Forbes I received an explanation from Foreign Minister Shidehara that the Foreign Minister, the Army Minister and the Chief of the General Staff had been in agreement not to allow military action against Jilin province, and had ordered the local Commander to desist." He thus explained that he had issued neither a warning nor an attack on the Japanese government.

In Japanese diplomacy while this book is being written (2011), the view that foreign countries should understand the particular local circumstances of Japan is often seen. But when Japan's local circumstances differ too much from those of foreign countries, the Japanese government has a responsibility to explain itself. It was the same with the pre-war Manchurian Incident. In the case of America, when it is announced that the Secretary of State, the Secretary for War and the Joint Chiefs of Staff are 'of the same opinion', then both in the 1930s and today this would cause no domestic problems.

But in pre-war Japan, where article 11 of the Meiji Constitution established 'independence of the right of command', even if the Foreign Minister and Chief of the General Staff conferred directly over the military actions of the *Kantōgun*, or if they both assured foreign countries that they were "of the same opinion", this clearly constituted 'interference with the right of command'. Moreover, since the American Secretary of State officially announced this in an open press conference, not only the Foreign Minister, Shidehara, but also the Chief of the General Staff, Kanaya Hanzō, lost out in relation to the *Kantōgun*. Both of them lost their power to prevent the *Kantōgun* from invading Jilin province.

On 7th December, an order was transmitted to the *Kantōgun* by the Army Minister that it was permitted, not only to 'mop up bandits', but to engage in battle with regular Chinese forces. Incidentally, warfare limited to defence of the areas alongside the Manchurian Railway fell within the category of independent command, and therefore was within the jurisdiction of Chief of the General Staff, but since warfare between independent states fell under the foreign policy power

Crisis, 1925–1937 199

according to article 13 of the Meiji Constitution, the order was issued by the Army Minister. This meant an expansion of the Manchurian Incident, and the defeat of Shidehara diplomacy.

Grand coalition plan by the Home Minister, Adachi

At the same time, the Minister of Home Affairs in the same *Minseitō* Cabinet, Adachi Kenzō, was greatly concerned about a military coup d'état, symbolised by the October Incident, and about the threat of terror from the civilian right wing. Moreover, against the backdrop of these incidents, there was social unrest from the difficulties farmers faced in making a living, as well as increasing labour unemployment, both resulting from the return to the gold standard. In order to curb the young officers' movement and abolish the gold standard, seen as the cause of social unrest, what Adachi proposed was a grand coalition of the *Minseitō* and the *Seiyūkai* (a cabinet of cooperation).

Japanese politics in the early years of Shōwa (from 1926) is known for its two-party system and attacks on it by young officers, but the concept of a grand coalition, premised on the abandonment of what had been another plank of the *Minseitō* Cabinet, the financial policies of Inoue Junnosuke, was a powerful option for the *Minseitō*. The second Wakatsuki Cabinet resigned and the Inukai Tsuyoshi Cabinet was formed, but in March 1932, before the May 15th Incident, Baba Tsunego wrote as follows about Home Minister Adachi's concept of a 'cabinet of cooperation':

> In the Diet before dissolution, the *Minseitō* Cabinet had an absolute majority of 260. But despite having an overall majority, the Cabinet lacked the self-confidence to overcome the situations it was faced with. It was threatened by an atmosphere of social unrest. For this reason the Home Minister, Adachi, proposed a cabinet of cooperation. It is difficult to overcome this atmosphere of social unrest with the power of the *Minseitō* alone. Maybe the existence of parliamentary politics itself is threatened. The *Seiyūkai* indeed is likely to support the protection of parliamentary politics. It is a question of defending parliamentary politics by combining the forces of the two major parties. Various ideas are bandied about regarding the motives for proposing a cabinet of cooperation, but this seems to be the fundamental motive. The atmosphere of social unrest incapable of solution even by the 260 parliamentary members of the *Minseitō* eventually destroyed the *Minseitō* Cabinet. Has the *Seiyūkai* acquired the self-confidence to solve it, or has it not?
>
> (*Minsei*, 1st March 1932)

As everyone knows, in the general elections of 20th February 1932, the *Seiyūkai* exceeded the previously cited '260' total for the *Minseitō* and won no fewer than 303 seats. But the fact that, as Baba pointed out, the social unrest, incapable of solution with 260 seats, was no more capable of solution with 303 seats, was shortly to be demonstrated by the May 15th Incident.

200 *Japan's Modern History*

The question is, why did the 'cabinet of cooperation' idea put forward by the Minister of Home Affairs, Adachi, and backed by Baba Tsunego, not materialise in December 1931? As a result of the fact that Adachi's idea was accepted neither by the *Minseitō* nor by the *Seiyūkai*, the *Minseitō* Cabinet (2nd Wakatsuki Cabinet) left the stage and the one-party *Seiyūkai* Cabinet (Inukai Cabinet) that followed was overthrown as a result of the May 15th Incident, after which there were no more party cabinets in pre-war Japan.

Of course, had Adachi's 'cabinet of cooperation' actually come about, there would have been absolutely no guarantee that the May 15th Incident by young naval officers could have been avoided. As can be seen from the diary of Fujii Hitoshi, cited several times above, probably nobody could have prevented the May 15th Incident from taking place. As Adachi asked, however, if the young naval officers had shot the prime minister of a 'cabinet of cooperation' between the *Minseitō* and the *Seiyūkai* working together, and commanding some 98 per cent of seats in the House of Representatives, would it in fact have been able to kill off party cabinets as such?

Opposition to coalition by the Finance Minister, Inoue

The determination, however, of the Finance Minister, Inoue Junnosuke, to stay on the gold standard made such a cabinet impossible. At the time the closest adviser to the Emperor was the Elder Statesman (*genrō*) Saionji Kinmochi, and the Lord Keeper of the Privy Seal, Makino Nobuaki, was second only to Saionji in influence. Moreover, Makino had high expectations of Adachi's cabinet of cooperation. Kido Kōichi, who served as Secretary to the Lord Keeper of the Privy Seal under Makino, was of the same opinion, but regarded the most difficult problem of a coalition between the two major parties as being whether or not the gold standard system were retained. In his diary entry for 17th November 1931, he wrote the following:

> When I think about constructing a coalition government, the most difficult problem between the *Seiyūkai* and the *Minseitō* lies not in foreign policy, but in financial policy, specifically issues centred on abolishing the ban on exporting gold. It is particularly important to listen to the candid opinions of the Finance Minister, Inoue.
>
> (Kido Kōichi, *Kido Kōichi nikki* ['Kido Kōichi Diary'],
> Tokyo Daigaku shuppankai, 1966, vol. 1, p. 11)

Nevertheless, when Inoue met with Kido, he made no reply at all to questions on the gold standard, and from a position critical of the military, he rejected the idea of a cabinet of cooperation.

> The concept of a so-called 'national unity' cabinet that is recently being advocated, or of a *Seiyūkai – Minseitō* coalition cabinet, are neither of them strong enough to restrain the military, but rather flatter the military, and when we

think of the future of our country, they contribute absolutely nothing. Moreover, in that the military is developing plans in ignorance of international relations, this will inevitably lead our country to destruction. Even though the present government has limited power, we are using all means to control the activities of the military. Accordingly, it is sincerely inevitable that we are unpopular among the military, and it is at present impossible to imagine that a stronger cabinet than ours could be formed.

(Ibid.)

This is a high-sounding argument, but the idea that "we are using all means to control the activities of the military" became even more impossible after the aforementioned Stimson discussion following the meeting on the 10th. Also, under the gold standard that Inoue adhered to, the lives of farmers and labourers became seriously impoverished, and the fact that this brought about the *Minseitō* rout in the March general elections is well known. This fine argument, which failed to comprehend the situation properly, drove the political parties into a bottomless pit.

As a result of the lack of unity over a cabinet of cooperation and the gold standard system, on 11th December the second Wakatsuki Cabinet resigned en masse.

Concerning a successor cabinet, it was clear that there was disagreement between the Elder Statesman Saionji Kinmochi and the Lord Keeper of the Privy Seal, Makino Nobuaki. Saionji believed in alternation between two major parties, whereas Makino was a supporter of a cabinet of cooperation. I shall omit detailed description about this, but just before it fell to the lot of Inukai Tsuyoshi, President of the *Seiyūkai*, to form a cabinet, Makino said to Saionji: "My hope was that Your Excellency would form a cabinet on the basis of a spirit of cooperation." In order to understand the later period of national unity cabinets, one should bear this phrase in mind (Itō Takashi, Hirose Yasuaki [ed.], *Makino Nobuaki nikki* ['Makino Nobuaki Diary'], Chūō Kōronsha, 1990, p. 492).

Formation of the Seiyūkai *single-party Cabinet*

Saionji, however, took no notice of this, and entrusted the formation of a new cabinet to Inukai Tsuyoshi, President of the *Seiyūkai*, which held just 37 per cent of the seats in the House of Representatives. The primary emphasis of the *Seiyūkai* electoral campaign had been on the resumption of developmental policies by coming off the gold standard. Also, the fact that Araki Sadao, as a condition for his joining the Cabinet as Minister for the Army, demanded that "Cabinet must not put restrictions on military actions in Manchuria" attracted the attention of the Emperor through the newspapers (ibid., p. 493). This condition imposed by him on his entry into the Cabinet was probably a quid pro quo for young Army officers not mounting a coup. In fact, he prohibited young Army officers from joining the May 15th Incident.

If things had progressed according to this scenario, and the *Seiyūkai* had won a convincing victory at the general elections of February 1932, the May

202 *Japan's Modern History*

15th Incident might well not have occurred even if the Manchurian Incident had been further expanded.

The 1932 general elections

When the *Seiyūkai* Cabinet of Inukai Tsuyoshi was put in place in December 1931, the Finance Minister, Takahashi Korekiyo, took Japan out of the gold standard on that very day. This meant a shift from the tight money policies of the *Minseitō* Cabinet to the traditional developmental policies of the *Seiyūkai* Cabinet. And then on 21st January 1932, the Prime Minister, Inukai, dissolved the House of Representatives.

The Seiyūkai, as the minority government party, which at the time of dissolution controlled 171 out of the total 466 seats, played it as a single-issue election based on escape from economic depression and restoration of prosperity. This is demonstrated in an extreme form by the following discourse by the party Secretary-General, Kuhara Fusanosuke:

> I think the main issue in the current political struggle is clear. Do you like prosperity or recession? Do you want to work, or do you want to be unemployed? Do you desire a stable livelihood, or an unstable one? Do you wish for industrial revival or industrial bankruptcy? Should taxes be reduced, or should they be increased? Should we have an autonomous foreign policy or a servile foreign policy? etc. etc.
>
> *(Seiyū*, February 1932, p. 2)

For an electoral campaign based entirely on economic policy to be effective, quite special conditions need to apply, but at the beginning of 1932 such special conditions actually existed. Because of Inoue's financial policies of returning to the gold standard in the middle of the Great World Depression, depressed economic conditions had grown worse both in cities and in rural areas, and the unemployed were crowding the streets. Continuing his earlier comment, Secretary-General Kuhara went on:

> Since the choice to be made is affected by the destructive policies of the *Minseitō* Government, on account of which everyone equally has tasted bitterness, the choice facing the people is extremely clear.
>
> (Ibid.)

The result was as Kuhara had predicted. The *Seiyūkai* picked up 132 extra seats, arriving at a total of 303 seats out of 466. On the other hand, the *Minseitō* lost 103 seats, becoming a minority party controlling no more than 144 seats out of 466.

As we have already seen, what drove the *Minseitō* Cabinet from office was three crises on different dimensions. Among these a way out of economic crisis was found with the overwhelming victory of the *Seiyūkai*. The two remaining crises were the crisis in foreign relations and the crisis of military coup d'état. But the

Crisis, 1925–1937 203

Seiyūkai thought that, for the Cabinet to include as Army Minister Araki Sadao, who carried with him the hopes and expectations of the young Army officers, the latter two crises could be avoided. In respect of the crisis of foreign relations, the word 'avoid' may well have been inappropriate. Since the Inukai Government on 1st March finally recognised the establishment of the puppet regime of Manchukuo, the crisis in relations with Europe and America became worse. On the other hand, a domestic crisis relating to foreign relations, whereby the Army, including especially the *Kantōgun*, might have attacked the *Seiyūkai* Cabinet over the Manchurian and Mongolian question, was indeed avoided.

Continuation of a coup d'état crisis: the May 15th Incident

The question was a crisis of coup d'état and of terrorism. As for the young Army officers, they had aimed to create a 'legal revolution', in which they would get rid of the *Minseitō* Cabinet, bring about a Cabinet of the *Seiyūkai*, and then have Araki Sadao in the Cabinet as Army Minister. Kita Ikki's expression that "[i]n this revolution there would be no victims, in other words no space fillers (*umekusa*, i.e. victims)" is remarkable given that he was later executed as ringleader in the February 26th Incident (*Kensatsu hiroku* ['Secret Record of the Prosecution'], vol. 1, p. 89; present writer's italics). Moreover, the statement of Andō Teruzō, who played a central role in the later February 26th Incident, that "we intend to keep victims to a minimum, according to our plan. Now, since our plan is steadily progressing, we do not wish terror to be committed", was similar to Kita's statement (ibid., p. 88).

By contrast, the young naval officers, who aimed to bring about the idealistic peasant society of Gondō Seikyō, from the very beginning intended to create "space fillers". Their central figure, Fujii Hitoshi, while recognising the change of policy on the part of the young Army officers, confirmed his resolution to "carry out the *heroic 'Sakurada Gate' deed* on National Foundation Day (11th February)" (ibid., vol. 3, p. 721; present writer's italics). The fact that this diary entry asserting his resolve was written on 14th January 1932 is important. When the Cabinet changed from *Minseitō* to the *Seiyūkai*, the young Army officers for the time being supported the *Seiyūkai* Cabinet, and the latter abandoned the gold standard which its predecessor had so firmly supported, the young Navy officers, with no concern for these events, were planning to replay the assassination of the *Tairō* Ii Naosuke (Sakurada Gate Incident), carried out by samurai adventurers in 1860.

Fujii himself, on 5th February 1932, as an airman involved in the Shanghai Incident, was killed in battle, but two days before National Foundation Day, the Blood League (*Ketsumeidan*) of Inoue Nisshō and others, shot dead Inoue Junnosuke with a pistol, and on 5th March the Chairman of the Board of Directors of the Mitsui Partnership, Dan Takuma, was shot dead, also by the Blood League. It is said that the young Navy officers group, having close relations with Inoue Nisshō, hatched the plan to carry out these acts after the ceremonial return of Fujii from the Shanghai front.

If we compare the scale of the May 15th Incident of 1932 with the February 26th Incident that occurred six years later, it is clear that the latter was a bigger

204 *Japan's Modern History*

event. Those who participated in the former were, apart from civilian pupils of the Patriotic School (*Aikyō juku*), 6 naval officers, 12 Army officer cadets, in all no more than 18 young officers of the Navy and Army. By contrast, in the February 26th Incident of 1936, even though the number of young officers was about the same (20), following them were around 1,500 lower-ranking officers and soldiers, so that the scale was some 84 times as great.

In terms, however, of its effect shifting the ethos of the age radically to the right, the two incidents were almost at the same level. Subsequently, and until the defeat in 1945, no single-party cabinet was formed. Over the 13 years until the end of the war, Japan continued to expand its aggression in China, and at the end of 1941 Japan embarked upon a war with Britain and America. Terror and coups d'état by military men occurred for the last time in the February 26th Incident, but the influence of the military in domestic politics continued to increase, and the end of the war in August 1945 was just 14 years from the Manchurian Incident and 13 years from the May 15th Incident. This was why the title of 'Fifteen-year War' took root.

Democracy in a vortex of crisis

With the three crises of 1931 and 1932, the attempt to create parliamentary democracy in pre-war Japan was frustrated. But over the five years up to the Marco Polo Bridge Incident of July 1937, neither the *Seiyūkai* nor the *Minseitō* abandoned their attempts to return to power, and the Social Masses Party, which was a party based on socialism, was looking at opportunities for a breakthrough. Unlike the 'Age of Breakdown', between 1937 and 1945, in the 'Age of Crisis' the forces that were exposed to attacks from military fascism showed full-scale resistance. With the start of post-war democracy, as it was called, following the defeat in 1945, those who supported it were mainly the opposition forces of the 'Age of Crisis'.

Calming of crisis under a national unity cabinet

The successor to the *Seiyūkai* Cabinet that resigned at the May 15th Incident was a national unity Cabinet under the Prime Minister, Saitō Makoto, a Rear Admiral in the Navy. The meaning of 'national unity' was that four ministers were appointed from the *Seiyūkai*, which held a majority in the House of Representatives, and three from the *Minseitō*, which was the second party (and up to this point it was the same as the previously discussed 'cabinet of cooperation'), but the post of Prime Minister was not accorded to a political party.

Under the Saitō Cabinet, the three crises referred to above moved towards solution. First of all, the idea of overthrowing a Cabinet in which Araki Sadao had been retained as Army Minister was impossible for the young Army officers. So far as the young Navy officers were concerned, since they had already perpetrated the May 15th crisis, they lacked the strength to commit more terrorist acts. A threat of a crisis of terror and coup by the military had receded for the time being.

As for the economic crisis, it had settled down as a result of the positive developmental policies of Takahashi Korekiyo and the individual efforts of private companies. The rice price had started to return in 1932, and in 1934 it reached 1.6 times the price in the worst period (1931). The level of unemployment fell from around 6.9 per cent in 1932 to 4.7 per cent in 1935.

In regard to the rapid rise in exports, it is easier to understand if, rather than giving the figures, I cite the unions' demands for wage increases. The organ of the largest union federation of the time (*Sōdōmei*), in its issue of November 1935, published the following opinion piece:

> Since 1932, Japanese industry has made spectacular advances, trade is on an upward trend, and in the situation as it is in the middle of this year (1935), it is predicted that later this year there will start to be an export surplus. When we look at industrial production, in silk we have overtaken Britain and become the first in the world, in rayon we have overtaken France and Italy and become the world's number two and we are competing fiercely with the United States, which is the number one. Japanese goods are flooding into the furthest corners of the world. What is the reason for this rise in Japanese exports? . . . The main reason is the low level of Japanese wages. Since wages are cheap, the cost of production falls, and this makes them competitive.
>
> (*Rōdō* (Labour), no. 292, p. 21)

Following on from this, the passage where *Sōdōmei* demanded higher wages can be omitted here. Between 1932 and 1935, in silk, rayon and miscellaneous goods, Japan was overtaking the top producers, and the economic crisis of the early 1930s was resolved.

Of the three crises, the one in which no path to resolution was to be found was the crisis of foreign relations. In September 1932 the Japanese Government officially recognised as an independent State Manchukuo, which had been arbitrarily created on Chinese territory by the *Kantōgun*. The arbitrary establishment of an independent State by another country on Chinese soil and within the area of Chinese sovereignty, was for China quite unacceptable. Even though at times China was silent in recognition of difference in military strength between it and Japan, it was impossible that this silence would last indefinitely.

The process and result of Japan's departure from the League of Nations is rather complex; we cannot be sure that it was the worst choice, and the view that for this single reason Japan became the 'world's orphan' is an illogical reading of the situation. As is clear from the work by Inoue Juichi entitled *Senzen Nihon no 'gurobarizumu'* ('"Globalism" in pre-war Japan'), Shinchōsha, 2011, if it proved impossible to suppress military actions by the *Kantōgun*, then the only method of avoiding economic sanctions by Britain and America was to leave the League (pp. 83–4). According to the Charter of the League of Nations (in this case article 16), sanctions could only be applied to states that were members of the League. Moreover, once Japan had departed from the League, not only was a systematic basis for interfering just in the question of Manchuria and Mongolia forfeited, but, as Inoue argues, interest in the matter was also lost (ibid., p. 88).

206 *Japan's Modern History*

Counterattack by the political parties

So far as this understanding was concerned, there was a common feeling among the political parties of resentment at the military that was playing up the idea of 'crisis' and then interfering in domestic politics. Uehara Etsujirō of the *Seiyūkai*, in that party's organ in January 1935, argued as follows:

> Where is the emergency in Japan at present? Even though they call it a continuous emergency, the nature of it two years ago and today are completely different. Two years ago externally, there was the Manchurian Incident and our departure from the League of Nations, and domestically we had the economic crisis, in other words it was reasonable to call it a time of emergency. By contrast today the Manchurian Incident has reached a pause, and the issue of leaving the League has been calmly resolved.
>
> (*Seiyū*, p. 83)

As we have already maintained, the economic crisis was coming to an end, and the crisis brought about by the military coup d'état was calming down. In addition to this, at a time when people felt that the external crisis had been resolved, the political parties began their counterattack against the military and against fascism.

The citation from Uehara's essay was from January 1935, but as is clear from what we have seen already, resolution of the three crises was already apparent in 1933. In October 1933, a speech meeting sponsored by the *Seiyūkai* was held in the Hibiya Public Hall, and Hamada Kunimatsu, later well known for his debate over ritual disembowelment with the Army Minister, made the following speech:

> Fascist ideas have become extreme, they take no notice of public opinion and are arbitrary, they damage personal freedom and have already destroyed State order. You can see examples of this in recent events in Japan. . . . This way of thinking is advancing, freedom of speech guaranteed in the National Constitution, freedom to publish, security of residence, all rights under public and private law – all of these are being subjected to increasing pressure directed at all of the people, and if you are deprived of these rights, are you prepared to put up with this?
>
> (*Seiyū*, November 1933, p. 69)

Split in the kensei no jōdō argument

Those political parties that realised that the three crises had been resolved did not only begin to criticise the military and fascism. Even in the House of Representatives at the end of 1933, the *Seiyūkai* controlled 291 seats out of 466. According to the regular procedures of constitutional government (*kensei no jōdō*), which had become a familiar concept since the end of the Taishō period (1926), that party's President, Suzuki Kisaburō, should have been occupying the position of

Prime Minister. That being impossible, the reason why, together with the *Minseitō* (119 seats), it was backing Admiral Saitō Makoto as Prime Minister was entirely because of the threefold crisis. Calls for constitutional procedures to be followed and for power to be handed back to the *Seiyūkai* were becoming stronger within that party. Here was the reason why the party was strongly criticising the military and fascism.

For the critic Baba Tsunego, who among pre-war intellectuals most consistently advocated that the regular procedures of constitutional government should be followed, a national unity Cabinet was a worthless regime without freedom of political choice. In 1933, when the *Seiyūkai* began to raise voices of criticism of the military and of fascism, Baba developed the following criticism of the national unity Cabinet in the journal *Chūō Kōron*:

> The strong point of parliamentary politics in peacetime is that the parties are divided into a government party and an opposition party and compete with each other. For instance, in the Diet the *Seiyūkai* and the *Minseitō* put forward opposite propositions, and outside the Diet they denounce and attack each other. . . . When they take opposite positions, and struggle in open conflict, one may at least advance arguments in the middle between their two positions. In other words, at least this breadth of freedom of speech exists.
>
> Freedom of speech now, however, exists only along one line, and horizontal breadth is hardly there at all. The government says something. Since both the *Seiyūkai* and the *Minseitō* together support the government, they express no contrary opinion. This unity of national argument is a strength of the national unity Cabinet, but is also a weakness of the State.
>
> (*Chūō* Kōron, August 1933, p. 70)

The expression that "a strength of the Cabinet" is also "a weakness of the State" is something that would only be expressed by a top-ranking journalist. But in Baba too there was a "weakness". According to his 'regular procedures of constitutional government' position, after the Cabinet of national unity were removed it would be necessary to form a majority *Seiyūkai* cabinet. But as we have already touched on, he hated the pro-military and pro-fascist positions of the *Seiyūkai*. After the national unity Cabinet was overthrown, the argument that a government should be formed, not by the majority *Seiyūkai*, but by the *Minseitō*, which controlled a mere 119 seats out of 446, only made sense if the *Seiyūkai* had no lust for power. But the *Seiyūkai*, which had had to relinquish power because of terror on the part of young naval officers, was anxious to return to power.

Even so, Baba pressed home this difficult argument on the basis of "opposing fascism".

> Since the gap between the *Seiyūkai* with 300 Diet members and the *Minseitō* with 120 is too great, there are calls for us not to hope for a *Minseitō* Cabinet, and to stay silent. But if we hope for a return to the regular procedures of constitutional government, we arrive, not at a *Seiyūkai* government but one formed

208 *Japan's Modern History*

by the *Minseitō*. . . . When the people firmly resolves to oppose fascism, this natural demand will point in the direction of the *Minseitō.*

(Ibid., pp. 72–3)

In the medium term, circumstances developed in the direction expected by Baba. Since the previous general elections were held in Febrruary 1932, four years later in 1936, irrespective of whether the Diet would be dissolved, elections were held at the end of the electoral mandate. As we shall once again discuss later, the *Minseitō* won a great victory, and the *Seiyūkai* was soundly defeated.

From 1933, however, before the mandate ran out, until 1936, the Elder Statesman Saionji Kinmochi acknowledged neither the basis for allowing the minority *Minseitō* to form a cabinet, nor his own readiness to do so.

Behind the majority *Seiyūkai* were the Army Minister, Araki Sadao, and the Deputy Chief of the General Staff, Masaki Jinzaburō, and others, who maintained warm relations with the young officers. There was no such fear in the *Minseitō*, but it was too small a party to put it in charge of the government. And yet, in a national unity cabinet with the two major parties both in office, but with differences in their basic policies, they would not be able to bring in new policies and the people's interest in politics would decrease.

Minobe's idea for a 'round table top leaders conference'

The solution to this triangular impasse put forward by the constitutional scholar Minobe Tatsukichi and the Head of Military Administration in the Army Ministry, Nagata Tetsuzan, was implemented in May 1935 by the Cabinet Council and the Cabinet Research Bureau, under the Cabinet of Okada Keisuke.

Minobe, famous as a liberal constitutional scholar, in the journal *Chūō Kōron*, proposed as a substitute for *kensei no jōdō* the idea of a 'round table meeting of top leaders' (*entaku kyotō kaigi*):

> "The greatest weakness of the current Saitō Cabinet is that it has no firm base in the Diet. . . . In terms of a cabinet having a firm base in the Diet, this would have to mean a Cabinet of the *Seiyūkai.* But it is extremely doubtful that a *Seiyūkai* cabinet could perform the crucial task of overcoming the national crisis, and gaining the trust of the people. . . . What we should like to hope at this juncture is that the leaders of each party, the military leaders, representatives of the commercial world, representatives of the labouring classes and so on, should come together and hold a round table top leaders' meeting. . . . Acting with humility and frankness, giving due consideration to the State and the People, it should propose concrete policies to place our finances and economy on a firm footing. In order to accomplish these major policies, it would for the time being put an end to political warfare and support a national unity cabinet.

(Minobe Tatsukichi, *Gikai seiji no kentō*
['A Study of Parliamentary Politics'], Nihon Hyōronsha, pp. 37–8)

Crisis, 1925–1937 209

The first half of this passage expressed, like Baba, a dislike for the *Seiyūkai*, showing that just as post-war intellectuals disliked the Liberal Democratic Party, so pre-war intellectuals disliked the *Seiyūkai*.

The problem lies in the second half of the same passage, since here, unlike Baba, Minobe broke with *kensei no jōdō*. Baba's insistence on ignoring the majority party and handing power to the minority party did not contradict the pre-war concept of 'regular procedures of constitutional government' (*kensei no jōdō*). In the cases of the cabinets of Tanaka Giichi, Hamaguchi Osachi and Inukai Tsuyoshi, all of them at the time of their formation were based on minority parties, but once they had come to power they dissolved the House of Representatives, since holding an election while it was in power would ensure that it became the majority party.

Minobe, however, in his 'round table top leaders' meeting' idea, denied not only *kensei no jōdō*, but the Diet itself. Under the Meiji Constitution, within 'finance and the economy', only in finance did the House of Representatives possess overwhelming power, as we explained repeatedly in Chapter 4. Minobe was proposing that power should be transferred to a representative body of political parties, the military, finance and labour.

His argument that at a time of economic crisis the Diet's power should be transferred temporarily to a body representing occupations was often followed after the war in advanced countries, so that it would be going too far to call Minobe in this respect 'fascist'. Even so, seen from this book's perspective, which has traced his anti-militarist and democratic position, there is no doubt that this was for Minobe a huge conversion. This idea of Minobe was in part realised under the Okada Keisuke Cabinet (1934–6), which we shall discuss in the next section.

From 'Crisis' to 'Breakdown'

The non-national unity Okada Cabinet

The Cabinet formed in 1934 by the retired Admiral Okada Keisuke, in contrast to the Saitō Cabinet, was not a 'Cabinet of national unity'. The majority *Seiyūkai* expelled those of its members who, departing from the principles of *kensei no jōdō*, joined the Cabinet (Tokonami Takejirō, Yamazaki Tatsunosuke and Uchida Shinya), and made it obvious that its position was that of an opposition party.

The economist Ishibashi Tanzan, who belonged neither to the *Seiyūkai* nor to the *Minseitō* tendencies, welcomed this move of the *Seiyūkai* into opposition. Just after the Cabinet was formed, he published an editorial in the *Tōyō Keizai Shinpō* (Eastern Economic News), arguing as follows:

> The opinion of this correspondent (Ishibashi) is that the formation of the Okada Cabinet not as a cabinet of national unity but with the *Seiyūkai* in opposition is something to be welcomed. . . . This correspondent probably yields to nobody in the extent of his dissatisfaction with our country's political parties. But even so, rather than entrusting politics promiscuously (*mizuten de*) to military

210 *Japan's Modern History*

bureaucrats, whose policies we cannot know, I am somebody who feels that it is far safer to entrust the political programme to parties which make clear the main lines of their policy publicly, however bad their programmes may be. There is nothing that can be done about the fact that the Okada Cabinet has already been formed. But the people devoutly wish that next time a party cabinet should be formed. Here the fact that the *Seiyūkai* . . . is now in opposition has created the most important condition for the next cabinet to revert to the political parties . . .

> (Ishibashi Tanzan, *Ishibashi Tanzan zenshū* ['Collected Works of Ishibashi Tanzan'], Tōyō keizai shinpōsha, vol. 9, pp. 57–8)

It was unlike Ishibashi to use a vulgar term such as 'promiscuously', but it demonstrates the depth of his hatred for 'military bureaucrats'. For him, who strongly believed in *kensei no jōdō*, meaning the system of alternation in power between political parties, so long as it was a party cabinet it did not matter if it were based on the *Seiyūkai*. Even for Baba Tsunego, a believer in *kensei no jōdō* who disliked the *Seiyūkai*, the Okada Cabinet, with the *Minseitō* as party in government, may be seen as partial fulfilment of his principal belief. For Baba, it was important that it was in July 1934 that the Okada Cabinet was formed. Whether or not there were a dissolution, there would be general elections for the House of Representatives within 18 months. If the *Minseitō*, being a minority party, but in government, were to win a convincing victory, the version of *kensei no jōdō* favoured by Baba, who inclined towards the *Minseitō*, would be fulfilled.

Nevertheless, for Baba, who believed in *kensei no jōdō* even though the meaning and content of his argument differed from that of Ishibashi, the 'round table top leaders meeting' of Minobe was unacceptable.

Cabinet Council and Cabinet Research Bureau

The 'round table top leaders meeting' proposed by Minobe came about in May 1935, in the form of a Cabinet Council and a Cabinet Research Bureau. The Cabinet Council consisted of all members of Cabinet, two members from the world of finance, four members of the *Minseitō* outside the Cabinet, three who had been expelled from the *Seiyūkai*, one from the *Kokumin Dōmei* of Adachi Kenzō and others, and five other members. Apart from the omission of the *Seiyūkai*, this was little more than a resurrection of the Saitō Cabinet, and could hardly be called a substitute for a 'round table top leaders meeting'.

The Cabinet Research Bureau, on the other hand, was a national legislative organisation that received support from a new force within the military (the *tōsei ha*, or control faction) centred on the Chief of the Military Administration Bureau, Nagata Tetsuzan, based on progressive government officials known at the time as the 'new bureaucrats', as well as from the Social Masses Party, a socialist party that in three successive elections under universal suffrage had failed to grow. We may well say that Minobe's concept of gathering together 'military leaders' and 'representatives of the labouring classes' was reflected in this arrangement. On

Crisis, 1925–1937 211

this point, a contemporary member of the Social Masses Party, Kamei Kanichirō, reflected on this after the war:

> Our party agreed with Nagata (Tetsuzan), in a general way, and brought about an understanding in relations between the military, the parties and the Diet. At that time, members of the Diet did not engage in party political tactics, but in the Diet, on a supra-partisan basis, a Policy Council (Cabinet Council) was established. Also at government level a Research Bureau was instituted. This is how it was.
>
> (Nihon kindai shiryō kenkyūkai [ed.], *Kamei Kanichirō shi danwa sokkiroku* ['Transcript of discussions by Kamei Kanichirō'], Nihon kindai shiryō kenkyūkai, p. 140)

At that time in the armed forces, under Major General Nagata Tetsuzan, a group (*tōsei ha*, control faction) centred on Major General Tōjō Hideki, Colonel Imamura Hitoshi and Lieutenant-Colonel Mutō Akira was increasing in influence. Unlike the former Army Minister, Araki Sadao, and the Inspector General of Education, Masaki Jinzaburō, they advocated strengthening military control without actually putting out to pasture the young military officers who wanted direct action. Moreover, in order to prepare for war against the Soviet Union and against China, they wanted legally to construct a total war regime taking into account the views of various forces outside the military. They had also, as we have seen, made overtures to the Social Masses Party, so that we may say that they were aiming by legal means to create national socialism.

The *tōsei ha* and the *kōdō ha* (Imperial Way faction) hardly existed as organisations, but if we distinguish Nagata Tetsuzan and his friends, who wanted a total war regime by legal means as *tōsei ha*, but Araki and Masaki, who showed a permissive attitude towards the direct action of the young officers, as *Kōdō ha*, this makes the divisions within the armed forces easier to understand.

The group of government officials known as the 'new bureaucrats' positively supported the Cabinet Research Bureau. Since the 1920s as officials of the Ministry of Home Affairs, they sympathised with the reformed capitalism tendency in the bureaucracy and exerted great efforts to conciliate labour disputes as well as disputes over tenancy. Thus under the Okada Cabinet, they took responsible positions as Home Minister (Gotō Fumio) and Head of the Cabinet Secretariat (Kawada Isao).

When we look at this, we see that the Okada Cabinet enjoyed support from the *Minseitō*, the Army *tōsei ha*, the new bureaucrats and the Social Masses Party, and had made enemies of the *Seiyūkai*, which was the majority party, and also of the Army *kōdo ha*. The question is how we should evaluate such a political situation.

Leadership class torn asunder

In this writer's view the political world had entered a period of what may be called 'liquefaction'. The Army, the parties, the bureaucracy – all had come to

212 *Japan's Modern History*

suffer from internal division, and the political forces were being fragmented. Even though it was sometimes possible to put together some of these fragmented forces as a temporary majority, it had become difficult to create a stable regime for the medium term.

Ugaki Kazushige, who came from the elite of the Chōshū domain, had served as Minister of Defence and as Governor-General of Korea, reflected on this. In his diary at the end of April 1935, he wrote as follows:

> In the political process of which I am aware, starting with the struggles of Satsuma, Chōshū, Tosa and Hizen after the Restoration, it progressed to the struggles between the bureaucracy and the parties, then struggles between the two major parties, today the parties, the military, the bureaucracy, move to the left, move to the right, and now we have come to internal struggles in the *Seiyūkai*, conflict within the *Minseitō* over whether to enter a coalition or not enter a coalition, factional fighting within the military, we have come to a situation of many small slices. What on earth does this tell us?
>
> (Ugaki Kazushige, *Ugaki Kazushige nikki* ['Diary of Ugaki Kazushige'],
> Misuzu Shobō, 1970, vol. 2, p. 1014)

Within this observation of Ugaki is to be found the *Minseitō* cooperation faction, not so far referred to in this book. It was similar to the 'cabinet of cooperation' of the late *Minseitō* cabinet, and argued that elimination of the non-party cabinets of Saitō and Okada would be difficult whether it were with a Cabinet of the *Seiyūkai* or of the *Minseitō*. Therefore he advocated a coalition of the two parties in order to resurrect party cabinets. At the end of 1934 when the Okada Cabinet was formed, this faction held a meeting of about 300 Diet members from both parties.

However this may be, the splits within many forces that Ugaki had observed as 'small slices' in April 1935 prompted his question: "What on earth do they tell us?"

What Ugaki meant by the "right wing" was the civilian right wing of Kita Ikki and Nishida Mitsugu, while the "left wing" for him meant the Social Masses Party of Kamei Kanichirō (in fact, the real 'left wing' had been eliminated by the Peace Preservation Law). In this way, in the political map under the Okada Cabinet, there were two factions in the *Seiyūkai*, two factions in the *Minseitō*, two factions in the military, two factions in the bureaucracy, two factions between left and right – in all ten factions in the political forces that he was depicting.

In this situation, it was obvious that political security was not to be expected. But things do not appear to have ended there. If we divide the ruling forces into ten parts, even if we count only those at the top, it means that there were ten leaders. The situation showed that the quality of the political elite must be deteriorating.

In the history of political conflict from the Meiji Restoration that Ugaki was describing, the top men of the Satsuma, Chōshū, Tosa and Hizen domains were four in number, in the 'struggle between the bureaucracy and the parties' there were two, in the 'struggle between the two major parties' there were two. This rapidly grew to 10, and a concatenation of political conflicts did not cease to increase.

Crisis, 1925–1937 213

Japanese politics in 1935 faced increasing global instability and a decline in the quality of the elite.

Exacerbation of struggle between Seiyūkai *and* Minseitō: Seiyūkai *attack on the organ theory of the Emperor*

The installation in May 1935 of the Cabinet Council and the Cabinet Research Bureau, was a wonderful opportunity for the leadership of the *Minseitō* to suppress those in the party that wanted a *Seiyūkai –Minseitō* coalition, and to force the *Seiyūkai* into opposition. Immediately after these two bodies were set up, Kawasaki Takukichi, Secretary General of the *Minseitō*, warned Matsuno Tsuruhei, Secretary General of the *Seiyūkai*, of the termination of the coalition between the two parties, in the following terms:

> Hitherto we have had cooperation between our two parties, with the aim of conducting investigations in national policy, but now the Cabinet Council has been established with the same goal, our party has joined it whereas your party has not. Therefore our party on the one hand participates in the Government Council, but on the other hand cooperation with your party, opposing the government, as well as investigation into national policy separately, we fear would frequently cause unacceptable situations.
>
> (*Minsei*, June 1935, p. 106)

Since the previous general elections were in February 1932, irrespective of whether or not to dissolve, elections had to be held by February 1936. From the time when the *Minseitō* had announced the rupture of its coalition with the *Seiyūkai*, there would have to be general elections in a mere nine months, and there was hope that the *Minseitō* would win a majority and the *Seiyūkai* would be relegated to opposition party status.

If such a situation were to be avoided, for the *Seiyūkai* it was essential to return to power before the elections. To this end that party developed two strategies.

The first, it goes without saying, was to insist that the party controlling a majority in the House of Representatives should be put in charge of the government, in other words, 'regular procedures of constitutional government' (*kensei no jōdō*) should be followed.

The second strategy was to attack the 'Organ Theory of the Emperor' of Minobe Tatsukichi. Expressing this criticism in a positive sense, it was to 'clarify the nature of the national polity' (*kokutai*) (demonstrate clearly the Japanese national polity centred upon the Emperor).

To our ears, schooled in post-war democracy, *kensei no jōdō* sounds progressive, whereas 'clarifying the national polity' rings out as reactionary. As we have already seen, however, under its President Tanaka Giichi, and under its President Inukai Tsuyoshi, the *Seiyūkai* advocated 'Emperor-centrism' and 'independence of command', and made clear its total opposition to Minobe's position.

Moreover, in 1935, in anticipation of the general elections due the following year, attacking the organ theory of the Emperor was valid in terms of political

214   *Japan's Modern History*

strategy. Even if the Okada Cabinet were pressured by the *Seiyūkai* into banning Minobe's publications and punishing him, on the stage of the Diet, the Cabinet would not move to dissolve the House of Representatives.

Previously Mr Kuno Osamu pointed out the two-sided nature of the Emperor system, between 'surface teaching' and 'hidden teaching'. The Emperor at the popular level (surface teaching) was not an 'organ' of the State, but was ruler of the Japanese State. The 'organ theory of the Emperor', holding that the Emperor stood at the highest point among the various organs of the State, but was no more than a single organ of the State, was merely 'hidden teaching' that was believed secretly among the corridors of power (Kuno Osamu, Tsurumi Shunsuke, *Gendai Nihon no shisō*, Iwanami Shinsho, 1956, pp. 118–82). Since it was impossible to question prevailing public sentiment in which 'secret teaching was attacked and which was controlled by 'surface teaching', the Cabinet would not be able to dissolve the Diet.

If we pursue this question right to the end, the Okada Cabinet had no choice but to resign en masse. If this was the case, then it was possible for the *Seiyūkai* to expect to come to power according to the arguments of *kensei no jōdō*, which as we have seen was another pillar, and become the party in power in the general elections of February 1936.

Exacerbation of conflict within the military

Nevertheless, as I have already explained, the political forces of the time were split in several ways, and did not move according to the opinions just of the *Minseitō* and the *Seiyūkai*. Rather than conflict between those two major parties both targeting the general elections due in February of the following year, conflict between the *tōsei ha* and the *kōdō ha* within the Army soon became the principal focus.

The confrontation between these two factions was initiated from the side of the *tōsei ha*, which we may consider one of the forces supporting the Okada Cabinet. At the conference of the Chiefs of the Army (Army Minister, Chief of the General Staff, Governor-General of Education) on 15th July 1935, the Army Minister, Hayashi Senjūrō, and Prince Kan'in Kotohito, Chief of the General Staff, demanded of Mazaki Jinzaburō that he resign as Governor-General of Education. When Mazaki refused, Hayashi on the 16th had an audience with the Emperor and received approval for the dismissal of Mazaki.

The *Seiyūkai* and the Army *kōdō ha*, considering Mazaki's dismissal to have stemmed from the judgement of the Emperor's close advisers who at the time were called the *jūshin*, made efforts to attack the *jūshin*.

Battles over the '**jūshin** *bloc*'

The addition of the *jūshin* to the elder statesmen (*genrō*) Saionji Kinmochi, in choosing a successor to the Prime Minister, as a priority item, occurred when the Okada Cabinet was formed in July 1934. At that time the *jūshin* consisted of those who had served as President of the Privy Council and Prime Minister. But the only

Crisis, 1925–1937 215

living former Prime Minister who had belonged to the *Seiyūkai* was Takahashi Korekiyo, and Takahashi at that time had broken with the *Seiyūkai* (his formal defection from the party occurred in November of the same year). Hara Takashi, Tanaka Giichi and Inukai Tsuyoshi had all died. In other words, the voice of the *Seiyūkai* in the '*jūshin* conference' had almost disappeared.

This was why the *Seiyūkai*, which had gone fully into opposition having broken with the *Minseitō* over the issue of the Cabinet Council, redoubled its attacks on the '*jūshin* bloc'. The *Seiyūkai* President, Suzuki Kisaburō, made a speech in June 1935, in which he said: "Since the reactionary and negative policies of the *jūshin* bloc harm the development of our national destiny, and contradict the positive policies of our party, I believe that this kind of leadership spirit must be abolished" (*Seiyū*, July 1935, p. 50).

As mentioned above, *jūshin* can be defined. But what is the meaning of *jūshin* bloc? About a month after this speech, the Governor-General of Korea, Ugaki Kazushige, returning to Tokyo from his post, collected information with this very question in mind, and defined it as the Lord Keeper of the Privy Seal, Makino Nobuaki, the former Prime Minister, Saitō Makoto, the Prime Minister, Okada Keisuke, the Minister of Finance, Takahashi Korekiyo, the Navy Minister, Ōsumi Mineo, the former Imperial Household Minister, Ichiki Kitokurō, the Principal Chamberlain, Suzuki Kantarō, and some of the 'new bureaucrats'. As he put it: "They are trying to monopolise and fully control the Palace and the government" (Ugaki Kazushige, *Ugaki Kazushige nikki* ['Diary of Ugaki Kazushige'], Misuzu Shobō, 1970, vol. 2, p. 1025).

Of the seven names he listed, five of them – Makino, Saitō, Okada, Takahashi and Suzuki – were attacked by the young Army officers in February 1936, and two of them lost their lives. The '*jūshin* bloc' that the opposition *Seiyūkai* aimed to 'destroy', was also the target of the young Army officers.

But unlike cooperation between political parties, relations between parties and the military – two different kinds of organisation – did not amount to 'cooperation' but were limited to a tacit alignment of activities. Mazaki, of the Army *kōdō ha*, said to Kuhara Fusanosuke of the *Seiyūkai*: "For the Army and for military men, there is no way of talking of cooperation with political parties. The important thing is that if what is right is strongly advocated, then the military will naturally go along with that in an unstructured fashion" (Itō Takashi et al. [ed.], *Mazaki Jinzaburō nikki* ['Diary of Mazaki Jinzaburō'], Yamakawa shuppansha, 1981, vol. 2, p. 96, 11th May 1935).

For the pro-government forces of the Okada Cabinet, the situation was the same. Even if in the general elections of February 1936 the pro-government *Minseitō* had won, this would not have meant that the Army *tōsei ha* would have prevailed over the *kōdō ha*. It is true that if the *Seiyūkai*, continuing its attacks on the '*jūshin* bloc', had lost the elections, one wing of the enemies of the *jūshin* would have collapsed. But the young Army officers' attacks on the *jūshin* would not have been controlled by the results of the elections. Given the 'liquefaction' of the political world referred to earlier, it was not possible for a decisive change in the political direction to result from some single 'incident'. On the contrary,

216   *Japan's Modern History*

through a succession of 'incidents', the political world staggered to the left and to the right.

'Leftward stagger' at the 1936 elections

The nineteenth general elections on 20th February 1936 were hardly seen as part of the normal course of history, since just six days later the most serious military coup d'état in modern Japanese history took place.

Seen, however, from the perspective of 21st February, when the coup had not yet been experienced, the elections were a rather significant political 'leftward stagger'. First of all, the *Seiyūkai*, which together with the Army *kōdō ha* had worked hard to attack the organ theory of the Emperor of Minobe Tatsukichi, was soundly defeated. Whereas the *Seiyūkai* held a small majority of 242 seats out of 466 at the time of dissolution, at the elections it lost 71 seats, reducing its total to 171 and relegating it to the status of a small party.

On the opposing side, even though one hesitates to state definitively that this was a party based on liberalism, the *Minseitō*, which at least opposed militarism and fascism, gained 78 seats and rebounded to the position of largest party.

We also need to consider the positive evaluation by progressive intellectuals of the leap forward of the Social Masses Party, a legal socialist party. That party's leadership group, which had a close relationship through the Cabinet Research Bureau with the Army *tōsei ha*, can hardly be called a purely social democratic party, and even though we talk of a 'leap forward', it only amounted to 18 seats out of 466. Compared, however, with three seats at the time of dissolution, this was a six-fold increase, and moreover 11 candidates came first in their [multi-member] districts, while many of those who failed to be elected were only one place below those elected. With a larger number of candidates and better distribution of them, the party would have probably won more seats (*Shakai undō no jōkyō* ['The Situation of the Socialist Movement'], vol. 8, p. 634).

At the February 1936 elections, the people said a decisive 'no' to the Army *kōdō ha*, accorded winning points to the *Minseitō* which though a party of capitalists, was liberal in nature, and showed some appreciation of the Social Masses Party, which was critical of the capitalist party ethos.

The February 26th coup d'état

Nevertheless, in the political situation characterised by 'liquefaction', the importance accorded to a general election lacked the level of decisiveness that it had enjoyed during the two-major-party period between 1928 and 1932. A mere six days after these general elections, young Army officers linked with the *kōdō ha* conducted a military coup d'état (Hayashi Shigeru et al. [eds], *2/26 jiken hiroku* ['Secret History of the February 26th Incident'], Shōgakkan, 1971, vol. 1, op. cit; see especially Matsuzawa Tetsunari, *Seinen shōkō undō no gaiyō* ['Outline of the Young Officers Movement'].

At five o'clock in the morning of 26th February, the first and third regiments of the first division, the third infantry regiment of the Imperial Guards, the seventh

Crisis, 1925–1937 217

regiment of field artillery and others, led by company and platoon commanders (about eight individual companies, totalling 1,847 men), attacked the Prime Minister's residence, the residence of the Lord Keeper of the Privy Seal, the residence of the Finance Minister, the office of the Principal Chamberlain, the residence of the Superintendent of Education, the inn where a former Lord Keeper of the Privy Seal was staying, the office of the Army Minister, the Police Department, the Army Ministry, the office of the Chiefs of Staff, and the Tokyo Asahi Shinbun Company and other buildings. As a result the Lord Keeper of the Privy Seal, Saitō Makoto, the Finance Minister, Takahashi Korekiyo, and the Superintendent of Education, Watanabe Jōtarō, were killed, and the Principal Chamberlain, Suzuki Kantarō, was injured. Prime Minister Okada, as the result of mistaken identity on the part of the attackers, was able to evade danger. Thus, as a result, the previously discussed '*jūshin* bloc' suffered serious aggression.

Since about 14,000 soldiers of the Imperial Guard and the First Division remained on the side of the government, the roughly 1,500 insurgents could not attain military supremacy. The '*jūshin* bloc', however, which controlled the core of the Palace and the government, suffered a deadly attack in the insurgency. The scenario whereby the '*jūshin* bloc' would enjoy the support of the *Minseitō* and Army *tōsei ha*, and would overcome the two great right-wing forces (the Army *kōdō ha* and the *Seiyūkai*), was destroyed by the February 26th Incident.

On the other hand, the idea that the *kōdō ha* and the young Army officers, with support from the *Seiyūkai*, would quickly establish a military regime was equally impossible.

Many of the coups seen in developing countries since the war have in some form or other enjoyed popular or mass support. The February 26th Incident, however, was a Palace revolution conducted by young army officers, lacking popular support. Once they had carried out their military coup, they appealed, not to the people, but to the Emperor personally, telling him that they had "destroyed the evil in Your Administration".

As we have already seen, the majority of the approximately 12,000,000 electors six days earlier had voted at general elections for 'anti-fascist' forces, as was shown by the victory of the *Minseitō* and the spectacular advance of the Social Masses Party. The leadership of the latter party aimed to align itself with the Army *tōsei ha*, but they had no links at all with the *kōdō ha* or the young officers. And above all, many of the electors who had granted 18 seats to the Social Masses Party, wanted it to 'oppose fascism'. The Police Administration Bureau of the Ministry of Home Affairs found the reason for the leap forward of the Social Masses Party at the elections to be "demonstrated in the sense of outrage in popular sentiment against recent fascist tendencies" (Naimushō keihokyoku hoanka, *Tokkō gaiji geppō* ['Security Police Monthly Bulletin of External Events'], February 1936, Appendix, p. 3).

The February 26th Incident not only lacked popular support, but was also rejected by the all-important Emperor. The expectation of the insurgent officers that if they attacked the evils of the Imperial Administration, namely the '*jūshin* group', the Emperor would deign to understand the true feelings of the young

218   *Japan's Modern History*

officers, was rejected by the Emperor himself. On the second day of the insurgency, 27th February, the Emperor spoke decisively to Honjō Shigeru, Chief of the Military Chamberlains, as follows: "My trusted senior retainers have been slaughtered. Even in their spirit what excuse do these brutal officers have?" (Honjō Shigeru, *Honjō nikki* ['Honjō Diary'], Hara Shobō, 1967, p. 275).

Isolated from both the Emperor and the people, the insurgent forces were on their own, and their defeat was merely a matter of time. Three days after the revolt, the Army leadership resolved to suppress them by military force, and at five o'clock in the morning on 29th February, 24,000 men of the Imperial Guard, the first and fourteenth divisions, were ordered to be mobilised. The insurgents amounted to about 1,500 men. On the same evening, apart from Company Commander Nonaka Shirō who committed suicide and Company Commander Andō Teruzō who was wounded in an unsuccessful suicide attempt, 17 serving officers and three former officers (Muranaka Kōji, Isobe Senichi and Shibukawa Zensuke) gave themselves up and were imprisoned.

Formation of the Hirota Kōki Cabinet

When we consider the political situation before and after these events, it was a natural result that as successor to the Okada Cabinet, which resigned en masse, the former Foreign Minister, Hirota Kōki, should have been chosen, and that a cabinet of national unity was formed, including two cabinet members each from the *Minseitō* and the *Seiyūkai*. To organise a military cabinet, activating the forces that had suppressed the insurgents, was impossible given the 'anti-fascist' verdict of the people in the general elections held six days earlier. Hiranuma Kiichirō (Deputy Head of the Privy Council) and Konoe Fumimaro (President of the House of Peers), whose names were mentioned as possible successors, had an excessively deep relationship with the behind-the-scenes manipulator of the affair, Mazaki Jinzaburō. Considering also foreign countries concerned with the direction of Japanese politics following the suppression of the military coup, selection of the former Foreign Minister was a safe choice.

The national unity Cabinet of Hirota was, in both rationale and form, similar to that set up after the May 15th Incident under Saitō Makoto, and amounted to no more than a temporary truce in the political world. What had been eliminated from the fragmented ruling elite under the Okada Cabinet about which Ugaki Kazushige had been concerned, were just the young Army officers and the *kōdō ha*. To replace this, there was increased demand within the *Minseitō* and the *Seiyūkai*, which had been forced to relinquish *kensei no jōdō*, for a cabinet that would include both parties, under Ugaki Kazushige, a military elder with experience during the party cabinet period.

Another point is that the Social Masses Party, which had given up on increasing its parliamentary strength during the Okada Cabinet period, but had become a supplementary force for the Army *tōsei ha* and the new bureaucrats, added two more members to its total, which was now 20 members, and thus came to be recognised as a parliamentary grouping (*kaiha*) in the Diet. Since the two planks of this party's platform were improving the standard of living of the people and strengthening national defence, it was not clear whether it was aiming at socialism or at militarism. Moreover, within the Army, which had suppressed the so-called 'fascist' forces within its ranks, Ishiwara Kanji succeeded Nagata Tetsuzan, taking control of the General Staff, and aimed to build up national defence with careful planning, taking the Soviet Union as potential enemy. Also, the mainstream faction of the *Minseitō*, which had won the elections of 20th February, sharpened its position opposing militarism.

The political situation that a year before Ugaki had deplored in the phrase "we have come to a situation of many small slices" was still continuing after the February 26th Incident.

Diet counterattack after the February 26th Incident

When we speak of 1,500 armed men shooting the Prime Minister and advisers to the Emperor, what resonates is that Japan in 1936 was controlled by men outside the law and was a disordered society. But the Japan of those days was a constitutional State under the Great Japan Imperial Constitution, of which article 45 stipulated that within five months of a Diet dissolution a special session must be convened. Since the previous dissolution took place on 21st January, a special session had to be convened before 21st June.

Moreover, there are plenty of people who believe erroneously that in pre-war Japan, which was controlled by the Special Police (Tokkō) and the Military Police (*Kenpeitai*), freedom of speech on the part of members of the House of Representatives was limited, and that the censor's hand penetrated the House records, whereas in fact the House of Representatives, together with the government, was an organ of State, and the Police Administration Department of the Ministry of Home Affairs was merely a single part of government, without the right to censor the records of the House or to arrest those members who spoke out. In other words, in the special session of the House convened on 4th May, the members were at liberty to make trenchant criticism of the handling by the Army of the February 26th Incident and its aftermath.

A representative example was the speech made by Saitō Takao on 7th May of the same year, representing the *Minseitō*, criticising the government's keynote address. This is what he said:

> What I would like to say in conclusion concerns the feelings of the people about this incident (the February 26th Incident). . . . So far as I can see, both nationally and locally, among higher-class people and lower-class people, there is the most extreme anger (applause). . . . In particular, the Finance Minister Takahashi, the Home Minister Saitō, the Superintendant Watanabe, the Emperor's retainers who were regarded by everyone as exceptionally sincere, and who had devoted themselves to their country, were butchered by the bayonets of soldiers who were under orders to defend our country (applause). For the people, who have trust in the Army, this has been a bitter

220   *Japan's Modern History*

experience, difficult to bear (applause). . . . Even so, the people have been silent and the political parties have maintained their silence. But if we think about it, how long is this situation going to endure? People are emotional beings. There is a limit to their patience.

(*Teikoku Gikai Shūgiin giji sokkiroku* ['Record of the Proceedings of the House of Representatives in the Imperial Diet'], vol. 66, p. 48)

The *Minseitō*, which had returned to the position of largest party in the general elections of 20th February, had now clarified its anti-fascist and anti-militarist position.

A pro-military socialist party

The Social Masses Party, however, which together with the *Minseitō* had made spectacular progress in the elections, did not share the position of the *Minseitō*. Around the year 1935 the party linked itself to the Army *tōsei ha* led by Nagata Tetsuzan, and at that time began to advocate in the Diet the doctrine of 'broad-based national defence' (combining military development and improving people's standard of living). This did not mean that they supported the kind of Army extremists revealed in the February 26th Incident, but they harboured hopes for the Army forces that suppressed the insurgency. On the next day after Saitō's speech, Asō Hisashi, representing the Social Masses Party, asked the following question:

Recently the Army Ministry issued a pamphlet entitled "(A Proposal for) The Basis of National Defence and its Reinforcement". The future of national defence should not stop simply with armaments, since if it does not become the basis for stabilising the standard of living of the people, national defence in the true sense will not be accomplished. If *current economic organisation* is an obstacle in the path of national stability of living standards, I believe that it should be reformed, and our conclusion should be that economic organisation capable of delivering stability of people's livelihoods should be put in place. In relation to the broad principles of the military, we express our total approval, but . . . in some senses we feel that the military itself acts in a spirit of trampling on the principles of broad national defence (applause).

(Ibid., p. 82; present writer's italics)

The phrase "current economic organisation", which we have italicised, meant 'capitalist economics'. Its 'reform' may have touched upon the 'private financial and industrial system', denial of which was forbidden under the Peace Preservation Law, but this part of the Peace Preservation Law that may have protected capitalists did not enjoy a good reputation among nationalists from the time of its introduction [in 1925]. Since Home Ministry bureaucrats in particular, from the 1920s on, were passionate about controlling the excessive pursuit of private profit by capitalists, the target of the Peace Preservation Law was mainly focused on those who proposed 'reforming' the 'national polity', in other words denying the Emperor system. For this reason, the Police Administration Bureau of the Ministry of Home Affairs came to take a favourable attitude towards the words and actions of the Social Masses Party, which did not reject the Emperor system.

The problem is not Asō's socialism, but his pro-military policies. Of course what Asō meant by 'the military' was the part of it that suppressed the February 26th Incident, and not the fascist forces criticised by Saitō Takao. But while *Minseitō* representatives attacked the fascist faction in the Army, the Social Masses Party representatives expressed support for the national socialist elements in this same military. The attitudes expressed by the two parties, which had both done well in the elections of 20th February, in the May special session of the Diet, were almost diametrically opposed to each other.

Anti-fascist trend in the Seiyūkai

The *Seiyūkai* as well, which up to the February 26th Incident had been aligned with the Army's *kōdō ha*, following its defeat in the elections and after the February 26th Incident began to reveal changes in its position. The faction favourable to cooperation between the two major parties and opposing the military was becoming dominant. At the 70th regular Diet session of January 1937, the so-called '*kappuku* question and answer' following the question by Hamada Kunimatsu, representing the *Seiyūkai*, expressed the view of this faction. He spoke as follows:

> It is true that military men, for the most part, are proud of their leadership in our country's politics, believing that without their leadership our people will lose their way. This inclination has been consistent in the May 15th Incident, in the February 26th Incident, and in their broadcasting of autocratic thought through various military organisations. . . . What underlies this may be called fascism, or perhaps autocratic thought, . . . and what we perceive is that this autocratic thought increases in parallel with *the progress of the Army purge.*
>
> (Ibid., vol. 68, p. 36; present writer's italics)

He was pointing to the contradiction that, after the purge, in other words the suppression of the fascist faction within the Army, the Army as a whole was moving towards fascism.

As we have earlier pointed out, within the powers granted by the Meiji Constitution, since the legislative branch was a government organ alongside the executive branch, there was freedom of expression in the House of Representatives. Hamada perceived this, and before his criticism of the military, he prefaced his remarks with: "Having unrestricted freedom (of a Diet member) in all respects, I propose to ask without reserve about current national politics" (ibid., p. 35).

But even if we accept this as a premise, Hamada's speech going so far as to call it military fascism was too much. The Army Ministry, Terauchi Hisaichi, angrily retorted: "Very recently I have heard Mr Hamada make various speeches here, and

222 *Japan's Modern History*

I feel that in these speeches he has spoken rather insultingly concerning the military" (ibid., p. 43). From this point the '*kappuku* (ritual disembowelment) question and answer session' began. Hamada pressed Terauchi, saying: "I do not retreat in face of the quarrel he has picked with me, saying that I have insulted the glorious Army of our Nation." Terauchi then merely replied, "I have given my advice," whereupon Hamada delivered the following explosive speech:

> I do not intend to receive advice from a man like you, younger than myself. You are the prestigious Minister of the Army under His Majesty the Emperor. Nevertheless . . . I, Hamada Kunimatsu, an unworthy, immature member of the House of Representatives, am an official under the Emperor. . . . If I my ageing self had to receive advice from you, I should have to consider it with great care. . . . If I, on searching the stenographic records, were to discover words that had insulted the Army, I should commit *kappuku* and apologise to you for it. If it is not there, you must commit *kappuku*.
>
> (Ibid., p. 45)

Terauchi Hisaichi was the first Army Minister up to that time to be denounced in such an extreme fashion in a plenary session of the House of Representatives. In his anger, Terauchi pressed the Prime Minister, Hirota Kōki, to dissolve that House.

In a national unity Cabinet, however, where there was no distinction between a party in power and a party out of power, the election was meaningless. Moreover, there was no way of determining through an election whether to support the military or the *Seiyūkai*. The Prime Minister, Hirota, said, in relation to the mission of the Elder Statesman Saionji: "In the emergency situation of the February 26th Incident, I have received the Imperial Command, and so far I have come through unscathed, but since in today's situation I feel that I am unable to fulfil the Command, I now think it would be appropriate to resign", and on 23rd January the Cabinet resigned en masse (*Saionji kō to seikyoku* ['Harada Kumao, Prince Saionji and the Political Situation'], vol. 5, p. 140). This was two days after Hamada's speech.

The abortive Ugaki Cabinet

In the background to the '*kappuku* question and answer session', which seemed to be a sudden impetuosity by Hamada Kunimatsu, the *Seiyūkai* and the *Minseitō* coordinated their efforts and moved to form a government to be led by Ugaki Kazushige, the Governor-General of Korea, and Ugaki himself was positive about it. Moreover, the former Lord Keeper of the Privy Seal, Makino Nobuaki, who since the February 26th Incident had been forced into silence, and the current Lord Keeper, Yuasa Kurahei, also aimed to support Ugaki.

But when Ugaki became a de facto candidate, he had lost the clear power of analysing the world that he had a year and a half earlier. At the end of April 1935, Ugaki analysed the contemporary situation in terms of "the parties, the military,

Crisis, 1925–1937   223

the bureaucracy, the right wing, the left wing and now we have to add internal struggles in the *Seiyūkai*, conflict within the *Minseitō* over whether to enter a coalition or not enter a coalition, factional fighting within the military, we have come to a situation of small slices" (see p. 212). In the meantime, in January 1937, when Ugaki stood as successor to Hirota, the only thing that had been cancelled was "factional fighting within the military", whereas what he had called the "the left" showed a notable leap forward by the Social Masses Party.

Of course, if Ugaki had placed the *Seiyūkai* and the *Minseitō* completely under his own umbrella, this would have been a very considerable force. But "internal struggles within the *Seiyūkai*" and "conflict within the *Minseitō* over whether to enter a coalition or not enter a coalition" were still current issues. In his diary just before the Imperial Command to form a cabinet was issued (17th January 1937), Ugaki revealed his relations with "so-called hard-line faction people" such as Koizumi Matajirō and Tomita Kōjirō of the *Minseitō* (vol. 2, p. 1123). Concerning the '*kappuku* question and answer session' of Hamada Kunimatsu, he wrote: "I was able to observe Hamada's determination about ten days ago" (ibid., p. 1125). On 25th January, he accepted the Imperial Command, based only on the 'cooperation factions' of the *Minseitō* and *Seiyūkai*.

While the *Minseitō* and the *Seiyūkai* were continuing their internal conflicts, Ishiwara Kanji, Head of the War Leadership Section of the Chiefs of Staff Headquarters, was controlling the Army, which had suppressed the *kōdō ha* and the young officers. Ishiwara, on 18th January, proposed as a condition for approving the organisation of Ugaki's cabinet – and this was approved by the Chiefs of Staff Headquarters on the 23rd (two days after the Imperial Command) – that his five-year plan for heavy industry should be accepted by the incoming Prime Minister This was clearly set out in writing (ibid., p. 1134). He had made a move to stop the formation of an Ugaki Cabinet.

Buffeted by the demands of Ishiwara and others, the Army Minister and the Superintendant of Education informed Ugaki that they would not be able to endorse the Army Minister, and on 29th January Ugaki abandoned the task of forming a Cabinet (Renunciation of the Imperial Command).

Alliance between the Army and the Zaibatsu (national defence narrowly defined)

As we have seen, the support base for the abortive Ugaki Cabinet was not at all strong. It was not a 'great political alliance', but only brought together parts of the two major parties.

But the Cabinet of Hayashi Senjūrō, created by the Army after Ugaki was forced to abort his attempt to form a Cabinet, had no support base whatsoever in the House of Representatives, and was to be quite fragile. The *Minseitō* and the *Seiyūkai*, which between them accounted for 80 per cent of the seats in that House, harboured strong resentment against the Army, which had forced the abandonment of the Ugaki Cabinet. The Social Masses Party, which in the course of the Diet session had acquired two extra seats, bringing its total to 20, suspected that

224 *Japan's Modern History*

the Army had lost interest in the 'broad-based defence' that it was advocating. In the previous Diet session, the SMP representative, Asō Hisashi, after he had fully endorsed the Army's 'broad-based defence', revealed his doubts about it in the following terms, which need to be remembered:

> Nevertheless, if henceforth we recall the circumstances of the budget, we feel that in some senses the military itself seems to be acting in a spirit of trampling on the principle of broad-based defence (applause). To some small extent, among the people, the military speaks of stabilising the people's standard of living and so on, but in fact, the military will be satisfied once its budget passes, and this sounds miserly (applause).
>
> (*Teikoku gikai shūgiin giji sokkiroku*, vol. 66, p. 82)

The opposite of 'broad-based defence' is 'narrowly based defence', Among commentators at the time, the view was current that the term 'narrowly based defence', which sounds rather negative, should be regarded positively, and that it should be a matter of satisfaction that the Army, which backed the Hayashi Cabinet, was beginning to distance itself from national socialism. The liberal critic Baba Tsunego, whom we have already introduced several times in this chapter, was a typical example. In a review published in the journal *Kaizō* just after the formation of the Hayashi Cabinet, he wrote as follows:

> The most important aspect of change in current trends is that the Army has come to place greater emphasis on narrowly based national defence than on broad-based national defence. They have been too enthusiastic about broad-based national defence, they preach renovation of all aspects of government, and in relation to administration, industry and the parliamentary system the opinions of the military are being broadcast to all sections of society. In these circumstances, it is of course problematic to overcome frictions between the various parts of society and the military, and thus to attain unity between the military and the people. . . . Recently, therefore, the military has been showing much more interest in narrowly based national defence, and is tending more to concentrate on traditional military duties. Not only is this to be welcomed, but it should be seen as an intelligent approach for the military itself.
>
> (Baba Tsunego, in *Kaizō*, April 1937, pp. 88–93)

What Baba was concerned about here in the background of the Hayashi Cabinet was the five-year plan of Ishiwara Kanji against the Soviet Union, (published as the *Five-Year Plan for Heavy Industry* by the Army Ministry in May 1937), as well as Ishiwara's approach to the Mitsui *zaibatsu* (financial conglomerate). As for the first of these, over the five years between 1937 and 1941, spectacular development of military procurement industries and heavy industries was envisaged, and so far as the latter was concerned, the central figure in the Mitsui *zaibatsu*, Ikeda Shigeaki, was appointed President of the Bank of Japan. Baba felt that for the central figure in Mitsui, which had been a target of attack before the May 15th

Crisis, 1925–1937 225

Incident in 1932, a mere five years later to have been appointed President of the Bank of Japan on the demand of the military represented "a change in the trend of the times". Ikeda himself, in response to a message from Saionji Kinmochi, explained in the following words how he had accepted the post of President of the Bank of Japan as the result of his part in assisting the drafting of the five-year plan:

> In relation to the concrete proposal that came from Ishiwara, there were various circumstances involved, but in particular I was requested by the Army to prepare for possible international situations and decide how much military build-up was needed. Moreover, it was essential not to destroy the present economic structure. This being the case, if the Bank of Japan did not act intelligently in relation principally to finance, a very dangerous situation might eventuate. . . . I am too senior now, but I thought that I should serve in this capacity, and gave my assent. So I have ended up assisting Yūki (Toyotarō, Finance Minister).
>
> (Harada Kumao [ed.], *Saionji kō to seikyoku* ['Prince Saionji and the Political Situation'], Iwanami Shoten, vol. 5, p. 254)

Since as payment for defending 'the base of the economic structure' the *zaibatsu* had to assist the five-year plan, this was Baba's 'narrowly based national defence'. The Army had announced its abandonment of national socialism, and demanded a build-up of national defence through national capitalism.

Today we regard failed models combining 'nationalism' and 'socialism' with distaste. But within 'national socialism' there was the dream of socialism. However in 'national capitalism' combining the Army and the *zaibatsu*, there was only profit. Even though the Army were derided as fascists, socialists had lost their expectation of 'broad-based national defence'. When the Social Masses Party, which pinned its hopes on 'broad-based national defence', turned into their enemy, the Army and the *zaibatsu* counted 85 per cent of the House of Representatives as its enemies. Even though what Baba termed 'narrowly based national defence' had meaning in the calculations of the Army and financial circles, their alliance meant they were treating 85 per cent of the House of Representatives as enemies, and thus popular opinion was being ignored.

The Hayashi Cabinet, supported by the Army, bureaucracy and financial circles, though it had no political prospects, on 31st March 1937 dissolved the House of Representatives. For a Cabinet that had no party in power supporting it, the election results from the start had no meaning. Although the gap in seat totals between the *Minseitō* and the *Seiyūkai* narrowed (180 to 174), this had no influence on the support base of the Hayashi Cabinet. The Social Masses Party, which had proclaimed its support for the Army but had been betrayed by the Army, in the elections of 30th April nearly doubled its seat total (from 20 to 36). Moreover, after the Army had moved to 'narrowly based national defence', the SMP slogan of 'broad-based defence' changed its meaning from a pro-Army symbol to a banner of democracy.

'Broad-based national defence' and democracy

The meaning and content of political slogans is not determined entirely by the intentions of those who devise them. The expectations of electors in relation to slogans is of comparable significance. When the SMP jumped ahead once again, going from 20 seats to 36, 'broad-based national defence', for critics and electors alike, turned sharply from a pro-fascist symbol into an anti-fascist banner.

When the Hayashi Cabinet dissolved the House of Representatives on 31st March, the SMP brought out an electoral slogan reading: "Broad-based national defence or narrowly based national defence? *Seiyūkai – Minseitō* alliance or Social Masses Party?" The first part of it was a criticism of the convergence between the Army and the *zaibatsu*, while the second represented opposition to any revival of the Ugaki Cabinet proposal that had been squashed by the Army. The idea that Ishiwara Kanji had aimed to improve relations with the two major parties, in my personal view, did not exist, and historical materials give no backing to the view that the 'cooperation faction' in the two major parties wanted to align themselves, not with Ugaki, but with Ishiwara. The two SMP slogans were essentially separate from each other.

These two slogans, however, give the impression that the party opposed the Army, opposed the *zaibatsu* and opposed the 'established parties' (*Minseitō* and *Seiyūkai*).

The Social Masses Party, which was opposing the four existing power centres, leaped forward at the general elections, increasing its seat total from 20 to 36. The *Minseitō* saw its total decrease by 24 to 180, and the *Seiyūkai* won three extra seats, lifting its total to 174, so that the two parties were evenly balanced in terms of their power.

Liberalism or national socialism

The fact that the two major parties had disappointing results but that the SMP nearly doubled its seat total left the critics of the time divided. The liberal Baba Tsunego entertained doubts about the two-sided nature of the SMP, which opposed both 'narrowly based national defence' and 'alliance of the two major parties'. In a round table discussion held in the journal *Chūō Kōron* on 8th August, Baba expressed his doubts to Miwa Jusō of the SMP as follows:

> The SMP opposes the government and opposes the established parties. To oppose both government and the parties when they are confronting each other head on, must surely end up assisting the government?
>
> (*Chūō Kōron*, June 1937, p. 100)

On the other hand, Kawai Eijirō, who in the post-war period was respected as a representative of liberalism but also attacked for it (at the time he was Professor in the Faculty of Economics at Tokyo University), confidently regarded the advance of the SMP "with a feeling of joy". In an article published in *Chūō Kōron*, Kawai argued in the following way:

Thirty-six Diet members amount to less than a mere one tenth of the 466 members of the House of Representatives. Despite this fact, why is it that we greet the advance of this small party with a feeling of joy? It is because this small party has a character not seen in other small parties that continue to appear. One of its characteristics is that, like a socialist party in any other country, it possesses a clear ideology, a second is that it has a progressive attitude towards contemporary society, and a third point is that it is a party that, far from retreating, is constantly improving its position.

(Kawai Eijirō, in *Chūō Kōron*, June 1937, p. 123)

As Kawai said, even though the SMP had advanced, it still only controlled 36 seats out of a total of 466. This party's activities were regarded sceptically by Baba Tsunego as the emergence of a fascist party, but were greeted by Kawai in a spirit of 'joy'.

As we have already explained, the Army under the Hayashi Cabinet had linked hands with the *zaibatsu*, and had begun to concentrate on 'narrowly based national defence'. On the other hand, the *Minseitō* and the *Seiyūkai* after the failure of Ugaki's attempt to form a cabinet, as the SMP said, were not moving in the direction of a mutual alliance. When it came to elections, the *Minseitō* fought as the *Minseitō*, and the *Seiyūkai* fought as the *Seiyūkai*, each competing with its own particular characteristics. And the Social Masses Party, increasing its strength by embroidering in the interstices between the four great forces, for some people appeared to represent a revival of fascism, and for others to represent the advance of a Western-style legal socialist party. The political characteristics that the former Governor-General of Korea, Ugaki Kazushige, two years earlier, regarded quizzically as 'small slices' may be said to have become even more prominent following the general elections on 30th April 1937.

The weakness of national leaders and the Japan–China war

On 7th July 1937, at a time when the situation in the political world was one of division in all directions, the Marco Polo Bridge Incident occurred, and in an instant full-scale war broke out between Japan and China. The historical judgement that the Marco Polo Bridge Incident was the direct cause of the attack on Pearl Harbor four and a half years later is today not so widely believed. If we follow the materials month by month concerning the vicissitudes of those four and a half years, we will understand that history was not as simple as that.

Nevertheless, for those who study the history of the First World War, and in addition have placed the Japan–China war in the context of the international situation of 1937, it is practically self-evident that the outbreak of the Japan–China war was the reason for the Pacific War in 1941, and that the result of the Pacific War breaking out in 1941 was the wasteland of 1945.

As for this horrifying future scenario, it is hard to find those who sought to avoid the Japan–China war, or sought to avoid the war between Japan and the United States. There was just one pro-war individual who was prepared for the Japan–US

228   *Japan's Modern History*

war, and as the result of it was ready for the wasteland that resulted from it, and from the perspective of 1937 he was able to describe the wasteland of 1945.

Just two months after the Marco Polo Bridge Incident, a book by Mutō Teiichi, entitled *Nisshi jihen no tsugi ni kuru mono* ('What is going to come after the China Incident'), was published by Shinchōsha. Inside the cover is written "published 7th September 1937", and "first edition 50,000 copies". The author, Mutō, while working for the *Asahi Shinbun*, was famous as a military commentator, calling for national preparedness against China, and against war with Britain. Those who are four or five years older than the present writer remember him at that time as a jingoist, and even today turn their faces away from him. He seems to have been a typical 'get up and go' type of journalist.

However right wing he may have been, Mutō had this capacity for rational argument about national defence and about war. Before the outbreak of Japan–China war, he criticised the *Kokusaku no kijun* (Foundation of National Policy) of August 1936, which regarded the Soviet Union as a potential enemy for the Army and the United States as a potential enemy for the Navy, argued that "National Defence Plan, which envisages a simultaneous war against Russia, Britain and America" was entirely "beyond Japan's capacities", and he declared sharply that "the National Defence Plan which depends on 'the Yamato [Japanese] spirit' and 'the divine wind' is a load of nonsense" (Mutō Teiichi, in *Chūō Kōron*, March 1937).

The Japan–China War and the Pacific War

In the book that this pro-war, rationalistic military commentator published on 7th September 1937, the most astonishing predictions are set out.

As for the present writer, I was born in May 1937, and was eight years old when the war was lost in 1945. Eight months before the defeat I was in Toyama as part of mass evacuation, and thus had little access to information, but I retain some memories of the whole of 1944 as a precocious primary school pupil. Almost all of what I experienced in 1944 was predicted by Mutō Teiichi writing in 1937, the year of my birth. First of all, he argued that if the Japan–China war developed into a war between Japan, Britain and America, bombing raids by the US air force on Japanese soil would occur, and moreover, young men in the prime of life would go to the battlefield, and the role of the 'home front' would double.

> Young men in the prime of life will go to the front, Old men, children and women will remain in the home territory, and as for their relationships, the reception of women into all kinds of productive organisations will increase to an amazing extent. . . . The crucial air defence industry will rest on the shoulders of the home front. In order to combat a rain of incendiary bombs, poison gas and bacteriological weapons, the apron image of the current Women's National Defence Association will be hopelessly inadequate. . . . According to European experience, the majority of burns from incendiary bombs affect the lower half of the body, especially the legs. Since Japanese

Crisis, 1925–1937 229

women's dress (kimono) and bare feet are the most inappropriate and dangerous apparel, this must absolutely be replaced. Planning new clothing devoted to new ideas in the *monpe* worn by women in Tōhoku, must be given immediate priority.

> (Mutō Teiichi, *Nisshi jihen to tsugi ni kuru mono* ['The Japan–China Incident and what is to come'], Shinchōsha, 1937, pp. 55–6)

At that time, when the Japan–China war had only just begun, members of the Women's National Defence Association, in their aprons, were waving rising sun flags for departing soldiers at railway station entrances. At that time Mutō was working out how these same women could extinguish fires in monpe-type clothing under a rain of incendiary bombs. In 1944 my mother, in monpe clothing, worked in relays with buckets.

Mutō predicted rationing and shortages of rice in the final period of the Pacific War: "Rice will be distributed at one *koku*, one *shō*, or just one *koku*, per person, and strict control by the State will have to be imposed" (ibid., p. 54). If we take one *koku*, since it amounts to 1,000 *gō* per year, it would be two *gō*, seven *shaku* per day (about 421.2 grams). In fact, I remember that it was rather less than two *gō*, four *shaku* (about 374.4 grams). Indeed, my health suffered and all my hair fell out.

When war broke out, metal items in households were requisitioned, and made into weaponry. In other words, "A time will come when perhaps gradually things will disappear, nickel silver coins, the steel handrails of park and bridge girders. Many other items in steel, copper, lead, tin, etc. will be taken from streets and from families to be sent to the field of battle and mobilised in greater quantities than men" (ibid., p. 52). People of this writer's generation will probably remember the copper statues, other than those of loyal patriots and military men, all reduced to their pedestals.

The basis for describing the picture of all-out war that Mutō had drawn up to this point was that the Marco Polo Bridge Incident had developed into full-scale war between Japan and China, and involved the prospect that Japan's total war would turn into all-out war between Japan on the one hand and Britain, America and the Soviet Union on the other. He wrote as follows:

> In the case of the earlier Manchurian Incident, or the Italian occupation of Ethiopia, or the Spanish [civil] war, they were no more than explosive events in one location, but the present affair has several times the dimensions of these, and if it develops into total war between Japan and China, it will necessarily go further, and there is no guarantee that it will not cause a huge catastrophe on a global scale.
>
> (Ibid., p. 7)

The world has entered the crucible of an entirely interconnected war. If the Japan-China situation does not reach some unexpected complete reversal, it is in a situation where it will have to proceed to the place where it is going. So

230　*Japan's Modern History*

to this point, whether it is the Soviet Union, whether it is Britain, or whether it is America, if countries having close relations with China take action, even to a limited extent, then the situation between Japan and China in a short while will light the fuse of a global emergency.

(Ibid., p. 14)

From 'crisis' to 'breakdown'

Immediately after the Marco Polo Bridge Incident of 7th July 1937, Mutō Teiichi seems to have been the only person to have penned such a dark future scenario. Mutō himself may have made his heart beat faster at this prospect, but for the present writer it can only be assumed that the 'Age of Crisis' had become the 'Age of Breakdown'.

Might it have been possible to avoid the 'Age of Breakdown' described by Mutō? Had the Ugaki Cabinet not proved abortive, perhaps it could have been avoided. Ugaki was supported by part of the Army and by a majority in the House of Representatives, while Ugaki, the *Minseitō* and the *Seiyūkai* opposed both fascism and war. Even with the 'narrowly based national defence' line of Ishiwara Kanji, total war between Japan and China might have been avoided. This is because those who over a five-year period preparing for a war against the Soviet Union gained the cooperation of the *zaibatsu* in producing aircraft and tanks and the heavy and chemical industries for that purpose did not think in advance that they would become involved in total war between Japan and China. The failed negotiations conducted by Ishiwara after the outbreak of war between Japan and China are a well known episode.

Even so, in the aftermath of two cabinets and a failed attempt to make a cabinet, the first Cabinet of Konoe Fumimaro, formed on 4th June 1937, published the following statement: "To continue the kinds of conflict and rivalry in our country that have been occurring invites the scorn of foreign countries. We shall act so far as possible to calm down rivalry and frictions" (Harada Kumao [ed.], *Saionji kō to seikyoku*, Iwanami Shoten, 1951, vol. 6, p. 383). Critics at the time turned it into the slogan: "Calming domestic conflict and rivalry". Following this slogan, the Konoe Cabinet appointed cabinet ministers not only from the *Minseitō* and the *Seiyūkai*, but also from the financial world and the new bureaucrats, and was supported both by the Army and by the Social Masses Party. According to a phrase that we have used repeatedly, this was a Cabinet that subsumed all the various political forces that had become "small slices".

In this Cabinet supported by all political forces, there was no basic line of policy, nor a ruling political force capable of attracting trust. It had a cabinet structure that, according to changing circumstances, could only move now to the right, now to the centre and now to the left. About a month after its formation, the danger of total war with China, introduced in Mutō's book, became apparent. The 'Age of Breakdown', making one nostalgic for the 'Age of Crisis', had begun. An old friend of the present writer continues to suggest to me that since we had bitter experiences of the 'Age of Breakdown' ourselves over the period of the

Japan–China war and the Pacific War, without an analysis of that period it must be impossible to bring 'Japan's Modern History' to a conclusion.

Nevertheless, the greatest reason why Japan entered the 'Age of Breakdown' was that the domestic rulers were split in multiple directions, and were unable to control foreign relations. This situation of multiple divisions deepened over the five years from 1932, and it developed into one of divisions without winners. The Konoe Cabinet did not overcome these divisions, but merely entrenched them and subsumed them exactly as they had been. Leaders who might have restructured the political system so as to stop the Japan–China war in its tracks, and then avoid war between Japan, Britain and America, essentially did not exist.

As for the eight years that were to follow, those prepared to express dissent in the political parties, bureaucracy, financial world, the world of labour, among critics and academics, were nowhere to be found, and above all, it was the 'Age of Breakdown'. I lack the ability to describe this 'Age of Breakdown', in which those expressing dissent had been extinguished.

I conclude this book, which has described Japanese modern history, dividing it into six periods, namely: Age of Reform → Age of Revolution → Age of Construction → Age of Management → Age of Reorganisation → Age of Crisis, as it was entering its Age of Breakdown.

Conclusion

As I have shown in the last chapter, Japanese leaders at the outset of the second decade of Shōwa (1935–45) had become separated out into small elements. It was in this domestic situation that war broke out between Japan and China, which Mutō recognised as the beginning of a great war. The Japanese people at the outset of the second Shōwa decade stood at the entrance to a double national disaster, in both domestic and foreign policy.

It goes without saying that what simultaneously liberated Japan from this double national disaster was 15th August 1945. Those military men and politicians who, lacking vision, only knew how to expand the war further were purged, and the people were liberated from war.

Many people when they discuss the triple disaster of 11th March 2011, combining a great earthquake, a great tsunami and a nuclear reactor accident, naturally compare it with a revival of the national disaster of the 15th August. The Japanese, who resuscitated Japan, a wasteland at the defeat, believed that they could conquer the national disaster of 11th March.

Nevertheless, for this writer, having analysed the transition, in Chapter 6, from the 'Age of Crisis' to the 'Age of Breakdown', this looks rather like 7th July 1937, when the Japan–China war broke out. While Japan on 7th July 1937 stood at the entrance to the 'Age of Breakdown', Japan on 15th August 1945 was at the end of the 'Age of Breakdown' and entering the 'Age of Reform'. The Japanese people, liberated from stupid leaders and a stupid war, burning with hope, accepted post-war reforms, and put all their efforts into reconstruction.

In Japan, confronting the third national disaster of 11th March 2011, there was no hope of 'reform' nor any trust in leaders. Of course, restoration and reconstruction in the Tōhoku region is the united desire of the Japanese people. But the political leaders who are supposed to lead this, just like those in the mid-1930s, are divided all ways into small elements. The belief that in order to face a national disaster you must have a 'Meiji Restoration' or a 'Post-war Reform' conspicuously lacks historical analysis and is simply a case of excessive optimism. The Meiji Restoration and the Post-war Reform both promoted Japan's development, but the 'Shōwa Restoration' merely deepened the crisis and led to 'breakdown'.

In order to overcome the 'national disaster' that began on 11th March 2013,

Conclusion 233

the emergence of new leaders is essential. Under small-minded leaders split every way, the chances of either restoration or renewal are slim.

In the course of history, however, 'renewal' and 'destruction' go hand in hand. Beginning with the 'renewal' of the Meiji Restoration, and after the 'destruction' of the Shōwa Restoration with which this book ends, the 'renewal' of the post-war reforms continued. In these 66 post-war years that began with the Post-war Reform, and now seem to have concluded a single cycle, perhaps the next generation of leaders in politics, the bureaucracy, finance, labour, journalism and academia, having overcome 'destruction' and now seeking 'renewal', are awaiting their turn.

It was in March 2010 that the present writer resolved to write this book, as the result of enthusiastic persuasion from Mr Masuda Kenji of Chikuma Shobō publishers. Around August of the same year he began writing, and completed the manuscript a whole year later, in September 2011. For this writer, who had been retired from the task of teaching for nine years, a whole year was literally a whole year.

Every time that I had completed 100 pages of manuscript, each accounting for 200 characters, he looked over what I had written and made comments. This means that when I had finished 1,200 pages of 200 characters each, he had commented on the manuscript 12 times. So there is not simply a division of labour between author and publisher in which the author writes the manuscript and the publisher publishes the book.

However this may be, for one person to write about 80 years of Japanese history was a more complex task than I had expected. Of course, from the beginning I was not aiming to write a straight history in which everything would be balanced. This book is a history of 80 years of modern Japan composed with the personal judgements and prejudices of this writer. But however much I may have resorted to personal judgement and prejudice, history from 1857 to 1937 was too long and too complicated. The book may be full of mistakes, but I can now calmly rejoice at being liberated from this penance.

Glossary

Bakufu   military government during the Tokugawa Shogunate period
Bakumatsu   the final period of the Tokugawa Shogunate, up to 1867
bansei ikkei   'lineal succession for ages eternal' (of the line of emperors)
bugyō   military or finance administrator in the feudal period
bushi   warriors
chokurei   Imperial ordinances
chōzen, chōzenshugi   transcendental, transcendentalism (doctrine that governments should not be answerable to parliament)
daimyō   feudal lord, in charge of a domain
fukoku kyōhei   'prosperous country, strong military'
gasshō renkō   multi-party alliance (Saigō Takamori)
gekokujō   inferiors overwhelming superiors
genrō   elder statesmen
gijō   senior councillor
gōgisei   consultative system
goshinpei   Imperial Forces (early Meiji)
Gosho   Imperial Palace in Kyoto
gunbu   military authorities
gunfuyaku   military service official
gunrei   military ordinances
haihan chiken   abolition of domains, establishment of prefectures
han   domain (to 1871)
hanbatsu   'domain-clique' [government]
hatamoto   'bannerman': senior retainer belonging directly to the Shōgun
heimin   commoners
iaku jōsō   direct appeal to the Throne by the military
jikan nōchi   resignation of the Lord Privy Seal and return of territory (from the Bakufu)
jūshin   senior statesmen (1930s)
kaikoku   opening the country
kangun   Imperial Army (in early Meiji period)
kashin   retainers

Glossary of Terms 235

kensei no jōdō regular procedures of constitutional government (implying that government should be based on a majority in Parliament)

karō chief retainer

ken prefecture (from 1871)

kōbu gattai alliance of Court and Bakufu

kōgi yoron fairness and public opinion

koku 0.18 cubic metres of rice (or other grain), sufficient to feed one person for one year

kokutai 'national polity'

kuge Court noble

kusetsu jūnen decade of fidelity in adversity (*Kenseikai*, 1916–24)

minryoku kyūyō mitigation of people's burdens

monpe women's trousers, gathered at the ankles

ōsei fukko restoration of imperial rule (1868)

sabaku kaikoku support the Bakufu, open Japan

sankin kōtai 'alternate residence' between domains and Edo

sanyo Junior Councillor

seihen political change (especially that of 1881)

seihi setsugen reduction of government expenditures

sekkyoku seisaku positive policies; developmental policies

shizoku former samurai

Shōgun de facto military ruler of Japan, up to 1867

shokusan kōgyō promotion of investment and development of industry

sonnō tōbaku revere the Emperor, overthrow the Bakufu

sonnō jōi 'revere the Emperor, expel the foreigner'

sōsai President (e.g. of a political party)

tairō 'Great Elder' (position held by Ii Naosuke in the Bakumatsu period)

taisei hōkan cession of political power by the Shōgun to the Emperor (1867)

tōsuiken right of command

yūshi brave warrior (samurai, comrade)

Index

absent government 63
Adachi Kenzō 194, 199–200
administration: principles/philosophy
of 91; reorganisation of 118
administrative expenditure/retrenchment,
and Meiji Constitution 114, 116
Aichi prefecture 84
Aikoku Risshisha 85
Aikokusha 83–4, 86–7, 92, 97, 98, 99, 112
Aikoku Shinshi 97
Aikokushi rin 97
Aizu Castle 48
Aizu domain 3, 21, 22, 25, 44, 45, 46, 47,
48
Aizu war 44
Akashi Motojirō 160, 163
Akita, George 96
alliance: Anglo-Japanese Alliance 137,
174–5; assembly establishment
alliance 54; between Court and
Bakufu (*kōbu gattai*) 23, 40; grand
alliance concept 13, 14, 15, 21–4;
horizontal/army and navy officers and
right wing 189; horizontal of samurai
from domains 21; multi-party alliance
(*gasshō renkō*) 4–10, 10–13, 15, 23,
25, 28; of retainers 18; of samurai 16,
17, 18, 21; Satsuma-Choshu 22, 27,
28–34; Satsuma–Tosa 8–9, 18, 36;
two-level 35
Alliance of Chambers of Commerce 144
American fleet, arrival of/1853 2
Andō Nobumasa 10
Andō Teruzō 203, 218
Anglo-Japanese Alliance 137, 174–5
Ansei Purge 2, 3, 4, 5, 6, 10, 12
Ansei Reform 4, 20
Anti-Communist Pact 196
anti-foreigner sentiment, collapse of 14, 28

anti-war socialists 138–9
Aoki Shūzō 56
Aomori peasant association 86–7
Arahata Kanson 139
Araki Rokushi 188
Araki Sadao 188, 201, 203, 204, 208,
211
Argument for Popular Politics, The 106
Arima Shinshichi 16
Arisugawa Taruhito 93
arms race, over Korea 104
Army *see also* military: and the
Dōshikai 151, 153; *kōdō ha* (Imperial
Way faction) 211, 214, 215, 216, 221;
moving to fascism 221; and the Social
Masses Party 223–4, 225; *tōsei ha*
(control faction) 210, 211, 214, 215,
216, 218, 220; and *zaibatsu* 223–5,
226, 227–30
army and navy, young officers'
movement 187–9
army camps 52
Army expansion: beginning of 102;
following Russo-Japanese war 145–6;
funding of 105; and Manchuria/
Mongolia 147–8; operating costs
of 131; rejection of 137; and World
War I 159–60; and World War I
boom 161
Army Minister, requirement to be serving
officer 152, 153, 186–7
Army Ministry 52, 79, 221, 224
Army national reconstruction movement
see Sakurakai
Army officers: attempts to control 203;
case for territorial conquest of
Manchuria/Mongolia 180–1; February
26th Incident 216; and *jūshin*
bloc 215; November Incident 196;

Index   237

and Seiyūkai 208; young officers'
movement 187–9
Ashio mine pollution issue 102, 124
Asō Hisashi 220, 224
assembly: argument 62, 74, 87;
controversy over 67; establishment of
landlord 130–1; and Inoue Kaoru 68;
and Itagaki/Saigō 63; peasant assembly/
samurai assembly 83; petition to
establish 54, 62, 63, 68, 83, 110;
popularly elected 68, 69, 71, 86
assembly establishment alliance 54
assembly politics 26–8
Azuma Noboru 195

Baba Tatsui 100
Baba Tsunego 183, 199, 200, 207–8, 210,
224–5, 226
Bakufu (Shogunate) *see also* Shōgun:
military power of 37–9; and opening
the country 1, 2, 3; overthrow of 34–9,
41–2; reform of 6, 17; restoration of
power to 22, 23; rule of 5; term 234
Bakumatsu-Ishin (Restoration)
revolution 52
Bakumatsu period 1, 4, 5, 55, 58, 67, 234
Bakumatsu seiji to Satsuma han 21, 35
balance of payments 79, 80, 150
Bank of Japan 102, 224
Bank of Taiwan 175, 192
bansei ikkei 234
Banzai Ichirō 181
Battle of Goryokaku (Hakodate) 22
Black Thursday 192
Blood League Incident 188, 196, 203
Boshin Imperial Edict 137
Boshin sensō 45
Boshin war 22, 35, 42, 44, 45, 62, 67, 135
Boxer Rebellion 124
Breakdown, age of 230–1
British consulate, arson attack 18–19, 68
British faction 97
British-style 'cabinet within parliament'
system 94, 97, 109, 111
British two-party system 112, 155–7, 179
broad-based national defence 220, 224,
225, 226
budgets: 1924 172; positive budget
1920 165; rejection of naval
budget 153–4; right to implement the
budget of the previous year 96, 105,
114
bugyo 234
Bunkyū era, political uprising 10

bureaucracy: and conservative party 122;
era of 106–8; and *Jiyūtō* 121;
reconciliation with parties 131–3; and
rural landlords 122
bureaucratic clique: and
constitutionalists 149; and Hara
Kei 166, 167; and Katsura Tarō 151;
move to get rid of 149; and
Seiyūkai 144–5, 150, 171
bureaucrats: military 210; new 211, 215,
218
bushi 234
businessmen: attack on *Seiyūkai* 144;
urban/tax reduction demands 144–5
business tax 144, 151

Cabinet Council 208, 210–11, 213, 215
cabinet decisions, v. Emperor's
opinion 125, 126
cabinet of cooperation 204 *see also*
national unity cabinet
Cabinet Research Bureau 196, 208,
210–11, 213, 216
cabinet(s) *see also* Diet (Parliament):
coalition 199–201; Hamaguchi 175,
182, 191, 209; Hara 152, 162–73;
Hatoyama 177; Hayashi 196, 223,
224, 225; Hirota *see* national unity
cabinet; Inukai 199, 200, 201–3,
209; Katō 162, 172, 173, 174, 182;
Katsura 137, 144, 148, 149, 151, 171;
Kiyoura 152, 172; Konoe 196, 230,
231; Matsukata Masayoshi 116, 130;
national unity cabinet 196, 204–5, 207,
208, 218; Navy 151, 153; Okada 196,
208, 209–10, 211, 212, 213, 215, 218;
Ōkuma 131, 154–5, 157, 160, 163;
party 131, 157; Saionji 137, 145,
146, 148, 151; Saitō *see* national unity
cabinet; and State 207; Tanaka 175,
177, 179, 180, 181, 192, 209;
Terauchi 152, 161–2, 161–3, 164;
three-faction Cabinet 152, 173, 174,
175, 179; Ugaki 189, 196, 222–3,
230; Wakatsuki 196, 199, 200, 201;
Yamagata 133–4; Yamamoto 151, 152,
153, 154, 171, 172
cabinet system: launch of 102; within
parliament 93, 98, 105, 109–10,
156, 157; parliamentary 91; within
parliament system/British-style 94,
97, 109, 111; party 121; and political
parties/parliament 94; researching
of 56; responsible cabinet 111

238 *Index*

Calming domestic conflict and rivalry 230
capitalism, national defence through 225
capitalist economics 220
Chamber of the Left 62
Charter Oath 1, 22, 56
Chiang Kai-shek 175, 178
Chiang Tso-Lin 175
Chichibu Incident 102
Chikujō kenpō seigi 184
Chikuzen domain 7
China: advocates of making war on 65–8;
 China policy 182; compatibility
 clause with 54; as hypothetical
 enemy 101, 147; indemnity paid
 by 123, 127; Japanese aggression
 towards 204, 205; military capacity
 of 103; non-interference in policy 163,
 175, 176, 182; relations with Japan
 over Korea 73, 100–5; reparations
 payments by 128; Republic of China
 founded 137; and Ryūkyū islands 64;
 threat argument 101, 102, 103–4;
 twenty-one demands to 152, 160, 161,
 163, 174–6
Chinese revolution 1911 137, 147, 148
Chishima, treaty exchanging 54
chokurei 184, 234
Chōshū, and Tosa alliance 68
Chōshū domain: abandonment of the anti-
 foreigner position 28; civil war 49;
 confrontation with Satsuma domain
 13–16; direct action by 14, 25; and
 Imperial Army 48–9; lower-ranking
 samurai 18; *Mitategumi*, the 18;
 national interest argument 3; opposition
 to Nagai 15; pro-Emperor/anti-foreigner
 faction 7, 13–15, 14, 21; punishment
 of 22, 25; restoring honour of 31,
 32, 34; second assault of 1866 31;
 supporting *sonnō jōi* 3; violence in 22
chozen 234
chozenshugi 234
Chūō Kōron 156, 157, 164, 183, 207, 208,
 226
City system 102
Civilian Officials Appointment Law
 1988 124
Civil servant appointment law 1893 102
coalition cabinet 199–201
coalitions, post-war permanent
 coalition 119
*Commentaries on the Constitution of the
 Empire of Japan* 95
commoners (*heimin*) 63, 234

communication systems 80, 165
Communist Party 152, 169, 193
compatibility clause, Japan/China 54
conference of councillors (*sanyo kaigi*)
 1863 23
conference of four domain lords 31, 32
conscription 52, 54, 78, 178
consensus diplomacy 175
conservative constitutionalism, Inoue
 Kowashi 98, 105
conservative faction 39–41; and the
 constitution 98–9
conservative finance policies 191, 193
conservative party, and government
 bureaucracy 122
constitution: agreement to principle of 69;
 argument 74, 87, 88–9; as basic law
 of Japan 62; and collective/individual
 responsibility 95; conservative/
 progressive factions 98–9; drafts
 of 84, 92; executive power in 98; and
 financial arguments 88–9; and Fukuzawa
 Yukichi 92, 93, 97; Great Japan Imperial
 Constitution *see* Meiji Constitution;
 and Inoue Kaoru 68; and Inoue Kowashi 57,
 84, 92, 94–7, 98, 99, 102, 105; Meiji
 Constitution *see* Meiji Constitution;
 and Ōkuma Shigenobu 91–2, 97, 99;
 promulgated under the name of the
 Emperor 91; and prosperous country
 factions 65; Prussian-style Great
 Japanese Imperial Constitution 57, 95;
 rather than parliament 55–8
constitutional defence movement:
 first 137, 144, 146, 148–9, 150–1, 171;
 second 152, 171–2, 173
constitutional government 55–8, 69
constitutional interpretation, of Minobe
 Tatsukichi 184, 185–7
constitutionalism: German-style 95; and
 Ozaki Yukio 149
constitutionalists, and bureaucratic
 clique 149
Constitutional Liberal Party 102
constitutional monarchy, German-/British-
 type 94, 95
Constitutional Progressive Party 102, 113,
 128
constitutional research 56–7, 93, 102
constitutional system: 1890–1900 114–15;
 proclamation on establishment 54; and
 tax reform 129–30
constitution factions: and foreign invasion
 factions 73–4; losing ground 75

Construction, age of 53–8, 82, 88, 94, 100
consultative system (*gōgisei*) 1
corruption, *Jiyūtō* 115
corruption scandal, navy 153, 154
cotton prices 191–2
councillor system 22, 37
counter-revolution, and revolution 189
country gentlemen 110; age of 108–9;
   and *Daidō Danketsu Undō* 111, 112,
   113; and *Jiyūtō* 113
coup d'état: 18th August 1863 3, 21,
   22–3; crisis of military 195, 202–3, 204,
   206; fear of 199; February 26th Incident
   see February 26th Incident; by Kim Ok
   Kyun 105; Restoration of Imperial Rule
   (ōsei fukko) 31, 34, 41
'creating an industrial nation policies' 192
crises: economic 204–5; financial 81, 82,
   149 *see also* financial panic; of foreign
   relations 202–3, 205; of military coup
   d'état 195, 202–3, 204, 206
Crisis, age of 175, 180, 204

Daidō danketsu 102, 110–20
daimyō 234
Dalian, lease of 160
Dan Takuma 196, 203
Date Munenari 32
decade of fidelity in adversity (*kusetsu
   jūnen*) 162, 173, 235
deflationary policies: Matsukata
   Masayoshi 89, 90, 94, 96, 102, 108–9,
   116; and rice prices 108; and tax
   revenues 80
democracy: and broad-based national
   defence 226; loss of interest in 167,
   168; parliamentary 111, 204
democratic party, *Kenseikai* as 174
democratic political system, in a public
   opinion 107
democratisation, in domestic politics 179
demokurashii (democracy) *see* democracy
Den Kanjirō 154, 159–60
depression: Great 192, 202; post-war 137,
   152
development dictatorships 75
Development Office property, sale of 84
Diet (Parliament) *see also* cabinet(s);
   House of Representatives: compromise
   with government 119–20;
   confrontation/compromise in 114; as
   constitutional organ 118; establishment
   of 96, 102; inauguration 116; twisted
   Diet 113

diplomacy, consensus 175
direct appeal to the Throne by the military
   (*iaku jōsō*) 183, 234
discontent, and businessmen 141, 144
Dōhō 168
domain-clique (hanbatsu)
   government 122, 129, 131, 132
domain faction 116
domain lords (*daimyō*) 3, 7, 10, 15, 52, 113
domains: abolishment of 22, 49, 51–2, 56,
   59; pro-Emperor 7
domestic goods, production of 55
domestic politics 14–15, 179, 204, 206
Dōshikai, and the Army 151, 153
Draft of a Japanese constitution, Ueki
   Emori 84

Eastern Conference 175
Eastern Congress (*Tōhō kaigi*) 178, 180
Echizen domain 4, 5, 6, 7, 10, 21, 22, 33
economic crisis 204–5
economic development 64, 65, 79 *see also*
   industrial development
economic panic, 1889 102 *see also*
   financial panic
economic policy, confusion in 191
economics, capitalist 220
Edo Castle, opening of 22, 42–4, 46
education, developing 165
Education law 1886 102
education ordinance 54
18th August 1863 coup 3, 21, 22–3
1862, the confused year 16–20
eight ministry system 50
eight shipboard policies 33
elections *see* general elections
electoral law: and land tax 108, 109;
   revision of 124, 137, 142, 152
electorate: increasing numbers of 142,
   166; large/medium landlords 109;
   qualifications of/limiting 87–8, 124,
   130, 137; rural landlords as 143
Emperor: Emperor's opinion v. cabinet
   decisions 125, 126; Manchukuo
   Emperor system established 196;
   Meiji 117, 125, 126, 137; organ
   theory of the Emperor 170, 196,
   213–14, 216; petitioning to establish a
   parliament 86, 87; rejection of February
   26th Incident 217–18; restoration of
   see Restoration of Imperial Rule (ōsei
   fukko); role of 179; system/disputes
   over 182; system/surface and hidden
   teaching 214

240 *Index*

Emperor-centrism, of *Seiyūkai* 179, 213
Engineering Ministry 22, 55
Enlightenment faction, *Bakufu* 27
Enomoto Takeaki 39
equality: of the four classes 136; of military service 136; political/and equality of servicemen 136, 138, 139
establishing a parliament from above 89–91
Etō Shinpei 44, 63
Europe, inspection tour to 53–8
executive power, in constitution 98
expansionism, policy of/Nagai Uta 15
Expedition High Command 45
expelling the foreigner/opening the country, shelving of dispute between 5–7
expelling the foreigner, Shimazu Hisamitsu's opinion 19
expenditure: on Army/Navy 145; and Meiji Constitution 114, 115, 117
exports: falling US 191–2; post Sino-Japanese war 130; rapid rise in/1932 205; traditional industries 55; and World War I boom 161
Ezochi, becomes Hokkaido 22

facism: and the Army 221; Japanese 183, 189; military 204; political parties countering 206; and Seiyūkai 207, 221–2; and Social Masses Party 217, 227
factories: inspection tour of Great Britain's 53–5; setting up new/modern 55
Factory law 1911 137
Factory Sale edict 82
fairness/public opinion (*kōgi yoron*) 1, 68, 70–82, 235
farmers: demand for a parliament 89; farmer class/breaking up of 108; independent/small 108; political participation of 90; social unrest 199, 201; tax reduction demands 144; wealth of 90
farmers' rights associations/movement 90, 92, 93, 94, 96
February 26th Incident 188, 196, 203–4, 216–20
feudal assembly argument 62
feudal parliament 24–8, 34–9
fidelity in adversity (*kusetsu jūnen*) 162, 173, 235
15th August, national disaster 232

Fifteen-year War 204
finance: balance of payments 79, 80, 150; and constitutional arguments 88–9; financial deficits 80; inconvertible paper money 79, 80, 89
Finance Ministry 192
financial crisis: 1912 149, 150; following Seinan war 81, 82
financial panic *see also* economic panic: 1927 175, 192, 194; post Russo-Japanese war 144
financial policies: conservative 191, 193; of Hara's *Seiyūkai* 165, 166; Matsukata Masayoshi 84, 89, 94, 100, 104, 105; Meiji Government 82; Ōkuma Shigenobu 80, 89, 90
fishermen, violence against/Ryūkyū islanders 64
five-power Disarmament Treaty *see* Navy Disarmament Treaty
Five-Year Plan for Heavy Industry 223, 224, 225
flagship policies, new/replacing positive policies 145
foreigners: anti-foreigner sentiment/collapse of 14, 28; argument to expel/shelving of 3; Satsuma domain/expulsion of 18
foreign invasion argument 58–62
foreign invasion factions 73–4, 75
foreign loans 88–9, 149
foreign policy(ies): of Hara Kei 163; of Japan 177; of *Kenseikai* 174, 176–7; of Meiji Government 125; of *Seiyūkai* 176, 177–8; of Shidehara Kijūrō 175, 176–7; of Tanaka Giichi Cabinet 177; of Terauchi Masatake 163, 164
foreign relations: crisis in 202–3, 205; inability to control 231
Four Nation Treaty 152, 174, 175
France, reducing influence of 163
freedom of speech, in House of Representatives 219, 221
Fuchibe Gunpei 77
Fujii Hitoshi 187, 190–1, 195, 203
Fujita Tōko 9
fukoku kyōhei see prosperous country, strong military (*fukoku kyōhei*)
Fukui prefecture 87
Fukuoka Takachika 32
Fukushima Incident 102
Fukushima prefecture 90
Fukuzawa Yukichi: and British two-party

Index 241

system 179; and constitution 92, 93, 97; defeat of 98, 99; and Gotō Shōjirō 111; and *Kōjunsha* 98, 99, 100; and Ōkuma Shigenobu 91, 94
Furuzawa Shigeru 63, 68, 69

Ga Noriyuki 56
gasshō renkō 234
gatherings, regulations on 54
gekokujō 234
general elections *see also* electoral law; electorate: 1st/1890 102; 2nd/1892 102, 115; 3rd/1893 115; 5th/1898 131; 12th/1915 152, 159; 13th/1917 152, 161; 14th/1920 152, 169; 18th/1932 196, 199, 201, 202–3; 1908/1912 143; 1930 192–4; 19th/1936 196, 208, 216; 20th/1937 196, 225–6, 227; interference in 102, 115, 116
General Staff Bureau 67
General Staff Office, and Takahashi Korekiyo 170–1
genrō 234
Genrōin 52, 102
Germany: German autocratic constitution 97; German faction 97; German-style constitutional monarchy 94, 95; Nazi regime established 196
Gessho 10
gijō 234
global instability 213
Glover, Englishman 28
Gneist, Professor Rudolf von 57
Godai Tomoatsu 80, 81, 85, 90
gōgisei 234
gold exports 152, 175
gold standard: established 124; and Great Depression 202; return to/and depression 192, 193, 194; return to/ secession from 175, 191–2, 196, 199, 200, 201, 202, 203
Gondō Seikyō 190, 203
Gōshikai 195
goshinpei 234
Gosho 234
Gotō Fumio 211
Gotō Shinpei 163, 172
Gotō Shōjirō 33, 40, 58, 62, 63, 102, 110–20
government: in 1874/Sat-Cho domain government 67; absent government 63; bureaucracy 121, 122 *see also*

bureaucracy; compromise with Diet 119–20; conflict with House of Representatives 115; constitutional 55–8, 69; domain-clique (hanbatsu) 122, 129, 131, 132; fragility of new 49–50; revenues 88, 89
Government Decree No. 48 82
Governor-General's office in Korea 137
grand alliance concept 13, 14, 15, 21–4
grand coalition 119, 199–201
Great Britain: inspection tour/of factories by Iwakura Mission 53–5; reducing influence of 163; treaty of harmony and friendship 2
Great Depression 192, 202
Great Japan Imperial Constitution *see* Meiji Constitution
Great Kanto Earthquake 152, 172, 191
Great Pacific War *see* Pacific War
Great Treason Incident 137
Great War boom *see* World War I
Guandong Army *see Kantōgun*
Guardian of the Shogun 10
gunboat diplomacy, and Kanghwado Treaty 73
gunbu 40, 234
gunfuyaku 234
gunrei 184, 234

Hachirin tsūkō 190
Hagi uprisings 54
Hague, incident of Korean secret agent at 137
haihan chiken 234
Hamada Kunimatsu 206, 221, 222, 223
Hamaguchi Osachi 119, 120, 181, 185; Cabinet 175, 182, 191, 209
Hama Yuji 189
han 234
Hanabusa Yoshimoto 101
hanbatsu (domain faction) 116, 138, 141, 144, 154, 234
Hara Kei: assassination of 152, 169; Cabinet 152, 162–73; collapse of the power of 154–5; decline in influence 145; foreign policies of 163; and House of Representatives 153; and Itō Hirobumi 141; and Katō Takaaki 166–7; and Katsura Tarō 140–1; and military clique 166, 167; party cabinet 121; and peace settlement 149; positive policies of 134, 136; and public works 149; reconciling officials and

242 Index

Hara Kei (cont.):
politicians 140–1; return of 151, 161; and *Seiyūkai* 122, 152; and Taishō Democracy 119–20; and two-major-party system 166–7; and universal suffrage 164–6, 167; and Yamagata Aritomo 166–7; and Yoshino Sakuzō 164
Hara Kei botsugo 170
harbours 80, 134, 135 *see also* ports
Harris, Townsend 2
Hashimoto Kingorō 195
Hashimoto Sanai 2, 4, 5, 6, 10, 13, 14, 15
hatamoto 234
Hatoyama Ichirō 183, 185
Hatoyama Yukio Cabinet 177
Hayakawa Wataru 29
Hayashi Senjūrō 214; Cabinet 196, 223, 224, 225
heavy industry, five-year plan for 223, 224, 225
heimin 63, 234
Heimin Shinbun 137
Hibiya arson incident 137, 139, 141, 144, 148
hidden teaching 214
High Command: Imperial Army (*kangun*) 47–8; Strategy for Preparedness against Neighbouring Countries 1880 105
Higo domain 7, 21, 22
Hiranuma Kiichirō 218
Hirota Kōki 222; Cabinet *see* national unity cabinet
Hirotsu Hironobu 60–1, 70, 71
Hisamitsu *see* Shimazu Hisamitsu
Hitotsubashi Keiki 2
Hitotsubashi Seishi faction 6
Hitotsubashi Yoshinobu 9, 10, 13, 19, 20, 25, 31
Hizen domain 44, 55
Hokkaidō Development Ministry 79
Hokuriku region 86, 110, 111, 135
home front, role of 228
Home Ministry 55, 64, 79, 80
Honjō Shigeru 218
Hori Chūzaemon 7
Hoshi Tōru 117, 122, 124, 132–3, 134, 135–6
Hotta Masayoshi 6
House of Elders (*genrōin*) 54, 102
House of Peers 96, 113, 114, 152, 153–4
House of Representatives: 1933 206; and centrist parties 98; conflict with government 115; dissolution of

1894 115; dissolution of/Hara 165; dissolution of/Hayashi 225; dissolution of/Inukai 202; dissolution of/Itō 132; dissolution of/Matsukata (second) 129; dissolution of/to gain majority 209; and domain-clique government 122; elections for 109; and electoral law 108; freedom of speech in 219, 221; and Hara Kei 153; and House of Peers 114; and Imperial Diet 96; and Imperial Proclamation for Harmony and Co-operation 117; and the *Jiyūtō* 113, 115, 128–9, 131; and land tax 132; and large/medium landlord electors 109; membership of 36; rejection of budgets/military expansion 105; and *Rikken Kaishintō* 113; and *Seiyūkai* 137, 159; and Socialist parties 112; and Ueki Emori 97
Hyōden: Hara Kei 165
Hyogo (Kobe), port 32
Hyōron Shinbun 76
hypothetical enemies 101, 145, 147, 228

iaku jōsō 183, 234
Ibaragi peasant association 86–7
Ichiji Masaharu 24
Ichiki Kitokurō 215
Ichiki Shirō 77
Iida Taizō 157
Iida Yasuzō 156
Ii Naosuke 3, 4, 6, 10, 203
Ijichi Masaharu 33, 34, 36, 40, 48, 67
Ijūin Kanehiro 67
Ikeda Shigeaki 224, 225
Ikedaya riots 22, 25
Imamura Hitoshi 211
Imo (Jingo) Incident 102, 105, 123
Imperial Army (*kangun*): cost of/to domains 46–9; dissolution/reconstruction of 47–52, 54, 59; formation of 34–5, 40; and Tōhoku war 44; weakness of 52
Imperial Constitution *see* Meiji Constitution
Imperial Defence Policy 137, 145, 147
Imperial Diet *see* Diet (Parliament)
Imperial Edict on harmonious cooperation 102
Imperial Guard 22, 54, 59, 60
Imperial Headquarters 196
Imperial Household Law 1889 102
Imperial Instructions on establishing a parliament 84

Imperial ordinances (*chokurei*) 184, 234
Imperial Proclamation for Harmony and
  Co-operation 1893 117–19
Imperial Reconstruction Organisation 172
Imperial Rescript on Education 102
Imperial Rescript, soldiers/sailors 102
Imperial Restoration 1868 22
Imperial treaty sanction 1865 22
Imperial universities law 1886 102
Imperial Way 33
Imperial Will, and cabinet decisions 125
imports 58, 80
import substitution, industrialisation for 55
Inada Masatsugu 56, 57, 58
Inba domain 7
income tax, and eligibility to vote 166 *see
  also* taxation
inconvertible paper money 79, 80, 89
indemnity, paid by China 123, 127
independence of the right of
  command 182–4, 185, 198, 213
Independent Club 115
industrial bonds 79
industrial development *see also* economic
  development; *Five-Year Plan for
  Heavy Industry*: and communications
  network 80; and financial issues 88;
  and Ōkubo Toshimichi 75; and Ōkuma
  Shigenobu 89; post Sino-Japanese
  war 130
industrialisation: and establishing a
  parliament from above 90; for import
  substitution 55; issuing of industrial
  bonds 79; promoting traditional
  industry 55, 80
industrial loans 80
industrial power, Japan–China Agreement
  as 178
industrial production, 1932 205
industry(ies): development of
  traditional 55, 80; investment/
  promotion of 18, 53–5
inflation 80, 89, 90
infrastructure, expanding of 134–5
infringement of the right of command 183,
  184, 185, 198
Inoue Juichi 182, 205
Inoue Junnosuke 192, 194, 195, 196, 199,
  200–1, 203
Inoue Kaoru: arson attack on British
  consulate 68; and constitution 68;
  and financial retrenchment 82;
  inspection tour/Western countries 74;
  and Kanghwado Treaty 74; and Kido

Kōin 52, 68, 69; and Korea 72,
  101; and the *Mitategumi* 18; Ōsaka
  conferences 69; and Taiwan 68
Inoue Kowashi: and cabinet within
  parliament 93; conservative
  constitutionalism 98, 105; as
  a conservative leader 100; and
  constitution 57, 84, 92, 94–7, 98, 99,
  102, 105
Inoue Nisshō 188, 203
Inoue Yoshika 71
insurrection movements, fear of 81
Interior Ministry 55
Inukai Tsuyoshi 149, 173, 196;
  Cabinet 199, 200, 201–3, 209
invasion force, Taiwan 64
investment: and establishing a parliament
  from above 90; and Ōkuma
  Shigenobu 89; renewed recognition
  of 53–5
Ishibashi Tanzan 209
Ishigami Ryōhei 170
Ishii–Lansing agreement 152
Ishiwara Kanji 180, 181, 195, 219, 223,
  224, 225, 226, 230
Isobe Senichi 218
Itagaki Taisuke: and constitution 98,
  99; and Gotō Shōjirō 110–11, 112;
  as Home Affairs Minister 132; and
  indemnity paid by China 127; and
  Itō Hirobumi 114; and Iwakura
  Mission 63; and *Jiyūtō* 129; and
  Kido Kōin 68–9; and Korea 59,
  61, 62; and military expansion/
  funding 122; as military leader 48;
  and national assembly 58; and Ōkubo
  Toshimichi 70; Ōsaka conferences 69;
  and overthrow of *Bakufu* 42, 43; and
  Petition to Establish a Popularly Elected
  Assembly 83; and Popular Rights
  Movement 98, 100; resignation of/as
  councillor 63; return to government 67;
  and the *Risshisha* 86, 97; and Saigō 51;
  and strong military 62, 63; as Tosa
  domain/military authorities 40;
  white paper for the establishment of a
  popularly elected assembly 56
Itakura Katsukiyo 38, 39
Italy, fascist regime in 175
Itō Hirobumi: arson attack/British
  consulate 19; assassination of 137;
  cabinet/resignation of 132; as
  a conservative leader 100; and
  constitution 92, 95; constitutional

244 *Index*

Itō Hirobumi (*cont.*):
 research of 57, 102; and election interference 116; and financial reform 51; and financing the military 52; and German faction 97; and *hanbatsu* forces 141; and Hara Kei 141; and Imperial Proclamation for Harmony and Co-operation 117, 118; inspection tour/Europe and America 53; and Itagaki Taisuke 114; and *Jiyūtō* 99, 129–30; and *Kenseitō* 134, 135; and Mutsu Munemitsu 123–4, 125; and Ōkubo Toshimichi 68, 72; and Ōkuma Shigenobu 93; petitioning the Emperor 126; and *Seiyūkai* 122, 124, 136, 141; and Yamagata Aritomo 141
Iwakura Mission 53–8, 63, 65, 94
Iwakura Tomomi 47, 50, 51, 53, 78, 93, 94, 97, 99
Iwase Tadanari 9

Japan–China Agreement 176, 178
Japan-China Friendship Treaty 22
Japan–China war 180, 196, 227–30, 232
Japan, designated a lawless country 61
Japanese Federation of Labour (*Nihon Rōdō Kumiai Sōdōmei*) 194, 205
Japan Farmers Union 152
Japan–Korea Agreements 137
Japan–Korea friendship pact *see* Kanghwado Treaty
Japan-Korea relations 70–1
Japan–Manchukuo Protocol 196
Japan's Lower Society 124
Japan Socialist Alliance (*Nihon Shakaishugi Domei*) // 152
Japan Socialist Party 137
Japan–Soviet Basic Treaty 175
Japan–US Security Treaty, revised 140
Japan–US Treaty of friendship and Commerce 2
Japan–US Treaty of Harmony and Friendship 2
Japan–US war 181
jiban 112
Jichi minpan 188
jikan nōchi 234
Jikyōsha 87
Jilin province 197–8
Jiyōtō 102 *see also Rikken Jiyōtō*
Jiyūtō: as centralist party 98; change of direction 116–17, 122; corruption 115; defeat of 131; formation of 99–100, 102; and House of Representatives 113,

115, 128–9, 131; and Itagaki Taisuke 129; and Itō Hirobumi 99, 129–30; *jiban* of 112; and land tax 129, 131; and village landlords 127
Jiyūtō shi 59, 83–4
Jiyūtō–Shinpotō coalition: rejects land tax increase 124
journalists: National Journalists Alliance 149; and Tsuzuki Keiroku 107
jūshin 234
jūshin bloc: battles over 214–16; February 26th Incident 217

Kabasan Incident 102, 111
Kabayama Sukenori 77, 102
Kagoshima party 76
Kagoshima prefecture 77
kaikoku 234
Kaishintō 115, 119
Kaizō 224
Kakushin Club 152
Kamei Kanichirō 211, 212
Kanaya Hanzō 197, 198
Kaneko Nobutaka 195
Kanghwado (*Kokado*) Incident 54, 70–2
Kanghwado Treaty 54, 72–3, 74, 101
kangun 235 *see also* Imperial Army (*kangun*)
Kan'in Kotohito 214
Kanto Earthquake 152, 172, 191
Kantōgun 175, 178, 195, 196, 197–8, 203, 205
kappuku (ritual disembowelment) debate 196, 221, 222, 223
Kapsin (*Kōshin*) Incident 102, 105, 123
karō 235
kashin 235
Kataoka Kenkichi 84
Katō Hiroharu 183, 185
Katō Takaaki: and 21 demands 160, 175–6; Cabinets 162, 174, 182; conservative finance policies 191; foreign policies of 163; and Hara Kei 166–7; popularity of 155; and regular procedures of constitutional government (kensei no jōdō) 161–2; and three-faction Cabinet 173; and Yamamoto Gonbei Cabinet 172
Katō Tomosaburō 169
Katsu Kaishū 16–18, 26–8, 42, 43
Katsura-Saionji era 142–3
Katsura Tarō 119, 140–3, 148, 150, 151, 152; Cabinets 137, 144, 148, 149, 151, 162, 171
Katsura Uemon 29

Index 245

Katsuta Magoyasu 6, 11, 23, 45
Kawada Isao 211
Kawai Eijirō 226
Kawamura Sumiyoshi 50, 66, 67, 77
Kawasaki Takukichi 213
Keiō University 92
ken 235
Kenkyūkai 154
Kenseihontō 124, 133, 141, 144, 150, 175
Kenseikai 119, 152, 161–2, 165–6, 174–7, 179–80, 192
Kensei kōron 179
Kensei no hongi o toite sono yūshū no bi o sumasu no michi o ronzu 152
kensei no jōdō 235 *see also* regular procedures of constitutional government (*kensei no jōdō*)
Kenseitō 124, 131, 132, 133, 134, 135–6
Ketsumeidan Incident 188
Kido Kōichi 200
Kido Kōin: and autocratic constitution 62; and constitution 63, 94; and Finance Ministry 51; and governmental fairness 57–8; and Inoue Kaoru 52, 68, 69; inspection tour/Europe and America 53, 56–7; and Itagaki Taisuke 68–9; and Kanghwado Treaty 73; and Korea 72; and Ōkubo Toshimichi 65, 68, 70; and Ōkuma Shigenobu 52; Ōsaka conferences 69, 70; resignation of/as councillor 65; return to government 67, 71; and Saigō 25, 29, 50; six articles 29–31
Kim Ok Kyun, coup d'état by 105
Kinmon Incident 3, 22, 24–6
Kirino Toshiaki 59–60, 61, 64, 73–4
Kishū faction 6
Kita Ikki 137–9, 183, 188, 190, 203, 212
Kiyoura Keigo 172; Cabinet 152, 172
Koba Dennai 11–13, 15
kōbu gattai 235
Kōchi prefecture 83, 85
kōdō ha (Imperial Way faction), Army 211, 214, 215, 216, 221
Koga Kiyoshi 195
kōgi yoron 235 *see also* fairness/public opinion
Kogosho Conference 37
Koizumi Matajirō 223
Kōjunsha 84, 91–2; of Fukuzawa 93, 94, 98, 99, 100
Kōjun zasshi 92
Kokkai Kisei Dōmei 84, 87, 92–3, 96, 97, 98, 99

koku 235
Kokumin Kyōkai 129
Kokumin no Tomo 102, 109, 110
Kokumintō 149, 151, 165
Kokusaku no kijun (Foundation of National Policy) 228
kokutai 193, 196, 235
Kokutai ron to junsei shakaishugi 138
Kokuyūkai 100
Komatsu Taiteki 24, 26, 27, 29, 33, 36
Komuro Shinobu 63, 68, 69
Kongo ('Diamond') cruiser 153
Konoe Fumimaro 218; Cabinet 196, 230, 231
Konoe Tadahiro 9, 10
Kōno Hironaka 84–7, 90, 99
Korea: 3/1 independence movement 152; assimilation of 71, 137, 147–8; conservative faction/pro-China 101; establishment of Governor-General's office 137; failure of military coup 102; incident of a Korean secret agent at Hague 137; invasion argument 59–60, 72, 73; and Itagaki Taisuke 59, 61, 62; and Japan-China 73, 101, 104, 123, 124; Kanghwado Treaty 54, 72–3, 74; pro-Japan faction in 100–2, 104; Saigō's invasion argument 60–2; split over invasion 54, 63, 64, 65, 67; withdrawal of troops from 102
Kōtoku Shūsui 115, 137
Kuga Katsunan 139
kuge 235
Kuhara Fusanosuke 202, 215
Kumamoto Castle, attack by Saigō forces 77, 78
Kumamoto domain 27
Kuno Osamu 214
Kurihara Yasuhide 188
Kuroda Godai 81
Kuroda Kiyotaka 29, 45, 59, 60, 61, 80, 106; and Korea 64, 66, 72; and war against China 67
Kusaka Genzui 15, 18, 25
kusetsu jūnen 162, 173, 235
Kuwana domain 25
Kwantung Army *see Kantōgun*
Kyoto, march to 10–11, 25

labour disputes 194
Labour Farmer Party (*Rōdō Nōmintō*) 194
Labour Union Promotion Society 124
landlord assembly, establishment of 130–1

246 *Index*

landlords *see also* rural landlords: large/
medium 108–9; parasitic/working 108;
rising standard of living 86; and small
farmers 108; taxation 116, 143
land rent, freezing of 54
land tax: amendment law 1884 102;
demands for reduction 144; and
electoral law 108, 109; increase 114,
133–4; and inflation 89; and
Jiyūtō 129, 131; law amended 124; and
Meiji Government 88; opposition to
increasing 131; ordinance 54; people
paying 83; reduction 54, 90, 114;
reform 80, 81–2, 85; and rice prices 80,
128, 143; rising/Russo-Japanese
war 136; and rural landlords 127
leadership: establishing political 121, 153;
political to bureaucratic 106; weakness
of 227–30
League of Blood (*Ketsumeidan*)
Incident 188
League of Nations: Japan joining 152;
Japan's departure from 196, 205;
Lytton Commission 196
left wing, of Social Masses Party 212, 223
legislative drafting 106
Levellers Association 152
Liaodong peninsula 127
liberal coalition government, three-faction
Cabinet 174
Liberal Democratic Party 119, 120, 121,
157
liberalism 226–7
Liberal Party *see Jiyūtō*
Li Hong-Zhang 127
liquidation of paper money 105
Liutiaohu Incident *see* Manchurian
Incident
loans: domestic/foreign for war 136,
149; foreign 88–9, 149; public/for
projects 128; public/for the Army and
Navy 102, 105
London Naval Disarmament
Conference 119, 175, 182–4, 194
London Treaty 175, 182–5, 186, 187, 196
Lushun, lease of 160
Lytton Commission 196

Maki Izumi 25
Makino Nobuaki 200, 201, 215, 222
Management, age of 84, 88, 94, 100, 102,
106, 108
Manchukuo, State of 196, 203, 205
Manchuria: case for territorial conquest/

Army officers 180–1; military actions
in 201; rights of/Army expansion
147–8, 160; withdrawal from 178
Manchurian Incident 113, 191, 196–9
manufacturing, fostering traditional 55
Manufacturing Ministry 80, 82
Marco Polo Bridge Incident 196, 227,
229, 230
Masaki Jinzaburō 208
mass movement(s): following Russo-
Japanese war 139–40, 144, 149, 151;
and House of Peers 153–4; and Yoshino
Sakuzō 155–6
Masuda Danjō 6
Matsudaira Katamori 23
Matsudaira Shungaku (Yoshinaga) *see*
Matsudaira Yoshinaga
Matsudaira Yoshinaga: and the Bakufu 13;
and *gasshō renkō* 6; and Hashimoto
Sanai 4; political president 2, 10, 19,
20, 27; poor reputation of 22; standing
of 5
Matsuda Masahisa 144
Matsuda Michiyuki 25
Matsukata Masayoshi: Cabinet 116, 130;
deflationary policies 89, 90, 94, 96,
102, 108–9, 116; financial policy 84,
89, 94, 100, 104, 105; and military
expansion/funding 128; and Ōkuma
Shigenobu 93
Matsumoto Yawara 153
Matsuno Tsuruhei 213
Matsuoka Komakichi 194
Matsuo Takayoshi 138–9, 150, 167
May 15th Incident 188, 191, 195, 196,
199, 201–2, 203–4
Mazaki Jinzaburō 214, 215, 218
mechanisation, post Sino-Japanese
war 130
Meiji 6 nen seihen 61
Meiji Constitution: article 10 95; article
11 113, 126, 184, 198; article 12 184;
article 13 199; article 33 96; article
37 114, 129; article 39 114; article
45 219; article 55 95, 113, 125–6;
article 67 114, 115, 116, 117, 118;
article 71 96, 114; and expenditure 114,
115, 117; finance and the economy 209;
and freedom of expression/Diet 221;
and government/Diet 117; and Inoue
Kowashi 94–5; and land tax 132; and
Ōkuma Shigenobu 91–2; promulgation
of 102, 106, 112, 113–15; right to
implement the budget of the previous

Index 247

year 96, 105, 114; and taxation 96, 108
Meiji Emperor 117, 125, 126, 137
Meiji Government: and China threat 103; financial policy 82; flexible frame government 82; foreign policy of 125; and inflation 90; and Kanghwado Incident 71; and land tax 88; Meiji political change 99; and Ōkubo Toshimichi 55; right/left confrontations 40; security law 110; and Taiwan 70
Meiji ishin 55
Meiji kenpō seiritsu shi 56, 58
Meiji Restoration 1–2, 4, 5, 14, 24, 56, 232, 233 *see also* Restoration of Imperial Rule (*ōsei fukko*); and Shōwa Restoration 189–91
Meiji socialism 115
Mie prefecture, peasants uprising 54
military *see also* Army: conflict within 214; and domestic politics 204, 206; inability to control 201; *kōdō ha* (Imperial Way faction) 211, 214, 215, 216, 221; and national defence 224; and national socialism 224, 225; and political parties 209–10, 215; and politics 201, 204, 206; powerful military argument 100–5; pursuit of strong 55; and Seiyūkai 207; *tōsei ha* (control faction) 210, 211, 214, 215, 216, 218, 220
Military Administration Bureau 181, 210
Military Affairs Council (*bōmu kaigi*) 159
military authorities (*gunbu*) 40, 234
military bureaucrats 210
military capacity, of China 103
military clique, and Hara Kei 166, 167
military expansion: expenditure 104–5, 119, 122; following Russo-Japanese war 145–6; and Itagaki Taisuke 122; operating costs of 131; post Sino-Japanese war 130; and tax rises 128–9
Military High Command 185
military ordinances (*gunrei*) 184, 234
Military Police (*Kenpeitai*) 219
military power: of *Bakufu* (Shogunate) 37–9; Japan's goal of becoming 145; and political power 186
Military preparation strategy for neighbouring areas (*Rinpō heibi ryaku*) 103
military service: equality of 136; and universal suffrage 138, 139

Minami Jirō 197
ministerial responsibility 95, 113–14
Minister of Home Affairs 115
Minister of the Left 90, 93, 99
Minister of the Right 78, 93, 94
Ministry of Agriculture and Commerce 130
Ministry of Finance 51, 128, 191
Ministry of Foreign Affairs 178
Ministry of Home Affairs 65, 80, 211, 219, 221
Ministry of the Interior 54
Minjō isshin 94
Minobe Tatsukichi: constitutional interpretation of 184, 185–7; organ theory of the Emperor 170, 196, 213, 214, 216; round table meeting of top leaders (*entaku kyotō kaigi*) 208–9, 210
minponshugi 151–9, 162–73, 169, 179
minryoku kyūyō 123, 235
Minsei 181
Minseitō 119, 179, 181–2, 212, 220
Minseitō Cabinet *see* Wakatsuki Reijirō Cabinet
Minshūteki jii undō o ronzu 157
Mitategumi, the 18
mitigating people's burdens (*minryoku kyūyō*) 123, 235
Mito domain 7, 10
Mito school 1, 13
Mitsui Bussan 153
Mitsuoka Hachirō 21
Miura Tetsutaro 150
Miwa Jusō 226
Miyoshi Guntarō 29
Mokuyōkai (Thursday Society) 180
Mongolia 147–8, 160, 178, 180–1
monpe 235
Mōri Motonori 14, 18
Mōri Toshihiko 61
multi-party alliance (*gasshō renkō*) 4–13, 15, 23, 25, 28
Muranaka Kōji 218
Murata Shinpachi 76
Murayama Matsune 21–2
Mutō Akira 211
Mutō Teiichi 228, 229, 232
Mutsu Munemitsu 123–5

Nagai Naoyuki 38
Nagai Uta 14, 15
Nagaoka Kenmotsu 6
Nagata Tetsuzan 180, 181, 196, 208, 211, 219, 220

248 *Index*

Nakae Chōmin 97, 102
Nakane Yukie 33, 38, 41
Nakano Buei 151
Namamugi Incident (Richardson murder) 2
Nanba Taisuke 171
Nanbu domain 45
Narahara Shigeru 16
Nariakira, Lord *see* Shimazu Nariakira
Narod 168
narrowly defined national defence 223–5, 227
national assembly, and Saigō Takamori 58
national bank law 54
national capitalism, national defence through 225
national defence: broad-based 220, 224, 225, 226; improving 165; and Meiji Constitution 184; narrowly defined 223–5, 227; and standard of living 220, 224; through national capitalism 225
National Defence Plan 228
national disaster 15th August 232
national foundation culture 54
national interest argument, Yokoi Shōnan 17–18
nationalisation, of railways 137, 143
nationalism, following Sino-Japanese war 123
nationalists, and military service/universal suffrage 138–9
National Journalists Alliance 149
national labour union movement 194
National Polity (*kokutai*) 193, 196, 235
national security, and two-party system 182
national socialism 224, 225, 226–7 *see also* socialism
National *Suiheisha* (Levellers Association) 152
national unity cabinet 196, 204–5, 207, 208, 218
naval development programme, of Katsu Kaishū 18
naval disarmament 176, 182
Naval Disarmament Treaty 152, 175, 183, 185, 186
Naval High Command 187
naval officers: assassinations by 203; and May 15th Incident 203–4; and *Seiyūkai* 207; young officers' movement 187–9
naval weakness, of Japan 67

navy: corruption scandal 153, 154; young officers' movement 187–9
Navy cabinet 151, 153
navy expansion: beginning of 102; expenditure 119; following Russo-Japanese war 145–6; and liquidation of paper money 105; operating costs of 131; post Sino-Japanese war 130; public loans for 102, 105; and World War I 159–60
Navy General Staff 186
Navy General Staff regulations 183, 184
Navy Minister, requirement to be serving officer 152, 153, 186–7
Nazi regime, Germany 196
Nemoto Hiroshi 181
new bureaucrats 211, 215, 218
New Deal policies, US 196
New Party *see Rikken Dōshikai*
newspapers, and Tsuzuki Keiroku 107
New York stock exchange, collapse of 192
Nihon oyobi Nihonjin 146, 148, 151, 157
Nihon Rōdō Kumiai Sōdōmei see Sōdōmei
Nihon Rōdō, Yūaikai changes its name to 152
Nihon Shakaishugi Dōmei (Japan Socialist Alliance) 152
Nine-Power Treaty 152, 175
1955 system 119
Ninomiya Harushige 197
Nippon 139
Nishida Mitsugu 188, 195, 212
Nishida Yoshiaki 194
Nishiyama Yukizumi 86
Nisshi jihen no tsugi ni kuru mono 228
Noda Matao 195
Nonaka Shirō 218
North China Incident 124
Northern Expedition, of Chiang Kai-shek 175, 178
November Incident 196
Numa Morikazu 100

October Incident 196, 199
Oda (Okayama) Prefecture 64 *see also* Okayama domain
Ogawa Heikichi 171
Ōgishi Raikō 195
Oguri Bungo (Kōzukenosuke) 16
Ōhara Shigenori 13
Ōhara Shigetomi 10
Ōi Kentarō 102
Ōishi Masami 100

Index 249

Okabe Suruga (Nagatsune) 16
Okada Keisuke 215, 217; Cabinet 196,
208, 209–10, 211, 212, 213, 215, 218
Okayama domain 21, 22 *see also* Oda
(Okayama) Prefecture
Okinawa prefecture 54
Ōkubo Ichiō (Tadahiro) 16, 27, 28, 33, 43
Ōkubo Kaname 6, 7
Ōkubo Toshimichi: age of 74–5;
and anti-foreigner position 28;
assassination of 54, 80; averting war
with China 68; and constitutional
government 70; dictatorship 65;
expedition to Taiwan 54, 63–5;
and Ijichi Masaharu 36; and Inoue
Kaoru 72; inspection tour/Europe
and America 53, 58; investment/
promotion of industry 18, 75; and
Itagaki Taisuke 70; and Iwakura
Tomomi 50; and Kido Kōin 65, 68,
70; and Korea 62, 71, 72; and Meiji
Government 55; and Murayama
Matsune 21; national foundation
culture 54; and prosperous country 57,
63, 79; and public assembly concept 33;
representing the anti-Bakufu forces 35;
and restoring the honour of Chōshu 34;
and reverence for the Emperor 16; and
Saigō 6–7, 8–9, 10, 12, 24, 26, 50,
63–5; and Sat–Chō alliance 29;
and strong military argument 64–5;
and transfer of troops to Court 51;
and war on China 65–8; and Yoshii
Tomozane 27
Ōkuma Shigenobu: attack on 102;
Cabinet 131, 154–5, 157–9, 160, 162;
and constitution 91–2, 97, 99; criticism
of 92–4; defeat of 98, 99; dismissal
of 100; and financial policy 80, 89,
90; and Fukuzawa Yukichi 91, 94;
and Gotō Shōjirō 111; and Hoshi
Tōru 133; investment/industrial
development 89; and Itō Hirobumi 93;
and Kido Kōin 52; leader of Meiji
Government 89; leaving office 84;
and Matsukata Masayoshi 93; and
Ministry of Finance 51; petition
of 90–1, 93; petitions for a constitution/
parliament 84; as Prime Minister 132;
and *Rikken Dōshikai* 155; and
Yamagata Aritomo 161
Ōmeisha 100
Ōmura Masujirō 40, 42, 44
Ōmura Masutarō 48

one-party *Seiyūkai* Cabinet *see* Inukai
Tsuyoshi Cabinet
Ōno Kenichi 55
opening the country 1, 3, 4, 16, 17
opening the country/expelling the
foreigner, shelving of dispute
between 5–7
Opinion on a constitution, Inoue
Kowashi 84
Opium War (1840–2), Chinese defeat 2
organ theory of the Emperor 170, 196,
213–14, 216
Ōsaka Castle 37, 41, 42
Ōsaka conferences 54, 69–70
Ōsaka Incident 102
ōsei fukko 235 *see also* Restoration of
Imperial Rule (*ōsei fukko*)
Ōsumi Mineo 215
Ōtsu Incident 102
Owari domain 7, 10, 43
Ōyama Ikuo 194
Ōyama Tsunayoshi 45
O-yura 9
Ozaki Yukio 149

Pacific War 1941 180, 227, 228–30
parasitic landlords 108
Paris Anti-War Treaty 175
Paris Peace Treaty 176
parliament *see also* Imperial Diet:
advocacy for/Tosa Domain 62–3;
cabinet system 56, 91, 94, 131, 157; and
constitution/assembly 69; constitution
rather than 55–8; establishing a
parliament from above 89–91;
establishment of 96; farmer's demands
for 89; feudal parliament 24–8;
Imperial Instructions on establishing
a 84; Ōkuma Shigenobu's petition 90–
1; peasant parliament/assembly 83, 88;
political parties controlling 97; powers
of 96; two-chamber system 32, 36
parliamentary democracy 111, 204
parliamentary politics 111
parliamentary rights argument, of Ueki
Emori 97–8
parties, political *see* political parties
Patriotic School (*Aikyō juku*) 204
Patriotic Society (*Aikokusha*) 54
Patriotic Women's Association 124
Peace Preservation Law 1925 175, 193,
212, 220–1
peace settlement, Russo-Japanese
war 139–40, 144

250 *Index*

Pearl Harbor 227
peasant assembly/parliament 83, 88
peasant associations 86–7 *see also*
  Sanshisha
peasant rights 110; and samurai rights 84,
  87–8, 97
peasantry: political participation of 83–8;
  taxation/prosperity of 81, 85, 86
peasants uprising 54
peerage establishment law 1884 102
people-based politics (*minponshugi*) *see*
  minponshugi
Perry, Commodore 1, 16
petition His Majesty to establish a
  parliament in our Empire, March
  1880 87
petitioning the Emperor, and Chiefs of the
  General Staff/Naval Command 183
petition movement, over the Sandai (three
  big issues) Incident 102
Petition to establish a parliament 1880 87,
  90
Petition to Establish a Popularly Elected
  Assembly 1874 54, 62, 63, 68, 83, 86,
  110
petition to the Emperor for the
  impeachment of the Cabinet 153
P'yŏngyang 126
philosophy of administration 91
pluralism, demands for 146
Police Administration Bureau, and Social
  Masses Party 221
Police Administration Department 219
Policy Affairs Research Council 116
policy(ies): based on research 106;
  changes and *Seiyūkai/Kenseikai*
  (*Minseitō*) 192; confusion in
  economic 191; Construction
  period/conflict in 82; 'creating an
  industrial nation policies' 192;
  foreign/defence 14
political change: of 1881 84, 89, 98, 99–
  100; 18th August 1863 coup 3, 21, 22–3
Political Change of Meiji 14 *see* political
  change, 1881
political choice, freedom of 151
political elite, deteriorating quality
  of 211–13
political leadership: to bureaucratic
  leadership 106; establishment of 121, 153
political liquefaction 211–13, 216
political participation: of farmers 90; by
  the peasantry 83–8; and rising standard
  of living 86

political parties: alternation of
  power between 169, 210; and the
  cabinet 94; controlling parliament 97;
  establishment of 91; and military 206,
  209–10, 215; reconciliation with
  bureaucracy 131–3
political power, and military power 186
political reform: 1857/1858 failure of 20;
  by Hoshi Tōru 135–6
political society 130, 131
political uprising, Bunkyū era (1861–4)
  10
politics: assembly politics 26–8; centred
  on Emperor 179; centred on public
  works 136; domestic 14–15, 179, 204,
  206; guided by public opinion 107; after
  Meiji Constitution promulgation
  113–15; and the military 201, 204, 206;
  parliamentary politics 111
popularly elected assembly 68, 69, 71, 86
popular rights associations 83
popular rights based on samurai *see*
  samurai popular rights
popular rights for farmers 90
popular rights for former samurai 90
Popular Rights Movement 48, 85, 87, 90,
  92, 98, 100, 115
pork barrel policies, of the *Seiyūkai* 142
ports *see also* harbours: opening of 55;
  port at Hyogo (Kobe) 32
positive finance, of Hara's *Seiyūkai* 165
positive policies: and financial
  crisis/1912 150; and Hoshi Tōru 132,
  136; and land tax increase 131;
  mitigating people's burdens (*minryoku
  kyūyō*) to 123; replaced by new flagship
  policies 145; of the *Seiyūkai* 134,
  142, 143, 165, 192; of Takahashi
  Korekiyo 134, 151, 204; of Tanaka's
  Seiyūkai/changing to creating an
  industrial nation 192; and Tōhoku
  region 134–5
postal system 102
post-war depression 152
post-war permanent coalition 119
post-war reforms 233
power: alternation between political
  parties 169, 210; centralisation of 51;
  of China 101; military/political 186; of
  taxpayers 96
powerful military argument, rehabilitation
  of 100–5
prefectures: establishment of 22, 46, 49,
  51–2, 56, 59, 102; new laws for 54

Index 251

prices: and inflation 89; rice prices *see* rice prices; after Seinan war 88
prime minister, responsibilities of 95
principles of administration 91
private draft constitution 84
Privy Council 102
production, of domestic goods 55 *see also* manufacturing
pro-Emperor alliance, setback for 15–16
pro-Emperor/anti-foreigner argument/ faction 1, 13–15, 21
pro-Emperor movement, Satsuma domain 16
pro-Emperor samurai 12, 13
progressive faction, and the constitution 98–9
Promotion of investment and development of industry (*shokusan kōgyō*) 55, 235
prosperity, and tax reform 85
prosperous country (*fukoku*) 55, 65, 70–82, 103–4
prosperous country, strong military (*fukoku kyōhei*) 1, 28, 64–5, 68, 103, 127
Prussian Constitution, article 109 96
Prussian model, of constitutional monarchy 57, 95
public assembly, multi-party alliance becoming 28, 33, 37
public loans, for projects 128
public officials employment law 152
public opinion, in a democratic political system 107
public works: and financial crisis/1912 149; funding of 128; politics centred on 136; and tax reduction 145

Qing (Ch'ing) China, as hypothetical enemy 101
Qing (Ch'ing) dynasty, end of 148

railways: building of 79–80; expansion of 123, 128, 130, 134; expenditure on 165; foreign loans for 149; Manchurian Railway 175, 196, 198; Mongolia 175; nationalisation of 137, 143; Ōsaka/Kōbe 54, 80; Shinbashi/ Kōbe 102; Shinbashi/Yokohama 54, 80; Tōhoku rail network 135
rationing 229
Reckless courage speech, Kabayama Sukenori 102
reconstruction 232
reform: 1857–1863 2, 232; of *Bakufu*

(Shogunate) 6, 17; change in the reform marketplace 4–5; land tax 80, 81–2, 85; period 5; reform faction 39–41
Reform, age of 2, 232
reformers, inside/outside the system 4, 5
regular procedures of constitutional government (*kensei no jōdō*) 161–2, 173, 206–8, 209, 210, 213, 218, 235
Renunciation of the Imperial Command 223
Reorganisation, age of 124, 137, 147, 150–1, 152
reparations payments, by China 128
research: based policies 106; constitutional 56–7, 93, 102
responsibility, ministerial 95, 113–14
Restoration of Imperial Rule (*ōsei fukko*) 22, 31, 33–5, 36, 39, 41, 49–50 *see also* Meiji Restoration
retainers, powerful 7, 15
return of political rule to the Emperor (*taisei hōkan*) 8, 34–5, 36, 235
revenue: government 88, 89; income tax 128; and Meiji Constitution 114; from taxation/for war 136; and World War I boom 161
Revere the Emperor and Overthrow the Bakufu (*sonnō tōbaku*) 5, 30
Revere the Emperor, Expel the Foreigner (*sonnō jōi*) 1–2, 4, 13–16, 17, 189, 325
revering the Emperor (*sonnō*) 3, 7, 10–11, 12, 16, 18, 25, 189
revolution: and counter-revolution 189; ending of 39–47, 52; by lower-ranking samurai 24; Meiji Restoration as 4
Revolution, age of 22, 52
revolutionary army 58
rice prices: collapse of 194; and deflationary policies 108, 116; following Russo-Japanese war 144; and government revenues 89; increasing 128; and land tax 80, 128, 143; returning/1932 205; and rural landlords 89, 96, 127, 194; and World War I boom 161
rice riots 152, 162, 164
rice shortages, in war 229
right of command: independence of the 182–4, 185, 198, 213; infringement of the 183, 184, 185, 198
rights of former samurai 92
right wing (civilian) 212; terrorism 199
Rikken Dōshikai 119, 150, 151, 152, 153, 155

Index

Rikken Jiyōtō 102
Rikken Kaishintō 102, 113, 128,
Rikken Kokumintō 137
Rikken Minseitō see Minseitō
Rikken Seiyūkai see Seiyūkai
Risshisha 83, 84, 85, 86, 87, 97, 99
Risshisha petition 54, 84
Risshō Gokokudō 188
roads, construction/repair of 80
Rōninkai 168
round table meeting of top leaders (*entaku kyotō kaigi*) 208–9, 210
Rousseau, Jean-Jacques 97
Rōyama Masamichi 167, 168
rural landlords *see also* landlords:
alienation of 144; and government bureaucracy 122; as majority of electorate 143; and rice prices 89, 96, 127, 194; special rights of 121; taxation 127, 136, 144; and war expenses 136; and World War I boom 161
Russia: as hypothetical enemy 145, 147; Russian revolution 152, 163–4, 168, 169; and Sakhalin issue 60; treaty of harmony and friendship 2
Russo-Japanese war 109, 127, 136–46
Ryūkyū domain, abolition of 54
Ryūkyū islands 64, 65

sabaku kaikoku 1–2, 235
Saigō Takamori: alliance of retainers 18; attack on Kumamoto Castle 77, 78; discussion with Katsu Kaishū 26–8; and Edo Castle 42, 43; end of his time 52; exiles of 2, 6, 8, 10, 13, 14, 15, 19; foreign invasion faction 75; grand alliance concept 13, 14, 21–4; and Hisamitsu 12, 15, 23–4, 77; and Imperial Army 51; and Imperial Guard 59; insurrection of 81; and intellectuals 189; invade Korea argument 60–2; and Iwakura Mission 63; and Kawamura Sumiyoshi 67; and Kido Kōin 29; and Kirino Toshiaki 73–4; letter to Koba Dennai 11–13, 15; as military leader 40; as military service official (*gunfuyaku*) 23; and 'multi-party' alliance 4–10; and Nariakira 2, 9–10; and national alliance of samurai 17; and national assembly 58; and Ōkubo Toshimichi 6–7, 8–9, 10, 12, 24, 26, 50, 63–5; pardon of 23–4; private army

of 76–7; private school 54, 76; release of 22; resignation of/as councillor 63; and restoration of Emperor 36; returning to government 67; revering the Emperor (*sonnō*) 7, 25; and Sat-Chō alliance 33, 34; and Shimazu Nariakira 2, 9–10; support for 76–7; tactical failures of 45–6; and Tōhoku war 44–5; and Yoshinobu as councillor 42
Saigō Takamori den 6, 23, 25
Saigō Tsugumichi 51–2, 64
Saionji Cabinet, second 137, 145, 146, 148, 151
Saionji Kinmochi 137, 142–3, 149, 200, 201, 208, 214, 225
Saionji kō 222
Saitō Makoto 196, 215, 217; national unity cabinet 196, 204–5, 207, 208, 218
Saitō Osamu 82
Saitō Takao 219–20
Saitō Toshiyuki 50
Sakai Toshihiko 137
Sakamoto Ryōma 28, 29–30, 33
Sakhalin issue 54, 59–60, 64
Sakuma Shōzan 9, 26
Sakurada Gate Incident 2, 10, 203
Sakurakai 195
samurai: alliance of 16, 17, 18, 21; and assembly politics 27; extremist movements 112; pro-Emperor 12, 13; salaries of 54; samurai assembly 83; samurai descendants (*shizoku*) 63; samurai rights/popular rights 62, 83–4, 87–8, 97, 109–10; in Shonai/Wakamatsu 77
Sandai (three big issues) Incident, petition movement 102, 111
Sanjō Sanetomi 44, 61, 66, 67, 93
sankin kōtai 235
Sanshisha 84, 85, 86, 90
sanyo 235
Sasaki Katsu 21
Sasaki Suguru 35, 45
Sasaki Takayuki 50
Sasa Tomofusa 61
Satake domain 45
Sat-Cho domain government 67
Sat-Chō High Command 44
Satsuma-Chōshu alliance 22, 27, 28–34
Satsuma domain: alliance with Tosa domain 8–9, 18, 36; confrontation with Chōshu domain 13–16; declining influence of 24; and exile of Saigō 6;

Index 253

and Imperial Army 49; independent actions of 14; policy of alliance 7, 21; pro-Emperor movement 7, 16; radical faction 10; restraining of 68; reverence for the Emperor 16; and revering the Emperor/overthrowing the Bakufu 3–4; Shimazu Nariakira 9; supporting union of Court and Shogunate 3; and Tōhoku war 46

Satsuma rebellion *see* Seinan war

Satsuma–Tosa Agreement 1867 22

Satsuma–Tosa alliance 8–9, 18, 36

Sawa Club 154

schools, Saigō Takamori/private 54, 76

school system proclamation 54

Security law 1887 102, 110

Security police law 1900 124

Security Treaty, Japan-US 140

Seichūgumi 15, 16, 18

seihen 235

seihi setsugen 235

Seinan Incident 175

Seinan war 54, 61, 75–7, 79, 82, 88, 89, 100

Seiron 111

Seiyūhontō 152, 172

Seiyūkai: age of 140; and aggression/ Emperor-centrism 179–80; anti-fascist trend 221–2; and Army officers 208; and bureaucratic clique 144–5, 150, 171; Cabinet one-party/single-party *see* Inukai Tsuyoshi Cabinet; departure from government 174; disillusionment with 144; Emperor-centrism of 179, 213; and fascism 207, 221–2; and financial crisis/1912 150; foreign policies of 176, 177–8; formation of 114, 122–36; and Hara Kei 122, 152; and House of Representatives 137, 159; and independence of command 213; and Itō Hirobumi 122, 124, 136, 141; and *jūshin* bloc 215; and Katsura Tarō 140–1, 150; and *Kenseikai* (*Minseitō*) policy changes 192; and land tax 144; loss of status of 159; and mass movement 149; and the military/ fascism 207; and naval officers 207; and organ theory of the Emperor 213– 14, 216; political control of 143–5; positive policies of 134, 142, 143, 150; return to office 161–2; and *Rikken Dōshikai* 119; split of 152; support system of 135–6; and Takahashi Korekiyo 170, 171–2; three-faction

constitutional defence Cabinet 152; and universal suffrage 138, 158, 173; views/ evaluation of 120

Seiyūkai–Minseitō coalition 213

Sekiyōsha 84–5, 86, 87

sekkyoku seisaku 235 *see also* positive policies

Sendai domain 45, 48

Senku 168

Senzen Nihon no gurobarizumu 182, 205

Sera Shūzō 45

Shakai Minshutō (Social Democratic Party) 124, 169

Shandong Peninsula: return of leasehold to China 175; return to China 175, 176; Shandong expedition 175, 178, 181–2; withdrawal from 178

Shanghai Incident 196, 203

Shibukawa Zensuke 195, 218

Shidehara diplomacy 176–7, 179, 197; defeat of 198–9

Shidehara Kijūrō: foreign policies of 175, 176–7; and Hara Kei 163; and Jilin province/US 197, 198; pro-US line 163, 198

Shimazu Hisaakira 23

Shimazu Hisahiro 24, 29

Shimazu Hisamitsu: conference of domain lords 32; independent action of/Edo 14, 16; march to Kyoto 10–11, 13; and Saigō 12, 15, 23–4, 77; single domain action of reverence for the Emperor 18; and supply of troops 50–1; written opinion of 19–20

Shimazu Nariakira 2, 5, 7, 9–10, 12, 13, 189

Shimazu Tadayoshi 46

Shimazu Zusho (Hisaharu) 24, 29

Shimonoseki peace conference 124, 127

Shimonoseki Treaty 126–7

Shimonoseki, attack 1864 14, 22

Shinagawa Yajirō 29, 115

Shinagawa Yojirō 40, 45

Shinjinkai (New Man Society) 152, 167, 168

Shinohara Kunimoto 64, 76

Shinpotō 124, 128–9, 131, 138, 141, 155

Shinsengumi, of Kondō Isamu 25

shipbuilding programme, following Russo- Japanese war 146

Shiroyama, attack on 79

Shishido Samanosuke 15

shizoku 235

254 Index

Shōgun: resignation of 33, 34; return of power to the Court 22; succession to the 3; term 235
Shogunate succession 1856–7 6 *see also* Bakufu (Shogunate)
Shōgun Iemochi, death of 31
shokusan kōgyō 55, 235
Shōwa era 121, 232
Shōwa Restoration 189–91, 232, 233
Siberian expedition 152, 162, 163–4
Siemens Incident 151, 152, 153, 155
silk industry 130
silk prices 191–2, 194, 205
Sino-Japanese war 65–6, 102, 104, 105, 115, 123–7
six articles, Kido Kōin 29–31
social contract argument 97
Social Democratic Party (*Shakai Minshutō*) 124, 169
socialism: creating national 211; Meiji 115; and the military 224, 225; national 224, 225, 226–7
socialist movement 168–9
socialist parties 112, 193–4
Socialist Party 97, 137
Socialist People's Party (*Shakai Minshutō*) 193
socialists, anti-war 138–9
Social Masses Party: advance of 193–4, 196, 216; anti-fascist banner 226; and the Army 223–4, 225; beginning of 204; and broad-based national defence 225–6; and Cabinet Research Bureau 210–11; and facism 217, 227; leap forward of 218–19; left wing of 212, 223; and Police Administration Bureau 221; as pro-military socialist party 220–1; and socialism 227; and Ugaki Kazushige 212; and *zaibatsu* 225
social unrest 199
Society for the Promotion of Universal Suffrage (*fusen jikkōkai*) 165
Society to Revere the Emperor (*Keitenkai*) 188
Sōdōmei 194, 205
Soejima Taneomi 63
sonnō jōi 235 *see also* revere the Emperor, expel the foreigner (*sonnō jōi*)
sonnō tōbaku 235 *see also* Revere the Emperor and Overthrow the Bakufu (*sonnō tōbaku*)
sōsai 235
South Manchuria Raiway Co. 137

Soviet Union, as potential enemy 228 *see also* Russia
Special Police (*Tokkō*) 219
spinning machines 80
standard of living: and national defence 220, 224; rising/and political participation 86
State, and Cabinet 207
status system, of samurai/peasant/artisan and merchant 62–3
Stimson, Henry 197, 198, 201
Strategy for Preparedness against Neighbouring Countries 1880 105
strong military: in Age of Construction 100; argument 101, 103, 104–5; in Bakumatsu period 67; change in meaning of 58; faction/defeat of 79; and Itagaki Taisuke 62, 63; of Meiji period 59, 67; pursuit of 55; and Saigō 63; trumping prosperous country (*fukoku*) 103–4
strong military, prosperous country (*fukoku kyōhei*) 57, 58
Suehiro Shigeyasu 100
suffrage, universal *see* universal suffrage
Suganami Saburō 188, 195
Sugita Teiichi 87, 98
Suiheisha (Levellers Association) 152
Sun Yat-sen revolution 190
support the Shogun, open the country (*sabaku kaikoku*): v. revere the Emperor, expel the foreigner (*sonnō jōi*) 1–2
Supreme Command, self-restraint by 184–5
surface teaching 214
Suzuki General Trading Company 175, 192
Suzuki Kantarō 215, 217
Suzuki Kisaburō 179, 206, 215
Suzuki Shōsaku 181
Suzuki Teiichi 180, 181, 182
swords, banning of wearing 54
system of irresponsibility 95, 113–14
system of *sanyo* 39, 40, 41

Tachibana Kōsaburō 195
Taguchi Ukichi 100
tairō 235
taisei hōkan 8, 34–5, 36, 235
Taishō Democracy 119, 121, 150, 164, 166
Taishō Emperor, death of 175
Taishō political change 137, 145–51
Taishō seikyoku shiron 142

Index 255

Taiwan: and Inoue Kaoru 68; invasion
argument 60, 67, 68; and Kirino
Toshiaki 59–60; Ōkubo Toshimichi
expedition 54, 63–5; subjugation
of 124
Taiwan Bank 175, 192
Taiyō 157
Takahashi Kitao 195
Takahashi Korekiyo: and alternation of
power arrangement 169; assassination
of 196, 217; foreign policies of 177–8;
and General Staff Office 170–1;
and gold standard 202; and *jūshin*
conference 215; positive budget
of 165; positive policies of 134, 151,
204–5; and role of Emperor 179; and
Seiyūkai 170, 171–2; and three-faction
Cabinet 173; and Yamamoto Gonbei
Cabinet 172
Takashima Tatsuo 181
Takasugi Shinsaku 15, 18, 24–5, 27, 29
Takechi Hanpeita 15
Takeda Kōunsai 6, 13
Takeichi Hanpeita 15
Takigawa Incident 196
Tamiya Jo-un 6
Tanaka diplomacy 175
Tanaka Giichi 163, 170, 174, 178;
Cabinet 175, 177, 179, 180, 181, 192,
209
Tanaka Shōzō 124
Tang gu ceasefire agreement 196
Tani Tateki 35, 40, 42, 43, 47, 48, 64, 77
tariff autonomy, restoration of 137
taxation: argument for maintaining
existing 95–6; business tax 144,
151; and commoners 63; falling
revenues/land tax 89; first post-war
tax rise 124; income tax exceeding
land tax 161; income tax revenue 128;
increase/and landlords 143; increased
revenue 136; indirect 105; lack
of demand for reduction 127; and
landlords 116, 143; land tax *see* land
tax; and Meiji Constitution 114; new
taxes 144; and public works 145;
revenues/and deflationary policies 80;
rural landlords 127, 136, 144;
special taxes 136, 144; tax rises/and
military expansion 128–9; and voting
rights 142; and war funding 136
tax payers: power of 96; right to political
participation 88; and voting rights 88
tax-raising powers 49

tax reform, and constitutional
system 129–30
teaching, surface/hidden 214
Teichū jōranki 77
telephone network 165
tenancy disputes 194
Teradaya Incident 2, 16
Terashima Munenori 73
Terauchi Hisaichi 221–2
Terauchi Masatake 160, 161, 163, 164;
Cabinet 152, 161–3, 164
territorial issues, emergence of 59
terrorism, right wing 199
textile industry 130, 205
textile tax 144
third national disaster 11th March
2011 232–3
three-domain mobilisation (sanhan
shuppei) 36
three-faction Cabinet 152, 173, 174, 175,
179
3/15 Incident 175
Three Great Incidents Petition movement
1887 102, 111
3/1 independence movement, Korea 152
Three-power intervention by Russia,
Germany and France *see* Tripartite
Intervention
three-rank system 40
Thursday Society 195
Tianjin Treaty 123
Tientsin Treaty 102
Toba-Fushimi, fighting in 35, 38, 42, 47,
49
Tōhoku Imperial University 135
Tōhoku region 86, 110, 111, 134–5, 232
Tōhoku war 44–6, 47, 49
Tōjō Hideki 180, 181, 211
Tōkaidō Expedition High Command 43
Tokonami Takejirō 152, 209
Tokudaiji Sanetsune 126
Tokugawa domain 33
Tokugawa Yoshinobu 8, 23, 34, 35, 36,
38, 39–41, 42
Tokushima domain 21, 22
Tokutomi Sohō 102, 109–10, 111–12,
113, 142
Tokutomi Tadasuke 21, 22
Tokyo, becoming capital 22
Tokyo Chamber of Commerce 151
Tokyo Imperial University, *Shinjinkai*
at 152
Tokyo Keizai Zasshi 100
Tomita Kōjirō 223

256   *Index*

Tonghak uprising 123, 124
Toranomon Incident 152, 171, 172
Tosa domain 8–9, 13–15, 22, 40, 47, 49, 55, 62–3, 68 *see also* Satsuma-Tosa alliance
Tosa Imperial Party 15
Tosa visit, of *Kōno Hironaka* 84–7
tōsei ha (control faction), Army 210, 211, 214, 215, 216, 218, 220
tōsuiken 235
total war, Japan–China war 229, 230
total war regime, by legal means as *tōsei ha* 211
Tottori domain 21, 22
towns/villages system 102
Tōyama Mitsuru 185
Toyama women's riot 164
Tōyō Keizai Shinpō 150, 151, 209
trade *see also* exports; imports: in fields/ rice paddy 54; Japan/Korea 61; and Okubo Toshimichi // 75; trade deficits 81
trade treaty, US/Japan 2, 3
transcendentalism 106, 113, 129, 131, 133, 234
transport network 86, 165
Treaty of Portsmouth 137
treaty revision conference, first 102
Tripartite Intervention 127
triple disaster 11th March 2011 232–3
Tsuchiura domain 7
Tsuzuki Keiroku 106–8
twenty-one demands, to China 152, 160, 161, 163, 174–6
twisted Diet 113
two-chamber system, parliament 32, 36
two-major-party system: and 12th general election 159; beginning of 174, 179–80; British-style 112, 155–7, 179; and Hara Kei 166–7; and national security 182

Uchida Shinya 209
Uehara Yūsaku 137, 146, 149
Ueki Emori 84, 97–8, 111
Ueno Kagenori 61
Ueno Shōgitai attack 47
Ueno war 43, 44
Uesugi Shinkichi 188
Ugaki Kazushige 212, 215, 218, 219, 227; Cabinet 189, 196, 222–3, 230
unemployment 194, 199, 202, 205
union of Court and Shogunate argument 3
unions 194, 205

United Kingdom *see* British; Great Britain
United States: arrival of American fleet 1853 40; collapse of New York stock exchange 192; as hypothetical enemy 145, 228; inspection tour to 53–8; mistrust of 197; New Deal policies 196; Pearl Harbor 227; pro-US line/Terauchi Cabinet 162–3; trade treaty with Japan 2, 3
Unity Movement 111
Unity of Court and Bakufu (*kōbu gattai*) 4, 5, 10, 13
universal suffrage: and Age of Reorganisation 150; demonstration movement 152, 168; and Hara Kei 164–6, 167; implementation of 109, 112, 174, 175; and Kita Ikki 137–9; and Matsuo Takayoshi 138–9, 150; and military service 138, 139; qualifications of/limiting 87, 124; and second constitutional defence movement 173; and *Seiyūkai* 138, 158, 173; and Taishō Democracy 121; and Yamakawa Hitoshi 169; and Yoshino Sakuzō 155–7
Universal Suffrage Law 1925 175
Unyō warship 71
upper/lower house system 36, 37, 39, 40, 41
urban businessmen, dissatisfaction of 144–5
US Consul-General 2

Versailles Treaty 152
veto-type parliament 109, 111, 112–13
Vickers 153
village landlords 88, 127
voting rights, and taxation 142 *see also* electorate

wages, low level of 205
Wakatsuki Reijirō 159, 191; Cabinet, second 196, 199, 200, 201
War Ministry 181
wars: Aizu war 44; averting/with China 68; Bakufu and Choshu as private quarrel 27; Boshin war 22, 35, 42, 44, 45, 62, 67, 135; on China/ and Mutsu Munemitsu 123–5; civil war/Chōshu domain 49; Fifteen-year War 204; first Chōshu 27; inability of Japan to declare war 19; Japan–China war 180, 196, 227–30, 232; Japan–US

Index 257

war 181; Opium War (1840–2) 2;
Pacific War 1941 180, 227, 228–30;
Russo-Japanese war 109, 127, 136–46;
Satsuma and Britain 1863 22; Seinan
war 54, 61, 75–7, 79, 82, 88, 89, 100;
Sino-Japanese war 65–6, 102, 104,
105, 115, 123–6; Tōhoku war 44–6, 47,
49; total war 136, 211, 229, 230; Ueno
war 43, 44; World War I 152, 159–60,
161–2, 165, 166; World War II 114,
204
warships, funding of 118
Washington Conference 152, 174–6
Washington Treaty 196
Watanabe Jōtarō 217
Watanabe Kunitake 128
wealth: of farmers 90; of peasants 81, 85
weaponry, Imperial Army (*kangun*) 48
Weihaiwei 126
White Paper for Return of Political Power
to the Emperor 33
white paper for the establishment of a
popularly elected assembly 56
Wŏnsan port 101
women, and Pacific War/changing role
of 228
Women Association 152
Women's National Defence
Association 228, 229
workers, appalling conditions of 130
working landlords 108
World Depression 175
World's Final War. The 180–1
World War I 152, 159–60; boom 161–2,
165, 166
World War II 114, 204

Yamada Akiyoshi 67
Yamagata Aritomo: and abolition
of domains/establishment of
prefectures 52; and avoiding further
wars 68; China threat argument 101,
102, 103–4, 147; and Hara Kei 166–
7; inspection tour 108; and Itō
Hirobumi 141; and making war with
China 67; and Ōkuma Shigenobu 161;

second cabinet of 133–4; and supply of
troops 50; and tax increases 132
Yamagata clique 119, 141, 143
Yamaguchi Naoyoshi 53
Yamakawa Hitoshi 169
Yamamoto Gonbei 151, 171–2;
Cabinet 151, 152, 153, 154, 171, 172
Yamamoto Shirō 165
Yamanouchi Toyonori 15
Yamanouchi Yōdō 32, 35, 40
Yamaoka Tetsutarō 43
Yamazaki Tatsunosuke 209
Yano Fumio 91
Yasuoka Masahiro 188
Yawata steelworks 124
yen: decline in confidence in 80; value
of 105
Yŏngjongsŏng (Eishūjō) Castle 71
Yodo domain 22
Yokohama 69
Yokoi Shōnan 16–18, 27, 28
Yokoyama Gennosuke 124
Yokoyama Shizuo 181
Yonezawa domain 21, 22, 45, 48
Yoshida Shōin 1, 10
Yoshida Tōyō 15
Yoshii Tomonari 24
Yoshii Tomozane 24, 26, 27, 28, 29, 36,
63
Yoshino Sakuzō 152, 155–7, 164, 167–8
Yotsumoto Yoshitaka 188
young officers' movement, Army and
Navy 187–9
Yoyogi 188, 189, 195
Yūaikai 137, 152
Yuan Shikai 61, 105
Yuasa Kurahei 222
Yūbin Hōchi shinbun 92
Yūki Toyotarō 225
Yuri Kimimasa 22
yūshi 235

zaibatsu, and the Army 223–5, 226, 227,
230
Zen'ei (Vanguard) 169
Zusho Hirosato 9

Lightning Source UK Ltd.
Milton Keynes UK
UKOW06n0609150416

272301UK00011B/292/P